THE BOOK OF™ INKSCAPE

THE BOOK OF™
INKSCAPE

The Definitive Guide to the Free Graphics Editor

by Dmitry Kirsanov

no starch press

San Francisco

THE BOOK OF INKSCAPE. Copyright © 2009 by Dmitry Kirsanov.

13 12 11 10 09   1 2 3 4 5 6 7 8 9

ISBN-10: 1-59327-181-6
ISBN-13: 978-1-59327-181-7

Publisher: William Pollock
Production Editor: Megan Dunchak
Cover Design: Octopod Studios
Developmental Editor: Tyler Ortman
Technical Reviewers: Tim Cole and Joshua A. Andler
Copyeditors: Kathleen Mish and Megan Dunchak
Compositor: Alina Kirsanova
Proofreader: Alina Kirsanova

For information on book distributors or translations, please contact No Starch Press, Inc. directly:
No Starch Press, Inc.
555 De Haro Street, Suite 250, San Francisco, CA 94107
phone: 415.863.9900; fax: 415.863.9950; info@nostarch.com; www.nostarch.com

Library of Congress Cataloging-in-Publication Data:

Kirsanov, Dmitry.
  The book of Inkscape : the definitive guide to the free graphics editor / Dmitry Kirsanov.
      p. cm.
  Includes index.
  ISBN-13: 978-1-59327-181-7
  ISBN-10: 1-59327-181-6
 1. Computer graphics. 2. Inkscape (Electronic resource) I. Title.
  T385.K491256 2009
  006.6'8--dc22
                                        2009023973

SUSTAINABLE FORESTRY INITIATIVE   Certified Fiber Sourcing
Label applies to the text stock   www.sfiprogram.org

BRIEF CONTENTS

CONTENTS IN DETAIL

4
OBJECTS   51

5
SELECTING   67

6
TRANSFORMING   81

9
STROKE AND MARKERS 135

10
GRADIENTS AND PATTERNS 149

11
SHAPES 165

14
DRAWING 237

15
TEXT 255

23
TUTORIAL: TECHNICAL DRAWING

24
TUTORIAL: THE ROSE

A
AN SVG PRIMER

B
IMPORT AND EXPORT

ACKNOWLEDGMENTS

This book would not exist if not for the help and encouragement of the staff of No Starch Press, in particular Megan Dunchak, Tyler Ortman, Kathleen Mish, and Magnolia Molcan. I am also indebted to the technical reviewers, Tim Cole and Joshua Andler, whose suggestions really improved the book.

I owe gratitude and respect to the Inkscape development team—dozens of dedicated volunteers who spent countless man-hours creating one of the best vector editors now in existence. It was a pleasure and honor to work with you.

Finally, special thanks go to my wife, Alina, for her unwavering support, constant prodding, and the huge work she did compositing, indexing, and proofreading the book.

INTRODUCTION

This book has two main goals.

First, this is a book about Inkscape, a powerful open source SVG-based vector graphics editor. It describes the stable version 0.47 (released in summer 2009) in great detail, covering all of its features (excluding only a few that are clearly experimental or incomplete).

The second, perhaps more ambitious goal of this book is to evangelize the vector way of creating graphics and share the joy of thinking in vector. Once the exclusive domain of professional designers, in the recent years vector graphics software has grown much more visible and accessible. A vector editor is not yet a standard accessory of a computer in the same way a bitmap editor like Photoshop is, but it's getting there—and Inkscape has been a major part of this "vector revolution."

Much of Inkscape's appeal lies in its being the only professional-level vector editor which is fully open source and cross-platform. There's more to it than that, however. Simple and accessible at the basic level, Inkscape is also extremely powerful if you dig deeper; it is vast and inexhaustibly hackable—from customizable keyboard shortcuts (Appendix D) and a command-line language (Appendix C), to powerful chainable path effects (Chapter 13), to arbitrarily complex vector filters that push the envelope of vector graphics (Chapter 17). This book swims the Inkscape ocean from shore to shore without leaving any island unvisited.

What's in This Book?

Chapter 1 is a high-level description of Inkscape, its capabilities, and its place in the world of vector graphics (and, to some extent, computer graphics in general). Next, Chapter 2 (page 17) gives an absolutely down-to-the-basics primer on the first steps in the program (installation, opening, creating objects, transforming them, saving); you can safely skip this chapter if you have ever completed even a small Inkscape project.

The bulk of the book, Chapters 3 to 18, is written to be read more or less in sequence. These chapters present all aspects of Inkscape functionality (objects, transformations, style, paths, text, and so on) with detailed explanations, illustrations, and practical tips.

The second part of the book (starting from Chapter 19) contains several complete step-by-step tutorials demonstrating real-world uses of Inkscape (such as an animation, a business card, and the cover illustration for this book). The book ends with several appendices (page 369) with reference information, including a complete list of keyboard and mouse shortcuts.

Inkscape is a work in progress. So is this book. New stable versions of Inkscape are released approximately once a year, and I will try to keep this book up to date. For the latest updates, visit *http://www.nostarch.com/inkscape.htm*.

Who Is This Book For?

You don't need to be a graphics professional to find this book useful. Even if you are entirely new to vector editors, this book should be a gentle enough introduction to get you started on your vector graphics journey. You will have some new concepts to grasp and some terminology to learn, but that should come naturally if you practice what you learn. As you read, I'd recommend that you run Inkscape and immediately try the techniques described in this book.

On the other hand, even an experienced user of Inkscape or another vector graphics program should find enough to chew on in this book. I am writing from two perspectives—that of a user of Inkscape and that of a developer, and I hope my experience of contributing to the Inkscape project allows me to more clearly see the logic of the program's interface and behavior, to identify its particularly strong and weak points (and to suggest workarounds for the weak points).

1

INKSCAPE AND THE WORLD

This may be your first encounter with vector graphics. Or, you may have used vector graphics before and are now checking to see what else it can do for you. Or, you may be considering Inkscape after having used other vector editing applications and would like to know what sets it apart. Whatever your situation is, you may find some background information useful. What is SVG? What is Inkscape? Where does it come from and where is it headed? What can you use it for? What is Inkscape's place in the world of computer graphics? This introductory chapter attempts to answer these and other questions.

1.1 What Vector Graphics Is and Why It Matters

Inkscape is a *vector graphics editor*. What does that mean?

The majority of images stored and processed on computers today are represented as *rasters*, also called *bitmaps*. A raster image is a rather primitive representation—just a lattice of small rectangular areas called *pixels*. For each pixel, the only information a raster file stores is its color and, possibly, its transparency.

For example, if you have a bitmap image with a black circle on white background (Figure 1-1, left), there is in fact *no* black circle stored in the image at all. It's only you, when viewing this image, who may (or may not) get the *idea* of a black circle. All the computer knows about the image is that some of its pixels are black and some are white (and a few are an in-between gray).

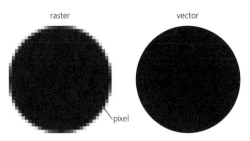

raster vector

pixel

Figure 1-1: A circle as a bitmap (left) and vector (right)

As a result, there is precious little that the computer can do with such an image without human guidance. It can paint all the white pixels blue, but it cannot move or transform the circle because it does not *see* it as a separate object. These kinds of tasks may be difficult even for humans, as anyone who has used the GIMP or Photoshop would attest; you'll have to use complex and unreliable tools to "select" the circle, and you can hardly ever do this perfectly if, for example, the edge of the circle is *antialiased* (so that some pixels on the edge have intermediate values between black and white) as it is in Figure 1-1.

It's all different with *vector graphics* (Figure 1-1, right). In a vector format, the actual circle can be stored along with its properties as an *object*. This means you can easily separate it from other objects and do whatever you please with it. Moreover, with such an image, your computer can do many smart things automatically—for example, it can automatically delete all circles, paint all red objects with green, or scale all black circles to twice their size.

No more frustrating pixel selections: Just pick any object and edit it as needed. That's how Inkscape works, and this is its main point of difference from raster editors such as Photoshop.

Let's look at the most prominent advantages of the vector approach:

Vector images are scalable.
   Scalability means you can view or export your drawing at any resolution, and you'll never see any jaggedness, pixelation, or unwanted blurring. Everything remains perfectly crisp regardless of size. This is often cited as the main advantage of vector graphics, although in my view, other advantages are no less important.

Vector images are editable at any time.
   No matter how complex your drawing is, you can always pick any object in it and edit away. It's a bit like a Photoshop file in which every single brush stroke is placed on a layer of its own—automatically. Furthermore, in a raster editor, you are supposed to eventually "flatten" your image, so that all separate layers are merged. By contrast, there's no need—indeed no possibility—to flatten a vector drawing (except by exporting it to a raster image).

Vector images are easy to create and read.

Vector objects conform much better to human visual perception: When we look at a scene, we tend to mentally separate it into objects, just as is done in a vector drawing. This makes vector graphics a very natural medium to work in. Also, since many vector formats (including SVG) are text-based, it is easy to *write* a simple vector drawing manually (without a graphic editor of any kind) or to program a script to generate or modify such a drawing.

Vector images are laconic.

Since you don't have to store information about every pixel, a vector image usually takes much fewer bytes to store and transmit than the corresponding raster image. As a nice side effect of this, Inkscape has unlimited undo history, simply because each undo step takes much less memory as a vector than it would as a raster.

Vector images are infinite.

A raster always has a fixed size in pixels—for example, 468 by 60 pixels. In an uncompressed bitmap, doubling the dimensions will quadruple the size of the file because the extra pixels need to be stored even if they are empty. Not so with vector images. A vector image is virtually *boundless*, and expanding it by moving an object an inch or a mile away costs nothing in terms of file size or computer memory. Similarly, a vector document is virtually infinite in terms of *depth*: You can zoom in as close as you want and create any number of microscopic-sized objects in any given space. (In reality, of course, both canvas size and zoom level are limited, but these limits are much, much larger than in a raster editor.)

Vector images can be animated.

Since objects are stored separately in a vector drawing, it's easy to animate them by moving them, transforming them, changing their colors, and so on. That's why some vector formats such as SVG or Flash naturally provide animation capabilities as well. Although Inkscape does not yet support animated SVG, this feature is planned for implementation in a future release.

Vector images can be interactive.

Not only can you animate objects, but you can make them interactive as well. A drawing can change the properties of objects in response to user actions, which makes it possible to implement complex user interfaces with buttons, links, drag-and-drop, and so on. Again, Inkscape's current capabilities in this area are limited, but you can manually edit an SVG file created in Inkscape, adding interactivity which can then be played in an SVG viewer.

Vector objects are reusable.

It's very easy to pick an object from one drawing, transform or restyle it without any loss of quality, and then insert it into another drawing.

If you are into digital music, you may better understand the distinction between vector and raster graphics if I liken vector graphics to a MIDI sound file and raster graphics to a WAV sound recording. Another analogy, suited to programmers, might be to compare vectors to the source code of a program and rasters to compiled binaries.

Of course it can't be all roses and no thorns. Here are the two main disadvantages of vector graphics compared to rasters:

Formats are fundamentally limited.

A vector image format (of which there are many, just as there are many different raster formats) always limits you to a certain repertoire of objects and their properties. New versions of formats invent and introduce new capabilities, but that only highlights the fact that perfection is unattainable. Vector formats are always "under construction."

There are many images that are very difficult or even impossible to reproduce exactly in vector form. For example, images that require complex textures, such as human skin, hair, or wood, are not vector-friendly. The world of vectors is traditionally made up of precise shapes, flat colors, and smooth gradients; if what you like is naturalistic noise, scratches, or dirt, you will probably have a hard time rendering that in a typical vector editor.

Still, with Inkscape's transparency, gradients, and filters, you can create amazingly photorealistic vector images (see Figure 1 on the color insert). Also note that, being a higher-level abstraction, a vector drawing may include raster images as a special kind of object. Thus, you can always insert a photo into an Inkscape drawing and freely combine it with vector objects.

Vector format conversions are unreliable.

For the same reason, it is never trivial to convert an image from one vector format into another. The repertoires of object types and capabilities of the formats always differ, sometimes in less than obvious ways; different versions of formats muddy the picture even more. For example, SVG supports blurring objects (**17.1**) while PDF does not; on the other hand, PDF supports gradient meshes (**1.5.4**), a feature presently missing in SVG. This makes any kind of vector conversion an iffy business. In the best case, you get an approximation of the source object that the target format cannot represent directly (for example, for exporting SVG to PDF, you may need to replace blurred objects with embedded rasters). In the worst case, you'll simply get a broken image after the conversion.

This is one of the reasons Inkscape's vector format, SVG, is so important. It is an acknowledged international standard with rich and well-defined capabilities, which therefore has the potential to become the lingua franca of vector graphics (although Adobe's PDF is still much more common in this role). We will discuss SVG in more detail later in this chapter.

So, what is actually stored in a vector drawing? Apart from the embedded raster objects just mentioned, the most common vector object type is a path. A *path* is just a sequence of commands like "draw a straight line to such-and-such point" and "draw a smooth curve through such-and-such points." There may be any number of such commands in a sequence, which means a path can approximate any geometric figure or real-world shape with any desired accuracy. A path can have *fill* (paint in the area enclosed by the path) and *stroke* (paint along the path itself), as well as many other properties that define how the path looks (Figure 1-2).

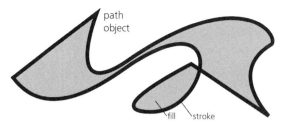

Figure 1-2: A path object can represent any shape.

There are several other object types (such as text objects, clones, and groups) and many other object properties (such as font size, visibility, and blur). Many properties can apply to all kinds of objects, while others are specific to particular object types. A drawing is just a collection of objects of various types; these objects can be placed whenever you need them, including on top of each other, and they can even be made partially or fully transparent so that whatever is beneath them shows through. Figure 1 on the color insert shows an example of a complex Inkscape drawing that makes heavy use of opacity, gradients, and blur to achieve realism (you can load it from Inkscape's *examples* directory if you want to examine it in full glory).

1.2   What Can You Do with Inkscape?

A lot.

Schemes, charts, diagrams. Plans and drafts. Scientific illustrations and data graphs. Icons, symbols, logos, and emblems. Heraldry, flags, road signs. Comics, cartoons, anime characters and scenes. Maps of lands both real and imaginary. Typography of all kinds. Banners, leaflets, posters. Web graphics. (Ads, too.) Book covers, holiday cards, headings, and vignettes. Kids' scribbles and stunning photorealistic art. Fantasy art, fan art, games art, and simply art of all flavors and varieties.

One of the goals of this book is to demonstrate that vector editing tools are applicable to a much wider range of tasks than is usually acknowledged. In fact, instead of trying to list all of the purposes for which Inkscape may be used, it's easier to describe situations where its use may *not* be appropriate. Let's try to define the borders of the Inkscape universe:

- Many tasks with photos or any other **preexisting raster graphics**, such as color corrections, retouching, and format or size conversions, are better done in raster editors such as the GIMP or Photoshop. Of all the limitations of vector images, this one is the best known because it separates the two commonly contrasted kinds of graphic tools: vector and raster. Note that some raster-related tasks—such as adding callouts or marks, drawing shapes over a bitmap background, masking (18.4), or even simple retouching (18.5)—can still be done quite naturally in Inkscape.

- Drawing with **natural-media tools**—those emulating oils, pastels, watercolors, and so on—is best done in specialized raster tools such as Krita, Corel Painter, or ArtRage. More generally, this applies to any art where the *texture* of the colored surface is paramount. Still, if you care more about shape and color than about texture, or if your art looks good with just flat color, gradients, and blurs, Inkscape is one of the best tools for "simply drawing" (Chapter 14).

- Producing **text-rich multipage documents**, especially with complex features such as footnotes, index, or a table of contents, is naturally the domain of page layout software (such as Scribus or Adobe InDesign) or batch formatters (such as TeX or Apache FOP). Inkscape, however, works very well for graphics-rich single-page documents such as posters or leaflets, and you can even use it for some multipage designs by storing each page in a separate document or layer (it does not yet support multiple pages within one document). Also, as of this writing, Inkscape lacks proper CMYK support, which limits its usefulness for print work.

- While Inkscape's 3D Box tool (11.3) can be used for simple **three-dimensional drafts and scenes**, it implements the approach of a traditional artist working on a 2D drawing depicting 3D objects, not of a 3D artist creating a 3D world. In other words, if you need a one-time drawing of a simple 3D scene, you can use Inkscape to get a nice-looking and geometrically correct result. If, however, you want several renditions of the same complex scene from different angles or a 3D animation, use some real 3D software instead (Blender, Maya, or SketchUp, to name just a few).

- You can do some simple **CAD** (Computer-Aided Design; this term usually applies to engineering drawings) work in Inkscape. Inkscape provides ways to draw and transform objects precisely, as well as a plethora of snapping, alignment, and distribution features. However, Inkscape does not support features like parametric modeling, nor does it yet have any libraries of CAD elements (such as screws or tubes) that are essential to professional CAD work. While you may try to borrow such elements elsewhere, in most cases it is still better to use a specialized tool such as QCad or AutoCAD.

- Inkscape has a dedicated Connector tool that you can use to draw pretty complex **diagrams and flowcharts** with automatically routed connectors. However, this tool is currently rather limited, and there are no collections of predefined diagram elements that you can easily reuse in Inkscape. So, if you need to create many standardized diagrams, look into specialized tools such as Visio or Dia.

- Some people have successfully used Inkscape for **presentations**. With its ease of manipulating objects and its many eye candy effects, Inkscape is a very attractive choice when you need to quickly build a presentation. You can create and reuse a page template with headers and placeholder text (3.2). Inkscape even includes a stand-alone SVG viewer (Inkview) with fullscreen mode and Space key for the "show next" command, which is typically all you need for displaying a presentation whose pages are saved in separate SVG documents. An office presentation application such as PowerPoint or OpenOffice.org Impress may still have its advantages, although these programs tend to feel quite clumsy once you get used to Inkscape's graphic power. Some people use Inkscape for drawing the graphics and a presentation application for adding text and creating the actual presentation. Also, a third-party extension called JessyInk (*http://code.google.com/p/jessyink*) will turn your multilayer SVG document into an multipage presentation that can be viewed in Firefox or another SVG-capable browser.

- Inkscape's extension effects (13.3) can render a lot of interesting graphic artifacts such as Lindenmeyer systems, random trees, spirograph curves, or barcodes. New effects are easy to program, too. However, if what you need is some complex **algorithmic art** (such as fractals), you may want to use specialized software and import the result into Inkscape.

- Inkscape does not yet support **animation**. So, while you can use it for drawing animation scenes, characters, and even complete frames, you will still need a different application (such as Adobe Flash) to combine these elements and manage the timeline of your animation.

Admittedly fuzzy (and quickly changing), these are the current frontiers of the vector graphics land. Everything within these boundaries is the rightful domain of a modern vector editor such as Inkscape.

Note that only some of these limits are inherent in vector graphics as such. Others are just current limitations of Inkscape, likely to be overcome with time. (They may be already obsolete by the time you're reading this—check out the latest version.)

Curiously, a lot of people roam the outer graphics lands but are quite unaware about the vector heartland. As a result, they often frustrate themselves trying to use their favorite specialized tool for the wrong generic task. Well-known examples are Microsoft Office users struggling with PowerPoint whenever they need to make any kind of picture or layout, or novices complaining in forums about how difficult it is to draw simple geometric shapes in the GIMP. These are typical cases of acute vector blindness; do not fall prey to this disease!

The vector land is also the place where a lot of project roadmaps begin. No matter what kind of project I am starting and what software I will eventually use, my first step is usually to open Inkscape and start making quick drafts. Only when I run into some of the limitations listed above might I move on to more specialized applications to complete my project. And, increasingly, I find that I don't really need to leave Inkscape to finish what I started. Inkscape's universe keeps expanding.

1.3 Sources of Inkscape Art

A tool is dead without a community of users, and a community of users is nonexistent without a body of work that can be studied and reused. Inkscape wouldn't be quite as fun to use if you always had to start a project from an empty page, or if you had no one to share your work with.

The two main reasons to seek SVG art are *learning* and *reusing*. Reusing is simple; this is what the whole idea of "clipart" is about. Instead of drawing everything from scratch, you take elements created by someone else and combine them with your own stuff (only if the license for those elements permits that, of course).

When reusing others' art, source format is not too important as long as Inkscape can read it (Appendix B). Not only SVG, but PDF and AI files[1] can be the source of vector images for your designs. PostScript and EPS (Encapsulated PostScript) are supported to a lesser extent. CDR (CorelDRAW) files can also be imported, and future versions are likely to support the XAR (Xara Xtreme) format as well.

Also, nothing prevents you from importing a bitmap file into Inkscape and either using it "as is" in your design, or taking advantage of Inkscape's versatile bitmap tracer (18.8.2) to convert it to vector shapes.

Even if you don't use clipart, learning is always a good reason to download the SVG source of an image you find interesting. Unlike a bitmap, a vector image contains a lot of information about the way it was created, and in Inkscape you can examine that information in detail. The correspondence between visible areas and objects, the types of these objects, their properties, grouping and layer structures—all these aspects are very instructive for anyone studying Inkscape or SVG techniques.

Inkscape's files are easy to find online compared to most other vector tools. It shouldn't be surprising given that its native format, SVG, is human-readable and naturally web friendly (it is directly supported by most recent browsers). Moreover, as open source software, Inkscape promotes a culture of sharing that extends to its graphics as well. There is tons of SVG content on the Web already (search Google for *filetype:svg*)—much more than AI, CDR, or XAR files (but still a far cry from Flash[2]).

Apart from searching the Web for SVG content, you might try the following resources:

- Open Clip Art Library (*http://www.openclipart.org*) is a community site with a lot of public domain clipart in SVG format. Inkscape can even import art directly from and export directly to OCAL.

- Wikimedia Commons (*http://commons.wikimedia.org*) contains thousands of SVG images of all sorts, most of them created in Inkscape.

- InkscapeForum.com (*http://inkscapeforum.com*) and the Inkscape group at *http://inkscape.deviantart.com* are two of the places where Inkscape artists share and discuss their creations.

- The Inkscape Wiki (*http://wiki.inkscape.org/wiki/index.php/Galleries*) contains a list of online galleries for individual artists.

1.4 A Brief History of SVG

Inkscape uses SVG as the format for saving its vector files. What is SVG?

The SVG (Scalable Vector Graphics) standard was born at the height of the XML revolution of the late 1990s. In those days, when the lure of simple yet

---

[1] Only PDF-based AI files are supported, which means AI files saved in versions 9 or newer of Adobe Illustrator (B.6).

[2] Ironically, these days Flash is more often used for video than for its original purpose—animated vector graphics.

infinitely expressive XML was fresh, people wanted to create XML vocabularies for *everything*. Vector graphics presented itself as a natural candidate. In 1998, a new working group was formed at W3C, the international consortium that is behind the most commonly used Web standards, including HTML and XML. That group included representatives of (among others) Adobe, Microsoft, and Macromedia. The first fruit of their labors, SVG 1.0, appeared in 2001; the most recent official version is 1.1, published in 2003. The next version, 1.2, is under development, and parts of it are already finalized.

Stemming from the long and often convoluted history of vector formats, SVG tried hard to do things the right way from the beginning. It inherited a lot of good stuff from PostScript and PDF (1.5.1.1) but was designed to be free from their limitations. SVG natively supports transparency, gradients, Unicode for text, and many other conveniences that are taken for granted in the 21st century. It also adds unique filter effects (Chapter 17), which are basically raster operations (such as blur) that can be applied to an object without losing its vector editability and resolution independence.

Since SVG was designed for the Web, and the most common vector format on the Web was (and is) Flash, SVG also includes quite comprehensive animation features. Version 1.2, still under development, adds more goodies: flowed text, vector effects including nondestructive Boolean operations, device-independent CMYK color, and more.

Currently, all modern browsers support SVG to a varying extent, the only exception being (you guessed it) Microsoft's Internet Explorer. (For IE, SVG viewer plugins exist, one of which—now discontinued—was developed by Adobe.) This means that you can load any of your Inkscape SVG files into Firefox the same way you would load a JPG or HTML file, and the browser will display your vector graphic exactly as it looked in Inkscape.

SVG is a large and complex standard, and few software supports all of it. Inkscape's support of SVG is also limited; most notably, it ignores SVG fonts (just like PDF, an SVG document can embed its own fonts) and cannot do animation. Some smaller features are also missing; for example, references to resources (such as gradients or symbols) only work within the same document. It is a stated goal of the Inkscape project to eventually support all of SVG.

When you save an Inkscape document, you have a choice of two SVG formats: *Plain SVG* and *Inkscape SVG*. Plain SVG is just that: pure SVG 1.1 code and nothing else. Inkscape SVG, however, adds quite a number of elements and attributes in Inkscape's private namespace.

Don't be afraid of Inkscape SVG! It is perfectly valid and standard-compliant SVG; the goal of these additional elements and attributes is just to provide Inkscape-specific metadata *about* the SVG objects, not to add some incompatible objects of Inkscape's own. Inkscape extensions may affect how objects *behave* when you edit them in Inkscape, but they never affect how the document is *rendered*. [3] Therefore, Inkscape SVG and Plain SVG versions of the same file will look exactly the same in any compliant SVG renderer. The only reason to use

---

[3] See 15.2.2 for an exception, however.

Plain SVG may be to reduce the file size or produce a document more suitable for manual editing by an SVG expert.

Inkscape can also save files as *compressed SVG* (both Plain and Inkscape varieties). Compressed files have the extension *.svgz*; unlike SVG, they are not human-readable but take much less space on disk. Most programs will read SVGZ files just as easily as they read SVG.

1.5   Inkscape and Its Competition

Of course, Inkscape is far from being the only game in town. There have existed and still exist dozens of vector editors: commercial and open source, for different platforms, generic and specialized, alive and dead. Only a few of them, however, deserve to be mentioned here. Currently, all of Inkscape's serious competitors are commercial (and often quite costly) applications, usually limited to the Windows and Mac platforms, which means Inkscape's zero cost and cross-platform availability immediately give it a competitive advantage.

1.5.1   Adobe Illustrator

Adobe Illustrator takes the indisputable first place in this list. An immensely powerful and feature-packed application, it is usually considered the leader in the field and a de facto standard in vector graphics. Even if you don't use Illustrator, you are likely to run across mentions of its features and versions, comparisons of other programs to it, and of course AI-created vector files in various formats (including SVG).

No doubt much of Illustrator's clout is channeled from its much more famous cousin, Adobe Photoshop. Positioned as parts of the same creative suite, Photoshop and Illustrator share many UI traits and are optimized for working together. However, compared to Photoshop, Illustrator's position in its field is fortunately much less of a monopoly. Even without Inkscape, it still has very serious competition, although its prominence has been growing in the recent years.

Dating from the late 1980s, Illustrator has had a long and winding history. It wasn't always the dominant player in vector graphics. Many of its features were pioneered in competing packages and, sometimes only after several years, were reimplemented in AI. By now, however, it's so big—and growing bigger with every version, especially if you consider the rest of Adobe's Creative Suite as well as a whole industry of third-party AI plugins—that any generalizations are risky. Illustrator is a lot of things to a lot of people.

And yet, I think I can risk one such generalization: Whatever its capabilities, few people will claim Illustrator's UI as a paragon of usability. Critics (admittedly mostly users of competing packages) cite a cluttered interface dominated by a swarm of floating dialogs, too many tools with too narrow functions, limited on-canvas editability of objects' properties, and scarcity of context information. Competing editors also often claim a speed edge over AI.

AI   *I'm not trying to write a comprehensive migration guide for AI users. Still, throughout the book, I will provide the AI equivalents and comparisons for some of Inkscape's features.*

1.5.1.1 Adobe's Vector Formats

Vector formats associated with Illustrator, and with Adobe in general, play a crucial role in the modern digital world. You need to have an idea of what PostScript and PDF are, how they are related, and what they are capable of, even if you're not planning to use anything but SVG with Inkscape.

Adobe's first claim to fame, back in 1984, was creating the grandfather of all vector graphic formats: *PostScript*. Designed as a standard for sending data to printers, it was ready just in time to become a major component of the "desktop publishing revolution" of the 1980s, driven by accessible personal computers and laser printers.

PostScript was (and is) quite unusual in that it is a complete *programming language* and not just a data format. A PostScript file is actually a program that a printer or computer must run in order to get an image. For example, a PostScript file may contain an instruction to print a text line, such as "I must not disrupt the class," and a loop that will repeat this line a hundred times. Unfortunately, this also means that, due to an error in the program or someone's malicious intent, a PostScript program might run indefinitely, tying up the system's resources.

On the positive side, PostScript's interpreter used little memory and could therefore be embedded in the hardware of the day. As a result, it became popular with printer makers and soon was the de facto standard for sending files to print.

It was also used as the base for the native file format of the first versions of Adobe Illustrator, which appeared about that time. Even though the AI file format changed in many ways with every version of the application, for a long time its foundation remained the same: An AI file was simply PostScript that followed certain conventions and used PS function libraries from Adobe.

Unfortunately for the users of Illustrator, PostScript's priorities as a print language were in addressing the concerns of printer makers rather than becoming a generalized vector graphics language. For example, Level 2 of PostScript (1991) added device-independent CMYK color, but it wasn't until Level 3 (1997) that such a basic thing as gradients became directly possible. (Until PS 3, applications wishing to create a gradient in PostScript had to "fake" it by overlaying many narrow strips of gradually changing color.) And even today, PostScript still does not support transparency natively.

This is undoubtedly one of the reasons why early versions of Illustrator were so slow to gain the new features that users demanded (and that competing vector editors were already providing). To this day, Illustrator's UI bears marks of being built with the PostScript feature set in mind, with everything else treated as an afterthought.

However, the biggest issue with PostScript is not its feature limitations. Over time, its being a programming language proved to be much more of a burden: What was once a clever hack in the late 1980s is now regarded as very cumbersome and dangerous. Since any PostScript file is a program, you simply cannot tell what exactly this file will display except by *running* that program. This means you need a complete PostScript interpreter in order to do even the simplest processing of PostScript files, and you cannot directly combine two PostScript files into a single document with predictable results.

Adobe tried to rectify this by imposing various limitations on PostScript files. One such limitation was the *Encapsulated PostScript (EPS)* format. An EPS file is simply a one-page PostScript document that can be reliably inserted into other documents. However, this was obviously not enough.

So in 1993, Adobe took a more drastic step: It introduced *Portable Document Format (PDF)*. This format, although based on PostScript, drops the idea of being a programming language. At first, PDF was just simplified PS rewritten in a declarative fashion with added compression and some top-level document management features. Later, Adobe went on to develop PDF well past what was ever available in PostScript; for example, transparency was added in PDF version 1.4 (2001).

Although PDF's stated goal was Internet document exchange, it became popular and eventually started gaining a foothold in print and design as well. The fact that PDF is an open format, standardized by ISO and free for implementation by anyone, also helped. By now, PDF has largely replaced PS in most commercial applications, including print.

More importantly for our discussion, with version 9.0 (2000), Adobe Illustrator switched its native AI file format to one based on PDF instead of on PostScript. This means that any AI file saved in a modern version of Adobe Illustrator is in fact PDF and can be viewed and imported by any software that supports PDF. For example, Inkscape's AI importer is actually the same as its PDF importer.

In summary, at this point in time it really makes no sense to use PostScript or EPS if you can use PDF instead. Inkscape can import PS and EPS, but only by converting them into PDF first, which requires the free cross-platform Ghostscript package (**B.4**) to be installed on your system. Exporting from Inkscape to PDF gives better results than exporting to PostScript.

1.5.2 CorelDRAW

Currently, Illustrator's biggest rival is CorelDRAW. Like Illustrator, it is a large, full-featured application and is part of a suite of graphic applications. Here, however, the similarities end.

CorelDRAW has always positioned itself as a vector editor "for the rest of us." Priced lower than Illustrator or Freehand (the main contender of Illustrator back in early 1990s, now bought out by Adobe and discontinued), CorelDRAW has always emphasized ease of use and, during the 1990s, greatly expanded the audience of vector editing tools. In some countries and communities, it was, and still is, more popular than Illustrator.

CorelDRAW pioneered some valuable UI concepts that were passed down to a number of other applications, including Inkscape. For example, the single Selector tool that can do all kinds of selections and transformations (move and scale, then click once and you can rotate and skew) first appeared in CorelDRAW; Illustrator and Freehand have separate "select," "scale," and "rotate" tools instead.

It has also introduced the notion of shapes (such as rectangles or ellipses) as separate object types, with the path editing tool acting differently on the shapes than on plain paths. Incredibly enough, Illustrator still has no concept of shapes; any rectangle in Illustrator is just a rectangular path, with no rectangle-specific properties.

1.5.3 Xara

CorelDRAW was, and still is, an impressive improvement over Illustrator in terms of usability. However, a lot more could be done in this area, as Xara Ltd., a small British company, managed to prove. In the mid-1990s, Xara ported its vector editor from the little-known Atari platform to Windows. The result was one of the most impressive debuts in computer graphics.

Xara's vector editor scored a number of important firsts. It featured complete on-screen antialiasing, on-canvas editing of gradients with convenient handles, convenient transparency support, and a context-sensitive panel with controls relevant to the current tool (despite the obviousness of the idea, it's something Illustrator didn't have until version CS2). On top of that, Xara was very fast, which was especially important with the hardware of the day.

In general, Xara had followed the CorelDRAW UI paradigm (so much so that for a time, Corel even distributed Xara under the name of CorelXARA, as a kind of a little brother to its CorelDRAW). However, the advantage in usability Xara held over CorelDRAW was even greater than the latter's advantage over the clunky Illustrator. Xara soon acquired a sizeable and very loyal user base. It's no wonder Inkscape has borrowed a lot of ideas and approaches from Xara.

However, over the years, Xara's novelty faded somewhat. Xara released several new versions, but so did its competitors, inventing new features and improving usability. By the mid-2000s, Xara was perceived by most people as a "nice little app"—very solid and usable, but somewhat passe.

In 2005, Xara Ltd. took an unprecedented step: It announced its plans to release as open source—and port to Linux—its flagship product, the vector graphic editor, whose most recent version was called Xara Xtreme. The Linux version was to be called Xara LX. This looked like, but actually wasn't, one of the "better to be open source than abandonware" scenarios. Xara remained in business, continuing to sell the Windows version of Xara Xtreme as well as other graphic products.

Interestingly, one of the reasons for the plunge quoted by Xara Ltd. was the rapid progress of Inkscape. Although much younger than Xara, Inkscape already had some unique features. Apparently, Xara wanted to tap into the open source talent pool to revitalize its product. On the other hand, Inkscape developers had always acknowledged Xara, with its consistent interface design and excellent usability, as one if its role models. So, even though these two applications had been aware of each other before, now for the first time they met face-to-face as competitors.

Indeed, due to its presence on Linux and general similarity of the UI, Xara is currently Inkscape's most direct competitor. At first, both projects declared themselves open and willing to exchange code and ideas, and there was even talk of an eventual merger. However, after the initial spurt of activity, Xara LX failed to attract significant attention from open source developers, mostly because

Xara Ltd. refused to release as open source one crucial part of the code—the renderer. Currently at version 0.7, Xara LX is basically usable, but its future is unclear.

1.5.4 . . . and Inkscape

Compared to its commercial competition, Inkscape still scores low in several respects. Of the missing features, perhaps the most important is the lack of native CMYK support, which makes it hardly usable for creating files for print (**8.2.2**). Also, Inkscape has no gradient meshes. This is a feature of AI and some other applications that allows different colors to be assigned to different points of a single object, with smooth transitions between the colors. Gradient meshes allow AI artists to create extremely photorealistic art with a minimum of objects. On the other hand, Inkscape already has some innovative features that are pretty much unique in its field, such as the clone tiler (**16.6**), 3D Box tool (**11.3**), path effects (Chapter **12**), and parts of the Tweak tool (**8.7**).

The most obvious reason why some features are not yet implemented in Inkscape is that they are missing in SVG. In particular, this is the case for the gradient meshes (although they are being considered for the next version of SVG standard). Similarly, Inkscape implements SVG's linear and elliptic gradients (**10.1**) but lacks other gradient types, such as conical supported by Xara. The same reason is behind the impossibility to create multiple-page documents in Inkscape. This is simply not provided for in the SVG standard at this time.

Fortunately, the only area where the limitations of SVG matter for Inkscape is the repertoire of basic object types. In its ways of manipulating these objects and combining them into higher-level objects, on the other hand, Inkscape is entirely free to innovate.

In interface and usability, Inkscape is often acknowledged to be quite easy to learn and work with. Inkscape's UI is comparable, and in fact quite similar, to that of Xara. Some things are done more conveniently in one of these programs than the other, but both feature an unobtrusive, streamlined interface with a lot of easily accessible power.

As a true open source application, Inkscape is coded mostly by geeks, and geeks' interests and priorities are sometimes quite different from those of commercial developers. For one thing, geeks hate dumbed-down interfaces and enjoy powerful controls and unlimited tweaking. They especially appreciate rich keyboard control, and Inkscape has an unprecedented number of keyboard shortcuts covering most of its modes, tools, commands, and features (Appendix **D**).

Not any less important than features and usability are an application's stability and speed. Inkscape's released versions may crash or freeze occasionally (save often!), but generally stability is not a concern for most users. Speed, however, is. Inkscape's screen update speed is far from stellar, and although it is improving with every new version, it may very well become a problem with complex graphics.

Ironically, a few years ago when Inkscape was, overall, significantly slower than it is now, complaints about its speed were rare; in fact, most users considered it pretty snappy. Now, however, even though the screen update is faster and the program is much more responsive, complaints about Inkscape's slowness and memory consumption are starting to really pile up.[4] The reason for this apparent paradox is simple: Inkscape has grown and matured enough to take on some really complex tasks, and artists using it on complex artwork start to hit the ceiling more and more often.

1.6   The Life of an Open Source Application

As you can see from this discussion of Inkscape's competition, it is rather unusual for a serious vector editor to be an open source application. What helped Inkscape succeed where other open source attempts (and there were quite a number of them) failed? Let's take a brief look at Inkscape's past.

The story of Inkscape begins almost simultaneously with that of SVG, except that that first chunk of code wasn't yet called Inkscape. It was called *Gill* and was the creation of a single person, Raph Levien, who in early 1999 hacked away at a simple viewer and editor for the new vector format, then under discussion by the W3C. It was a typical one-man project, and it suffered the fate of many one-man projects: Its author soon lost interest in it.

But the Gill code was publicly available, and another person picked up the development. Lauris Kaplinski renamed the project *Sodipodi* and set a much more ambitious goal for it: Develop a real vector editor with most of the bells and whistles usually associated with this genre, with the UI largely modeled on CorelDRAW but also influenced by the GIMP, a well-known open source bitmap editor.

The first releases of Sodipodi were done by Lauris alone and attracted little attention. By 2002, however, more and more people were discovering Sodipodi, and patches from other developers started flowing in. Yet, Lauris remained the sole maintainer of the application; he decided which patches would go in and when the releases would be made. Few people other than him had commit rights to the project's code repository.

Lauris did a great amount of work on Sodipodi; to this day, a sizeable portion of Inkscape's code bears his copyright. However, with time, his autocratic way of steering the project was becoming more and more of an obstacle. Patches being ignored for a long time and disagreements erupting over the development direction weren't healthy.

In October 2003, things came to a head. A group of dissatisfied developers, after failing to reach an agreement with Lauris, declared a fork. They took the latest Sodipodi codebase, added their patches, and coined a cool name for the new project: Inkscape.[5] For a short while, Inkscape and Sodipodi were being

---

[4] Along with every speed optimization, there usually comes some exciting new feature that increases the performance demands again. This is what happened in version 0.45, for example. That release introduced *interruptible display*, so you don't need to wait for it to finish redrawing the screen before you can issue a command. This greatly improved the responsiveness of the program. However, the same version also added Gaussian blur (17.1) which, especially in its original implementation, rendered dramatically slower than anything else in Inkscape. As a result, 0.45 received more complaints about slowness than any previous release.

[5] If you're wondering how it was possible to take someone's copyrighted code and start changing and renaming it, read the copy of the General Public License (the file *COPYING*) that comes with your copy of Inkscape.

developed in parallel, but the latter soon entered hibernation, unable to keep up with its young rival.

In contrast with its predecessor, the Inkscape project is very open. No single person has the supreme say on how things are to be done. To be granted full developer rights, including the right to commit directly to the code repository, you need to submit just two successful patches. Especially in Inkscape's early days, very little discussion was taking place at all; if someone took active interest in some aspect of the program, others just assumed that that person knew what he or she was doing and didn't interfere.

Over time, a number of guiding principles have emerged, and now it is not uncommon to see a contribution rejected if it contradicts the developers' idea of how things should work. However, there's still no top authority figure; everything is being decided by discussion and consensus. This means that anyone who's passionate enough to persuade others *and* can code efficiently still has a good chance of influencing the overall direction of the project.

Among the guiding principles of the project there's a simple rule: *Listen to the users.* This sounds commonplace, but it is surprising how few software projects, be they commercial or open source, actually follow this. In Inkscape, it really helps that many of the developers are themselves active users of the program. Also, in its early days, Inkscape had to win over Sodipodi's users in order to survive at all; fortunately, the tradition of taking user feedback seriously has continued even after Sodipodi stopped being a competitor (and it's not like Inkscape suffers a shortage of other competitors).

Another rule of the project is, *Patch first, discuss later.* That means if you have an idea and can code, don't try to talk others into implementing it; do it yourself and let others test it live in the program. If it's any good, your fellow developers will help you make it perfect. (If it's not, you will just have to back it out, that's all.)

One consequence of the "patch first" rule is the policy that development builds must always be workable; any regressions are noted and fixed as early as possible. A community of enthusiastic users downloads the most up-to-date code daily and tests it, long before an official release is even on the horizon. Developers encourage this constant testing and work to facilitate it by providing new compiled binaries for all major platforms every day.

The result has been fast and steady growth of the project, which is now widely acknowledged as one of the most important open source projects and a strong competitor in its software domain. In terms of numbers, as of this writing Inkscape has:

- Almost half a million lines of code
- Over 100 developers (though at any given time, the active core is about 10 people)
- Over 3 million downloads only from the official site
- A user interface translated into more than 50 languages

2

AN INKSCAPE PRIMER

This introductory chapter is for those who have no previous Inkscape experience and little to no experience with other vector editors. These are your first baby steps in the new world. If you have already worked with Inkscape and think you can easily recreate this chapter's final example (Figure 2-24) on your own, feel free to skip this chapter.

2.1 Installing Inkscape

The first question to ask yourself before installing Inkscape is whether you want a *stable version* or a *development build*. Stable versions have been officially released and have version numbers associated with them. Calling a version (for example, version 0.46.1) stable does not mean it's perfect and never crashes; it just means this version has received a decent amount of testing, is more completely documented, and is what most people use. In fact, apart from its stability, the biggest advantage of running a stable version is that this is what other users run, so fellow Inkscape artists are more likely to be able to help you.

Overall, I recommend that you start with a stable version, but consider upgrading to a development build if you find that you like Inkscape and want to support its development, or if you need the new features added since the release (visit the next version's Release Notes on *http://wiki.inkscape.org* to see what's being worked on).

Using a *development build* has its own distinct advantages. First of all, such builds have all the latest and best features, which are often quite significant compared to the latest stable version (especially if it's been several months since the stable release). These new features often include fixes for the important bugs of the stable version. Also, by running the development version, you help the development community to discover and iron out new bugs. Naturally, active developers are more interested in the development version, so you're more likely to receive prompt help directly from the developers.

But what about stability? Granted, development builds are, on average, buggier and crash more often. However, if you run into a bug that's really driving you crazy—and if that bug is not fixed quickly enough—you can always go back to the latest stable version. (Remember to save often, no matter which version you use!)

NOTE *Inkscape's stable releases are still numbered below 1.0, and each release increments the version number by just 0.01 (for example, 0.40 was followed by 0.41, then 0.42, and so on). Recently, several months typically pass between stable releases. Often, a 0.xx stable release is followed by a 0.xx.1 bugfix release (for example, 0.45 was followed within a month by 0.45.1), which adds no new features but fixes some bugs. Development builds after the 0.xx release are designated 0.xx+svn (for example, 0.46+svn), and each build has a revision number (for example, r20887). You can always find out the exact version number, revision, and build date of your installation of Inkscape by opening* **Help ▸ About** *(look at the top-right corner of the* **About** *window) or by running Inkscape from the command line with the* --version *parameter (not on Windows, Appendix C).*

Fortunately, the stable and development versions are equally easy to install. Just go to the Download section of the Inkscape website (*http://www.inkscape.org*) and follow the links to either a stable or a development version for your operating system.

Windows

You will download a *.exe* installer. Just run it and follow the prompts to choose the language, directory, and other options. At the end you will get a clickable icon of Inkscape on your desktop and in the Start menu.

NOTE *Sometimes, development versions for Windows are archive files with the extension .7z. Download the free unarchiver at* http://www.7-zip.org. *With such a build, all you need to do is unarchive the file into some directory and it will run nicely from there.*

Linux

There are several options. If all you want is a stable version, most Linux distributions already include one; just select it in your software installation application (for example, on Ubuntu, launch Synaptic or simply run `apt-get install inkscape` from the command line).

This version, however, is often quite old. If you want a newer stable version or the development bleeding edge version, download an autopackage for the version of choice. After you get the *.package* file, make it executable and run it. (The first time you do this, you will be prompted to download and install the Autopackage program itself; everything is done automatically once you allow it.) Follow the prompts. Once the package is installed, you will get Inkscape in your **System** menu and/or on the desktop (it will also be, of course, runnable from the terminal by typing inkscape).

Mac OS X

You will download a disk image (*.dmg*) file; just open it in the Finder and drag the contents somewhere on your system. Note that you need to install X11 from Apple's OS X installation disc for Inkscape to work.

New development versions are made available fairly regularly, normally every day. If, however, you want absolutely up-to-the-minute Inkscape, or if the above methods do not work for you for some reason, you can get Inkscape's code directly from the SVN repository and compile it yourself. Compiling Inkscape is possible on all major platforms; however, it requires an above average level of computer savviness, so we won't discuss it here.

2.2 Inkscape's "Hello, World!"

Studying a new programming language traditionally starts with a "Hello, world!" example. This is a minimal, yet real and working, program that simply outputs the string "Hello, world!" somewhere and then quits. Let's go through a minimal yet real Inkscape editing session which includes starting the program, creating some objects, editing them, and saving the result.

Starting Inkscape is no different from starting any other program. Depending on your OS and personal preferences, you can click the icon, select it from a menu, or type inkscape on the command line. Whatever you use, you will end up with a default Inkscape interface:

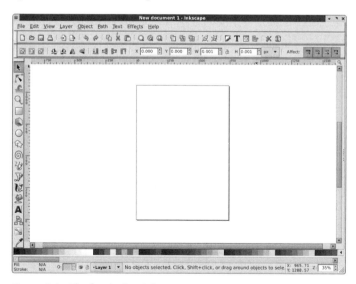

Figure 2-1: The first look at Inkscape

Inkscape's window displays a white work area, called the *canvas*, in the middle and a number of tools and controls at the edges. The canvas is what interests us now. It represents a new, empty, document Inkscape has created for us, so you don't need to select **File ▸ New**. We can start working on it right away.

In the column of icons on the left, click the icon with the blue square. This is the Rectangle tool that lets you create and edit rectangles. Now, click the mouse button anywhere on the canvas and drag. A blue rectangle will appear; when you release the mouse, the rectangle will be created as a new *object* in your document:

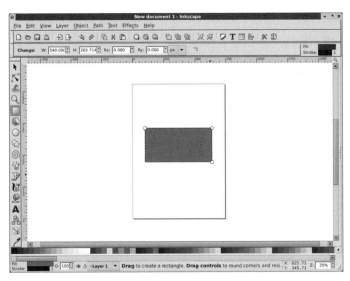

Figure 2-2: We have created a rectangle.

Now, click the **A** button on the left, which will switch you to the Text tool. Click (but do not drag) inside the rectangle. You will see a text cursor blinking where you clicked. Type Hello, world!. You have just created a text object, the second object in your document:

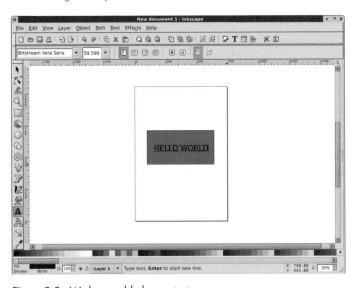

Figure 2-3: We have added some text.

Now, you probably have a better idea as for the size, position, or color of your objects. Easy fix! In the toolbar on the left, click the topmost button showing an arrow. This is the Selector tool. Now you can move any of the objects anywhere on the canvas by dragging with the mouse. To change the color of an object, simply drag that color from the color palette at the bottom of the window and drop it on the object.

Enough tweaking. The document looks perfect. The only problem with it is that it's not saved to a file yet. Just select **File ▸ Save**, navigate to the directory of your choice, and type a filename. That's all: You have just created a new SVG document with graphics and text. Congratulations!

2.3 Interface Overview

Now, let's take a closer look at the interface of Inkscape:

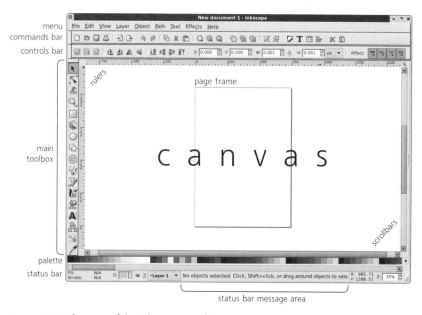

Figure 2-4: Elements of the Inkscape interface

Of course you don't have to work in the small window that Inkscape starts with by default. Feel free to maximize it to fill the whole screen. You can even press F11 to enter fullscreen mode.

Most of the window is occupied by the *canvas*, surrounded by rulers (top and left) and scrollbars (bottom and right). On the canvas, you can see a rectangular shade of a page (A4 paper size by default). This *page frame* defines the edges of your document. However, Inkscape allows you to freely draw anywhere, both on and off the page: The page frame is not a restriction, just a hint. This frame only matters when exporting into some vector formats and when viewing the SVG file in an external viewer; in both these cases you will see only the objects that overlap the page rectangle. You can easily hide the page frame if you don't care about it.

The part of the canvas you see is far from all the canvas there is. In fact, the canvas is so huge, it is almost infinite. You can see more of it by zooming out or by scrolling in any direction, as we'll see in the next section. You'll never run out of room in Inkscape! (In fact, you can even get lost in the vastness of canvas; to return to the page frame, just press the $\boxed{4}$ key at any time.)

To the left of the canvas, there's the vertical *main toolbox*. The buttons on this toolbox activate various Inkscape tools. Each tool has its own purpose, features, controls, keyboard shortcuts, mouse cursors, and other stuff. Some tools create new objects, others edit them in various ways, and still others help you navigate in your document. We'll briefly look at some of the tools in this chapter and explore them all in detail in the rest of the book.

Above the canvas you see two more toolbars, both horizontal. Of these, the top one, called the *commands bar*, is a regular toolbar of the type you'll find in many programs. It has buttons for actions such as **Save**, **Open**, **Undo**, and so on. The other toolbar, immediately above the canvas, is more interesting: It is called the *tool controls bar* (or simply the *controls bar*) and contains various options and controls applicable to the currently selected tool. Click some tool buttons on the left and watch the contents of the controls bar change.

Below the canvas, there's the *color palette*; it can be scrolled horizontally by a scrollbar of its own. Further below, there's the *status bar*, a motley bag of stuff whose components we will explore in detail later. For now, take note of the *message area* of the status bar, which always displays some message relevant to what you're doing now. Pay attention to what the message area is saying; it may save you a lot of time and frustration!

Finally, to the right of the canvas, there's the *dock* for Inkscape's dialogs. By default the dock is hidden, but if you call up a dialog (for example, the **Fill and Stroke** dialog by pressing $\boxed{\text{Shift-Ctrl-F}}$), it will appear in the automatically expanded dock:

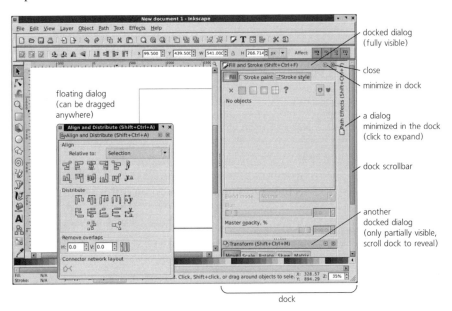

Figure 2-5: Several docked dialogs (and one floating)

The dock may contain many different dialogs; if there are too many of them to fit vertically, the dock gets a scrollbar. Each dialog in the dock can be minimized (the button with the triangle) or closed (the button with the X). You can drag dialogs around in the dock to rearrange them. You can also drag a dialog off the dock, in which case it becomes *floating* and can be placed anywhere on your screen. In most cases, however, working with docked dialogs is more convenient.

NOTE *As of version 0.47, not all Inkscape dialogs can be docked (see 3.7 for more on that).*

All elements of the interface except the menu, the canvas, and the dock can be shown or hidden using commands in the **View ▸ Show/Hide** submenu.

2.4 Panning and Zooming

With an infinite vector canvas, the ability to move around that canvas as well as to zoom in and out for a more convenient view is very important. Inkscape offers a plethora of ways to pan (scroll) and zoom, enough to satisfy every taste.

Of course, the canvas scrollbars work just fine to scroll the canvas wherever you want to go. However, these scrollbars aren't all that convenient, so I usually hide them by pressing Ctrl-B. Instead, what I use most often is *middle-drag*: Press the middle mouse button on any point of the canvas and drag it in any direction. Middle-drag works in any tool or mode.

NOTE *If you think your mouse does not have a middle button, try to press (not roll) the wheel that most mice have in between the left and right buttons. In most cases, this wheel can be clicked just as if it were a button. Of course, rotating the wheel also works to scroll the canvas vertically, whereas rotating it with Ctrl scrolls horizontally.*

Very often, however, my right hand is on the keyboard instead of the mouse. In that case, the most convenient way to scroll the canvas is by pressing Ctrl-→. If you press and hold Ctrl-↑, for example, the canvas starts scrolling downwards (i.e., your view starts going up), at first slowly but gradually accelerating. When you get the hang of it, it feels very natural.

Zooming in and out is also easy. With your keyboard, just press the plus + or minus – keys to zoom in or out (note that unlike most other programs, these are just plain plus and minus keys, either on the main keyboard or on the keypad; you don't need to press Ctrl or Shift with either.) With your mouse, middle click to zoom in and Shift-middle click to zoom out. Or, switch to the Zoom tool where you can use regular left click to zoom in, Shift-left click to zoom out, or drag with the left mouse button to zoom into a rectangular area.

For lots more zooming and panning information and tips, jump to 3.8.

2.5 Creating Objects

Now that you can navigate your way around the canvas, let's have a closer look at the tools available for creating objects.

Looking down the main toolbox, the first object-creating tool you see is the Rectangle tool. This and the next four tools—3D Box, Ellipse, Star, and Spiral—are collectively called *shape tools*, and the objects they create are called *shapes*.

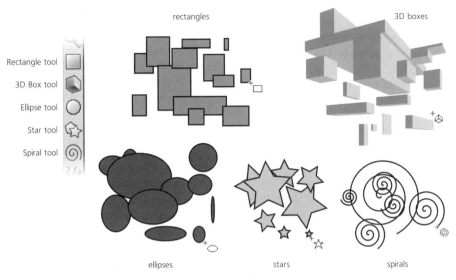

Figure 2-6: *Playing with shape tools*

A *shape* is a geometric object which you can not only move, scale, or rotate (as you can any other object) but also edit in some ways specific to its type. For example, a rectangle can have rounded corners; an ellipse can be turned into a segment (pie-slice shape) or elliptic arc; a 3D box can be moved and resized in its own 3D space. We will talk about shapes in Chapter 11; for now, choose any of the shape tools and start drawing on the canvas. Each mouse drag, from press to release of the left mouse button, creates a new shape.

Next down in the toolbox are the *Pencil* and *Pen* tools. Both create arbitrary paths, but do so differently. The Pencil tool works just like a real pencil: You draw on the canvas, and it leaves behind a trace. (Note that the trace is not exact; it's a bit smoothed out compared to the actual mouse trajectory.)

Figure 2-7: *Using the Pencil and Pen tools*

The Pen tool is more complex; it assumes that you understand how paths are composed of nodes connected by linear or curved segments. For now, just click several times with this tool at different points (this creates linear segments between click points), then click and drag a few times, and finally press Enter to finish the path. Both Pencil and Pen by default create paths with thin black stroke but no fill. We'll discuss these tools in Chapter 14.

The next two tools, *Calligraphic pen* and *Paint bucket*, also create paths, but unlike Pencil and Pen, they by default produce filled paths without stroke. The Calligraphic pen is one of the most versatile tools in Inkscape; its many options and parameters allow it to imitate not only calligraphic pen (which was its original purpose), but also various brushes and many other drawing implements and behaviors (some of which have no counterpart in the real world). This is the primary tool of those who use Inkscape to *simply draw* (Chapter 14).

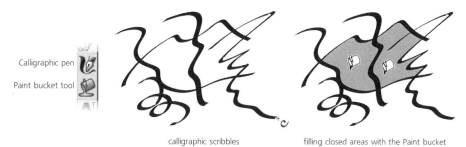

Calligraphic pen

Paint bucket tool

calligraphic scribbles   filling closed areas with the Paint bucket

Figure 2-8: Using the Calligraphic pen and Paint bucket tools

The Paint bucket tool is also a great help for a cartoonist or illustrator. Just as you'd expect, it fills in any bounded area, creating a filled vector path. For practice, draw around a closed area with several brush strokes of the Calligraphic pen, then click inside with the Paint bucket. (If you click in an unbounded area, the tool will fail to fill it and say so in the status bar.)

Finally, the *Text* tool creates and edits text objects. Creating a new text object is as simple as clicking anywhere and starting to type. Or, you can click and drag, in which case you're creating a *flowed text* object that will automatically wrap when you type up to the right edge. Editing an existing text object is just as easy: Click it with the Text tool to position the cursor and use all the familiar text editing keys (the arrow keys, Home, End, Delete, and so on). The Text tool is the subject of Chapter 15.

Text tool

Lorem Ipsum

Lorem ipsum dolor sit amet, consectetuer adipiscing elit. Vestibulum viverra varius enim. Sed a lorem ut est tincidunt consectetuer. Nullam sapien mauris, venenatis at, fermentum at, tempus eu, urna. Donec tempus quam quis neque.

regular text   flowed text

Figure 2-9: Using the Text tool

And what if you need to have a raster object, such as a photo, in your SVG document? This is done not with a tool but by the **Import** command in the **File** menu. Just select any raster image file (JPG, PNG, GIF, and TIFF all work), and it will be inserted into your document. It will, however, remain a raster; for ways to convert it to vector objects, see 18.6.

2.6   Selecting

As you may have noticed, right after you create a new object (for example, with the Rectangle tool or Calligraphic pen) that object has a dashed frame around it. That frame indicates that the object is *selected*.

Selection is a fundamental concept in Inkscape. Almost all tools, commands, dialogs, and shortcuts work only on those objects that are currently selected. Various informational displays, such as the status bar, always describe the selected objects. The ability to quickly and precisely select what you need, as well as to quickly figure out what is currently selected and where, is absolutely vital for effective work in Inkscape.

The main tool that allows you to select objects is called, appropriately enough, the *Selector* (Figure 2-10). It is also the first (topmost) tool on the toolbox, because selecting is so important. You can switch to this tool not only by clicking its button but also by pressing either F1, s, or Space. You really can't miss this tool!

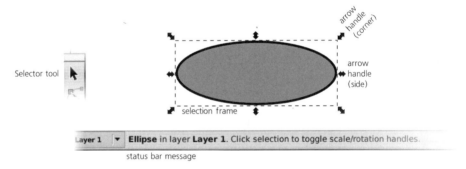

Figure 2-10: The Selector tool and a selected object

Basic selection with Selector is very easy (as is any other basic thing in Inkscape). You just click any object and voilà, it's selected. Try it now. Watch also how the status bar message immediately updates to tell you what exactly you have selected: a rectangle, a path, an ellipse, a text object, and so on.

More than one object can be selected at any time, as shown in Figure 2-11. Usually, when you already have something selected, clicking another object deselects the first. However, if you Shift-click any unselected object, you *add* it to the list of selected objects. (If you Shift-click an already selected object, you will *remove* it from selection.) Note what the status bar says about your new selection. Note also how each of the selected objects has its own dashed frame.

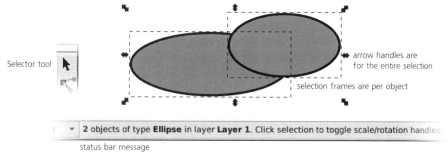

Figure 2-11: Multiple objects selected

Need to select 1,000 objects at once? No need to Shift-click 1,000 times. With Selector, just *drag* (press the mouse button and move the mouse without releasing the button) across all the objects you want to select. You will see a rectangular *rubber band* which follows your mouse. When you release the mouse, all objects that are completely inside the rubber band will get selected:

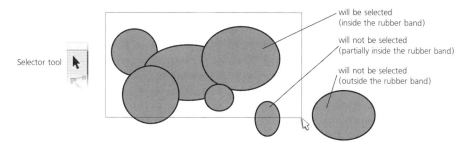

Figure 2-12: Using a rubber band to select multiple objects

You can select by keyboard shortcuts, too. The Tab key has the generic meaning of "going to the next one," so it's not surprising that in Inkscape, pressing Tab selects the next object (typically in the order of creation). Shift-Tab selects the previous object. The familiar Ctrl-A, which in many programs means *select all*, also works as expected.

Need a different selection? Deselect anything you have selected by pressing Esc or by clicking anywhere on the empty canvas (not on an object).

That's just a fraction of all the selection methods and techniques Inkscape offers, but it should be enough to get you started. Let's move on to actually changing what we have selected.

2.7 Transforming

The other function of the Selector tool, apart from selecting objects, is *transforming* them.

"Transforming" is simply an umbrella term for *moving, scaling* (resizing), *rotating,* and *skewing.* The first two of these—and especially moving—are extremely common in vector work because it's nearly impossible to create objects at once in the exact place and with the exact size you need. You will find yourself moving stuff around all the time, so you need to learn how to do this quickly and precisely.

NOTE *All four transformation modes treat an object as a whole. By transforming, you can move, squeeze, rotate, or skew the entire object, but you cannot move one part of the object relative to the other parts; that's a task for other tools. For example, if the nose in your drawing of a face is a separate object, you can make it larger on the face using nothing but the Selector tool. But if the nose is part of the same object as the rest of the face, you will need to use other tools to make the nose larger without also changing the face.*

Moving the selection using the Selector tool is very simple: Just drag any of the selected objects with your mouse. If you have more than one object selected, dragging any one of them moves them all together.

One very common operation is *duplicating* objects, or making an exact copy of the selection. To do this, press Ctrl-D; a copy is created and placed exactly over the original selection (so it does not seemingly change). Just drag it away with the Selector tool to where you want to place the copy. You can also use the traditional copy-and-paste method of duplicating objects (Ctrl-C, Ctrl-V).

Other types of transforming are a little more difficult. Notice that whenever you have anything selected, the selection is surrounded by eight arrow marks. Dragging any of these arrow marks performs *scaling*: This is how you make your selection larger, smaller, taller, wider, and so on. The four corner arrows can move in any direction, resizing the selected objects freely; the four others move only in one direction (the top center and bottom center marks move vertically, the left center and right center move horizontally).

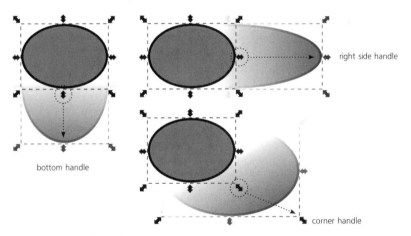

Figure 2-13: Scaling objects

For the remaining two transformation modes, *rotate* and *skew*, you need to click anywhere on any already selected object, or alternatively press Shift-S. Notice how the arrow marks change; now your selection is in the *rotate mode*, as opposed to the *scale mode* we used before (Figure 2-14). Now, dragging any of the four corner arrows rotates the selection around its center, while the four other arrows skew the selection. Also, you can still move your selection around by dragging while it's in the rotate mode. To go back to the scale mode, click the selection or press Shift-S again. Next time you select these or other objects, they will again be in the scale mode first.

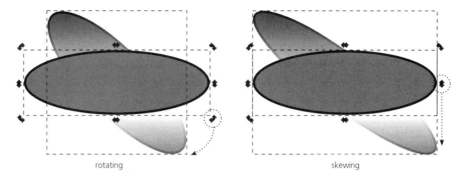

rotating   skewing

Figure 2-14: Rotating and skewing objects

If you prefer to control Inkscape from the keyboard, you won't be surprised to learn that the four arrow keys each move the selection in the corresponding direction. More interestingly, the left and right angle brackets (`<` and `>`) scale the selection down and up, correspondingly, while the square brackets, (`[` and `]`), rotate it. There are no shortcuts for skewing objects.

That's all there is to the basic transformations of objects with the Selector tool. Again, there are many more tricks, shortcuts, and rules of thumb that we'll discuss later, but for now this should suffice for getting a general feel of how Inkscape works.

2.8   Styling

Any object in Inkscape has some style. *Style* is a complex thing that includes many separate properties, from the color of the fill to the width of the stroke and to complex SVG filters that totally alter the way the object looks. Let's look at the basics of changing the style of objects.

First of all, you should have guessed by now that the style-changing actions, as any other actions in Inkscape, always apply to the *current selection*. That is, before you change the style of something, you must first select that something.

Once you select the objects you want to style, the simplest thing to do is just click the color palette at the bottom of the canvas. The color you click becomes the new fill color of all selected objects. Even if the object had no fill at all (like a path created with the Pencil tool), it becomes filled with that color too. (Note that you can scroll the palette to the right to see more colors than fit the screen.)

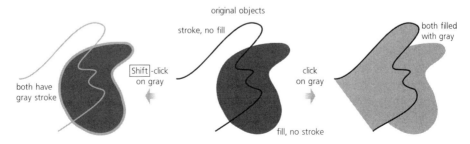

original objects

stroke, no fill

both filled with gray

Shift -click on gray

click on gray

both have gray stroke

fill, no stroke

Figure 2-15: Setting fill or stroke from the color palette

You can just as easily change the stroke color of the selected objects: Simply Shift-click instead of clicking a color. Again, if some objects have no stroke, they will get it now.

Now, pay attention to the complex control in the lower-left corner of your Inkscape window, on the left end of the status bar. This control (shown in Figure 2-16) is called the *selected style indicator*, and in full accordance with its name, it indicates the style of the selection (actually, it only shows the most important style properties; there's much more to an object's style than shown in this indicator). To put it simply, here you can see the fill and stroke colors of the selected objects.

Figure 2-16: Selected style indicator

Perhaps more importantly, here you can also change these style properties. One very common operation is *removing* the fill or stroke from selected objects. Just middle-click the **Fill** (top) or **Stroke** (bottom) swatch to do this, or right-click the corresponding swatch and choose **Remove** from the pop-up menu. Note that an object with no fill and no stroke is completely invisible: You can't see it and you can't click it to select (although you can drag the rubber band *around* it to select it).

Apart from the fill and stroke colors, one important style property is *opacity*. Think of stained glass which has its own color but still shows through what is behind it; this is how objects with opacity less than 100% behave in Inkscape. (Obviously, an opacity of 0% makes an object invisible.) Opacity is changed by the **O:** control in the selected style indicator. Try selecting an object which is on top of other objects and type in a different opacity value; notice how the object becomes semitransparent.

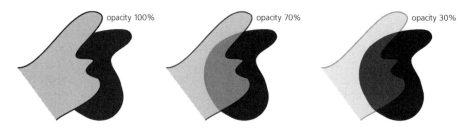

Figure 2-17: Changing opacity

If you just want two objects to have the same style, this is easy to do. Select the first object and press Ctrl-C; this places a copy of the object on the clipboard. Then select the other object (or objects) and paste the style of the clipboard object onto them by pressing Shift-Ctrl-V. This is the easiest way to make multiple objects look the same.

2.9 Saving and Exporting

Now, suppose you've created something in Inkscape that you would like to share with others. What is the best way to go about it?

Saving a document as SVG works as expected. Just press Ctrl-S or choose **File ▸ Save** from the menu, choose the directory, type the filename, and click **Save**.

As far as sharing goes, SVG isn't a bad format at all; for example, as already mentioned, it can be displayed directly, in all its vector glory, in any modern browser (except the one coded by Microsoft). However, for any number of reasons SVG may not be a viable choice in your situation. In that case, you need to *export* your document to some other format. Go to the **Save** dialog again. Note the drop-down list in the lower-right corner; now it displays *Inkscape SVG*, but you can see what else is available. Quite a lot, in fact! More than a dozen different vector formats are listed.

Don't get overexcited, though. Several of these formats are just variations upon the primary Inkscape SVG format (plain SVG, compressed SVG, etc.). Others are severely limited in various ways, either because the target format is itself limited compared to SVG, or because Inkscape's exporter for that format is less than fully developed, or both. These export formats are usable, but only if you know what the limitations are and design your documents with these limitations in mind.

Perhaps the safest export format, besides SVG, is PDF (Appendix **B**). It still cannot handle some SVG features (such as filters, which are by default raster-ized), but for the simple documents you're going to be creating at this early stage of learning Inkscape, it should be perfectly adequate. The big advantages of PDF are, first, that it is vector, and second, that Adobe Acrobat Reader and other PDF viewers have many more users than any program capable of viewing SVG.

As you may have noticed, the **Save** dialog only lists vector formats for export. But what about exporting as a raster image? This is done in a different dialog, called **Export Bitmap**.[1] Open it by pressing Shift-Ctrl-E or choosing **File ▸ Export Bitmap** (Figure 18-16).

At the top of the **Export Bitmap** dialog, there are four buttons for choosing *what* to export. If you drew your image paying respect to the page frame which thus nicely enframes your art, select **Page**. Otherwise, select **Drawing** to make the export area cover all the objects of your image no matter where they are. You can also export only the current selection if you wish.

Then, set either the desired pixel size of your raster image or the resolution of the bitmap (these two values are obviously interconnected: increasing one increases the other, and vice versa). Finally, type or **Browse** for the export filename

---

[1] Actually, this dialog should properly be called *Export PNG*, because as of 0.47, the only raster format it exports is PNG. It's not such a big problem in most cases, though. PNG is viewable in all browsers (even though Microsoft's Internet Explorer has some problems with it, it *can* view PNGs), supports full RGB color and gradual (alpha) transparency, and is just an all-around nice all-purpose format, perfectly suitable for renditions of any vector artwork. If you really need JPG, GIF, or TIFF, you can use any number of specialized tools for converting from PNG to your desired format.

and click **Export**. (After exporting, the dialog remains open, for reasons that will become clear in 18.9.1).

You're done! Take your saved or exported file and show it to the world.

2.10   A Final Example

Let's apply what we have learned so far to a slightly more complex illustration: a silly, South Park–style boy's face. This isn't much of a challenge, of course, but it should be useful for shaking down all the new knowledge you've acquired.

To start, run a new Inkscape instance, or press Ctrl-N to create a new empty document if you're already running Inkscape.

Choose the Ellipse tool and draw an ellipse (Figure 2-18). That will be the boy's head. Scroll the palette at the bottom, choose a suitable body color, and click it to assign it to the ellipse. (You can try several colors until you find the best one.) If the ellipse came up with a stroke, middle-click the **Stroke** swatch in the lower-left corner of the status bar to remove it.

Figure 2-18: One ellipse

Draw a smaller ellipse on top of the head ellipse. What's going on—is it invisible?! No. Ellipse (like most other tools) simply remembered the color you assigned to the head and now used the same color for the new ellipse, so it appears merged into the background of the larger head ellipse (although you can still see the selection frame around it). Scroll the palette back to the left and click the white color swatch to see the smaller ellipse:

Figure 2-19: Two ellipses

This smaller ellipse is supposed to be the white of the boy's eye. It's probably not exactly the size you want the eye to be and is in a funny place for an eye. Switch to the Selector tool and drag the small ellipse to approximately where you want it. Then drag one of the arrow marks at the corners to make it approximately the right size, as shown in Figure 2-20.

Figure 2-20: Positioning the second ellipse

Now we need yet another ellipse for the pupil of the eye. Instead of going back to the Ellipse tool, however, we will use duplication. With the white ellipse still selected, press Ctrl-D. Nothing visibly changed, but we know that we now have two ellipses there, the new one being selected. Click the black color swatch, then drag the arrow marks again to make the pupil smaller and drag it into place:

Figure 2-21: Head and one eye

The eye is ready—but we need two identical eyes. Let's duplicate the entire eye we created. The eye consists of two separate objects, so before duplicating we need to select them both. You can do this either by dragging a rubber band around the eye (but make sure to start dragging from an empty space and not from the head ellipse, otherwise you'll be dragging the head, which is not what you want!), or just click the pupil and then Shift-click the white. Press Ctrl-D and drag the second eye sideways (both objects move when you drag any of them).

Figure 2-22: Head and two eyes

Now, to finish the drawing, choose the Calligraphic pen tool and draw the nose, mouth, ear, and some hair (Figure 2-23). If the paths appear in some wrong color, click black on the palette; after that, all new calligraphic paths will be black too. If the pen draws too wide or too thin, adjust the **Width** value on the tool's controls bar above the canvas. If something turns out wrong, undo by pressing Ctrl-Z.

Figure 2-23: Welcome to the world!

The image is ready, but we're not finished yet with all the possibilities it offers. What you have done so far would be just as easy to do in a raster editor. But we're in vector, so let's use the specific vector advantages to play with the result. Using Selector, select both eyes' whites and scale them up or down. Or move the pupils around. Or scale, rotate, and move the mouth. All of this creates a wide range of facial expressions. You can also select, duplicate, and drag away the entire drawing to present several examples side by side:

Figure 2-24: Life and its many faces

Save or export the result. That's all!

3

SETTING UP AND MOVING AROUND

After the first introductory chapters, this one will finally get you started in Inkscape in a serious way. From here on, we will explore practical topics at a maximum level of detail, leaving no stone unturned. It is impossible to predict what features or techniques you will find most useful; this depends a lot on the nature of your work and your personal tastes. That's why this book tries to cover absolutely everything Inkscape has to offer.

In this short chapter, you won't be creating or editing any objects yet. Instead, you'll prepare your workspace, discuss some useful customizations, and learn techniques to navigate the document by zooming and panning.

3.1 Preferences

Inkscape is an extremely configurable piece of software. Throughout this book, we will mention all sorts of Inkscape *preferences* that you can change to explore the program's capabilities and better adapt it to the way you prefer to work. Before you begin using Inkscape for anything of consequence, therefore, let's see how and where all the various preferences are set and stored in Inkscape.

All user preferences in Inkscape belong to one of two main classes.

3.1.1 Inkscape Preferences

Inkscape preferences (sometimes called *global preferences* or just *preferences*) affect those aspects of the program which do not depend on the particular document you're editing. These preferences include the default behavior of various tools and shortcuts, details of treatment of various object types, display and color management options, and so on.

Most of these options are set in the **Inkscape Preferences** dialog (press Shift-Ctrl-P or select **File ▶ Inkscape Preferences**). Some preferences, however, are set by commands; for example, when you hide scrollbars by pressing Ctrl-B (or choosing the equivalent command from the **View ▶ Show/Hide** submenu), that setting is also remembered as a global preference.

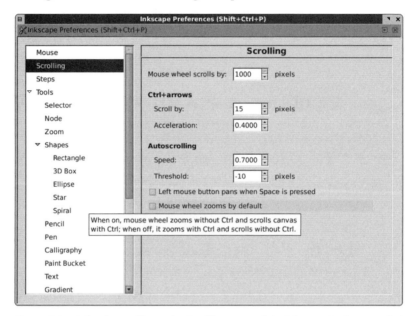

Figure 3-1: A floating tooltip on the Scrolling page of the Inkscape Preferences dialog explains one of the options.

Throughout the book, we will discuss specific global options where they are relevant, referring to the corresponding pages of the **Inkscape Preferences** dialog (the list of pages is shown on the left side of the dialog). All options in the dialog have useful descriptions; if you need help, hover your mouse over an option and read the floating tooltip (Figure 3-1).

Note that the dialog has no **Save** or **Apply** button. Most changes take effect immediately. A few require you to restart Inkscape, which will be mentioned in the option's description. All global preferences are automatically saved when you exit the program.

The file where the global preferences are stored is called *preferences.xml.* Its location depends on your platform; on Linux it's the directory *.config/inkscape* from your home directory; on Windows, it can be found at *Documents and Settings\ <your login>\Application Data\Inkscape.*

NOTE *Some little-used options have no UI; the only way to set them is by manually editing the* preferences.xml *file. This is an XML file with a simple and largely self-explanatory format. Typically, you will be given instructions to change a specifically named attribute of an element with a certain ID, for example,* printing. *You would then load that file in a text editor, search for the string* id="printing", *and edit the value of the specified attribute in that element, for example by replacing* attribute="old" *with* attribute="new" *(note that attribute values are always in quotes).*

3.1.2 Document Properties

Document properties, on the other hand, apply to individual documents. This category of options includes the size and orientation of the canvas, the default measurement unit, various snapping options, status of the snapping grid and guidelines, and so on. Most of these options are set in the **Document Properties** dialog:

Figure 3-2: The Page tab of the Document Properties dialog

Document properties are automatically saved as part of the Inkscape SVG document for which they are set. This means that, for example, if you change snapping modes in one document, they will be remembered the next time you load that document, but they will not affect other documents. To change the document properties for newly created documents, you will need to edit the document template used to create those documents, as you'll see in the next section.

3.2 Document Templates

When you run Inkscape, it automatically creates a new document for you, based on the default template. Inkscape's window cannot exist without some document loaded into it, so if you don't give it some existing document to load, it will create a new one for you.

If you need to create an empty document from a window where another document is being edited, just press [Ctrl-N] or go to the **File ▸ New** submenu. This submenu lists a number of document templates for new documents. The default template—the one that you call up by [Ctrl-N]—is the first on the list, but there are quite a few others.

A *document template* is just a regular Inkscape SVG document with a specific page size, default unit of measure, and other document properties saved into it. To create a new document, Inkscape simply makes a copy of a template. Usually a template is empty but it can contain any objects, as well as show any snapping grids or guidelines. Inkscape ships with a collection of templates for standard paper sizes, standard icon and web banner sizes, desktop sizes (for wallpapers), CD/DVD covers, and business cards. For example, here is the template for a 16-by-16 pixel icon (to create a website's favicon), with pixel grid enabled:

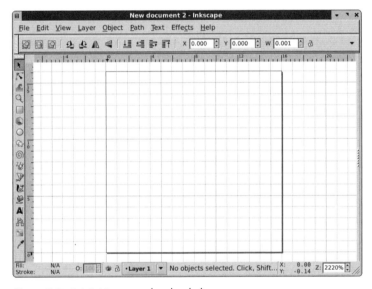

Figure 3-3: 16x16 icon template loaded

You can add your own templates to the list. Any document that is a better starting point than the default empty canvas can be turned into a template. For this, just copy or save the document to the user templates directory, which is *~/.config/inkscape/templates* on Unix and *share/templates* inside the Inkscape application data directory (*Documents and Settings\<your login>\Application Data\Inkscape*) on Windows. If this directory does not yet exist, create it. In the **Save** dialog in Inkscape, there's a shortcut in the left pane called **templates**; double-clicking it takes you to that directory (this shortcut is not available on Windows).

You can even override any of the standard templates if you use the same name for your custom template. For example, the default template is called *default.svg*; if you save a file under that name in your template directory, it will be used as the base for all new documents created when you run Inkscape or press [Ctrl-N].

3.3 Keyboard Setup

Inkscape is unusually rich in keyboard shortcuts. A complete chart of all keyboard and mouse shortcuts (you can view it in the browser by choosing the **Keys and Mouse Reference** command in the **Help** menu) contains more than 460 entries.

Normally, keyboard shortcuts don't require any setup: They just work. Sometimes, however, you may want to change some of these shortcuts or add new ones, perhaps because you're used to a different keyboard layout from another program, or simply because your work habits are not adequately covered by the existing shortcuts.

Most (although currently not all) of Inkscape's keyboard shortcuts can be configured by the user. You can also assign a shortcut to any of the commands that you see in the menus, including any extensions in the **Extensions** menu (13.3). There are even a few relatively obscure commands that are not included in any menu and do not have any shortcuts by default but can be accessed if you assign shortcuts to them.

NOTE *The shortcuts you cannot yet configure include those that involve mouse clicking or dragging, as well as those keyboard shortcuts that are limited to a single tool or mode (i.e., only* global *keyboard shortcuts can be configured).*

All of Inkscape's keyboard configuration files are stored in the directory *keys* which is inside the *share* directory of your Inkscape installation. There, the file *default.xml* is the only one that Inkscape reads when it is started; this is the standard Inkscape keyboard layout.

The *inkscape.xml* file is just a copy of *default.xml*. Other files in that directory provide keyboard layout emulations for all the major Inkscape competitors (Adobe Illustrator, CorelDRAW, Xara Xtreme, Macromedia Freehand) as well as for some minor vector editors (Zoner Draw, ACD Systems Canvas). The file *right-handed-illustration.xml* is a variant of the standard layout which places the most often used commands under the left hand so you can avoid lifting your right hand from the mouse or tablet.

You can enable any of these layouts instead of the standard one by copying the corresponding file over *default.xml* and restarting Inkscape. Note that the alternative layouts may not be as complete or up-to-date as the main one. Any help in improving these alternative layouts or adding new ones will be appreciated by the developers.

Changing existing shortcuts or adding new ones is possible by editing the currently used keyboard layout—the file *default.xml*. This XML file is quite simple in structure and contains extensive explanations in comments, so I will not describe it here.

3.4 Page Setup

The first tab of the **Document Properties** dialog, called **Page** (see Figure 3-2), contains some general settings that you will be changing quite often, so we'll look at them now. (All other tabs control grids, guides, and snapping modes; we will discuss them in detail in Chapter 7.)

3.4.1 Document Units

First of all, you can set the default unit for your document—for example, px (SVG pixel; see **A.6**) or mm (millimeters). This setting will affect all places where you see or can specify lengths or coordinates. For example, the **X**, **Y**, **W**, and **H** controls of the Selector tool display their values measured with the default unit of the document, although to the right of them there is a drop-down menu where you can choose any other unit (see Figure 6-10). Similarly, status bar hints (for example, when drawing a path with the Pen tool, **14.1**) indicate distances in the default unit.

3.4.2 Background

You can also change the background color and opacity of the document (the default is fully transparent white). Just click the color swatch and use the pop-up color selector menu:

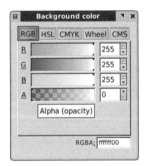

Figure 3-4: Choosing page background color and opacity

Changing the opacity of a white background has no visible effect on your screen, but it will affect the exported PNG files: They will only have transparent background if you have transparent background in your SVG document.

NOTE *The background color and opacity will not work in other SVG viewers, which will always show a transparent background. The Inkscape background color setting is limited to editing display and bitmap export in Inkscape itself. If you want a colored background that works everywhere, create a background rectangle underlying the entire drawing.*

3.4.3 Page Size

Next, you can change the page size—either by choosing from a list of standard sizes or by specifying a custom size—and the orientation (portrait or landscape). Inkscape's canvas is virtually limitless (**1.1**), and you can draw anywhere on it, be it inside or outside the page. However, most standard SVG viewers will only display what is on the page, ignoring anything outside the page boundaries.

So, if you're preparing your artwork to be published or shared in SVG format, you can use outside-the-page canvas as clipboard or work area, but then place the finalized artwork onto the page. Printing or exporting to most vector formats also ignores everything outside the page. Bitmap export, however, can take either the page, or the actual drawing (all objects), or just the selected objects no matter where they are located (2.9).

If you've been drawing without much regard to page borders but now want your drawing to fit precisely within the page boundaries, a convenient way to do this is to select the **Fit page to selection** button in the **Document Properties** dialog. Just select all objects that you want to have in the final drawing (Ctrl-A or rubber band selection, see 5.7) and click this button to make the page border frame the selected objects exactly.

As you resize the page, the objects in your drawing remain fixed relative to the top and left sides, whereas the right and bottom sides move.

At other times, however, you may not care about the size of the page at all. For example, you may be working on a collection of icons or logos, all in the same SVG file, not intending to share the SVG but exporting each icon to a separate bitmap file. In that case, the rectangle of the page is just a distraction. The page border controls at the bottom of the **Document Properties** dialog allow you to change the color and shadow of this rectangle or just hide it altogether. You can also place the border on top of the drawing so it remains visible over any objects that might otherwise obscure the edges of the page.

3.5   Instances, Documents, Views

An Inkscape window you see on your screen (such as the one on Figure 2-1) is not the same as Inkscape itself. A running copy of the program—an *instance*—may have many documents open, and each document is in its own editing window. Moreover, the same document can be loaded into more than one window, providing different views of the same drawing. Any changes made to a document in one window are immediately reflected in all windows (within the same instance) where the same document is loaded.

The easiest way to open multiple windows with different documents is to start with any existing window and use the **File ▸ Open** command (Ctrl-O) from it. If that window contained a new and unchanged document (i.e., just an empty canvas), it will be replaced by the opened document. Otherwise, a new window will be created for the newly opened document.

Alternatively, you can list the filenames of all documents you want to open in the command line when calling Inkscape (C.1):

```
$ inkscape portrait.svg ../path/to/document.svg another.svg
```

If you want to open a new window showing another view of a document you already have open, use the **View ▸ Duplicate Window** command from an existing window with that document. After that, you will have two windows with two views of the same document, but each with its own independent zoom level, active tool, and selection. Any changes made to the document in one window are immediately visible in the other.

To cycle through all the windows belonging to the same instance of Inkscape (whether they have the same or different documents), press Ctrl-Tab (forward) or Shift-Ctrl-Tab (backward).

For example, in one window you can work in close zoom on small details of your drawing, at the same time viewing the entire document zoomed out in another window:

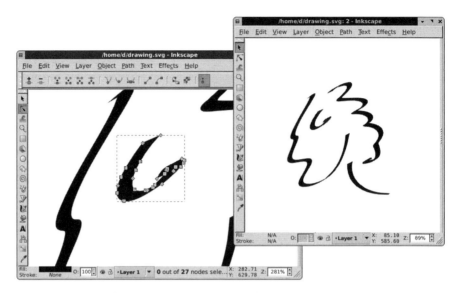

Figure 3-5: Using multiple windows with the same document

NOTE *If you just launch the Inkscape program twice, you will get two Inkscape windows, but these windows will belong to* different *Inkscape instances. Between such windows, automatic synchronization of the views of the same document does not work.*

3.6 The Document Window

The main components of Inkscape's window (Figure 2-4) are, from top to bottom: the menu, the commands bar, the controls bar (whose contents change when you switch tools), the main toolbox on the left and the dialog dock on the right with the document canvas between them, and, at the bottom, the palette and the status bar. By default, the canvas area has rulers (top and left sides) and scrollbars (bottom and right sides).

NOTE *Press* Alt-X *to access the first editable control in the controls bar.*

All parts of an Inkscape window, with the exception of the menu and the canvas itself, can be hidden by the commands in the **Show/Hide** submenu of the **View** menu, as shown in Figure 3-6.

Leave only what you need; the more you hide, the more room is left for your drawing. I usually hide the commands bar, rulers, and scrollbars. Most of the time I also hide the palette, unless I plan to use Inkscape for color-intensive tasks (such as coloring cartoons).

All these options are remembered in global preferences and will be restored when you next start Inkscape. Moreover, Inkscape's window can be switched to fullscreen mode (press F11 or go to **View ▸ Fullscreen**). In that mode, the set of

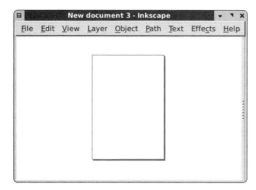

Figure 3-6: A minimal Inkscape window

visible interface elements can be entirely different. For example, you may show the toolbar and the tool controls in the regular mode where you do all the editing but hide them in the fullscreen mode that you use to view your artwork with minimum distraction.

3.6.1 Window Geometry

The phrase *window geometry* refers to something very simple: the size of an Inkscape window and its position on the screen. In its attempt to be as helpful as possible, Inkscape remembers this size and position for each document window and saves these values with that document. So, when you next load the document, the window is opened with the same size and position it had the last time the document was saved.

In most cases, this is helpful. Sometimes, however, this is more of an annoyance—for example, if you get Inkscape SVG files from someone who has a different screen resolution, the window on your screen may end up in a weird place. To disable this behavior, go to the **Windows** tab of the **Inkscape Preferences** dialog and change the **window geometry** option:

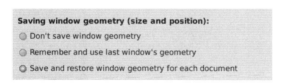

Figure 3-7: The window geometry option

The first choice disables both saving and reading window geometry. The second choice makes window geometry a global rather than per-document preference, so that the whenever you change the size or position of any Inkscape window, this geometry is then applied to all subsequently opened windows. The last choice—per-document window geometry—is the default.

For example, if you want each new document to open in a maximized window, there are two things you can possibly do. First, you can maximize the window with an empty document and then save the empty document as *default.svg* in your template directory; the maximized state of the window will be saved with it, and all newly created documents will then be maximized. Or, if you always maximize all your windows, just switch the window geometry option to **Remember and use last window's geometry** (the second choice).

Apart from window geometry, the current zoom level and the view area are always saved with the document, so you will be looking at the same place at the same zoom when you next load it into Inkscape.

3.7 Dialogs

Apart from the main editing window, Inkscape's user interface contains a number of smaller panels, called *dialogs*, each with a specific function. While Inkscape strives to make most editing operations accessible right on the canvas via tools and shortcuts, dialogs still exist and are used quite frequently.

For each dialog, usually there's a menu command and a keyboard shortcut that starts with Ctrl and Shift (for example, Shift-Ctrl-F opens the **Fill and Stroke** dialog). A newly opened dialog gets keyboard focus, so you can not only work with it using your mouse, but also navigate it using the Tab key, switch tabs with Ctrl-Page Up and Ctrl-Page Down, type values into fields, and so on.

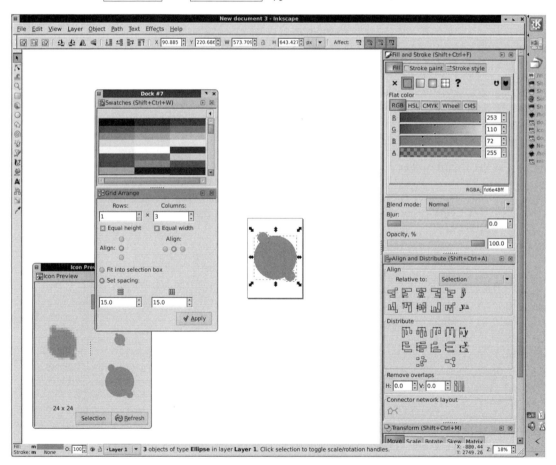

Figure 3-8: Floating and docked dialogs

To close a dialog, just click the "X" in the top-right corner or, if the dialog has keyboard focus, press $\boxed{\text{Ctrl-W}}$. To move keyboard focus back to the canvas without closing the dialog, click the canvas or press $\boxed{\text{Esc}}$. If a dialog is already opened, choosing its command or invoking the shortcut again does not close it but moves keyboard focus to it.

As of 0.47, most dialogs are dockable (a few which are not will be made dockable in future versions). A dockable dialog can be *docked*—placed into the docking area on the right-hand side of the editing window, or it may be *floating* in a small window of its own. (Nondockable dialogs are always in separate windows.) Moreover, floating dialogs can be docked together so that two or more dialogs are in the same floating window.

Each dialog remembers its status (docked or floating), so when you open it next time it will be in the same position. To dock or undock a dialog, simply drag its title bar to the docking area or away from it.

In Figure 3-8, one floating window contains two dialogs, another contains one, and the main dock in the editing window contains three more dialogs.

If you don't like the dock, go to the **Windows** page of **Inkscape Preferences** and change the **Dialog behavior** option from **Dockable** to **Floating**. This will disable the dock and make all dialogs floating.

On Windows, floating dialogs suffer from an annoying problem: They do not stay on top of the main editing window, and when you click the editing window all floating dialogs "sink" under it. There's an experimental fix for this problem that you may enable on the same **Windows** tab of the **Inkscape Preferences** dialog.

3.8   Basic Zooming

Zooming (in or out) is just temporarily magnifying your view on the drawing so you can examine the small details (when zoomed in) or look at the whole picture (when zoomed out). Zooming does not change the drawing itself, just your view on it.

The (almost) infinite scalability of vector graphics makes zooming one of the most common operations in vector work. It's not surprising that Inkscape offers a *lot* of different ways to zoom.

First of all, the current zoom level is always displayed in the lower right corner of your editing window, in the **Z:** editable field, as shown in Figure 3-9. You can always click there, type the desired level of zoom, and press $\boxed{\text{Enter}}$.

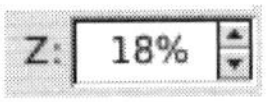

Figure 3-9: Current zoom indicator in the status bar

The simplest way to zoom in or out using the keyboard is by pressing the plus sign and minus sign keys ($\boxed{+}$ and $\boxed{-}$), correspondingly. The keys on the keypad (on the rightmost end of the keyboard on most desktop computers) work just as well as those in the main keyboard (above the letter keys). Moreover, the equal sign ($\boxed{=}$), usually located on the same physical key as the plus sign, also works for zooming in, and the underscore ($\boxed{\_}$), usually on the same key as the minus sign, works for zooming out; in other words, you never have to press $\boxed{\text{Shift}}$ to access the zooming keys.

Zooming by using the plus and minus keys works in all tools and modes, except when you are editing text. In text, the plus and minus keys on the main keyboard insert the corresponding characters, but the keypad $\boxed{+}$ and $\boxed{-}$ keys still work for zooming.

Often, your hand is on your mouse or tablet pen, and reaching for the keyboard is inconvenient. The simplest way to zoom in by mouse is by pressing the middle button (on many mice, this is not actually a button but a scroll-wheel that you can click as well as rotate). The point you click will keep its relative position in the window after the zoom, so by clicking some small object, you zoom into that object—unlike the plus sign and minus sign key zoom, which zooms into the center of the visible area. To zoom out, middle-click with the $\boxed{\text{Shift}}$ key pressed.

Additionally, with a scrollwheel mouse, you can rotate the wheel up to zoom in or down to zoom out. By default, you need to press $\boxed{\text{Ctrl}}$ for that, because the scroll wheel without modifiers scrolls the document, as in most other programs. There's an option, however, to make it zoom without modifiers and scroll with $\boxed{\text{Ctrl}}$; it is set in the **Scrolling** page of the **Inkscape Preferences** dialog.

You can adjust the amount of zooming in or out that the plus and minus sign keys, the middle click, and the single scrollwheel click perform. This value is set in the **Steps** tab of the **Inkscape Preferences** dialog. The default is 141 percent, which is 100 percent multiplied by the approximate square root of two, so that two subsequent zoom-in keystrokes zoom you in exactly 200 percent.

3.9 The Zoom Tool

More zooming methods are available via the Zoom tool (the fourth from the top in the toolbar on the left). Actually, in my work I never switch to this tool, because all of its commands and modes are also available in any tool via various shortcuts. Still, this tool is useful as an overview of the zooming capabilities of Inkscape.

First of all, in the Zoom tool, simple mouse-clicking zooms in, and $\boxed{\text{Shift}}$-click zooms out. Sometimes, however, you already know the area that you want to zoom into, and you don't want to go through all the intermediate zoom levels to reach your target zoom. In that case, simply drag with the tool, creating a rectangular rubber band around that area, and Inkscape will zoom directly into that area when you release the mouse:

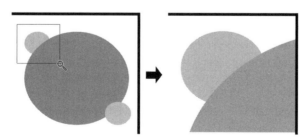

Figure 3-10: Zooming into an area with the Zoom tool

A couple versions back, this zoom-into-an-area capability of the Zoom tool was the main reason to occasionally use it. In recent versions, however, such zooming can be done without leaving your current tool: In any tool or mode, dragging the middle mouse button with Shift starts the same zoom area rubber band and zooms into it when you release the button.

Let's look at the controls bar of the Zoom tool:

Figure 3-11: Command buttons on the Zoom tool controls bar

The first two buttons do the same as the plus and minus sign keys. Then come three predefined zoom buttons: 100 percent (also available via the 1 key), 200 percent (the 2 key), and 50 percent. Next, there is the **Zoom to fit selection** button (also available by pressing the 3 key); it zooms in or out and scrolls the view so that your current selection entirely fits into the window. The next three buttons do the same for the entire drawing (the 4 key), the page (the 5 key), and the page width (the 6 key).

Perhaps the most interesting are the last two buttons on the Zoom controls bar. As mentioned above, zooming does not change the document and thus cannot be undone by the **Undo** command. However, there's another way to "undo zooming."

Every time you change your zoom level, Inkscape remembers the previous zoom and the area of the canvas you were looking at. The **Previous Zoom** and **Next Zoom** commands, accessible via the last two buttons on the bar, allow you to travel back and forth in this history of zooms. For example, if after viewing the entire drawing you zoomed close into an area, edited something, and then want to see the entire drawing again, you don't need to press the minus sign key repeatedly. Instead, just press the backstroke key (`) and you'll be taken to your previous zoom and view instantly. The same ` key, when pressed in combination with Shift, will then re-zoom you back into the same area. The zoom history is unlimited—it stores all your zooms from the beginning of your editing session.

Apart from the Zoom toolbar and the keyboard shortcuts, all the same commands are also available in the **Zoom** submenu of the **View** menu.

3.10 Panning

When you *pan* a document in Inkscape, you just shift the visible area inside the window without changing the zoom. It's basically the same as *scrolling*, except that scrolling assumes a single axis (e.g., up and down) whereas panning can be done in any direction. It is, right up there with zooming, one of the most common things you do when you work in a vector editor.

An Inkscape document window has the traditional scrollbars that you can use to scroll both horizontally and vertically to reach any point on the canvas. Scrollbars, however, are pretty clumsy, so I usually prefer other methods for panning and turn the scrollbars off (Ctrl-B) to free up some extra room for the artwork.

There are simple ways to pan using both the keyboard and the mouse. With the keyboard, press Ctrl with the arrow keys to scroll in any of the four directions. This is more handy than it may sound, because if you press and hold Ctrl along with an arrow key, the canvas movement accelerates. This means you can budge the canvas position a little by single strokes of Ctrl and an arrow key, or swoosh it quickly aside if you press and hold. The speed of Ctrl and arrow key scrolling (i.e., the distance for a single keystroke) can be set in the **Scrolling** tab of the **Inkscape Preferences** dialog.

With the mouse, the easiest way to pan the canvas is by dragging it around with the middle button. Again, this works in any tool or mode. There's no dedicated "hand" tool for panning in Inkscape. You can also scroll vertically with the scroll wheel on your mouse and horizontally by Shift-wheel.

Inkscape tries to make panning automatic whenever possible. For example, when you drag selected objects with the Selector tool and push them against the edge of the screen, the canvas will automatically scroll under you. Also, when you select a new object or path node with the Tab key, Inkscape scrolls to make this object or node visible.

AI *Canvas panning is one of the areas where Inkscape's user interface is noticeably different from that of its biggest competitor, Adobe Illustrator. Many Illustrator users are used to panning by pressing the spacebar and dragging with the left mouse button. In Inkscape, however, pressing the spacebar in any tool temporarily switches you to the Selector tool (hitting the spacebar again switches back to the tool you were in before). Specially for Illustrator refugees, Inkscape offers a compatibility option: With the spacebar pressed, the left mouse button will drag the canvas. Enable this option in the **Scrolling** tab of the **Inkscape Preferences** dialog.*

3.11 Rendering Modes

By default, Inkscape strives to render each document as close as possible to the way it should be rendered according to the SVG standard. However, sometimes you need to *work* with the document, not just look at it, and such complete rendering may then be an obstacle. This is when you switch to Outline view mode. In Outline mode, there are no fills, no transparency, no color, no gradients, no blurring, or any other filters. Any object is shown as a thin outline whose width (1 screen pixel) does not depend on zoom:

Figure 3-12: A few objects in the Normal view mode (left) and the Outline view mode (right)

The quick keyboard shortcut to toggle from Normal to Outline mode and back is to press Ctrl with 5 on the numeric keypad.

The most common reason to switch to Outline mode is to make working with complex slow-rendering documents faster. Also, in Outline mode it's much easier to find and access invisible objects (those that are completely transparent or hidden underneath other objects). In this mode, everything is visible, and you can select any object by clicking its outline.

Outline mode does use colors other than black, but they do not reflect the fill or stroke colors of objects. Instead, colors are used to differentiate object types. Regular paths and shapes use black outlines, bitmap objects (Chapter 18) are shown as red-outline rectangles with two diagonals, clipping paths (18.4) are green, and masks (18.4) are blue. Text objects are the only kind of objects that are not outlined (they are shown with black fill).

NOTE *Outline mode is not remembered in global or per-document properties; every time you need it, you must switch to it. However, if you* really *need it, you can force Inkscape to always start in outline mode. For that, you need to edit your* preferences.xml *file (see 3.1) by finding the element with* id="startmode" *and changing its* outline *attribute to* 1.

4

OBJECTS

Objects are the bread and butter of Inkscape graphics. Much of the rest of the book will be devoted to various types of objects, their properties, and techniques for working with them. However, regardless of type, all Inkscape objects have a lot of things in common.

This and the next two chapters will cover the fundamentals of objects and generic object operations in painstaking detail.

4.1 Object Properties

Inkscape has a number of dialogs for manipulating various properties of objects, but only one of them is so generic as to be called simply **Object Properties** (accessible by pressing Shift-Ctrl-O or by choosing a command in the **Object** menu). This dialog is quite small, as shown in Figure 4-1.

You need to select (Chapter 5) a single object to view its properties in this dialog. The *identifier (ID)* of an object is the id attribute of the corresponding element in the SVG source of the document (Appendix A). Its value is always unique inside this document; Inkscape provides unique IDs for all objects automatically. You can, however, change this value as long as it remains unique.

Figure 4-1: The Object Properties dialog

Assigning meaningful names to objects is a useful approach to organizing complex artwork. However, the ID is not the best place to do this, because according to XML rules, you can only use a very limited set of characters in element IDs: no spaces, only Latin letters, digits, hyphens, underscores, and dots. For a more human-friendly alternative, set the object's *label* in the **Label** field (which corresponds to the inkscape:label extension attribute in SVG). Here, you can compose an arbitrary label or description for your object; it can be any length, use any character, and need not be unique.

SVG *The **Title** and **Description** fields can contain additional freeform metadata about the object (they are the standard title and desc elements of SVG). Since these values are stored in elements, not attributes, they can even contain child elements such as text markup (though you cannot do this via the **Object Properties** dialog).*

*The **Interactivity** part of the dialog (folded up by default; click the triangular mark to unfold it) allows you to edit values of the interactivity attributes (such as onclick, onmouseover, and so on) which are used in SVG with Javascript. Inkscape does not support Javascript, but this can be useful if you want to view your SVG in a Javascript-enabled viewer.*

At the bottom of the dialog, two checkboxes control the locked and hidden status of the selected object. A *locked* object is visible, but most selection methods cannot select it, so it is therefore impossible to change. A *hidden* object is both invisible *and* unselectable.

I would not recommend hiding or locking individual objects. It is usually much more convenient to act on the layer containing the objects you want to hide or lock. Hiding and locking via layers is better not only because it affects multiple objects at a time, but also because a layer, even if locked or hidden, can always be easily accessed (via the **Layers** dialog, see **4.6.4**) and its status changed.

With objects, however, many users find themselves in a trap: You need to select the object to unlock or unhide it, but you cannot easily select it because it is hidden or locked. Specifically for such situations, the **Object** menu contains two commands, **Unhide All** and **Unlock All**, that will reveal and make selectable all objects in the current layer.

4.2 The Bounding Box

Generally, an object is just a visible thing on the canvas, a part of your drawing. Of course it's not always that simple; sometimes, what looks like a separate object is either a part of some other object or a combination of several objects. Identifying individual objects may require some work and Inkscape experience.

Nevertheless, whenever an object is visible on the canvas, we can measure its size and position, using the familiar rectangular coordinate system, with a horizontal X axis and a vertical Y axis. In Inkscape, the coordinate origin is always in the bottom-left corner of the page frame (usually visible as the gray frame on your canvas), with Y values increasing upward and X values increasing to the right.

NOTE *However, in SVG the coordinate origin is in the* top-*left corner of the page, and the Y coordinate grows* downward*. Inkscape moves the origin and flips the Y coordinate when displaying the coordinates to the user, but saves everything in the SVG document per SVG rules. You should always remember this when viewing or editing raw SVG code—for example, in the XML Editor (4.7).*

The rulers at the edge of your canvas area are one way to measure the coordinates (press Ctrl-R to reveal them if they are hidden). As you move your mouse over the canvas, small triangular markers on the rulers reflect its current position. Also, the X and Y coordinates of the mouse pointer are always displayed on the right end of the status bar, just before the zoom field marked **Z**:

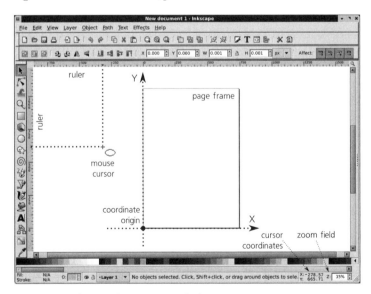

Figure 4-2: The coordinate system of Inkscape

The measurement unit used by the rulers is the same as the document unit that you can set in the **Document Properties** dialog (3.4). To figure out which unit the rulers currently use without opening the dialog, hover your mouse cursor over a ruler until a floating tooltip appears.

Now let's create some object; for example, draw an ellipse with the Ellipse tool. You will see that the object, when selected, is framed by a dashed rectangle (Figure 4-3). This rectangle is the visual representation of what is called the *bounding box* of the object—the smallest possible rectangle which completely encloses the entire object. The bounding box is always upright, that is, its sides are parallel to the coordinate axes; if you rotate an object, its bounding box may or may not change its size, but it won't rotate with the object. (Try rotating the ellipse by pressing the square bracket keys, [and].)

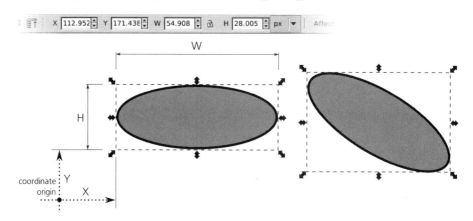

Figure 4-3: The bounding box of an object is always upright.

The width, height, and coordinates of the selected object's bounding box are always reported by the four editable fields in the controls bar of the Selector tool. The **X** and **Y** display the coordinates of the bottom-left corner of the box, and the **W** and **H** indicate its width and height. (If multiple objects are selected, the values reflect the overall bounding box of the entire selection.) The unit of measurement can be chosen in the drop-down menu on the right; initially it's the document unit which, by default, is SVG pixel (px, see **A.6**).

Of course, you can click inside any of these fields and type your own value, which will result in the object being moved (for **X** and **Y**) or scaled (for **W** and **H**). If you want the change in width to cause proportional change in height or vice versa, click the lock button between **W** and **H** to lock them together.

In Inkscape, bounding boxes of objects can be of one of the two types: visual (the default) and geometric. The program always uses only one of these types; to switch from one type to the other, go to the **Tools** tab of the **Inkscape Preferences** dialog. The difference is that the visual bounding box, unlike the geometric, includes *everything that's visible* about the object—most notably its entire stroke (**9.1**) but also markers (**9.5**) and filter margins (**17.4.4**), while the geometric box enframes only the *geometric outline* of the object's path.

Thus, with the geometric box, the outer fringe of a stroked object falls *outside* of the bounding box; this kind of box corresponds to the object as it is visible in the Outline mode (**3.11**). Usually, the geometric bounding box is preferred by those who use Inkscape for technical drawing, while the visual option makes more sense for almost everyone else. Figure 4-3 shows the visual bounding box; note that it fully encloses the black stroke of the ellipse.

4.3   Z-Order

The term *z-order* refers to the order in which objects are drawn on top of each other. An object on top in the z-order may obscure those below it, if they overlap and if the top object is not transparent. The term *z-order* derives from the notion of the third coordinate axis, Z, which is imagined to extend perpendicular to the X/Y plane of the drawing toward the viewer. Objects higher in the z-order are thus "closer" to the viewer.

Objects you create are always placed at the very top of the z-order of the current layer (and if you didn't create any new layers, this will be the top of the z-order of the entire document). For example, if you draw several ellipses, each new one will be drawn on top of the previous ones, as shown in Figure 4-4.

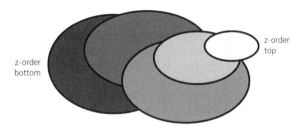

z-order
top

z-order
bottom

Figure 4-4: Z-order

NOTE *In the SVG source of the document, objects that are* higher *in z-order are those that are closer to the* end *of the document. Thus, new objects are always added to the end of the list of existing elements (usually within the current layer).*

No selecting, transforming, or style changing operations change the z-order of objects. This means you can move, scale, or paint an object while it remains upon its own "floor"—provided you've selected that object. (In **5.9**, you'll see that special methods exist for selecting objects that are at the bottom of the z-order and cannot be simply clicked to select.)

Quite often, however, you need to rearrange the stack of objects in your drawing. Inkscape has four commands for moving objects up or down in z-order, two absolute ones and two relative. They are used regularly, so they can be accessed via buttons on the Selector controls bar, via the **Object** menu, or via simple keyboard shortcuts. The absolute commands are:

Raise to Top (Home)
  Raises selected objects to the very top of the objects' layer.

Lower to Bottom (End)
  Lowers selected objects to the very bottom of the objects' layer.

The relative commands are:

Raise (Page Up)
  Raises selected objects up one step (past one other object).

Lower (Page Down)
  Lowers selected objects down one step (past one other object).

Figure 4-5 shows an example of how these commands work on the selected ellipse that is in the middle of a stack of rectangles.

Note that the relative z-order commands take into account only those objects that *overlap* the selection (more precisely, those objects whose bounding boxes overlap the bounding box of the selection). If your selected object or objects do not overlap any others, the **Raise** and **Lower** commands will just move the selection all the way to the top or bottom of the layer, correspondingly.

Another important thing to remember is that all z-order commands work only *within the layer*. If you have several layers in your document, these layers form their own z-order, and an object in a lower layer can never be on top of an object in a layer above. For rearranging the z-order of layers, use layer commands as described in **4.6.2**.

It is possible to have objects in different layers or groups selected at the same time. In this case, the z-order commands work on each selected object within its own layer or group. For example, it may be that a **Raise to Top** command will change the z-order of one selected object but will leave the other untouched if it was already the topmost object in its layer.

4.4 Copying, Cutting, Pasting, and Duplicating

Inkscape supports all the traditional clipboard operations: copying, cutting, and pasting.

Copying (Ctrl-C) remembers a copy of the selected object or objects in the program's clipboard; *cutting* (Ctrl-X) performs the same action as copying, but the object is then deleted. Finally, *pasting* (Ctrl-V) places the content of the clipboard back into the document (but retains it in the clipboard as well, so you can paste the same object multiple times).

The **Paste** command has two variants. The regular **Paste** (Ctrl-V) places the object in the point on the canvas where your mouse cursor currently hovers. This provides a handy method for moving an object to an entirely different place of the document; just cut it from where it was before, scroll and/or zoom to where you want it to be, hover your mouse over the exact location, and press Ctrl-V. You can even "paint" with copies of an object by moving your mouse around and pressing Ctrl-V repeatedly.

NOTE *Another command which places an object under your mouse cursor is **Import** (Ctrl-I); see 18.1.*

Sometimes, however, you want to paste an object exactly where it was copied from. That's what the **Paste in Place** (Ctrl-Alt-V) command does. For example, you can use it for moving an object from one layer to another without changing its position on the canvas: Copy it, switch to the target layer, and paste it in place.

Sometimes, people use **Copy** and **Paste** simply as a method to get a duplicate of one or several objects. In Inkscape, you don't need to use that workaround; there's a convenient **Duplicate** command (Ctrl-D) that creates a copy of your selection and places it in the same position on the canvas. This is equivalent to copying and then pasting in place, except that **Duplicate** does not change the contents of your clipboard.

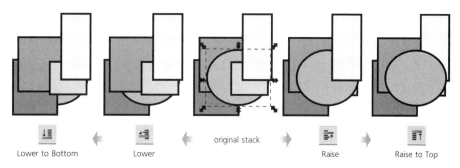

| Lower to Bottom | | Lower | | original stack | | Raise | | Raise to Top |

Figure 4-5: Changing the z-order

All pasting and duplication commands, just as any other methods of creating new objects, place the new object on top of the z-order in the current layer.

NOTE *What if you have selected an object somewhere in the middle of the z-order and want to duplicate it but keep the copy at the same level instead of jumping to the top? In general, this is a symptom that your document needs to use more layers. By placing such an object into its own layer, you will ensure that duplicating it will place the copy on top of that object's layer instead of on top of the document.*

Yet another method of creating copies of objects is *stamping*. Whenever you transform a selection (move, scale, rotate, or skew) by dragging the mouse in the Selector tool (see **2.7**), you can press `Space` to leave behind a copy of the selection without interrupting the interactive transformation. For example, if you grab and drag an ellipse and then press and hold the spacebar while dragging, the object being moved will leave a trail of its copies on the canvas. Stamping also works in the Node tool when you drag a selection of nodes (**12.5.7**).

All object copying methods discussed so far created new independent objects that are not linked in any way to their originals. If you want a *linked copy* that inherits some properties of the original and updates itself automatically, read about clones in Chapter **16**.

4.5 Groups

Grouping is a way to make a single object out of a number of independent objects. It is an easily reversible action; objects combined into a group can be ungrouped and made independent again. Moreover, many of the tools in Inkscape completely disregard grouping and allow you to work directly with individual objects regardless of whether they are grouped or not. The Selector tool by default selects the group as a whole, but even in it, there are methods to select an object inside the group without ungrouping it (**5.10**).

To group some objects, just select them and choose **Object ▸ Group** (`Ctrl-G`). Groups can be further grouped just like any other objects. You can even group a single object; for example, select a rectangle and press `Ctrl-G`. Now you have a group with a single rectangle inside (such groups may be useful in a number of situations, such as blurring a clipped object; see **18.4**).

When a single group is selected, the status bar indicates how many member objects are within this group, for example: *Group of 3 objects in layer Background.*

To ungroup a group, select it and choose **Object ▶ Ungroup** ($\boxed{\text{Ctrl-U}}$); the group no longer exists, but all its former members, now released, remain where they were on the canvas (both the coordinates and the z-order of the objects are preserved).

You can select any number of groups and ungroup them all at once. Moreover, you can select any number of different objects, only *some* of which are groups, and press $\boxed{\text{Ctrl-U}}$; groups will be ungrouped, but all nongroup objects will remain intact.

NOTE   *The **Ungroup** command removes only the topmost level of grouping. For example, if you have a group containing two other groups, pressing* $\boxed{\text{Ctrl-U}}$ *will release the two groups—they will stay selected but not ungrouped. You will need to press* $\boxed{\text{Ctrl-U}}$ *again to ungroup them. To ungroup all groups in a complex drawing, just select all objects and keep pressing* $\boxed{\text{Ctrl-U}}$ *until the status bar says,* No groups to ungroup in the selection.

XML   *In XML, a group is the* g *element (see **A.5**), which is a parent of its member objects. This means, among other things, that objects with unset style properties (**8.1.1**) will inherit these properties from their parent group or from an ancestor further up the tree.*

4.5.1 Uses of Grouping

Why group objects? There may be different reasons to use grouping.

- First, groups are an easy way to *select sets of objects*: With the Selector tool, click any object in a group and the entire group gets selected. In this sense, a group is a "saved selection." After selecting, it is easy to move, scale, or paint the group just as you would a number of separate selected objects.

- Second, grouping is a quick and simple way to *organize complex artwork*. When you have thousands of objects in your drawing, sorting out what belongs together is difficult. One way to structure such complex documents is via layers, as we'll discuss later in this chapter. However, often layers are too much hassle; if you just want to ensure that the objects of the nose and the eyes in your portrait are never accidentally moved relative to each other, the easiest way to achieve this is by grouping them together.

- Finally, sometimes groups allow you to achieve effects that would be impossible otherwise. The most common of these effects is *group transparency* (see **8.1.2** for more on transparency). When you apply transparency to a group, it is made transparent as a whole, which may look quite different from the effect of applying the same level of transparency to the individual objects (Figure 4-6).

    On the left, two independent objects are fully opaque (zero transparency). In the middle, they are made 50 percent transparent as individual objects; note that the corner of the rectangle shows through the ellipse. On the right, the same opaque objects are grouped and the group is made 50 percent transparent; note that now, the checkered background shows through, but the overlapping area of the rectangle is still obscured by the ellipse and does not show through.

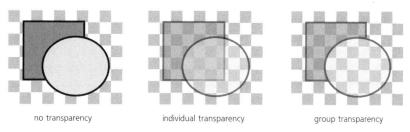

Figure 4-6: Group transparency

NOTE *Because of group transparency and other similar effects, ungrouping a group does not, in the general case, guarantee that the appearance of the document will not change.*

4.5.2 Groups and Z-Order

An important thing to remember is that a group, as an object in its own right, has its own place in the z-order stack of your document, and all the members of the group share its z-order position.

This means that if object A is on top of B and B is on top of C, you cannot group A and C without changing the z-order. If you attempt to do that, C will jump up under A, and you will have a group containing A and C lying on top of the object B.

Ungrouping a group in that case does not restore the original z-order. If you ungroup the "A and C" group, you will get three independent objects, but they will be now in the order A, C, B (top to bottom). (Of course, if you simply **Undo** (Ctrl-Z) right after grouping, both grouping and the z-order change will be reverted.)

For the same reason, you cannot group objects from different layers. Both layers and groups are branches of the XML tree of the document, and you cannot have a branch (group) growing from more than one parent branch (layer). If you try to group objects selected in different layers or within different groups, Inkscape will complain (with a message in the status bar) and do nothing.

4.6 Layers

Basically, layers in Inkscape are just what the name suggests: "levels" or "floors" within a document, stacked on top of each other and containing other objects. Every layer has a name; layers can be easily hidden, locked, or rearranged.

Every object belongs to one and only one layer. To find out which layer the object belongs to, just select that object and look at the status bar: It will say something like *Rectangle in layer **Layer 1*** (here, ***Layer 1*** is the name of the layer). You may easily select objects from different layers, in which case the status bar will say, *2 objects in 2 layers.*

One of the layers in the document is always *current*. Any new objects you create, paste, or import are always added to the current layer. To make layer switching in complex drawings easier, Inkscape follows selection: That is, if you are in layer A and select some objects in layer B (for example, by clicking it), layer B becomes your new current layer. Conversely, if you change the current layer, your selection is deselected.

Inkscape remembers the current layer when saving the document and restores it when you load it the next time. A new document template (see **3.2**) usually contains one initial layer called *Layer 1*; it is made current when you load the template, so if you don't create any new layers all your created objects will end up in Layer 1.

Just like individual objects, layers may be locked or hidden. In a *locked* layer, objects are visible but cannot be selected. In a *hidden* layer, objects are both invisible and cannot be selected. Also, you cannot add new objects to a hidden or locked layer.

Typically, layers are hidden when you want to temporarily simplify a complex artwork to work on some parts of it. Hiding complex layers may speed up screen redraw considerably and thus make your work more comfortable. Locking layers is useful when you want some background objects to be visible but not selectable, so it's easier to select the foreground objects by clicking or dragging around them.

4.6.1 Layer Hierarchy

At a more advanced level, layers in Inkscape are closely related to groups. In fact, a layer is just a kind of group that Inkscape treats in a special way.

XML *In XML, both layers and groups are represented by the same element,* g. *The only difference is that a layer has the attribute* inkscape:groupmode="layer" *(A.5).*

Just as groups may include other groups as members, layers may contain further *sublayers*. This makes it easier to organize complex artwork: Instead of a flat list of layers, you may have a hierarchical tree, where related layers are grouped by a common parent and it's easy to rearrange the structure by raising or lowering the entire branches of the tree instead of individual layers one by one.

Furthermore, you can temporarily *enter a group*, i.e., tell Inkscape to temporarily treat this group as a sublayer and to make that sublayer current. For that, just select the group and double-click it, or press Ctrl-Enter, or right-click it and choose **Enter group** from the pop-up menu.

This technique combines the advantages of groups (a group is easy to select, move, transform, style, view its bounding box, and so on) with the advantages of layers (a layer defines a context that you can enter and work inside, for example, by adding new objects to it). In particular, the easiest way to move some object *into* an existing group without ungrouping is to cut the object (Ctrl-X), enter the group, and paste the object there (Ctrl-V or Ctrl-Alt-V).

To leave a sublayer—whether it's a real sublayer or just a group that you entered—press Ctrl-Backspace, or right-click anywhere on the canvas and choose **Go to Parent** from the pop-up menu.

4.6.2 The Layer Menu

The most important layer commands are collected in the **Layer** menu:

- The **Add Layer**, **Rename Layer**, and **Delete Current Layer** commands do what they say they do. The two latter commands apply to the current layer; the first one creates a new layer and asks you to provide a name and decide whether to place it below the current layer (default), above the current layer, or inside the current layer as a sublayer (see Figure 4-7). Layer names need not be unique and can use arbitrary characters. Be careful: Deleting a layer deletes all objects that were in that layer!

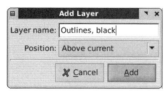

Figure 4-7: Creating a new layer

XML *In SVG source, the name of the layer is stored in the* inkscape:label *attribute.*

- The two **Switch** commands just switch the current layer to one below or above it. These commands simply define the context for other operations; they do not change anything visible on the canvas and cannot be undone (only the commands that actually change the document can be undone).

- The next two commands, **Move Selection to Layer Above** (Shift-Page Up) and **Move Selection to Layer Below** (Shift-Page Down), take the current selection and move it to the layer above or below the current one. (If there is no layer above or below the current layer, these commands do nothing and complain with a message in the status bar.) By crossing the layer boundaries, these commands are complementary to the regular z-order changing commands, such as **Raise** or **Lower** (4.3), that work within the same layer.

NOTE *Here's a method to move objects from one layer to any other, not necessarily adjacent: Cut the object* (Ctrl-X), *switch to the target layer, and paste it in place* (Ctrl-Alt-V).

- The four z-order commands—**Raise Layer** (Shift-Ctrl-Page Up), **Lower Layer** (Shift-Ctrl-Page Down), **Layer to Top** (Shift-Ctrl-Home), and **Layer to Bottom** (Shift-Ctrl-End)—are equivalent to the z-order commands for objects (4.3), except that they act on the current layer and move it (with all of its objects and sublayers) up or down among its sibling layers. Note that the keyboard shortcuts for these commands are the same as for the object z-order commands but with Shift-Ctrl added.

- Finally, the **Layers ...** command (Shift-Ctrl-L) opens the **Layers** dialog (4.6.4).

4.6.3 The Current Layer Indicator

Inkscape has two main UI controls for working with layers: the basic current layer indicator in the status bar and the more powerful **Layers** dialog.

The *current layer indicator* displays the name of the current layer and, by the two toggle buttons on the left, indicates if that layer is hidden (the eye button) and/or locked (the lock button):

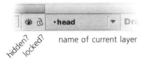

name of current layer

Figure 4-8: The current layer indicator in the status bar

It's an interactive control, not just a display; you can toggle the buttons and use the pop-up menu of all layers to switch the current layer:

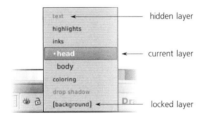

hidden layer

current layer

locked layer

Figure 4-9: The pop-up menu of all layers in the document

In the menu of the layers, the current layer is marked by bold face and a bullet. Locked layers have square brackets around their names (for example, *[Layer 1]*); hidden layers' names are gray. A temporary layer (such as a group that you entered) uses italics for its name.

4.6.4 The Layers Dialog

The current layer indicator's advantages are that it is always active and takes very little space on screen. However, it is only adequate if your layer structure is small and simple. In more complex documents, it quickly becomes unwieldy. That's when you should check out the **Layers** dialog (Shift-Ctrl-L), shown in Figure 4-10.

In its list of layers, branches of sublayers inside layers can be expanded and collapsed by clicking the triangle markers. Also, here you can lock or unlock and hide or unhide any layer, without making it current, by clicking the corresponding icon to the left of the layer name.

AI *Unlike Adobe Illustrator, Inkscape's Layers dialog cannot yet show individual objects within layers. To some extent, you can use the XML Editor (4.7) for viewing the entire tree of the document, including all layers and objects.*

Below the list of layers, the six buttons correspond to the following commands, left to right: **Create a new layer** (a name is requested), **Raise the current layer to the top**, **Raise the current layer**, **Lower the lower layer**, **Lower the**

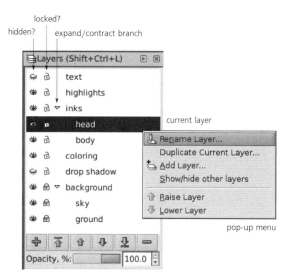

Figure 4-10: The Layers dialog

current layer to the bottom, and **Delete the current layer**. You can also rename a layer by clicking its name in the list and typing a new name.

By right-clicking a layer name, you will open a pop-up menu with commands for adding, renaming, lowering or raising, as well as duplicating a layer. The **Show/hide other layers** command toggles all other layers (except the current one) between visible and hidden states.

At the bottom of the dialog, there's a list of blend modes that can be applied to the entire current layer (see **17.2** for more on blend modes) and a slider control for setting the opacity of the current layer. This opacity affects all the objects in the layer and works the same as group opacity (**4.5.1**); it provides a handy way to peek under a layer by making it almost transparent but not entirely hidden.

4.7 The XML Editor

The XML Editor is what sets Inkscape apart from all other vector editors. This is where you can see the entire raw source of your document, with nothing hidden or (mis)interpreted. Quite simply, if something cannot be seen in the XML Editor, it's not in your document.

If you want to learn SVG or are simply interested in what is behind some of the objects or properties of your document, the XML Editor is your primary tool. Here, you can do absolutely anything to your document. One might claim that the XML Editor is the only essential part of the program, everything else being just optional conveniences!

The XML Editor is completely synchronized with the rest of the program. Any changes you make in the XML tree are immediately reflected on your canvas, and any changes you make with any other tools are immediately visible as element or attribute changes in the XML Editor.

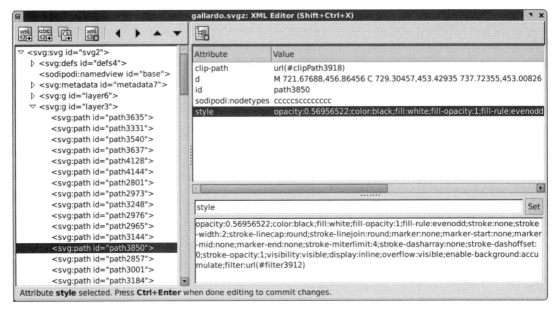

Figure 4-11: The three panes of the XML Editor

The XML Editor has three main panes, as shown in Figure 4-11. There's also a status bar of its own at the bottom, displaying various status information and hints.

Left pane

Shows the entire tree of the document you are editing. Each node of the tree (each line in this list) is either an XML element or a text node. In SVG, text nodes are only used for holding the text content of text objects; all other objects are element nodes. For example, svg:rect is a rectangle and svg:g is either a group or a layer (here, svg is the namespace prefix; see **A.2**).

Not every element in the list is an object, however; some elements represent things (such as metadata) that you don't see on the canvas. For more on various SVG and Inkscape elements, refer to Appendix **A**.

NOTE *In the XML Editor, all elements are listed in the* document order: *Objects and layers that are* topmost *in the z-order on the canvas are the* last *in the list. In particular, this means that the order of layers in the XML Editor is reversed compared to that in the* **Layers** *dialog or the current layer indicator.*

In the document tree, you can select any element by clicking on it. This selection in the list is synchronized with the regular object selection in Inkscape: If the selected element corresponds to a visible object, that object gets selected on the canvas; conversely, if you select an object on the canvas, the XML tree pane scrolls to the corresponding element and highlights it. This is one way to reach elements that are otherwise inaccessible, such as those that are locked or hidden (**4.1**).

Above the tree pane, there's a small toolbar with buttons for generic XML operations: creating new elements or text nodes and duplicating or deleting the selected node. The last four buttons are for moving the selected node (and all its children) in the tree: The up or down arrows reorder the nodes (you can also do this by dragging the selected node with your mouse), while the left and right arrows change their nesting. For example, to turn a node from a child of its parent to its sibling, click the left arrow button; conversely, the right arrow button turns a node into a child of its preceding sibling.

Top-right pane

Displays all the attributes of the selected element node. (If you select a text node instead of an element node, this pane will allow you to edit the text of the node.) Every attribute has a name and a value, which are listed in two columns of a table. The order of the attributes does not matter in XML, so the dialog shows them alphabetically sorted. Above the pane, there's a button for deleting the selected attribute.

Bottom-right pane

Allows you to edit the attribute you selected in the top-right pane. It consists of a single-line field for the name of the attribute, a bigger pane for its value, and a **Set** button (when done editing, you can press Ctrl-Enter instead of clicking **Set**).

You can add a new attribute to an element by editing both the name and the value fields. If the attribute name you entered matches that of an existing attribute, that attribute gets replaced with your value; otherwise, a new attribute is created and added to the element.

Note that the value editing pane wraps long attribute values to make editing easier. This is particularly handy when editing the style attributes (A.8), whose values tend to be quite long.

5

SELECTING

There are precious few useful things that you can do in
Inkscape without first selecting some object or objects.
Of all Inkscape operations, selecting has, by far, the
greatest number of methods, tools, dialogs, and shortcuts available. You need
to know a good portion of them to be able to work efficiently, and at least a few
of them to be able to work in Inkscape at all.

By itself, selecting or deselecting objects does not change the document in
any way. Therefore, none of the techniques described in this chapter are undoable
actions and none require the document to be saved.

5.1 The Selection Cue

As you probably know by now, Inkscape's selection is just a list of objects, which
may include anything—from no objects (empty selection, nothing selected) to
all the objects in the document. Selection is local to the editing window; if you
open a second window with the same document (3.5), that window will have its
own independent list of selected objects. Selected objects can be anywhere on
the canvas, in any layer or group; multiple selected objects don't have to be
children of the same parent. The only thing you *cannot* do is select an object
and its ancestor at the same time (5.10).

NOTE *Even hidden or locked objects can be included in the selection. While most tools will refuse to directly select a hidden or locked object, it is still possible, for example, by using the XML Editor (4.7).*

On the canvas, each selected object is marked by the selection cue. By default, this cue is a dashed frame around the object, showing that object's bounding box (4.2). This frame is painted on top of all objects using a contrasting color, so it is visible on any background.

You can switch to a different selection cue: a small diamond-shaped mark in the top-left corner of each object's bounding box, as shown in Figure 5-1 (this is similar to what the Xara vector editor uses). To change the type of the selection cue or to turn it off altogether, go to the **Tools ▸ Selector** subpage of the **Inkscape Preferences** dialog.

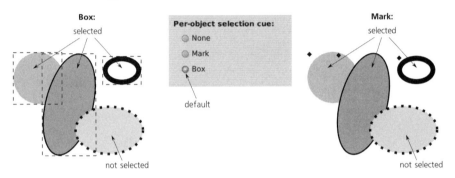

Figure 5-1: The two possible types of selection cues

Also, you can control which tools display the selection cue and which do not. For this, look for checkboxes labeled **Show selection cue** on each tool's page in the **Inkscape Preferences** dialog. By default, every tool shows the selection cue, except for the Calligraphic pen and Paint bucket tools, which are more artistic than technical—there, the cue is not very useful and may be a distraction. (Of course, the selection is still there whether the cue is displayed or not—it remains the same now matter how much you switch tools.)

5.2   Selection and the Status Bar

A lot of things happen throughout the program when you select or deselect objects. Inkscape instantly redirects all its attention to the new selection: It redraws the selection cues, scrolls the canvas to show the selected objects if necessary (3.10), and updates various displays and indicators all over the interface.

One of the most important sources of hints in Inkscape, the status bar, displays as much information about the selection as is reasonably possible to fit into it. For a single selected object, it tells you the type of the object, certain additional properties for some of the types (such as the number of nodes for paths, font family and size for texts), and the layer in which this object resides, as shown in Figure 5-2.

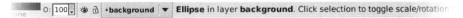

Figure 5-2: Status bar description of a single selected object

For multiple selections, Inkscape tells you how many objects are selected and, if there are no more than three different types of object selected, lists these types:

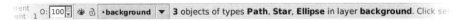

Figure 5-3: Status bar description of multiple selected objects

If there are too many object types to list and they are in more than one layer, Inkscape just gives you the number of objects, object types, and layers:

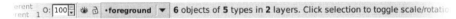

Figure 5-4: Status bar description of multiple selected objects of multiple types in multiple layers

To the left of the status bar message area is the current layer indicator (4.6.3). Since selected objects can be located in many layers, this widget is not directly connected to the selection. However, when you select an object by clicking, Inkscape assumes that you now want to work in that object's layer, so it makes that layer current, which the indicator reflects.

Further to the left is the *selected style indicator*, which always reflects the style of the current selection (if many objects with different styles are selected, it displays their *averaged* style). We will discuss this important widget in detail in 8.1.

5.3 Subselection

Some tools allow a finer-grained type of selection, so that they can work on a part of a selected object rather than the entire object. This selected part of a selected object is then called the *subselection*.

One example is the Text tool. You can select an entire text object, but then you can select a *fragment* of text inside that text object by pressing Shift and an arrow key or by dragging the mouse just like you do in a text editor (15.1.1). That selected part of the text is the text subselection.

Another example is the Gradient tool. A gradient can have many stops (10.5), and the tool can select one or more of these stops at a time. Naturally, gradient stops are only visible for selected objects, so if you select one stop, you're creating a subselection within the regular object selection.

When you change subselections, many things in Inkscape behave the same as when you change selections. Perhaps most importantly, the selected style indicator in the status bar (8.1) displays the style of the subselection—that is, the style of the selected text fragment and not the entire text, or the style of the selected gradient stop and not the entire object. Also, any style setting commands (such as clicking a color on the palette, or pasting a style by pressing Shift-Ctrl-V) will apply to the subselection if it is present. In other words, subselection allows you to deal with parts of your objects almost as though they are separate objects in their own right.

5.4 Selecting by Clicking: The Selector

Most likely you already know that the topmost tool in the toolbar is the Selector and that clicking an object with that tool selects that object. Of course, there is much more to the Selector tool than that, but let's look at this simple action in more detail.

First, note that clicking an object *deselects* any previous selection. Also, observe that with the Selector tool, you can not only select objects, but also *drag* the selected objects in any direction. Combined, these two features make it extremely easy and natural to move objects around, almost without thinking about "selection" at all: You see an object, and you click and drag it to where you want it. The click selects it, deselecting anything else, and the drag moves it.

Sometimes, this may be an annoyance. Especially if you use a tablet with a pen and not a mouse, you may find that it's too easy to accidentally nudge an object when all you intended to do was just select it by clicking. To make this less of a problem, go to the **Mouse** tab of the **Inkscape Preferences** dialog and adjust the **Click/drag threshold** value. This sets the allowed "slippage" in screen pixels, the default being 4; if you click and drag an object by less than this many pixels, your action is still considered a click and the object does not move. Increase this value if you often end up accidentally moving objects instead of clicking them; conversely, decrease it if you find that objects annoyingly "stick" more than you like when you really want to move them.

Before you can click anything, however, you want to be sure that you're clicking in the right place so that your click will not be wasted. Here, Inkscape is very helpful: It changes your mouse cursor when you are over a clickable area of an object, as opposed to an empty canvas where the cursor is an arrow. The exact shape of the over-the-object cursor is different on different platforms; for example, on Ubuntu Linux it looks like a hand, while on Windows it looks like a cross with arrows on the ends.

Play with this cursor-changing capability a little. You will discover that objects with no fill cannot be selected by clicking inside them and that fully transparent objects are not selectable by clicking at all (although you can select them with the rubber band, as you'll see in the next section). In Outline mode (**3.11**), you can select any object only by clicking its outline.

As you can imagine, this changing cursor is less helpful in complex drawings where the entire canvas is often covered with objects. However, if you separate all the background objects into a layer and lock that layer (**4.6**), then these background objects, now unselectable, will stop changing the cursor—and you can again sense the foreground objects by moving your mouse over them.

Also, you will notice that every clickable object has an invisible margin, several pixels wide, on all sides. A click in that margin will still select that object. This is very handy for selecting small objects which would otherwise be almost impossible to accurately click upon. On the downside, this also explains why it's sometimes so difficult to select the bottom object in a stack even if that bottom object protrudes a little from under the top one.

If you don't like the size of this clickable margin, you can change it on the **Mouse** tab of the **Inkscape Preferences** dialog: Adjust the **Grab sensitivity** value, the default being 8 screen pixels. Note that both this value and the **Click/drag threshold** are in screen pixels. This means they do not depend on zoom, so even if the values remain the same, you will find it much easier to perform small moves and select small objects simply by zooming in.

5.5 Selecting by Clicking: Other Tools

One of the most important principles of Inkscape's user interface is consistency: Unless there's a reason to do otherwise, all tools and modes must behave the same. In selecting, this means that many tools, just like the Selector, can select an object by clicking it.

The tools in which clicking to select works are: Node (12.5), all of the shape tools (Chapter 11), Text (Chapter 15), Connector (1.2), and Gradient (10.1). (The tools that *cannot* select by clicking are different for a reason: In those tools, a single click is reserved for a different function specific to each tool.)

Unlike the Selector, all these tools directly select individual objects, even if they are inside groups (in other words, in these tools simple clicking is equivalent to Ctrl-clicking in the Selector, see 5.10). This makes sense: All of these tools work on individual objects of various types, so in most cases selecting a group is not what you really want to do. For example, if you select a group with the Node tool, you would not be able to do anything useful with it—a group has no path nodes to edit. That's why this tool always directly selects the *path* you clicked, regardless of whether it is grouped with anything else or not.

Also, unlike the Selector, other tools don't change the cursor over selectable objects. The only exception is the Text tool, which switches to the text insertion cursor when over an editable text object (15.1).

5.6 Adding to a Selection

A selection may contain more than one object. Sometimes, you have spent some effort selecting several objects, and then you want to select a few other objects as well. Can you do that without starting the selection all over again?

Yes. To *add* another object to the current selection, Shift-click it. If, however, you Shift-click an already selected object, it will be *removed* from selection. In other words, this shortcut works as a toggle that reverses the selected status of the object on which you Shift-click.

5.7 Selecting with the Rubber Band

Another way to select multiple objects in the Selector is by dragging around them. Imagine a rectangle surrounding all the objects you want to select and drag from one corner of that rectangle to the opposite corner. (The exact direction of the drag—top left to bottom right versus top right to bottom left, for example—does not matter.) This rectangle (shown in Figure 5-5), which is visible while you're dragging, is called the *rubber band*, or *marquee*.

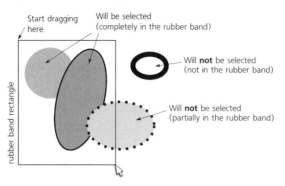

Figure 5-5: Using the rubber band (mouse drag) to select multiple objects

Selecting by rubber band is *not a toggle*; once you start a new rubber band, any previous selection is deselected. This is why, logically, single-clicking on empty space (not an object) deselects anything—this is just a zero-size rubber band that deselects the old selection but does not create a new one.

The rubber band selects enclosed objects in all visible and unlocked layers—in other words, across the z-order stack of the entire document, not the current layer only. (For this reason, selecting by rubber band does not change the current layer, even if it resulted in selecting a single object in a layer different from the current one.) Also, the rubber band allows you to select those objects that you cannot select simply by clicking them—those that are underneath others, those without fill and stroke, and those that are made fully transparent (with zero opacity). However, objects that are hidden or locked (4.1) still cannot be selected.

In short, if the object's bounding box is completely inside the rubber band rectangle and that object is at all selectable, it *will* get selected.

AI *In Adobe Illustrator, rubber band works slightly differently: It selects all objects whose bounding box lies within* or intersects *its rectangle. Inkscape's behavior, selecting only what is* completely *inside the rubber band, is shared by CorelDRAW and Xara vector editors. Inkscape can get a little closer to the AI-like behavior with* touch selection, *as described in the next section.*

You might assume that, like clicking, dragging the rubber band with Shift pressed would give you the toggle behavior. This is not the case, however. Pressing Shift and dragging with the Selector tool works exactly like simple dragging with one exception: It always creates a rubber band, even if you start from an object and not from an empty canvas. Without Shift, dragging from an object will simply select and move that object, but pressing Shift and dragging *forces* the rubber band, and thus makes it a lot more useful in complex drawings where empty canvas may be hard to come by.

5.8   Touch Selection

Touch selection is a close relative of the rubber band. With the Selector tool, if you drag from an empty canvas with the Alt key pressed, instead of a rectangle you will see a red trail left by your mouse cursor—the *touch path*. After you release the mouse, all objects *touched by* (not included in) this trail will get selected, as shown in Figure 5-6.

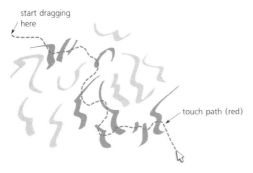

Figure 5-6: Using touch selection (Alt -drag): Objects that will be selected after you release the mouse are marked with darker gray.

So, you can literally "paint" over the objects you want to select, which is very convenient in situations where many objects are located compactly, but their bounding boxes are too big or too intertwined with those of other objects.

Unlike the regular rubber band, touch selection does not select completely transparent objects or those obscured by others—that is, those objects that you cannot really "touch." In fact, touch selection behaves exactly as if it were a series of Shift -clicks along the touch path, where each touched object receives one such click.

Note that if there is a selection, Alt -drag has a different function: It moves the selection regardless of where you drag (**6.1**). But what if you already have some selection and want to *add* to it by touch selection? Use Shift-Alt -drag: Just like Shift forces the rubber band even if you start from an object, with touch selection it forces the touch path even if you have a previous selection. The touched objects are then *added* to selection.

If you touch objects so that you can then delete them, the Delete mode of the Eraser tool performs both functions at once: Drag over objects and get them deleted once you release the mouse. This may be convenient if you want to use this functionality as a separate tool without having to hold Alt .

5.9   Selecting Objects from Underneath

One of the most common problems with selecting objects in complex drawings is that some objects obscure others. Even if the top object is partially transparent and you can see another object underneath, simply clicking it will still select the top object.

If the bounding box of the bottom object is smaller than that of the top one, you can Shift -drag a rubber band around the small bottom object, and this will select it without selecting the top object. However, this is not always possible.

Inkscape offers a convenient way to select objects that are not at the top of the z-order: Alt -click *selects under* the currently selected object. This means that the result of an Alt -click depends on the current selection; if nothing is selected, or if you Alt-click outside the current selection, the result is the same as if you simply clicked without Alt.

If, however, you click a selected object and there are other objects underneath it, Alt-click will deselect the selected object and instead select the object immediately beneath it. The next Alt-click will select a still deeper object, and so on. When you reach the bottommost object at the click point, the next Alt-click again selects the topmost one.

For example, suppose you have three stacked objects, numbered 1, 2, 3, from bottom to top. With nothing selected, Alt-clicking them selects the topmost one, 3. The next Alt-click selects 2, then 1, then 3 again, and so on.

Shift-Alt-click differs from Alt-click in the same way Shift-click differs from a simple click: It adds to the selection or removes from it without unselecting it completely. So, in our 1, 2, 3 stack of objects, the first Shift-Alt-click selects 3; after another Shift-Alt-click you will have 2 and 3 selected; finally, one more Shift-Alt-click adds the bottommost object to the selection as well—so, after three Shift-Alt-clicks you will have all of 1, 2, and 3 selected.

5.10   Selecting in Groups

Grouping is a wonderful thing when you need to treat a collection of objects as a whole. If you simply click any object in a group with the Selector tool, the entire group gets selected. However, quite often you want to select and edit an object inside a group without ungrouping it. This is possible by Ctrl-clicking an object in a group.

Ctrl-clicking completely ignores *any* grouping, no matter how many levels deep it is. For example, if object A is a member of group B which, in turn, is a member of top-level group C, then Ctrl-clicking A will select A, cutting right through both levels of grouping. There's no way to select group B by Ctrl-clicking; it will always select only the lowest-level nongroup object.

The only way to select group B, which is inside group C, is by *entering* group C (see 4.6.1). Entering C makes it a temporary layer. Once in that layer, you can select B by simply clicking.

Ctrl-click can be combined with Alt (select under). Logically, Ctrl-Alt-click does the same thing as Alt-click, except that it disregards any groupings and browses through the z-order stack of objects at the click point as if they were all ungrouped.

Similarly, Ctrl-click can be combined with Shift to add an object to selection or remove it from selection. Finally, you can Shift-Ctrl-Alt-click, which means "Add to selection the topmost nonselected object in the z-order stack at this point, ignoring grouping; if all objects at this point are selected, deselect the topmost one."

The only limitation to the power of selecting by clicking with various modifiers is this: You cannot have both an object and a group which contains that object selected at the same time. So, for example, if you Ctrl-click an object inside a group and then Shift-click (without Ctrl!) another object of the same group, thus trying to add the group to the selection, the group becomes selected, but the first selected object is deselected. A situation where both a group and an object inside that group are selected at the same time would lead to various logical impasses, so Inkscape does its best to prevent this from happening.

5.11   Selecting with Keyboard Shortcuts

Generally, selecting is a task for a mouse or pen, because in most cases it is done by indicating some points or areas on the screen. However, keyboard shortcuts can also be used for two very common selection operations: selecting the *next* or *previous object* (Tab or Shift-Tab) and selecting *all objects* (Ctrl-A).

The concepts of *next* and *previous* actually refer to the z-order of objects inside the document (see 4.3). When you press Tab, you select the object immediately *above* the currently selected object in the z-order (or above the topmost selected object, if several objects are selected). Correspondingly, Shift-Tab selects the object immediately *below* the (bottommost) selected object.

If nothing was selected, Tab selects the bottommost object in the current layer, and Shift-Tab selects the topmost one. Since objects are typically added to the top of the current layer's z-order, pressing Shift-Tab with no previous selection is therefore a convenient shortcut for selecting the most recently added (drawn, pasted, imported, etc.) object.

Some aspects of the behavior of these three shortcuts can be changed on the **Selecting** tab of the **Inkscape Preferences** dialog:

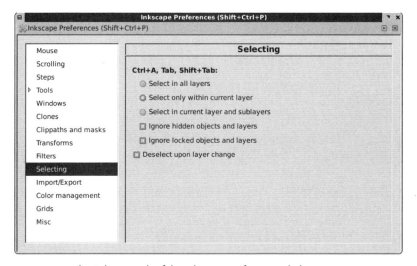

Figure 5-7:   The Selecting tab of the Inkscape Preferences dialog

- By default, these keys are limited to the current layer (which may be a group that you have entered, 4.6.1). That is, once you reach the topmost object of the layer by pressing Tab, next you will go back to the bottommost object in the same layer, and pressing Ctrl-A will select all objects only in the current layer. In the dialog, this behavior is described as **Select only within current layer**. Of the two other options, **Select in current layer and sublayers** works the same except that it enters inside the sublayers of the current layer (4.6.1), and **Select in all layers** allows Tab or Shift-Tab to cross the boundaries of layers and Ctrl-A to select all objects in the entire document.

- The two checkboxes, **Ignore hidden** and **Include locked objects and layers**, can be unchecked to allow the keyboard shortcuts to select those objects that are hidden or locked or, if you also chose **Select in all layers**, are in a hidden or locked layer (4.6).

5.12 Finding Objects

Searching for objects is something you will only need to do in complex documents—but when you need it, you will be glad Inkscape can do it. This chapter on selection is the best place to discuss object searching simply because it is, in essence, yet another way to select objects.

The main way to search is to use the **Find** dialog (Figure 5-8) that you can call by pressing Ctrl-F or by selecting **Edit ▸ Find**.

Figure 5-8: The Find dialog

You can search by typing your query in one or more fields, as described below. If you specify a value for more than one search field, they are combined using the logical "and"—that is, only those objects are found that satisfy *all* the specified criteria.

Text

This field applies only to text objects (Chapter 15) and searches within their text content. The search is case sensitive. If there are objects whose text exactly corresponds to the query string, only those objects get selected; otherwise, Inkscape tries to find *partial matches*—i.e., those text objects whose contents *contain* the query string.

ID

This searches within the id attribute of all objects (A.9). This only makes sense when some of your IDs are meaningful, that is, set by you and not generated automatically by Inkscape. As with text, Inkscape first tries to find exact matches and, failing that, looks for partial matches.

Style

This field allows you to search within the style of objects. Unfortunately, since this is a simple text field, to use this feature you need to have at least some idea of how style is written in SVG (see A.8). Here are a few examples:

Finding all red-filled objects

This is possible but only for one specific red color, which you must know how to convert into the RRGGBB form. For example, the "bright red" in the color palette is ff0000 in RRGGBB notation, and in an object's style string this is preceded by a hash mark (#) and the name of the property, fill, separated by a colon. So, the entire search string will be fill:#ff0000.

Finding all objects without stroke or fill

Search for stroke:none or fill:none.

Finding all fully transparent objects

Search for opacity:0; (note the separator semicolon at the end; without it, it will also find all *partially* transparent objects—for example, those with opacity:0.5; in their style).

Attribute

This field searches for objects that, in SVG, have an attribute with this *name* (regardless of its value). For example, all objects that you export to bitmap using selection export get the attribute inkscape:export-filename, which stores the filename of the bitmap export file. So, searching for this attribute will select all objects in the document that were ever exported (following which you can, for example, export them all again, see 18.9).

Type

This allows you to search for objects of specific types. Unchecking the **All types** checkbox opens up a column of other checkboxes corresponding to various object types:

Figure 5-9: Choosing object types in the Find dialog

Leave checked only those types that you want to find. You can combine this with the other search criteria listed above.

In addition to the search fields, four checkboxes at the bottom of the dialog enable various search options:

Search in selection
This allows you to narrow the current selection instead of searching the entire document.

Search in current layer
By default, Inkscape searches in all layers. Check this to limit the search to the current layer.

Include hidden and **Include locked**
By default, Inkscape's search ignores hidden and locked objects, as well as objects in hidden or locked layers. Check these to enable searching within hidden and/or locked objects.

5.13 Following Links

As you will see in the following chapters, objects in Inkscape can be linked to each other in various ways. You will often want to follow such links to find the object to which your current selected object is linked. Inkscape has a universal keyboard shortcut for this, Shift-D. Depending on what kind of object is selected, pressing Shift-D will select:

- The original of a clone (16.4), if a clone is selected
- The path to which the selected text-on-path object is attached (15.2.3)
- The path to which the selected linked offset object is attached (12.4)

Remember that some of the document objects may be stored in the defs (see A.4), in which case they can be referenced from the document but are not visible anywhere on the canvas. If your on-screen clone, text-on-path, or linked offset refers to an object in defs, Shift-D will fail with an error message in the status bar.

5.14 Deselecting

In almost any tool, context, or mode, pressing Esc will deselect the current selection. If you have a subselection, typically pressing Esc once will deselect the subselection and the second Esc will deselect the regular selection.

Another way to deselect is by clicking the empty canvas (or a locked object with nothing underneath it). This, however, works only in Selector and in those tools where a simple click selects objects (5.5). In complex drawings where accessing empty canvas may be difficult, Esc is by far the most convenient way to deselect.

Also, by default Inkscape deselects when you switch the current layer (see 4.6). This can be disabled on the **Selecting** tab of the **Inkscape Preferences** dialog.

5.15 Selection Miscellany

When you undo an action, sometimes, though not always, the current selection is deselected. (Whether this happens or not depends on what kind of action you're undoing.) This is not the intended behavior; in fact it is a bug, and future versions of Inkscape are likely to fix it.

Another similar problem is that selection is often lost after an extension (13.3) is run. Moreover, if an extension opens a configuration dialog and in it, you check the **Live preview** checkbox, you cannot change selection (or do anything else on the canvas) while that dialog is open.

Inkscape's powerful command-line interface has a special parameter for selecting objects, --select (C.5). To use it, you need to know the IDs of the objects you want to select. This makes it possible to script fully automated Inkscape editing sessions where a single command loads a document, selects some objects, performs some actions on them, saves the document, and quits—all without any user interaction.

6

TRANSFORMING

In Inkscape, *transformation* has a rather narrow meaning. Despite what the word might imply, it does not refer to *any* change of an object, but only to four simple operations that affect the entire object in the same way: moving, scaling, rotating, and skewing. Anything else is not transformation.

Metaphorically, transforming objects is simply moving around the furniture in your house without repainting the walls or opening up any cabinets.

SVG *Transformations applied to an object are often (but not always) stored as the* transform *attribute in SVG; for more on when it is or is not written, as well as the relevant preferences settings, see* **A.7**.

6.1 The Selector: Moving

After selecting objects, transforming them is the second most important function of the Selector tool. And of all the kinds of transforming, moving is the easiest: Just grab an object (if it is not selected yet, clicking will select it; you just need to be in the object's clickable area for this to work) and drag.

Such *free dragging* is easy and inspiring; you would normally use it at the early stages of your work where you need to move stuff around a lot to find the best overall composition. (Note that unlike many other vector editors, Inkscape moves the object itself in real time, not just its outline or frame.)

At later stages of your work, you will more often need *constrained dragging*. The most common constrained mode is horizontal or vertical dragging with Ctrl pressed. When you press and hold Ctrl while dragging, Inkscape creates two invisible "rails," one horizontal and one vertical, which intersect at the point where your dragging started. The selection can then move only along these rails, jumping from one to the other depending on which one is closer:

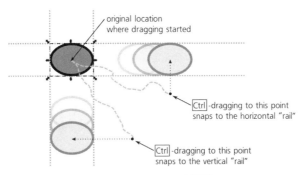

original location
where dragging started

Ctrl-dragging to this point
snaps to the horizontal "rail"

Ctrl-dragging to this point
snaps to the vertical "rail"

Figure 6-1: Constrained dragging with Ctrl

Ctrl has the general meaning of constraining your action in many other situations, too. In this, Inkscape is different from Adobe applications which normally use Shift for a similar purpose. Many more ways to constrain object movement are available via snapping, which we will discuss in the next chapter.

As you know from the previous chapter, sometimes selecting just the objects you need may be difficult; in particular, you may have to use Alt-clicks (selecting under) and Ctrl-clicks (selecting in groups) to get to the objects you need. And now, if you want to drag these selected objects around, you may run into a problem: Any drag starts with a click, and that click may very well ruin your carefully constructed selection by selecting some other object—such as the one that happens be on top of your objects, or the containing group.

In many cases, the easiest workaround for this problem is to move the selection by arrow keys, not by mouse drag (**6.5**). However, you can use mouse dragging too, if you start your drag with the Alt key pressed. This allows the current selection to be dragged without inadvertently selecting other objects. Therefore, you can start Alt-drag to move the selection from any point, not only from the selection itself but also from an empty canvas or any other object.

You might wonder how this Alt-drag can be compatible with Alt-click, which *does* change selection by "selecting under." The solution is simple: Unlike regular click-to-select, "selecting under" happens not when you click your mouse button but when you *release* it after a click; if, between click and release, you didn't move your mouse by more than the click/drag threshold (**5.4**, default is 4 screen pixels), this is considered a click, and "selecting under" is performed. Otherwise, the current selection is moved.

6.2 The Selector: Scaling

Now let's look at something more complex: *scaling* the selection, or making it bigger or smaller. This is not the same as zooming; when you zoom, you just view your drawing from closer up or from farther away without changing it in any way. Scaling means actually resizing the objects; this is an undoable action.

For scaling your selection, the Selector tool displays eight handles, four at the corners and four on the sides of the selection's bounding box. Dragging the side handles scales selection in one direction (horizontally or vertically); dragging the corner handles scales it in both directions:

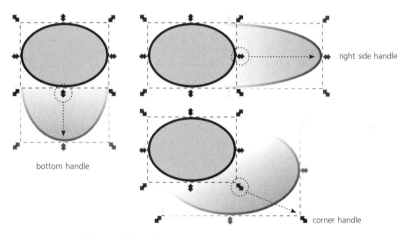

Figure 6-2: Scaling with the Selector tool

By default, the corner handles can move freely in any direction. This means that in the general case, the ratio between width and height (also called *aspect ratio*) of the selected objects will *not* be preserved. You can stretch or squeeze your selection, and you can even make it taller *and* narrower, or lower *and* wider, in a single drag. Side handles also do not preserve the aspect ratio, as they scale in one dimension only.

The simplest way to lock the aspect ratio is to scale with Ctrl pressed. This makes scaling proportional for both corner and side handles. Another way to achieve this is by clicking the lock toggle in the Selector controls bar above the canvas, between the **W** and **H** editable fields:

Figure 6-3: The aspect ratio lock in the Selector controls bar

When this lock is on (pressed), corner handles always scale proportionally. Side handles, however, are not affected by the lock and still scale in only one dimension.

Normally, scaling works in such a way that the opposite side (for side handles) or the opposite corner (for corner handles) of the selection's bounding box remain fixed. Sometimes, however, you will want the center of the selection to be fixed so that it is scaled symmetrically out from the center. This is what Shift does. Note that during any scaling, the fixed point is always visualized by a cross mark:

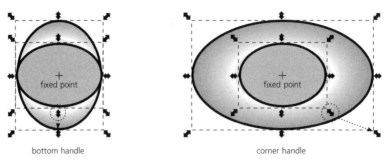

Figure 6-4: Scaling around the center of selection with Shift

NOTE *Here's a useful mnemonic: When typing text, pressing* Shift *makes the letters* bigger *(i.e., uppercase); when scaling, it also makes the result twice as big as it would be without* Shift *(since it scales on both sides of the center point).*

You can move the center of scaling anywhere, as described in **6.4** below.

The remaining modifier, Alt, also has a role during scaling. It allows you to scale the selection by integer multipliers: up to 2, 3, 4, and so on times the original size, or down to 1/2, 1/3, 1/4, and so on of the original size. Alt can be combined with Ctrl to lock the aspect ratio or with Shift to scale around the center of the selection.

6.3 The Selector: Rotating and Skewing

The question *How do I rotate objects?* is surprisingly common on Inkscape users' forums and mailing lists. To rotate the selection, you need to switch the Selector tool into *rotate mode*, and here's the little secret of how this switch is done: by a *second click* on the selection. (Note that this must be a distinct second click, not a quick double-click.) A third click toggles the Selector back into scale mode, a fourth returns it to rotate mode, and so on:

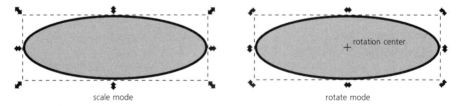

Figure 6-5: The scale and rotate modes of the Selector tool

AI *Inkscape didn't invent this; the separate Selector mode is borrowed from the CorelDRAW and Xara vector editors. Not surprisingly, most of the people who have problems with this convention are accustomed to Adobe Illustrator instead.*

There's one problem with the second click: Just like with moving, it may not always be possible to click the selection without selecting something else (if, for example, selected objects are in groups or under other objects). In these cases, just press Shift-S to switch to the rotate mode or back.

Once you are in the rotate mode, rotating the selection is as easy as dragging the corner handles. Dragging side handles skews the selection.

When rotating, Ctrl constrains the rotation angle to equidistant angle increments, by default every 15 degrees:

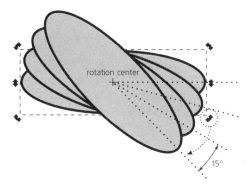

Figure 6-6: Rotation constrained by Ctrl

This constraint angle can be changed in the **Steps** tab of the **Inkscape Preferences** dialog (the **Rotation snaps every** drop-down menu). You can choose one of the many values from 0.5 degrees to 90 degrees.

Skewing with Ctrl honors the same constraint angle:

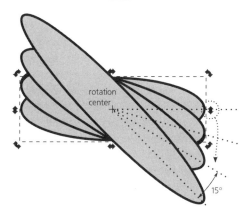

Figure 6-7: Skewing constrained by Ctrl

Shift-rotation temporarily moves the rotation center to the bounding box corner opposite to that of the corner handle being dragged.

6.4   Center of Rotation

When you switch the Selector tool into rotate mode, you will see a cross mark in the center of the selected object or objects. This is the center of rotation. This point is remembered for each object and is one of its permanent properties; moving any object's center is an undoable action, and when you save the document, the rotation centers of all objects are saved with it. Scaling, rotation, or skewing are performed around this point not only with the Selector tool but in most other places as well (such as in the **Transform** dialog or when transforming by keyboard shortcuts).

By default, the rotation center is in the geometric center of the bounding box of an object. With the Selector tool, you can freely drag it to any point (inside or outside the object itself). While being dragged, the center snaps to the edges of the object's bounding box, to the geometric center (its original location), and to the horizontal and vertical axes going through the geometric center. This makes it easy to quickly snap the rotation center back into the default position or to a corner of the bounding box. Drag it with Shift to suppress snapping; drag it with Ctrl to limit its movement to horizontal/vertical.

If you move the object (by any means, not only by dragging with the Selector tool), its center of rotation moves along with it, so it always stays in the same relative position to the object. Unfortunately, there's currently no way to move an object's center of rotation using the keyboard—you can only manipulate it by dragging it with the mouse.

When more than one object is selected, the selection as a whole also has a rotation center, which is that of the object which was selected *first* (if you selected objects one by one, by adding to the selection with Shift-clicks) or the one which is closest to the *bottom* in z-order (if you selected by rubber band or by Ctrl-A). If that first or bottommost object ever had its rotation center moved away from the default position, the entire selection will have the same rotation center as that object; otherwise the selection's rotation center will be in the default position—in the geometric center of the selection bounding box.

Moreover, if, with multiple objects selected, you drag the selection's rotation center, this applies to *all* selected objects: Each of them will have this new rotation center position. For example, if you draw a wheel with multiple spokes, you can select all the spokes and move the rotation center to the center of the wheel just once. After that, even if you select a single spoke, it will conveniently rotate around the center of the wheel.

Also, the rotation center is inherited when you duplicate or clone (**16.1**) the object. For example, you can draw a single spoke, move its rotation center to the center of the wheel, then duplicate (or clone) that spoke and simply rotate the copies by any method (by dragging corner handles with the Selector tool, by keyboard shortcuts, or by the **Transform** dialog). The new spokes will remain firmly set inside the wheel:

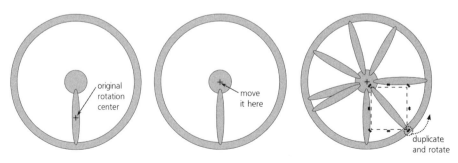

Figure 6-8: Using a rotation center to ensure spokes belong to the wheel

6.5   Transforming with Keyboard Shortcuts

Transforming objects by dragging them or their handles on the canvas is easy and intuitive, but it's not very precise (even when using various constrained modes) and may sometimes feel quite clumsy. Many long-time users of Inkscape prefer to use keyboard shortcuts for most of their transformations.

Keyboard shortcuts for transforming objects are easy to remember, and often, they will make your work a lot easier. Another reason to learn these keys is that, as we will see in the rest of the book, they are used consistently in many other tools and contexts to perform analogous functions—for example, to transform nodes with the Node tool, text characters with the Text tool, or gradient handles with the Gradient tool.

NOTE   *Skewing is not possible from the keyboard, which is understandable given that this operation is not used all that often.*

6.5.1   Moving

The ←, →, ↑, and ↓ arrow keys move the selection. The amount of move depends on the modifiers.

- Without modifiers, arrow keys move by 2 px (2 SVG pixel units, not screen pixels, **A.6**). This is the default value; you can change it in the **Steps** tab of the **Inkscape Preferences** dialog.

- With Alt, arrows move the selection by 1 screen pixel. This means the actual distance depends on the zoom level, and you can do finer moves when you are zoomed in or coarser moves when zoomed out. This is one of the most common and useful shortcuts because of its precision and adaptability: With it, you can always move your selection by the minimum distance that is still noticeable at the current zoom.

- With Shift, arrows move by 10 times the distance as they would without Shift. So, simple Shift-arrows move by 20 px (by default) and Shift-Alt-arrows move by 10 screen pixels at the current zoom.

The ease and predictability of the keyboard move commands make them useful in a lot of different situations. For example, sometimes I need to do something to objects obscured by some large foreground object. Alt-clicking to "select under" works, but it's often too cumbersome; moving the foreground object to a new layer and hiding that layer is also a good option, but it is even more cumbersome. In such cases, I often select the foreground object and move it off (to the right) by several → or Shift-→ keystrokes. When finished, I will select it again and move it precisely back into place by the same number of movement keystrokes in the opposite direction. (Just remember to not use Alt-arrows in this case because you may be at a different zoom level when moving the object back, and that would affect the distance.) The same "move away and then back" trick is useful for analyzing complex compositions when I'm trying to find out which parts of the drawing correspond to which objects.

6.5.2 Scaling

The $<$ and $>$ keys (angle brackets) scale the selection down and up, respectively. Keyboard scaling always preserves aspect ratio and is performed around the geometric center of the object's bounding box (not around its moveable rotation center). Again, the amount of scaling depends on the modifiers.

- Without modifiers, the $<$ and $>$ keys scale by 2 px (2 SVG pixel units, not screen pixels). This increment is applied to the biggest of the two dimensions of the bounding box; for example, if the object is wider than it is tall, its width grows by 2 px (the left and right edges of the bounding box move by 1 px each, in opposite directions), and its height grows by a proportionally smaller amount. The default value is 2 px; you can change it in the **Steps** tab of the **Inkscape Preferences** dialog.

- With `Alt`, the $<$ and $>$ keys scale by 2 screen pixels, so that in the larger dimension of the bounding box, the edges move by 1 screen pixel each in opposite directions. As with `Alt`-arrows, this means the actual distance depends on the zoom level, and you can scale finer when you are zoomed in or coarser when zoomed out.

- `Shift` has no effect on the $<$ and $>$ keys. This is because on some keyboards, you need to press `Shift` just to get these characters. By the way, $,$ (comma) and $.$ (dot) work as $<$ and $>$, respectively, because on many keyboards they are physically the same keys.

- With `Ctrl`, the $<$ and $>$ keys scale by a factor of 2—that is, they make the selection twice smaller and twice larger, respectively. This is convenient when you need to scale something by a large ratio; for example, start by pressing `Ctrl->` a few times to get within the ballpark of the required size, then adjust it more precisely using the same key with `Alt` or without modifiers.

6.5.3 Rotating and Flipping

The $[$ and $]$ keys (square brackets) rotate selection counterclockwise and clockwise, respectively. Rotating is performed around the moveable rotation center that is visible in Selector's rotate mode; unless you moved it, it's the geometric center of the object's bounding box. Again, the amount of rotation depends on the modifiers.

- Without modifiers, the $[$ and $]$ keys rotate by 15 degrees. This is the same angle constraint value that is used by mouse rotation with `Ctrl`. It is changeable in the **Rotation snaps every** drop-down menu in the **Inkscape Preferences** dialog.

- With `Alt`, the $[$ and $]$ keys rotate by such an angle that the bounding box corners of the selection move by 1 screen pixel. This means the actual rotation angle depends on the zoom level, and you can rotate finer when you are zoomed in or coarser when zoomed out.

- `Shift` has no effect on the $[$ and $]$ keys, for the same reason it has no effect on the $<$ and $>$ keys.

- With `Ctrl`, the $[$ and $]$ keys rotate by 90 degrees (one quarter of the full circle).

Also, four common transformations are accessible both as keyboard shortcuts and as buttons on the Selector tool's controls bar, as shown in Figure 6-9:

- Rotate selection by 90 degrees counterclockwise and clockwise, also accessible via the Ctrl-[and Ctrl-] shortcuts.
- Flip selection horizontally and vertically, also accessible via the h and v shortcuts.

Figure 6-9: The Selector tool's controls bar: transformation buttons

NOTE *Flipping is equivalent to scaling by −100 percent in the respective dimension.*

To make two objects *exchange places*, you can use double flipping: First, select them both and flip them as a whole; then, select each one in turn and flip it individually to restore it. To make the exchange two-dimensional, you will need to perform this procedure twice, once using horizontal flipping (h) and then using vertical flipping (v).

Artists sometimes use flipping to check their work. When you're drawing something, it's easy to grow progressively blinder to your errors exactly because you're looking at them for so long. In this situation, flipping the entire drawing horizontally or vertically gives you a fresh look at the drawing and makes many problems with shape, balance, or composition painfully obvious.

6.6 Transforming with Numbers: X, Y, W, and H

Sometimes, neither mouse nor keyboard methods of transforming are quite up to the task because you know exactly how far (or to what point) you want to move your objects or by what angle to rotate them. Inkscape allows you to specify exact numeric values for transforming selection.

There are two places where this can be done. One is the controls bar of the Selector tool:

Figure 6-10: The Selector tool's controls bar: the X, Y, W, and H fields

Here, the **X** and **Y** values specify the position of the selection and **W** and **H** specify its width and height. Not only do these values automatically update when you select and deselect objects or move or scale the selection, but they also allow you to type any values to have the selection moved or scaled correspondingly.

NOTE *The coordinate origin for the X and Y values is in the top-left corner of the page (3.4.3).*

After typing a value in the field, press Enter to activate it, or press Tab to activate it and move to the next field. To jump to the first field from the keyboard, press Alt-X.

To the right of the editable fields, there's a drop-down menu for selecting the unit in which the values are expressed. Inkscape supports a number of units, including **in** (inches), **pt** (points, each point being 1/72 of an inch), **mm** (millimeters), and **cm** (centimeters). The default unit is **px** (SVG pixel, **A.6**).

One of the most useful units is the **%** (percent). It allows you to scale an object not to some absolute size but as a percentage relative to its current size. For example, to scale selection to 1.5 times its size, switch the unit to **%** and type 150 in the **W** and **H** fields (if you click the lock button between them, setting only one of these fields to 200 will be enough).

6.7 The Transform Dialog

A more powerful tool for transforming objects numerically is the **Transform** dialog (Shift-Ctrl-M). It has separate tabs for each of the four transform types we've been discussing (moving, scaling, rotating, and skewing) as well as a tab for the complete transformation matrix. Generally, you choose one of the tabs, type the values you want, and click **Apply**.

Let's look at these tabs in order.

6.7.1 The Move Tab

Unlike the **X** and **Y** values in the Selector controls bar, which always show you the absolute coordinates of the selection, in the **Move** tab (shown in Figure 6-11) you can view and specify both absolute coordinates and relative displacements. By default, the **Relative move** checkbox is selected, so the **Horizontal** and **Vertical** fields initially display zeroes, and any numbers you type there will move the selection *by* that much (for example, the values of 3 and 0 move the selection by 3 units horizontally to the right).

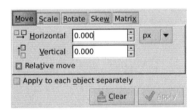

Figure 6-11: The Move tab of the Transform dialog

Now, uncheck the **Relative move** checkbox; you will see that the values in the fields have changed. They now display the current coordinates of the selection, which are the same as the **X** and **Y** fields in the Selector controls bar. The units drop-down menu also works similarly.

6.7.1.1 Moving to Adjust Intervals

If several objects are selected and both the **Apply to each object separately** and **Relative move** checkboxes are checked, each object will be shifted, not relative to its own previous position, but relative to its neighbor—the nearest selected object to the left (for X) or below (for Y). This makes it easy to "space out" or "tighten up" collections of objects.

For example, if you need to space out a horizontal row of objects, select them and move them horizontally by 5 px with both checkboxes checked. The leftmost object will shift by 5 px to the right, the next one by 10 px, and so on until the rightmost selected object is displaced by $5n$ px, where n is the number of selected objects. As a result, each interval between adjacent objects will increase by 5 px and the whole row will be spaced out, much like a letterspacing adjustment spaces out a text string (15.3.4). Moving these objects by −5 px will, conversely, squeeze them tighter together: The leftmost will move by 5 px to the left, the next one by 10 px, and so on. For vertical moves, the effect is the same except that it starts from the object closest to the bottom (i.e., with the smallest Y coordinate).

NOTE   *The order in which objects are shifted may not be obvious if they overlap. The rule is, either left edges (for horizontal moves) or bottoms (for vertical moves) of the objects' bounding boxes are sorted to determine which object to move relative to which. The order of selecting the objects or their z-order makes no difference.*

6.7.2   The Scale Tab

Here, the default unit is always %, which allows you to quickly scale selection by a given ratio (such as 200% to scale it up twice or 50% to scale it down to half the size). The units drop-down menu contains all the absolute units you may need (switching to them changes the displayed values from 100% to the width and height of the selection in the chosen unit), and the **Scale proportionally** checkbox is analogous to the lock button on the Selector's controls bar.

So far, everything this tab is able to do can also be carried out via the Selector tool's **W** and **H** controls. However, the important **Apply to each object separately** checkbox is unique to this dialog: It applies the same scaling to each selected object, scaling it around its own rotation center (6.4) instead of scaling the selection as a whole around its center. For the % unit, this means scaling each selected object by the same ratio; for all other units, this results in all selected objects getting the same specified width and height.

Unlike the **Move** tab (and the Selector controls), values on the **Scale** tab (shown in Figure 6-12) do not update automatically when you transform a selection by other means (such as by dragging handles), nor when you just select a different object; the values you typed stay put. This is convenient when you want to apply the same size to many different objects, but sometimes this may be a problem: You may assume that the displayed value in absolute units is that of the currently selected object, while that's not actually the case. To quickly reset the values back to 100% of the current selection, click the **Clear** button.

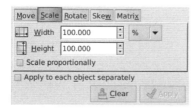

Figure 6-12: The Scale tab of the Transform dialog

6.7.3 The Rotate Tab

This tab (shown in Figure 6-13) contains a single editable field for the rotation angle. Positive values rotate counterclockwise, and negative values rotate clockwise. The default unit is degree (360 degrees to the full circle), but you can switch it to radians (2 × π = 6.283 radians to the full circle). The **Apply to each object separately** checkbox works as expected: Instead of rotating the entire selection around the selection's rotation center (6.4), it rotates each object separately around its own rotation center.

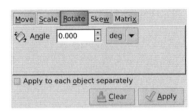

Figure 6-13: The Rotate tab of the Transform dialog

6.7.4 The Skew Tab

This tab (shown in Figure 6-14) contains two editable fields for horizontal and vertical *skewing*, which basically means displacing one of the four sides of the bounding box along itself, correspondingly slanting the adjacent perpendicular sides. The **Apply to each object separately** checkbox works the same as for scaling and rotating, skewing each object around its own rotation center.

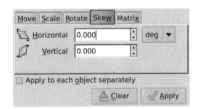

Figure 6-14: The Skew tab of the Transform dialog

The units drop-down menu contains absolute length units, percent, and angular units (degree and radian). Here's how they work:

Absolute units
With an absolute unit, the **Horizontal** value specifies the absolute displacement of the top edge of selection to the right (positive) or to the left (negative); the **Vertical** value specifies the displacement of the left edge down (positive) or up (negative).

Percent
With the % unit, values are specified in the same way as with absolute units, except that the amount of displacement is calculated as the given percentage of the adjacent perpendicular side of the bounding box. In other words, this percentage is equal to the *tangent of the skew angle*. For example, skewing

an upright rectangle vertically by 100% results in its formerly horizontal sides becoming slanted at 45 degrees.

Angular units

This allows you to directly set the slant angle—that is, the angle of the sides adjacent to the side being moved. For example, vertically skewing an object by 45 degrees is the same as skewing it by 100% or by the absolute value of the object's width.

NOTE   *Skewing by 90 degrees is a simple way to create an "infinite" object (in reality, of course, it will become very big in the direction of the skew but not infinite).*

6.7.5 The Matrix Tab

This tab (shown in Figure 6-15) allows you to directly edit the object's *transformation matrix* stored in its transform attribute (**A.7**). A detailed explanation of the algebra of transformation matrices is outside the scope of this book; for practical purposes, it's enough to know that the two rightmost values (labeled **E** and **F**) represent the displacement of the object (how far it has been moved), and the four other values collectively encode its scaling, rotation, and skew.

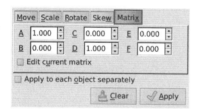

Figure 6-15: The Matrix tab of the Transform dialog

By default, the **Edit current matrix** checkbox is unchecked and the tab presents an *identity matrix* where **A** and **D** are 1 and all other values are 0. If you change any values and click **Apply**, this matrix will be *post-multiplied* with the current matrix of the object, that is, applied to the selected object on top of its current transformation. If you check the **Edit current matrix** checkbox, the tab will show and let you directly edit the current matrix of the selected object. (If multiple objects are selected, the matrix of the first or bottommost selected one will be displayed.)

The **Matrix** tab thus provides a way to reset the transform attribute of an object without going to the XML Editor: Check **Edit current matrix**, then click **Clear** (this resets the values to the identity matrix), and click **Apply**.

6.8 Pasting Sizes

One way to quickly assign a specific size to an object without using any dialogs is by *pasting* that size on it. For this, you must first copy (Ctrl-C) an object whose size you want to assign to other objects. After that, use the commands from the **Paste Size** submenu in the **Edit** menu.

The six commands of this submenu implement various combinations of pasting.

- Pasting either width only (height is unchanged), height only (width is unchanged), or size (both width and height).

- Pasting to the selection as a whole or pasting to each selected object separately (analogous to the **Apply to each object separately** checkbox in the **Transform** dialog).

For example, if you have imported a number of bitmap images and you want to create a gallery of thumbnails out of them, you can unify their sizes by drawing a rectangle of the desired thumbnail size, copying it to the clipboard, then selecting all the images and choosing **Edit ▸ Paste Size ▸ Paste Size Separately**.

6.9   Transforming with the Tweak Tool

The Tweak tool (w or Shift-F2) is a versatile instrument which applies the same "soft brush" metaphor not only to transforming objects but also to styling them (**8.7**) and editing paths (**12.6**). This tool has a number of *modes*; in this chapter, we will cover those modes that deal with transforming, duplicating, and deleting objects. Using these modes, it is easy to sweep, sculpt, and scatter collections of objects, such as clone tilings, into complex and naturalistic images—to *draw with scattering*.

All modes of the Tweak tool share a number of common features. No matter which mode you're in, you use a circular soft-edged brush (the orange circle you see under the cursor) controlled by the **Width** and **Force** parameters on the controls bar and affected by the pen pressure (if you have a pressure-sensitive tablet). You "paint" with this brush over the selected objects to change them.

The *width* of the brush varies from 1 to 100, but these aren't absolute units; regardless of zoom, 1 gives you a very small brush and 100 gives you a brush approximately the size of your screen. In this tool, you will always see the circular brush outline centered on your mouse cursor and demonstrating the current width of the brush. You can change this value by using the **Width** control on the toolbar or the ← (narrower) and → (wider) keys. The brush is soft; its action is maximum in the center and smoothly decreases towards the edge following a bell-like profile.

Similarly, *force* ranges from 1 (very weak; you need to stroke an object several times to achieve a visible effect) to 100 (very strong; the first stroke of the brush applies the maximum effect under the brush). To change the force, use the toolbar control or press the ↓ (weaker) and ↑ (stronger) keys.

To get a feeling of how the Tweak tool works, create a number of small objects in a test drawing. The easiest way to do this is to set up a small clone tiling (**16.6**) of about 10-by-10 clones, but you can also start with a single ellipse or path and manually duplicate (Ctrl-D) or clone (Alt-D) it several times, dragging away the copies. Now, select all the objects you created, switch to the Tweak tool, adjust **Width** so the circle covers several objects at once, set **Force** to a moderate value of 20, enable one of the modes by its toggle button, and start dragging over the objects. Figure 6-16 shows what will happen.

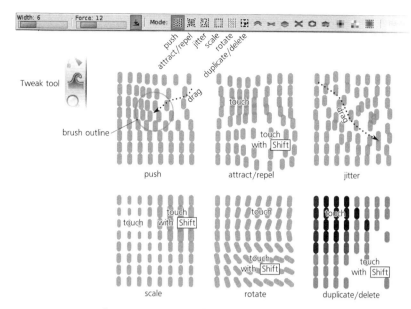

Figure 6-16: Transforming a scattering of semitransparent objects with the modes of the Tweak tool

Move mode

Moves those selected objects that are under the brush in the direction in which you drag the brush. This mode is similar to simply dragging objects around, except that instead of dragging each object individually, you drag a brush that softly and naturally "sweeps" all objects that it happens to run across. Note that non-selected objects are never affected; the easiest way to achieve this is to group all tweakable objects and simply select the group.

Attract/Repel Objects mode

Attracts those selected objects that are under the brush towards the cursor (default) or repels them away from the cursor (with Shift pressed). This is a way to "suck in" or "blow up" some areas of the scattering.

Move Jitter mode

Moves those selected objects that are under the brush in random directions and by random distances. The harder you press and the higher the **Force** is, the heavier the jitter is. This is a way to "shake up" your composition if it's becoming too solid.

Scale mode

Scales those selected objects that are under the brush down (by default) or up (with Shift pressed). This mode allows you to introduce scaled nonuniformities to your scattering—smoothly make the objects larger in some parts of the image and smaller in others.

Rotate mode

Rotates those selected objects that are under the brush clockwise (by default) or counterclockwise (with Shift pressed). This allows you to introduce rotation non-uniformities to your scattering, for example to "bend" your scattering texture to adapt it to the dominant directions in different parts of the image.

Duplicate/Delete mode

Randomly duplicates some of the selected objects under the brush (by default) or deletes some of them (with Shift pressed). The chance of an object to be duplicated or deleted, as always, depends on force and pen pressure. This completes the "scatter drawing" toolset by providing a way to thicken and thin your scattering wherever necessary.

As with the regular **Duplicate** command (4.4), duplicating with the Tweak tool places the copies right over the originals, so it is a good idea to use the Jitter mode after duplicating to ruffle them apart. The duplicates created by the tool are automatically added to selection if the original objects were selected (e.g., if you're tweaking a group of objects, they are duplicated within that group and are not by themselves selected).

6.10 What Transformations Affect

Now that you can transform your objects by a myriad of methods, it's time to look closer at what exactly gets transformed when you do it. As it turns out, Inkscape can optionally affect or not affect some specific parts of objects. This is controlled by the **Affect** toggle buttons on the right end of the Selector controls bar:

Figure 6-17: The Selector tool's controls bar: the Affect buttons

There are four **Affect** toggle buttons, in the following order:

Stroke width

This button applies only to scaling and has no effect on moving, rotating, or skewing. When this button is on, any scaled object that has stroke (8.1.1) will have the width of the stroke scaled by the corresponding ratio. For example, if you scale an object with a 2-px wide stroke to twice its current size and this button is on, the resulting object will have 4-px wide stroke. If the button is off, it will have the same unchanged stroke width of 2 px.

If you scale an object without preserving the aspect ratio, with the **Affect stroke width** button on, stroke gets scaled by the square root of the product of vertical and horizontal scale ratios. For example, if you scale an object to twice its width horizontally but leave its height unchanged, the stroke becomes wider by a factor of 1.415 (the square root of 2).

Keeping stroke width unscaled is more commonly useful. For example, in a plan or draft, you normally want all your objects to have the same fixed stroke width, unaffected by scaling, so there you would toggle this button off. It only makes sense to toggle this button on when you use stroke as a purely visual element (such as brush-like strokes in a freehand drawing).

NOTE *Profiled strokes that the Pen and Pencil tools create (Chapter 14) always scale their width when the object is scaled.*

Rounded rectangle corners

This button also applies only to scaling and has no effect on moving, rotating, or skewing. It controls whether Inkscape scales the rounded corners of rectangles (11.2.2). When it's on, a rectangle is scaled as a whole, just as it would be scaled if converted to path; this may lead to the rounded corner becoming larger, smaller, and/or nonround. When it's off, Inkscape preserves the rounded corners exactly as they were. This can be useful, for example, in a flowchart diagram where you want all your boxes to have the same rounded corners independent of their sizes.

Gradients

This button controls whether transformations are applied to the gradients in objects' fills or strokes (10.1). Since gradients (more precisely, positions of gradient stops) can be moved, rotated, and skewed as well as scaled, this button applies to any kind of transformations. When it's on, the gradient stops are transformed as a whole with the object carrying the gradient. When it's off, the gradient stays glued to the canvas (unchanged in position, direction, or scale) while the object is transformed.

For example, with this button toggled off, it is possible to move an object beyond its own gradient, or scale it up so that more of the gradient becomes visible. This is useful when the gradient's position is exactly coordinated with other objects in your drawing, while the object itself is simply a "window" onto that gradient, and you want to move or adjust the edges of that window without touching the gradient itself.

Patterns

This button is completely analogous to the **Affect gradients** button except that it applies to the patterns (10.8) instead of gradients.

NOTE *In future versions, more **Affect** buttons may be added—for example, for scaling or not scaling path effects (Chapter 13) or filter effects (Chapter 17).*

NOTE *There's an annoying but harmless bug: Regardless of the current position of the **Affect** buttons, interactive transforming of objects by the mouse in the Selector tool always shows stroke, rounded corners, gradients, and patterns as transformed while you're dragging the mouse. As soon as you release the mouse, however, everything is corrected according to the current state of the **Affect** buttons.*

7

SNAPPING AND ARRANGING

As a sequel to the previous chapter, here we will look at more advanced transformation topics. Inkscape allows you to not only freely transform objects but to do it quickly, precisely, and, to some extent, automatically.

Snapping refers to making some points, lines, or paths work as magnets, so that when you are transforming something in the vicinity of such a magnetic attractor, the object you're transforming "snaps" into the exact desired position. *Arranging* moves a large number of objects in a regular way so that they are aligned, distributed, scattered, or lined up into a table exactly as you want them to be.

7.1 Guidelines

The easiest way to snap objects to alignment is by creating a guide, or guideline. *Guides* are visible, infinitely long straight lines on the canvas, but they are not objects. They cannot be selected, they don't print, and they don't show up on bitmap exports. Although they are saved with the document, they are not part of the SVG standard and are therefore invisible in SVG viewers other than Inkscape. They are just Inkscape-specific helpers for organizing your artwork.

For example, guides may separate parts of your layout, helping you visualize the edges of the various areas or cells. A guide can be a centerline helping you draw symmetrically around it. Or you can use a guide to quickly check if several objects are *really* aligned or just *look* like they are.

To create a guide, you must have rulers visible. (If you've hidden the rulers, display them with Ctrl-R.) Click anywhere on a ruler and, without releasing the mouse, drag your cursor onto the canvas. You will see a new ruler appear which you can now drop (by releasing the mouse) where you want it. Naturally, dragging off the horizontal ruler creates *horizontal guides*, and dragging off the vertical ruler creates *vertical guides*; what's more interesting, dragging from the very ends of the rulers creates *diagonal guides*, slanted (by default) at 45 degrees.

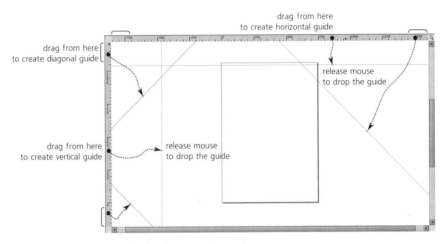

Figure 7-1: Creating guides by dragging from rulers

Moving a guideline is easy: With the Selector or Node tool, just grab the guideline and drag it to where you want it to be. (When you are hovering the mouse over a guideline, it turns from blue to red, which indicates that it can now be grabbed.) To delete a guideline, simply drag it back onto a ruler and drop it there, or Ctrl-click it.

To hide all guidelines in the document, press the | key (this is the vertical line character, usually on the same key as the \ but requiring Shift to be pressed as well). This does not delete anything, however; if you press | again (or try to create a new guideline), all hidden guidelines will be displayed again. This key controls both guide visibility and snapping to guides (you won't snap to invisible guides); if you want to disable only snapping without hiding the guides, use the % key (the global snapping toggle, **7.3**).

7.1.1 The Guideline Dialog

As often is the case in Inkscape, while you can move guidelines manually by dragging, there's also a way to specify the position and angle of a guideline precisely via numbers. This is done in the **Guideline** dialog (Figure 7-2), which is called up by double-clicking any guideline.

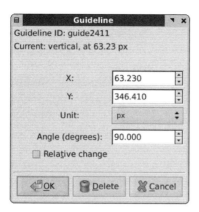

Figure 7-2: The Guideline dialog

- For horizontal guides, the **Angle** is 0, while **Y** determines the height of the guideline.

- For vertical guides, the **Angle** is 90, while **X** determines the horizontal position of the guideline.

- Finally, for diagonal guides, the **X** and **Y** values together determine the *anchor point* through which the guideline goes (which, initially, is the point where you released the mouse when creating the guide). On canvas, the anchor is shown as a small circle. The **Angle** sets the slant (default is 45 degrees).

The **Relative change** checkbox zeroes all editable fields in the dialog; now any value you type into them will *add* to the current values, not replace them. When done, click **OK** for your changes to take action; the **Delete** button deletes the guideline. Both buttons close the dialog.

This dialog is *modal*, which means it locks the rest of Inkscape while it is displayed.

7.1.2 Guideline Properties

A few general options that affect all guidelines can be found in the **Guides** tab of the **Document Properties** dialog (Shift-Ctrl-D), as shown in Figure 7-3. Why not the global **Inkscape Preferences** dialog? Because these options are considered to be local to the document and are saved with it. This means different documents can have different guide setups.

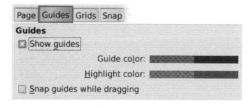

Figure 7-3: Guideline settings in the Document Properties dialog

Here you can see the global guide visibility checkbox. On by default, it allows you to quickly hide (but not delete!) all guides in the document. You can toggle guide visibility even without opening the dialog, by pressing the ⏐ key. Toggling guide visibility also toggles snapping to the guides.

Next, you can change the color and opacity of the guides in their normal state (default is half-transparent blue) and when the mouse is hovered over them (default is half-transparent red). Clicking the color swatches opens a small color chooser dialog:

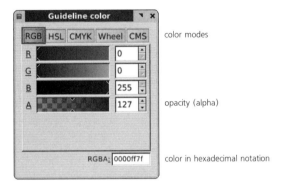

Figure 7-4: A color chooser dialog

The **A** slider sets *alpha* (transparency). You will see this dialog in many other situations as well (such as when choosing the page background color).

Finally, you can let guides snap when you drag them. Normally, guides are added so you can snap objects *to* them, but snapping guides themselves when you move them around is also useful. Guides will only snap to objects' bounding boxes, not to other guides or grids.

7.1.3 Guides from Objects

Converting an object to guidelines is a way to quickly create multiple guidelines at once. This is done by choosing the **Objects to Guides** command in the **Object** menu.

NOTE   *By default, this operation destroys the selected objects and replaces them with a bunch of guidelines. However, you can toggle on the **Keep objects after conversion to guides** checkbox in the **Tools** tab of the **Inkscape Preferences** dialog to prevent this, or simply press* Ctrl-D *before calling conversion.*

Figure 7-5 shows how this command works for different types of objects:

- For paths or rectangles, it replaces each straight path segment or rectangle side with a coincident guide. For example, if you just draw a rectangle and convert it to guides, you will have a rectangular area delineated by two vertical and two horizontal guides. Or, to quickly create a slanted guideline going through two given points, switch to the Pen tool (**14.1**), click one point, double-click the other (to finalize the straight line path), and convert this path to a guide.
- For 3D boxes (**11.3**), all 12 edges of a box are converted to guidelines.

- For anything else, the four sides of the object's bounding box are converted to two vertical and two horizontal guides.

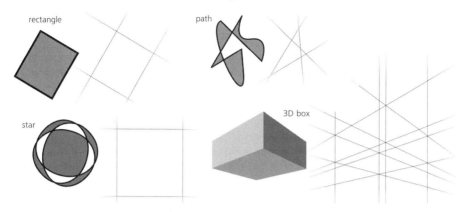

Figure 7-5: Converting various objects to guides

7.2 Grids

Grids can be seen as a development of the idea of guidelines. A *grid* is just a regular pattern of guidelines that covers the entire canvas. Grids are often used for snapping, for equispaced distribution of objects, for modeling of the pixel grid (see Figure 3-3), for axonometric drawing (Chapter 23), and for many other purposes.

Inkscape supports two types of grids: *rectangular* and *axonometric*. One document can display more than one grid, different in type and/or spacing. To create a new grid in your document, go to the **Grids** tab of the **Document Properties** dialog and under **Creation**, select the desired grid type and click **New**. A new grid will light up in the document:

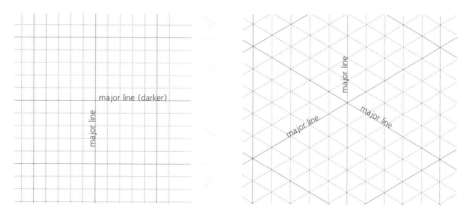

Figure 7-6: Rectangular and axonometric grids

As you can see in Figure 7-6, the rectangular grid consists of two perpendicular sets of guides, whereas the axonometric grid has three sets, one vertical and two others at an angle (by default both at 30 degrees). The rectangular grid is the most common type, whereas the axonometric grid is used mostly for drawing axonometric scenes (i.e., pseudo-3D drawings without vanishing points).

If you zoom in and out in a document with a grid, you will notice that Inkscape tries to maintain the visual density of the grid lines within certain limits. As you zoom out, the lines of course get closer to each other, but at some point Inkscape decides that the clutter is too much to bear and weeds the grid, switching to showing only every tenth grid line. Keep zooming out and this decimation of grid lines will happen again and again, so as to keep the grid manageable. As the default rectangular grid spacing is 1 px, at most zoom levels—if not for this adaptive hiding—the grid would cover the page so densely that you wouldn't be able to work.

Inversely, if you zoom in, Inkscape will gradually reveal more and more grid lines so as to evenly fill your screen. New lines only stop appearing when you reach a zoom level where all of the lines are visible: You now see the entire grid without any abridgement.

At close zooms, you will notice that every fifth line (called a *major line*) is a little darker than the rest (*minor lines*). This is another thing Inkscape does to make navigating in the grid easier, similar to a ruler that has some of its marks larger than others.

To hide all grids in the document, press the #️⃣ key. This does not delete anything; if you press #️⃣ again, all hidden grids will be displayed again. This key controls both grid visibility and snapping to grid (i.e., you won't snap to invisible grids); if you want to disable only snapping without hiding the guides, use the %️⃣ key (global snapping toggle, *7.3*).

7.2.1 Grid Options

Many aspects of grids can be changed in the **Document Properties** dialog. Once you create a grid, you will see a grid properties panel at the bottom of the dialog:

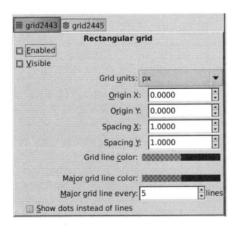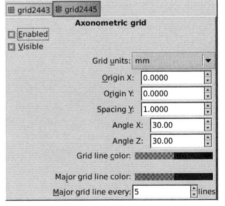

Figure 7-7: Grid properties (left, for a rectangular grid; right, for an axonometric grid)

Note that you can create more than one grid in the same document, and by default they will all be visible at once (although you can enable or disable any of them separately). In the dialog, each grid will have its own tab.

Let's look at what you can change for a grid:

- You can toggle between showing and hiding the grid as well as enable or disable snapping to it. If a grid is hidden, you cannot snap to it, so unchecking the **Visible** checkbox disables the rest of the properties.

- **Origin** and **Spacing** values define the position and the density of the lines in the grid. (Note, however, that if you make the grid too dense, Inkscape won't show all lines anyway until you zoom in close enough.) For a rectangular grid, there are two spacing values: **X** (horizontal) and **Y** (vertical). For an axonometric grid, there's only one spacing value—the distance along the Y axis between the slanted lines; the intervals between the vertical guidelines are completely determined by this distance and the axonometric angles. All these values are, as usual, coupled with a unit selector (a drop-down list).

- **Angles** are only available for axonometric grids. These two values set the angles of the two sets of diagonal lines; by default both are 30 degrees, but they can be anything from 1 to 89 degrees and don't have to be equal to each other.

NOTE *If you have added an axonometric grid to your document, new diagonal guides (7.1) will be created with the same angles as those used by the grid.*

- Colors can be set separately for the major and minor grid lines. By default they are both blue, but the minor lines are less opaque and therefore less visible.

- Frequency of the major lines can also be adjusted; by default, every fifth gridline is major.

- For a rectangular grid, you can select the checkbox to show a grid of dots instead of the grid of lines; dots are placed where the grid of lines would have intersections. Major line intersections display little circles instead of dots.

If what you need is not a snappable grid of helper lines but a grid of real objects (i.e., a grid that other SVG software will display just as Inkscape does), you can use the clone tiler (16.6) or the **Grid** extension (13.3).

7.3 Snapping

Now that you know everything about guides and grids, it's time to look at what guides and grids are most often created for: snapping.

The idea of snapping is simple: Inkscape can try to place things where you *want* them to be instead of where you actually move them with your inevitably imprecise mouse or tablet pen movements. As soon as you move a *snappable* (something that can be snapped) close enough to an active *snap target*, it jumps all the way into place. Snapping is a fundamentally interactive operation; it may only happen when you drag something with your mouse (but not, for example, when you move things by arrow keys on your keyboard or use the **Align and Distribute** dialog).

Snappables can be entire objects as well as different kinds of nodes or points (path nodes, gradient handles, center points, etc.) inside objects. Snap destinations, apart from guides and grids, can include other objects and their parts (i.e., objects can snap to objects, if you allow them).

Snapping is a big topic, but it's not deep; once you get the basic idea, the rest is just remembering the numerous modes and toggles. If you don't need snapping and do not use guides or grids, you will likely never be bothered by it. In any case, remember that there's a *master snap toggle*—the %⃞ key—that enables or disables all kinds of snapping in the entire program. (A mnemonic for remembering this shortcut is to view the % sign as two objects that are about to snap to a slanted guideline.) Unlike the |⃞ (guides toggle) and #⃞ (grid toggle), this key only turns snapping behavior on or off but does not hide or show anything.

7.3.1 The Snap Controls Bar

Most of the snapping controls are collected in the *snap controls bar*, by default displayed between the commands bar and the tool controls bar above the canvas. Use **View ▸ Show/Hide ▸ Snap Controls Bar** to turn this toolbar on or off.

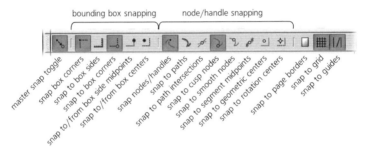

Figure 7-8: The snap controls bar

The leftmost button on the bar is the master snap toggle; if it's off, all other buttons on the bar are disabled.

Apart from grids and guides, the things that snap and are snapped to can be classified into two large groups, corresponding to the two largest sections of the snap controls bar: bounding boxes in the Selector tool (**4.2**) and nodes and handles in the rest of the tools. While in certain cases, things from one group can snap to things from the other, in general they tend to snap only within their own family. In particular, as of Inkscape 0.47, nodes and handles never snap to bounding boxes (though this may change in later versions). These two groups of options are detailed in the following sections.

Finally, the three last buttons on the bar control the major snap destinations that work for both groups: the edges of the page (**2.3**), grid (**7.2**), and guides (**7.1**). All of them only affect snapping but, unlike the |⃞ and #⃞ keys, do not hide the snapping aids.

In all icons on the snapping bar buttons, *blue* dots depict the *snappables* (i.e., what snaps), while *green* lines and circles correspond to *snap targets* (i.e., what you snap *to*). Some buttons enable/disable one kind of element in both these roles.

7.3.2 Bounding Box Snapping

If all you need is to align the whole objects and you're not interested in nodes or other special points, use bounding box snapping.

In the bounding box group of buttons, the first button enables *bounding box corners* as a snappable. (Unlike a snap target which can be either a point or a line, a snappable can only be a point.) Now, when you drag or transform anything with the Selector tool, the bounding box of the selection will snap to whatever snap targets you enable. Unless this button is on, all other buttons in this group are grayed out.

The next two buttons enable the *sides* of the bounding box and its *corners* as snap targets. This includes the boxes of all visible objects in your drawing, whether they are selected or not. (For example, if you want to snap corners to corners only, turn on the first and the third buttons in this group.) In situations like this, when you have both a line and a point on that line as a snap target, the point (i.e., the bounding box corner) takes over when you are close enough to it, but if you are close to the snapping line but far from the corner, you will snap to the nearest point on the line and easily slide along it.

The last two buttons in this group enable *centers of bounding box sides* and *centers of the entire boxes* as both snappables and snap destinations.

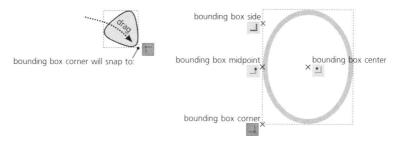

Figure 7-9: Bounding box snapping options

7.3.3 Node and Handle Snapping

This group controls snapping of not only path nodes (**12.1**) but gradient/pattern handles (**10.1**, **10.8**), rotation centers (**6.4**), text baseline origins (**15.3.3**), and some other special points.

Again, the first button in this group serves as a local master switch for the group; it activates nodes and handles as snappables, and without it, all other buttons in this group are grayed out.

The next button enables snapping to *paths*: You can snap and slide nodes along any path in your drawing (it need not be selected), but intersections, nodes, and midpoints on these paths do not hold any special attraction for the node you're dragging. These snap targets are turned on by the next four buttons: *path intersections* (**12.1.2**), *cusp nodes, smooth nodes* (**12.5.5**), and *midpoints* of straight line segments in paths (Figure 7-10).

The last two buttons add two more snap targets for nodes: *geometric object centers* and *rotation centers* (which are initially the same as geometric centers but can be moved anywhere).

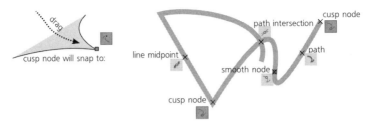

Figure 7-10: Node snapping options

7.3.4 Snapping Preferences

On the **Snap** tab of the **Document Properties** dialog, you can adjust the snapping distance—how close you must get to the snap target for snap to happen. This parameter is per-document and can be set separately for snapping to objects (i.e., to bounding boxes, path, nodes, etc.), grids, and guides.

For grids, the default setting is **Always snap**, which means snapping happens at any distance (which for a grid cannot be more than grid spacing anyway). If you zoomed out and some of the grid lines are hidden (7.2), snapping will happen to visible grid lines only.

For objects and guides, snapping is triggered, by default, at a distance of 20 screen pixels or closer. Using the screen pixel unit ensures that the snapping force is independent of zoom; if you want to move a snappable close enough to a snap destination but avoid snapping, work at a closer zoom level.

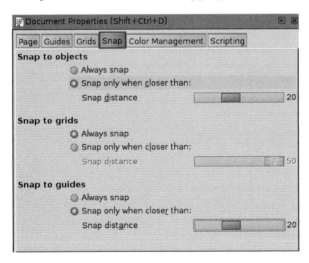

Figure 7-11: Snapping options in Document Properties

The global **Inkscape Preferences** dialog (3.1.1) also has a **Snapping** tab (Figure 7-12).

- **Snap indicator** (by default turned on) is the X-shaped mark in the snap point and the textual label, displayed right on canvas, telling you what has just snapped to what. Both the mark and the text pop up when snapping happens and disappear after one second. Snap indication greatly improves usability, but you can turn it off if you like.

- **Snap delay** is the time, in milliseconds, that Inkscape waits after your mouse pointer stopped before doing the snap. Increasing this value makes snapping more "reluctant," but this may actually be a good thing if your document is complex and you have many snapping modes enabled, so that everything wants to snap to everything. In this case, increasing the delay and decreasing the snap distance will make your work much easier.

- **Only snap the node closest to the pointer** tells Inkscape to ignore all other nodes you may be dragging except the one to which your mouse cursor is the closest. For example, if you plan to snap a corner of a rectangle, simply grab the rectangle near this corner for dragging, and all the other corners will not get in your way. This is another way to reduce "parasite" snapping and speed up work in complex documents. If this option is on, Inkscape will display a black round mark over the snap-enabled node while you drag.

- **Weight factor** is another parameter that controls Inkscape's decision about which of the dragged points to snap if more than one get within snapping distance of a target. When set to 0, Inkscape snaps whichever point is the closest to its target, ignoring the position of the mouse cursor. Setting it to 1 is similar to turning the **Only snap the node closest to the pointer** option on; now, among all nodes that *want* to snap, snapping will happen for the node which is closest to the cursor (which may or may not be the same as the closest node which *can* snap). Using a value in between 0 and 1 allows you to balance these two snapping strategies.

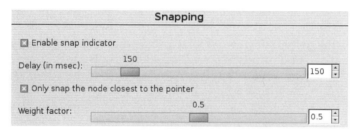

Figure 7-12: Snapping options in Inkscape Preferences

7.4 Aligning

Aligning is similar to snapping; the main difference is that for something to snap, you set up a snap target and use your mouse to move the selection close enough to that target, whereas aligning commands themselves move the selected objects by any distances necessary to arrange them in a certain way.

Alignment commands are collected in the powerful **Align and Distribute** dialog. Open it by pressing Shift-Ctrl-A or by selecting a command in the **Object** menu. The basic routine is: You select the objects you want to align, call up this dialog, and click one of the buttons to perform the alignment.

Figure 7-13 shows the **Align** part of the dialog with all buttons annotated.

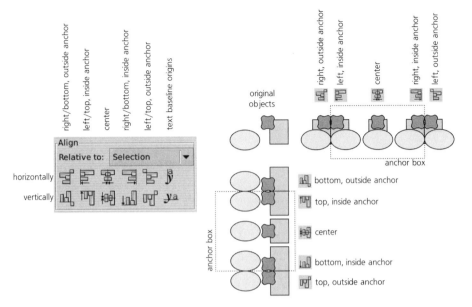

Figure 7-13: Aligning objects

To make sense of this plethora of buttons, observe the following:

- Buttons in the top line align things by moving horizontally; those in the bottom line, by moving vertically.

- All the alignment buttons move objects relative to the *anchor box*. What exactly is considered the anchor box is changeable by the **Relative to:** list. The default, which works in most cases, is **Selection**, which refers to the united bounding box of all selected objects. However, you can instead select the bounding box of one of the selected objects (the one which was the first or the last to be selected, or the biggest or smallest one) as well as the entire page or entire drawing's bounding box.

  For example, if you have a collection of small objects and you want to align them against the top of a large background object, select everything and choose **Biggest object** in the **Relative to:** list.

- Of the 10 buttons on the left, the middle ones in both rows align centers of selected objects at the center of the anchor box horizontally and vertically. The two buttons immediately to the left and the two to the right of the centering buttons press objects against the edges of the anchor box *on the inside*. Together, these six buttons are perhaps the most commonly used in the entire dialog. The four remaining buttons also align the objects at the edges of the anchor box but *on the outside*.

- The two buttons on the right—those with letters on them—only apply to *text objects*. Every text object has a *baseline origin point*, and these buttons align the selected text object by these points. This is sometimes necessary because if you align text objects as regular objects by their bounding boxes, the characters with and without *descenders* (such as the bottom stroke of *y*) and *ascenders* (such as the stem of *d*) will not keep the line:

Figure 7-14: Aligning text objects

7.5 Distributing

Distributing selected objects means moving them so that the intervals between them, when measured in a certain way, become equal. The same **Align and Distribute** dialog has eight object distribution buttons and two text distribution buttons, differing in how they measure these intervals. As with alignment buttons, half of these buttons (the top row) work horizontally and the other half (the bottom row) work vertically:

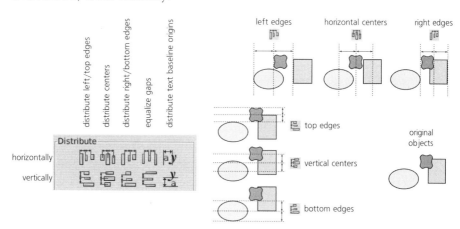

Figure 7-15: Distributing objects

Exactly under the centering buttons in the **Align** section, the **Distribute** section has the two buttons for *distributing centers*. By pressing one of these buttons, you move selected objects in such a way that their centers (more precisely, the centers of their bounding boxes) are at equal distances from each other horizontally or vertically.

Immediately to the right and left of these two buttons, four more buttons perform the same equispaced distribution for the right and left, bottom and top sides of the bounding boxes.

Two more buttons further to the right, instead of equalizing distances between same-named edges of bounding boxes, make the *gaps* between them equal. This means that, for horizontal gap equalization, the distances between the right edge of one object to the left edge of the next one will be the same. When objects are different in width, this usually makes more visual sense than evenly distributing their centers. Figure 7-16 shows the difference between distributing centers and equalizing gaps.

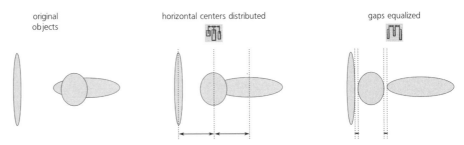

Figure 7-16: Distributing centers of objects vs. equalizing gaps between them

Finally, the two buttons furthest to the right distribute the baseline origins of the selected text objects.

Unlike alignment buttons, distribution buttons always use the selection bounding box as its anchor box (i.e., the **Relative to:** list does not affect the **Distribute** section of the dialog). In other words, distributing always preserves the bounding box of the selection because it never moves the leftmost and rightmost (for horizontal) or topmost and bottommost (for vertical) objects, but only those that fall between them. (One consequence of this is that distributing only makes sense for three or more selected objects.)

So, if after distributing you find that your objects are too dense or too sparse, just select one of the objects at the edge of your distribution, and move it toward others (to make it denser) or away from others (to make it sparser). Then, reselect all objects again and distribute them once more.

Note that selected objects may overlap, both before and after distributing. Even when equalizing gaps, objects' edges may overlap; in this case the gaps are considered to be negative, and they are still made equal to each other when you click the button (in other words, all adjacent objects are made to overlap by the same amount).

When you are using the Node tool (**12.5**), the **Align and Distribute** dialog shows four buttons that allow you to align and distribute, horizontally and vertically, the selected path nodes:

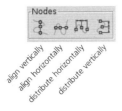

Figure 7-17: Aligning and distributing path nodes (for the Node tool)

7.5.1 Randomizing, Unclumping, and Removing Overlaps

So far we've looked at the basic alignment and distribution commands. They all have one thing in common: Each of them works only in one dimension, either horizontally or vertically. The same dialog, however, provides a number of more interesting capabilities that involve moving objects in both dimensions at once.

Randomizing simply moves each selected object to a random position within the selection's bounding box. Each click of the button will result in a new random arrangement; you can repeat this until you find a randomization you like the best:

Figure 7-18: Randomizing object positions

NOTE *When you click the **Randomize** button repeatedly, only the first click remembers the current bounding box of the selection; all subsequent clicks will use this remembered bounding box as the area within which to scatter objects, even if the bounding box changes because of the randomization. This prevents the objects from drifting away as you randomize them repeatedly.*

Unclumping is an operation that is similar to equalizing gaps (that's why its button is aligned under the equalize gaps buttons) but works in both dimensions at once, trying to equalize the closest distance between all pairs of adjacent objects in the selection. It works best for a large number of objects:

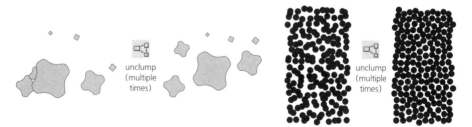

Figure 7-19: Unclumping objects

Unclumping is an imprecise operation, and you may want to use it not just once but repeatedly, until you are satisfied with the result. It does not replace your current arrangement entirely but improves it in small steps, nudging each object closer towards a point equidistant from its immediate neighbors. The most noticeable result of this is a reduction of *clumps*—areas where objects are too dense.

In most cases, the unclumping process converges—that is, visual unevenness in distribution of the objects reduces and each subsequent unclumping has less and less effect. After thorough unclumping is achieved, further attempts to unclump will just slowly disperse and migrate the swarm of the objects in a random direction without further improving its uniformity.

Unclumping objects produces a characteristic texture that appears, at the same time, both random and artificial. It is quite similar to what a human would produce if asked to evenly fill a space with random dots. Traditional examples of such textures include polka-dot patterns (**10.8.3**) and dot engravings where shading is created by smoothly varying the density of scattered dots.

NOTE   *Unclumping does not take into account the actual shape of your objects, only their bounding boxes. It therefore works best with multiple objects of simple consistent shape, such as circles or stars. We will see more examples of unclumping in the section on clone tiler (**16.6**).*

In contrast with unclumping, *removing overlaps* is a deterministic operation: It tries to move each selected object by a minimum distance necessary for all selected objects to be free from overlaps—and usually succeeds on the first attempt. The amount of moving it performs, of course, depends on the initial arrangement of objects, but in most cases, the layout of objects after removing overlaps will be still similar to the original layout, although less so than after unclumping. You can set the horizontal and vertical spacing (in px units) to be added to the objects' bounding boxes:

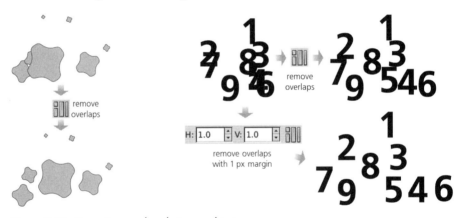

Figure 7-20: Removing overlaps between objects

Notice that objects that did not overlap with any other selected object did not move.

Finally, the **Connector network layout** button at the bottom of the dialog only works on diagrams with automatic connectors.

7.5.2 Arranging Objects in a Table

As a further development of alignment and distribution commands, the **Rows and Columns** dialog (accessed from the **Object** menu) arranges selected objects into a two-dimensional table with a number of spacing and layout options, as shown in Figure 7-21.

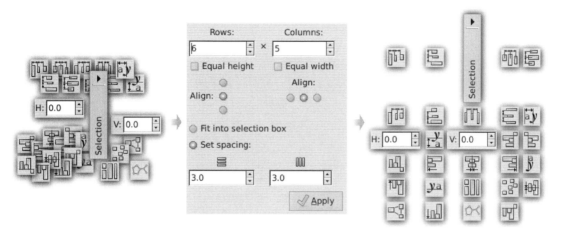

Figure 7-21: Using the Rows and Columns dialog to create a table from existing objects

Note that using this dialog only makes sense for *different* objects that you already have—for example, imported bitmaps from which you want to make a gallery of thumbnails. If what you need is just a pattern, table, or grid of identical objects (or objects different only in size or style), look into the clone tiler (16.6).

The first thing you need to decide on is the number of rows and columns in your table. The dialog senses the number of selected objects and, when you change the number of rows (or columns), it recalculates the columns (or rows) so that the table would be just large enough for all objects. For example, if you have 29 objects selected, at first the dialog will offer 1 row and 29 columns; if you increase the number of rows by scrolling up, the number of rows and columns will change to 2 and 15, 3 and 10, 4 and 8, 5 and 6, 6 and 5, and so on.

Under the **Rows** and **Columns** fields, two checkboxes control whether all rows and columns will be equal in height and width. For example, when the **Equal height** checkbox is selected, all rows in the entire table will be as high as the tallest of *all objects* (plus spacing, see below). If it's off, each row will be only as high as the tallest of all objects *in this row* (plus spacing).

Further down, groups of radio buttons control the alignment of objects within their rows and columns; by default they are centered in both dimensions.

The rest of the controls in the dialog define how large your table will be. The **Fit into selection box** option ensures that the table will be exactly as wide and as tall as your selection before you click **Arrange** in this dialog. In other words, after creating the table, Inkscape will set the spacing between rows and columns so that the overall dimensions of the selection don't change; this may result in overlaps (i.e., negative spacing). For example, if you want the table to be sparser, undo arranging, drag one of the objects away from others, reselect all objects, and click **Arrange** again. Alternatively, you can set spacing for rows and columns explicitly by choosing **Set spacing** and typing the desired values (in px units).

8

STYLING

Now that we know all about selecting and transforming objects, it's time to start a new topic that will entertain us for the next several chapters: styling. The way an object in an Inkscape document looks is determined by that object's *style*, consisting of separate *properties*. Mastering the program is impossible without familiarity with the available style properties and the tools for editing them.

In this chapter, we will look at the most basic style properties, including the common types of *paint* (fill and stroke) and opacity. This will be followed by Chapter 9 covering stroke style, Chapter 10 where we'll look in detail at gradients and patterns, and Chapter 15 where we'll explore text style properties. Filter effects, such as blurring, are also part of an object's style; we will discuss them in Chapter 17.

8.1 Style Fundamentals

Inkscape has quite a number of dialogs, commands, and tools that deal with the style of objects. If you're using Inkscape for anything practical, you're likely already using at least some of them. Instead of discussing these UI elements one by one, we will start by looking at the general style concepts and specific properties, examining the corresponding tools when they are relevant.

One style-related command you should know up front is **Edit ▸ Paste Style** (Shift-Ctrl-V). It takes the style of the object you last copied to the clipboard and applies it to all selected objects. This is a true lifesaver when you want some objects to be mostly but not completely identical in style; it is usually much easier to first paste the same style on all of them and then only change those properties that need to be different.

NOTE   *The way object style is expressed in the source of an SVG document is not defined solely by the SVG standard; for this purpose, SVG reuses another standard called* Cascading Style Sheets (CSS). *However, SVG uses only a subset of CSS properties and concepts; refer to the SVG standard* (http://w3.org/TR/SVG11) *as well as to Appendix* A *for details.*

8.1.1 Paint

As you probably already know, objects have *fill* and *stroke*, which are collectively called *paint*. One could say that an object is filled by one paint and stroked by another. A paint may take several different types, including:

None (no paint)
   An object with its fill set to none has only stroke, and an object with its stroke set to none has only fill. If both fill and stroke are none, the object is completely invisible (and cannot be selected by clicking, 5.4), just as it would be when set to zero opacity.

Flat color
   This is the most common option, painting the fill or stroke with a plain solid color. Later in this chapter, we'll look at the many ways to set and change fill and stroke colors.

Gradient or **pattern**
   Both fill and stroke may have various types of smooth color gradients or repeating patterns made from any objects. These complex paint types are the subject of a separate chapter (Chapter 10).

Unset
   This means that a fill or stroke is *not specified,* and therefore may be inherited from an object's ancestors. This is not the same as none, which simply forces invisibility. Since ancestors are normally layers or groups without their own stroke or fill, an object with unset fill or stroke will get the SVG defaults: an invisible stroke and a solid black fill. Unsetting is useful with clones (Chapter 16) because it allows creating clones painted differently from their originals.

The main tool for editing an object's style, the **Fill and Stroke** dialog (Shift-Ctrl-F), has a number of buttons on its **Fill** and **Stroke paint** tabs that correspond to the different paint types. The pressed button indicates the current paint type of the selected object; if multiple objects with different paint types are selected, no button is pressed and the dialog says *Multiple styles.*

Also, learn to use the *selected style indicator* (**2.8**) in the status bar to quickly determine the paint type of the selected object, as well as change it via the right-click menu of this control (note that to access this menu you need to right-click the fill swatch at the *top* to change *fill* paint and the stroke swatch at the *bottom* to change *stroke* paint).

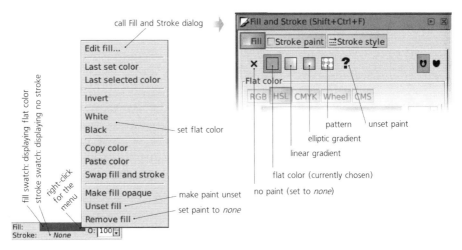

Figure 8-1: Paint types in the selected stroke indicator (left) and the Fill and Stroke dialog (right)

NOTE *A path need not be closed in order to be filled; unclosed paths (**12.1.1**) can still be filled, as if their ends were connected by an unstroked straight line segment.*

One important property which, unlike other paint properties, applies to fill but not stroke, is the *fill rule*. It may take one of the two values. The value of evenodd means that *any* self-intersections or inside subpaths (**12.1.1**) create holes in the fill of a path or stroke. The value of nonzero means that most holes are covered with fill (more precisely, if the inner subpath has the same direction as the outer one, the hole will be filled; otherwise it will still be a visible hole). To change this property, use the two toggle buttons in the **Fill and Stroke** dialog:

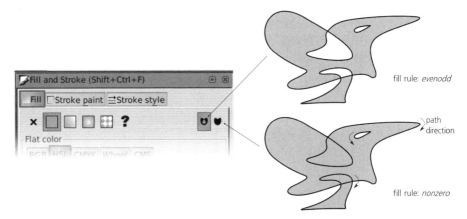

Figure 8-2: Changing the fill rule in the Fill and Stroke dialog

NOTE *Some of the inner subpaths can still produce holes even with* nonzero *fill rule. This depends on the direction of the subpath (12.1.1): If it is counterdirected relative to the outer path, the hole will remain unfilled.*

Not all object types can or should have fill and stroke:

Bitmaps

Bitmap objects (Chapter 18) cannot have either fill or stroke. However, you can easily convert a bitmap into a rectangular path filled by that bitmap as a pattern (just press Alt-I), which can then have a stroke applied to it.

Groups

It makes little sense to assign fill or stroke to groups by themselves, because the objects inside a group usually have their own paint and ignore what is set on their parent group. In fact, if you attempt to set a fill or stroke on a group in Inkscape, in addition to setting it on the group, it will assume you mean to assign fill or stroke recursively on all the group's members. Only explicitly *unset* fills or strokes of members are then left alone; however, they will inherit the new fill or stroke from their ancestor anyway.

Clones

If you try to set fill or stroke on a clone (Chapter 16), it won't have a visible effect unless the original of that clone has fill or stroke *unset*.

8.1.2 Opacity

On top of paint, objects may have *opacity*, editable by adjusting the **O** field in the status bar or the **Opacity** slider in the **Fill and Stroke** dialog. Just like filters (Chapter 17), opacity applies to the entire object without any distinction between fill and stroke.

Strictly speaking, the above is only true for the master opacity of an object. In SVG objects can have three kinds of opacity: *master opacity* (which is called simply *opacity* in most places in the UI as well as in this book), *fill opacity*, and *stroke opacity* (see Figure 8-3). The two latter kinds apply only to fill or stroke, respectively, and while Inkscape allows you to view and change them, it generally discourages them in favor of master opacity. Situations where you might need your stroke opaque but fill transparent or vice versa are not too frequent in practice, and in all other cases master opacity is a lot more natural and easier to use.

One consequence of using stroke opacity is that you can see the fringe of the object's fill, normally obscured by its own stroke. Per SVG rules, stroke is always drawn on top of fill in the object's own internal z-order, and fill is bounded by the midline of the stroke, so with a semitransparent stroke you will see three distinct boundaries: the outer boundary of the stroke, the stroke's midline where its fill starts, and the inner boundary of the stroke where it overlaps the fill.

Master opacity, unlike stroke opacity, has no such problems—it applies to the object as a whole, without revealing any untidy fringe. In the same way, when applied to a group, it makes the group transparent as a whole, which is often different from the same level of opacity assigned to individual objects in the group (see Figure 4-6).

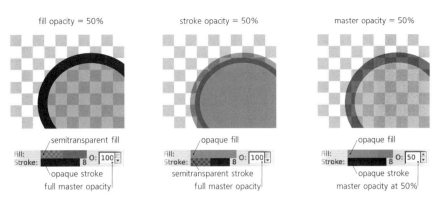

Figure 8-3: Fill opacity, stroke opacity, and master opacity

Also, unlike fill or stroke opacity, master opacity is applicable to objects that cannot have fill or stroke of their own, such as bitmaps and most clones.

NOTE *What is the difference between* opacity *and* transparency? *They simply look at the same thing from opposite angles: When an object's opacity is zero, it is fully transparent; conversely, when its transparency is zero, it is fully opaque. Yet another synonym for opacity that you may encounter is* alpha.

8.2 Color Models

The most basic and the most important building block of style is *color*. A discussion of representing color on the computer could easily fill a book; while Inkscape is not yet the most powerful program for working with color, it is still quite rich and complex in this area.

The first choice you will face is between *color models*. The same color can be represented differently by different color models.

8.2.1 RGB

You probably already know the most common color model, *RGB*, in which any color is represented as a mix of red, green, and blue components, or *channels*. This model is implemented by nearly all computer displays (which are typically composed of tiny light sources of these three colors) and is the primary color model used in SVG as well as most other computer graphic formats.

Depending on which software you use, the value of each of the three channels in an RGB color may be either a fractional number between 0 and 1 (such as 0.5) or an integer between 0 and 255 (such as 127). These two systems are equivalent; for example, a color with R = 0, G = 0.5, B = 1.0 is the same as R = 0, G = 127, B = 255. Inkscape normally uses the 0-to-255 integer format, which we will also prefer in this book. (However, in some parts of the Inkscape UI, you will see a choice to use either the integer or the fractional format.)

In RGB, higher values of the channels make the color lighter and lower values make it darker. Thus, RGB 0/0/0 is black and RGB 255/255/255 is white. Any RGB color where the values of all channels are equal is a shade of gray; making the channels unequal adds saturation to the color, and the bigger the inequality, the greater the saturation. Thus, pure colors such as red (RGB 255/0/0) or yellow (RGB 255/255/0) have maximum possible saturation.

The **Fill and Stroke** dialog lets you edit colors in RGB using either numeric input fields (with scroll buttons) or sliders that move within graduated-color grooves (see Figure 2 on the color insert). Note that the colors of the grooves change as you move the sliders; each groove shows you the the colors that you will get by moving the slider within it if the other sliders remain where they are. The fourth slider at the bottom, labeled **A** (alpha), represents the fill or stroke opacity (and thus is not, strictly speaking, part of the color).

An RGB color is often expressed as a string of the form RRGGBB where each of the three components is given by a two-digit hexadecimal (base 16, instead of the conventional base 10) number. Hexadecimal numbers can use digits 0 through 9 and letters A through F. The maximum integer value of a channel—255 in decimal—is represented as FF in hexadecimal. So, for example, 000000 is black, FFFFFF is white, 660000 is dark red. This form of representing colors is used in the SVG source of Inkscape documents, as well as in a lot of other software and languages (such as HTML). When you choose **Copy color** from the right-click menu of the fill or stroke swatch in the selected style indicator (Figure 8-1), the RRGGBB representation of the color is copied to the clipboard. Also, a RRGGBBAA representation (with two more digits appended representing fill/stroke opacity) can be viewed and edited in the **RGBA** field in the **Fill and Stroke** dialog.

If multiple objects are selected and they have different fill or stroke colors, both the **Fill and Stroke** dialog and the selected style indicator display the *averaged color*. If you change that averaged color, it will be assigned back to all the selected objects, in effect flattening any color differences these objects might have had.

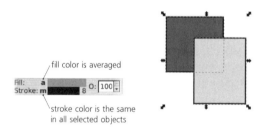

Figure 8-4: Averaged color in the selected style indicator

NOTE   *This averaging is done in RGB—that is, the averaged color's R, G, and B channels are the arithmetic mean of the corresponding channels in the input colors. The same averaging formula, per SVG rules, is used in gradients for interpolating between stop colors (10.2).*

8.2.2 CMYK

Similar to RGB, in the *CMYK* model a color is obtained by mixing color channels. However, CMYK has not three but four channels: *cyan, magenta, yellow,* and *black* (see Figure 3 on the color insert). This color model is best suited for printed output because many professional printers and printing presses use CMYK. Since Inkscape (and SVG itself) is not yet very well suited for producing printed output, the support for this color model in Inkscape is rather superficial. Most importantly, even if you specify a color in CMYK, what gets written into SVG is its RGB approximation, and conversion from CMYK to RGB and back typically introduces distortions because not all CMYK colors can be exactly represented in RGB and vice versa.

NOTE *Traditionally, numeric values of CMYK channels are in the range of 0 to 100, not from 0 to 255 as in RGB.*

The **CMS** (Color Management System) tab of the **Fill and Stroke** dialog allows you to edit colors in a *calibrated space*, which may include true calibrated CMYK (not the approximation of the **CMYK** tab) or Adobe RGB. This is currently an experimental feature; it requires the color management to be properly set up in **Inkscape Preferences** (3.1.1).

8.2.3 HSL

Neither RGB nor CMYK are very intuitive; they represent the way computers and printers deal with color, not the way artists use it. For this reason, Inkscape usually gives preference to another color model: *HSL (hue, saturation, lightness)*. Unlike RGB and CMYK, the channels of HSL are not individual colors that you mix together; rather, they are the properties of the color which, together, define it unambiguously.

The *hue* channel is the rainbow of maximum saturation colors, starting from red and going through yellow, green, blue, and back to red. *Saturation* varies the color in the range from maximum colorfulness, through drab and dull, to the pure gray of the same brightness level. Finally, the *lightness* channel goes from black to the given color and then to white. (This means any color with maximum lightness is white and any color with zero lightness is black, regardless of the hue and saturation.)

A similar color model you might have seen in other programs is *HSV (hue, saturation, value)*, sometimes also called *HSB (hue, saturation, brightness)*. Its most visible difference from HSL is that in HSV, the Value component changes only from black to the given color (e.g., red). In HSL, the Lightness component ranges all the way from black through the given color to white (i.e., it is symmetrical with regard to lightness and darkness).

The HSL color model, once you get used to it, is very natural. When you think that some color is not quite right, for example, you are likely to suggest making it "lighter" or "less saturated" rather than "add more green" to it. Therefore, most color-related tools in Inkscape use HSL for choosing and changing colors.

In the **Fill and Stroke** dialog, there are two different tabs that let you edit color in the HSL model (see Figure 4 on the color insert). The first one (titled **HSL**) uses traditional linear sliders, whereas the other one (titled **Wheel**) has a circular ring for the H channel (which has a better resolution simply because, if straightened, it would be longer than a linear slider fitting into the window) and a triangle that encodes the saturation and lightness channels. Rotating the mark on the hue ring rotates the triangle too, so that its maximum-saturation tip always points to the current hue on the ring.

8.3 The Palette

The simplest way to assign a color to the fill or stroke of the selected objects is by clicking one of the swatches in the *palette*, usually located at the bottom of the editing window, above the status bar (see Figure 5 on the color insert). Simply clicking assigns fill color to the selected objects; Shift-clicking assigns stroke color. The leftmost button on the palette *removes* fill or (with Shift) stroke.

Apart from clicking, you can drag and drop colors from the palette onto objects. This is one of the very few ways to change objects without selecting them; if you drop a color on some object, that object will change, even if it is not selected and even if some other object is selected. Dropping also works for changing stroke color, for which you need to drop the color swatch precisely onto the outline of a path or shape.

Inkscape does not yet allow you to edit the color swatches or add new swatches to the palette via the UI. However, you can choose one of the many different palettes that are included with Inkscape. On the right end of the palette, there's a button with a triangle mark; clicking it opens a menu listing available palettes, such as a web-safe palette, palettes used by Ubuntu and Windows for their UI, and various monochrome palettes (greens, golds, and so on). Inkscape will remember your choice of palette.

In the same menu, you can choose one of the standard *sizes* of the swatches, their *width* (narrow swatches are harder to click but may get rid of the palette's scrollbar by fitting the entire palette into your screen width), as well as enable the palette to *wrap around* (this makes it taller but also gets rid of the scrollbar).

Along with the docked horizontal palette, Inkscape has the **Swatches** dialog (Shift-Ctrl-W). It can show all the same palettes and has all the same size options, except that it has an additional **List** option where it lists all the colors along with their names. You might prefer it to the palette because as a dialog, it can be placed in the dock on the right and squeezed there into a narrow vertical strip.

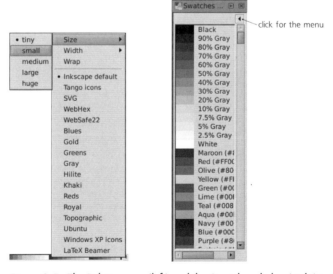

Figure 8-5: The Palette menu (left) and the Swatches dialog (right) in the List format showing colors with their names

You can edit your Inkscape palettes as well as add new ones. Each palette is a text file that can be edited by hand. On Unix, the palettes which ship with Inkscape are located relative to Inkscape's installation prefix, in the *palettes* directory (often */usr/share/inkscape/palettes*, or */usr/local/share/inkscape/palettes* if you compiled Inkscape yourself). Custom palettes can be placed in *~/.config/ inkscape/palettes*; you will need to create this directory if it does not exist. On Windows, palettes are located in *share\palettes* inside the Inkscape installation directory (usually under *Program Files\Inkscape*).

Inkscape borrowed the format of its palette files from the GIMP raster editor, so you can drop any palettes from a GIMP distribution into that directory to use them in Inkscape. Here's the beginning of the default palette file, *inkscape.gpl*; the color components (R, G, B) are in the 0..255 format:

```
GIMP Palette
Name: Inkscape default
Columns: 3
# generated by PaletteGen.py
  0   0   0  Black
 26  26  26  90% Gray
 51  51  51  80% Gray
 77  77  77  70% Gray
...
```

8.4 The Selected Style Indicator: Paint Commands

Apart from the commands to set various paint styles, the right-click menu of the selected style indicator (see Figure 8-1) has several useful commands for dealing with paint. Again, note that the fill swatch (top) and stroke swatch (bottom) are distinct even though their context menus are similar; be sure to right-click the half that you want to change.

Edit fill/stroke . . .
Choosing these commands, as well as simply clicking the fill or stroke swatch, will open the **Fill and Stroke** dialog.

Last set color
This assigns to the selection the color that was last set on the corresponding paint (e.g., fill or stroke) of any selected object. For example, if you just painted something a particular shade of blue and then realized that you want *all* your objects to have that fill, select all and call this command from the fill swatch's right-click menu.

Last selected color
This assigns to the selected object the corresponding paint (e.g., fill or stroke) of the object that was selected before the most recent selection change. For example, select an object whose fill color you like, then select some other object, and use this command on its fill swatch to assign the same color to it.

Invert

This replaces the flat color paint by the RGB inversion of the color—for example, white becomes black and yellow becomes blue.

White and **Black**

These commands simply assign these colors to the paint.

Copy color and **Paste color**

These commands allow you to exchange objects' colors via the system clipboard. For example, you can copy one object's stroke color and assign it to another object's fill, or paste the color (as a #RRGGBB string) into any other program where you might need it.

Swap fill and stroke

This command exchanges the fill and stroke paints on selected objects. For example, if a selected object had no stroke and blue fill, after applying this command it will have blue stroke and no fill. This command can be useful when you use both the Pencil (14.2) and the Calligraphic pen (14.3) tools for drawing and want the result to use the same color, even though the Pencil creates stroked paths without fill and the Calligraphic pen creates filled paths without stroke.

Unset fill/stroke

Make fill or stroke *unset* (8.1.1). Note that this is not the same as removing it.

Remove fill/stroke

Set fill or stroke to none (8.1.1). This command has a convenient shortcut: Middle-click the fill or stroke swatch to set the corresponding paint to none. If the paint is already removed, middle-clicking creates the default fill or stroke (usually black). Apart from the "no paint" swatch on the palette, middle-clicking the selected style indicator is the fastest way to get rid of stroke on selected objects.

Make fill/stroke opaque

Remove any fill opacity or stroke opacity from paint (8.1.2). Master opacity (shown by the **O** control to the right of the swatches) remains unchanged.

8.5　The Selected Style Indicator: Color Gestures

Apart from the right-click menu commands, the selected style indicator has a convenient method for quick adjustment of colors: *color gestures* (see Figure 6 on the color insert).

To use color gestures, grab the fill or stroke color swatch and drag it as described below. Note that this only works when the swatch displays a *flat color*; it does not work for a swatch showing *None* (i.e., no paint), *N/A* (i.e., nothing is selected), or displaying a gradient (although you can select one or more gradient stops in the Gradient tool and color-adjust them by color gestures just as you would with objects).

Color gestures work in the HSL color space. Dragging without any keyboard modifiers adjusts the hue channel, dragging with Shift adjusts saturation, and dragging with Ctrl adjusts lightness.

The adjustment is done by "rotating" the color swatch away from the original direction, which is assumed to be 45 degrees to the northeast, that is, from the swatch diagonally into the document window. Once you click and drag the color swatch, imagine a diagonal line going from the point where you clicked in the northeast direction, across the entire Inkscape window. By dragging *below* or *to the right* of that line, you *decrease* the corresponding color channel, down to the minimum at the lower edge of the window; by dragging it *above* or *to the left*, you *increase* it, up to the maximum at the left edge of the window. If you hover your mouse exactly over the 45-degree line, the change will be zero.

The mouse cursor changes when you're doing color gestures, reflecting the channel currently being adjusted, and indicating the directions for increasing and decreasing the value. Also, watch the status bar, which will indicate, as you drag, the channel you are adjusting, the original value of that channel, the new value, and the difference.

The angular nature of this adjustment means that you can easily vary the precision of the change. If you drag close enough to the swatch, any small movement results in a big change of the color. If you need a finer adjustment, just drag farther away from the swatch, toward the center of the Inkscape window or even to its upper-right corner, where the same movements will produce very small changes in the color.

You can switch channels while you drag—that is, you don't need to drag from the swatch again and again if you want to adjust all three channels. You can do it all in one drag, by pressing and releasing Ctrl and Shift as necessary. Note that when you change the keyboard modifiers during drag, the zero-change line is temporarily rotated to go through the current mouse position; this is done so that there are no sudden changes in color if you are switching modifiers away from the original 45-degree line.

The Alt modifier is special. Pressing Alt means "do nothing"; this allows you to move the mouse, without releasing, to a more convenient place from which you can continue tweaking the color after letting go of Alt. As with the other modifiers, releasing Alt temporarily redefines the zero-change axis to go through the point where Alt was released. For example, imagine you made your color darker by Ctrl-dragging toward the bottom edge of the window, and you now need to make it less saturated. You cannot, however, Shift-drag it any lower because there's not enough room for that. In that situation, without releasing the mouse, Alt-drag it upward to a convenient spot and then Shift-drag downward as needed. Also, you can start dragging from the swatch while holding down Alt to avoid any change of the color until you take a more convenient position for adjusting it.

For example, you can select a green rectangle and first turn it into a greenish-blue color by dragging away from the fill swatch and slightly above the 45-degree line; then, without releasing the mouse, press Ctrl and drag a bit to the right to darken the color; then press Shift, release Ctrl, and adjust saturation. You can press or release Ctrl and Shift as many times as necessary during a single drag; when you are finally satisfied with your color, release the mouse to commit the change.

Apart from precise adjustments, you can use color gestures to very quickly perform some common color transformations:

- Ctrl-drag the swatch to the right and down to paint all selected objects black.

- Ctrl-drag the swatch up and to the left to paint all selected objects white.

- Shift-drag the swatch to the right and down to desaturate the color of selected objects (turn them to gray).

- Shift-drag the swatch up and to the left to maximize saturation of the color of selected objects.

Note that when several objects or gradient stops with different colors are selected, the selected style indicator shows their *averaged* color. If you adjust that color by gesturing, the changed color will be assigned back to all selected objects or stops, in effect eliminating any difference between them. If you want to adjust many different-colored objects preserving their relative differences, use the color modes of the Tweak tool (8.7), color adjustment extensions (8.8), or color filters (17.3).

8.6 The Dropper Tool

The Dropper tool allows you to pick a color (and, optionally, opacity) directly from any point or area of the drawing and assign it to the selected objects (or to selected gradient handles, 10.4.2). With this tool, you can use your own drawing as a palette, easily reusing colors you have once created for something else. It is also indispensable when you need to combine and blend vector objects with an imported bitmap.

The important thing about this tool is that when picking colors, it pays no attention to what *object* you click; instead, it simply takes the color of the clicked *pixel* in the rendered screen image. This means you can easily pick colors from bitmaps, stacks of semitransparent objects, blur fringes (17.1), or from the middle of a gradient. This also means that if an object is too small to be rendered at the current zoom, you can't pick its color, and that if you click the edge of a black object on white background, chances are you'll pick a midrange gray color of the antialiasing pixel in that point (see Figure 1-1).

8.6.1 Sampling

When you switch to the Dropper tool (F7 or d), the status bar starts to report the color located directly under the cursor. So, if you want to know the color of some area, you don't even need to click: Just hover your mouse over that area and read the status bar. Also, at any time you can press Ctrl-C to copy the color under the cursor to the clipboard (in the form of a RRGGBBAA hex string); from there you can paste it to any text object in Inkscape or to an external program.

8.6.2 Assigning

Assigning colors to selected objects or gradient handles can be done either by clicking or by dragging. With a click, you just take the color of the screen pixel which happens to be under your mouse cursor. With a drag, you create a circular area whose center is in the point where you started dragging, and when you release the mouse, the tool *averages* the colors of all pixels inside this circle.

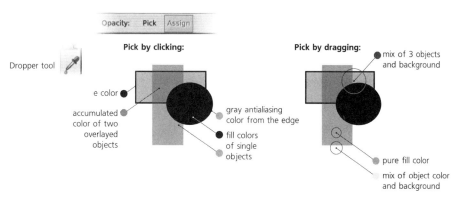

Figure 8-6: Using the Dropper tool

Picking with averaging is especially useful for sampling colors from bitmaps. For example, if you need to create a vector object that is the same color as the cheek of a face on a photo, picking single pixels from the cheek is unlikely to get you what you need; the picked colors will be too light or too dark due to the nonuniformity of the photo. If, however, you average the colors from a circular area covering most of the cheek, the result will be much more persuasive.

By default, Dropper assigns its colors to the fill of the selected objects. When you Shift-click or Shift-drag, it will instead change their stroke.

8.6.3 Opacity

Using the two toggle buttons on the controls bar of the Dropper tool, you can change the way it treats transparency. The **Opacity: Pick** button controls whether the opacity at the point under the cursor is picked, and the **Assign** button controls whether that picked opacity value is assigned to selected objects. (When **Pick** is off, the **Assign** button is disabled.)

NOTE *The opacity that the tool picks is the* accumulated *opacity of all objects at the click point. For example, if you click a single object with 50 percent opacity, the picked value is 50 percent. If two such objects overlay, the picked value is 75 percent. The opacity of the page background (as set in **Document Properties**, 3.4.2) is ignored by the Dropper tool.*

Let's look at a simple example. Suppose you have a bright red (FF0000) object with 50 percent opacity which makes it appear pale red. Now, you select some other object and try to pick the color from the red one. What will happen?

Opacity: Pick button is off

The tool will pick the pale red color (FF8080) and no opacity. In other words, the opacity will already be "multiplied into" the color. The status bar will report *FF8080 under cursor* and that is the color the selected object will get—whereas the opacity of the selected object, if any, will not change. Only in this case the visible color of the page background will be mixed in.

Opacity: Pick button is on

The tool will pick the actual bright red color (FF0000) and the 50 percent opacity *separately*. The status bar will display *FF0000 alpha 0.5 under cursor*. Now, what happens when you click depends on the other button, **Assign**:

- If **Assign** is on, both color (FF0000) and opacity (50 percent) will be assigned to the selected objects' fill or (with Shift) stroke. Note that the opacity will become the fill or stroke opacity of the selected objects, not their master opacity (8.1.2).

- If **Assign** is off, the bright red color (FF0000) is assigned to the selected objects' fill or stroke, whereas the picked opacity is simply discarded and 100 percent opacity is assigned. For example, if you select a semi-transparent object and click that object *itself* with **Pick** on and **Assign** off, the object will lose its opacity but keep its color.

8.7   Color Tweaking

We've already seen some of the capabilities of the Tweak tool in the chapter on transformations (6.9). Let's look at its two modes for changing colors of objects, *Color Paint* and *Color Jitter*. Both of these modes work on flat color paint as well as on gradients (10.7). Refer to 6.9 to review how the tool's **Width** and **Force** parameters work.

NOTE   *In future versions, these modes may be split off into separate tools.*

8.7.1   Color Paint

The Color Paint mode is used to apply color to the selected objects *under the brush*. The color being used—more precisely, the *style* because it includes both fill and stroke—can be seen in the style swatch at the right end of the tool's controls bar (above the canvas). To change this applied style, simply click the color palette or use any other style editing command (such as the **Fill and Stroke** dialog) while you are in this mode of the Tweak tool.

NOTE   *Unlike all other tools, in the Tweak tool in Color Paint mode you cannot assign style directly to selected objects; any style-setting commands are "intercepted" to change the tool's style instead.*

The fill from the tool's style applies to the fills of the painted objects, and the stroke applies to the strokes. If the tool's style has no fill or no stroke, it won't affect fills or strokes, correspondingly. For example, if you want to color the fills of objects blue but leave their strokes untouched, assign blue fill to the tool's style (just click blue on the palette) but set its stroke to none (middle-click the **Stroke** swatch in the status bar).

This mode literally paints on objects, *gradually* shifting their colors toward the target color. For example, if you keep painting with yellow fill over a blue-filled object, the object will first become greenish blue, then green, then yellowish green, and sooner or later end up being exactly the yellow color you're painting with.

Painting with Shift pressed *inverts* the color you're applying (e.g., when painting with yellow, Shift will gradually apply blue).

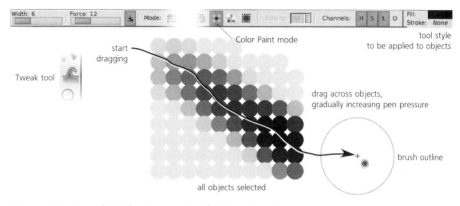

Figure 8-7: Using the Color Paint mode of the Tweak tool

The speed of this gradual transition depends both on the **Force** value and, if you have a pressure-sensitive tablet, the pen pressure. Also, since the brush is "soft," objects touched by the periphery of the brush are less affected than those hit by the brush center.

8.7.2 Color Jitter

The Color Jitter mode does not apply any color, but instead *jitters* (randomizes) the colors of the objects it touches. The force of the action determines how strong the randomization is—that is, how far the colors deviate from the original values:

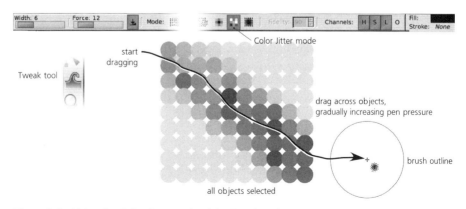

Figure 8-8: Using the Color Jitter mode of the Tweak tool

8.7.3 Channels

On the Tweak tool's controls bar, to the right of the **Mode** buttons, there are four **Channels** toggles: **H**, **S**, **L**, and **O**. They allow you to turn on and off the tool's action on the object's hue, saturation, lightness, and opacity, correspondingly.

For example, if you want to raise the saturation of some part of your drawing without changing the hue, select some maximum-saturation color (such as pure red) and turn off all **Channels** buttons except **S**. Similarly, you can replace the hues without affecting saturation or lightness (with only **H** turned on), or lighten/darken all colors without changing their hues and saturations (only **L** turned on). Enabling **O** applies the master opacity from the tool's style to the master opacity of objects (but not fill or stroke opacity).

8.7.4 Usage Notes

Color painting is quite similar to a soft brush in a raster editor (such as the GIMP or Photoshop). However, even though the tool itself works as a brush, it still applies its color to vector objects, which behave as vector objects usually do. For example, if you want to change the tint of the face in your drawing, and if a hand in the drawing is part of the same path object as the face, that hand will change its tint too, even if it's located far from the point you are painting. Still, even with this limitation, color painting allows you to quickly and intuitively make adjustments which would be awkward and slow with traditional vector tools.

Drawings containing patterns or scatterings of small independent objects are especially suitable for color painting with the Tweak tool. Examples include the following:

- Freehand drawings with the Calligraphic pen, consisting of many separate strokes.

- Gradient meshes imported from Adobe Illustrator's AI files (**B.6**), which Inkscape renders as lattices of small polygons. While there's no direct support for gradient meshes in Inkscape yet, color painting on such lattices is nearly as good.

- Text converted to paths, where each letter is a separate path (**15.7**).

- Patterns made with the clone tiler (**16.6**). Note that you need to unset the fill and/or stroke on the original object and use the **Color** tab of the **Create Tiled Clones** dialog to assign some initial color to the clones—this will make them paintable with the Tweak tool without unlinking.

Still, color tweaking can be useful for compositions with just a few objects or even for single objects. Unlike all other color selection methods, painting with the Tweak tool implements the *color mixing* metaphor, which is more natural for artists than RGB sliders or even the HSL color wheel. For example, start with a rectangle of pure blue color; then, pick different colors using Color Paint and apply light touches with minimum force and minimum pen pressure: Add a little green, a little brown, a little yellow, and so on until you have the exact mixed tint you need. Similarly, you can whiten or blacken any hue by adding white or black.

You can also use color tweaking to add a tint, darken, lighten, saturate, desaturate, or color-jitter your entire drawing. Just select all in all layers (5.11), zoom out, choose a large brush width so it covers all of the drawing, and apply a little color tweaking (with minimum **Force**) that will therefore affect all visible objects.

8.8   Color Extensions and Filters

So far, we've seen quite a number of style setting commands and tools in Inkscape, each with its own approach and capabilities. However, each of them has some downside. In particular, the **Fill and Stroke** dialog and the selected style indicator cannot edit many different colors without unifying them. The Tweak tool, on the other hand, which can adjust multiple colors at once, requires you to actually paint on canvas and can therefore be slow and imprecise for some tasks.

As a workaround, a group of extensions in the **Color** submenu of the **Extensions** menu allows you to adjust all colors of a selection at once. These commands affect both fill and stroke colors, including colors of gradient stops, but excluding bitmaps or patterns. They include:

- A full set of *HSL adjustments* (increasing and decreasing hue, saturation, or lightness by 5 percent)
- **Brighter** and **Darker** (adjust brightness up or down by 10 percent)
- **Desaturate extension** (set HSL saturation to zero)
- **Grayscale** (equalize the three RGB channels; the result is largely similar but different from that of Desaturate)
- **Negative** (for example, convert black to white, yellow to blue, and so on)
- Commands for removing or swapping the *Red*, *Green*, and *Blue* channels
- A **Custom** command which allows you to set your own formulas for modifying the color channels, using the values of other channels if necessary

Yet another way to change colors of objects is by using SVG filter effects (Chapter 17), in particular the preset filters from the **Filters ▸ Color** submenu, or any others using the **Color Matrix** primitive. Compared to extensions, SVG filters are better in that they are nondestructive (the original look and color of an object is preserved and can be restored simply by removing the effect) and work on everything, including bitmaps and patterns. However, filters slow down rendering, and custom filters may be cumbersome to create.

9

STROKE AND MARKERS

While relatively rare in artistic drawings, stroked paths—outlines, frames, arrows, connectors, and so on—are very common in technical drawings such as drafts or flowcharts. A sizable share of all SVG style properties control the appearance of stroke, which therefore deserves a chapter of its own.

While stroking in SVG is quite rich and adequate for a lot of purposes, some things you may be looking for are simply not there, or are only available via workarounds. In particular, SVG stroke always has *constant width* (it cannot get wider or narrower along the path); to emulate variable-width stroke, use the Calligraphic pen (14.3) or path effects (13.1). Also, while stroke can have a dash pattern (9.4) and markers attached to its nodes (9.5), you cannot stroke a path with a brush or repeated pattern that would follow the bends of the stroke—although, again, this is possible via path effects (13.1.3), and you can always apply the standard SVG rectangular pattern (10.8.1) to paint a stroke exactly as you would a fill (however, the pattern in this case is simply superimposed; it is not distorted to follow the trajectory of the stroke).

9.1 Stroke Width

The most important property of the stroke is its *width*. Like any other length value in Inkscape, width can be measured in a number of different units. There are currently two places in the UI where you can see and change the stroke width of the selected objects: in the selected style indicator in the status bar (at the right end of the stroke swatch) and in the **Stroke style** tab of the **Fill and Stroke** dialog:

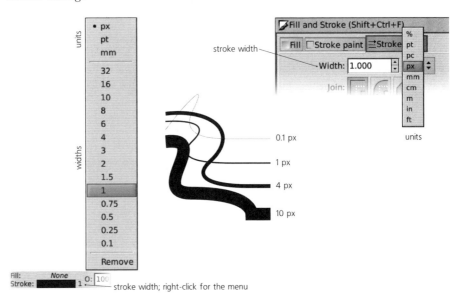

Figure 9-1: Stroke width in the selected style indicator (left; right-click to open the menu) and the Fill and Stroke dialog (right)

NOTE *If the contents of the **Stroke style** tab are disabled (grayed out), this means your selected object has no stroke paint. To enable it, in the same dialog go to the **Stroke paint** tab and choose a solid color or any other paint for the stroke.*

In the selected style indicator, one way to change the stroke width is by right-clicking directly on the numeric stroke width shown next to the swatch and choosing a value from the menu which pops up. In the same menu, you can choose the unit to be used for stroke width; by default it's px (SVG pixel).

Similar to editing fill or stroke colors by color gestures (8.5), you can also drag off the stroke width value in the selected style indicator, into the canvas, to change the stroke width of selection. Dragging above and to the left of the 45-degree line from the swatch makes the stroke in selected objects wider (up to twice the original width); dragging below and to the right makes it narrower (down to half the original width). For example, if you start with a 1 px stroke, dragging up and to the left will give you 2 px, and dragging to the right and down will yield 0.5 px. This way, you can adjust stroke width quickly and precisely without opening any dialogs or menus.

In the **Fill and Stroke** dialog, there's a regular editable field where you can type any value, as well as a unit selector.

NOTE *In Outline mode (3.11), the stroke width is ignored and all objects are shown with a stroke that is one screen pixel wide, regardless of zoom. However, this is only an Inkscape-specific editing convenience; in SVG, stroke width is always specified in absolute units, so you cannot make it independent of zoom. This may change in a future version of SVG. If it does change, Inkscape will eventually support this as well.*

When selection contains multiple objects with different strokes, the selected style indicator *averages* the stroke widths of those objects that have any stroke. For example, if one of the two selected objects has 3 px stroke and the other has 1 px, the indicator will show *2* (and the tooltip will say that this is an averaged value). Now, if you set any width via the right-click menu, the same width will be assigned to all selected objects that had any stroke in the first place. (For example, if one of the objects has 3 px stroke and the other has no stroke, it will display *3* as its stroke width and *Different* in the swatch on the left, but any new width you set will be assigned *only* to the object that had 3 px stroke.)

The **Fill and Stroke** dialog behaves differently. When different stroke widths are detected in selection, the stroke width unit switches to percentage unit (%) and the displayed value is 100 percent. Now, if you change it, for example, to 200 percent and press $\boxed{\text{Enter}}$, each stroke width in the selection will get two times wider than it was before. After that, all stroke widths that were different will remain different, and the displayed value will be reset to 100 percent.

Of course, in that dialog you can just as well switch the unit selector to any absolute unit and assign the same stroke width to any number of selected objects. On the other hand, even if you have a single object selected, you can still switch to the percent unit and specify a new width as a percentage of the old.

9.2 Join

Stroke always follows a path, and a path can have sharp turns, called *cusps*. Typically, a cusp is a nonsmooth node (12.5.5) where two path segments join, but you don't even need to have a node to make a cusp; it is possible to create a sharp cusp in the middle of a Bézier curve (13.1.7).

The way the stroke behaves at the cusps is determined by the two style properties: *join type* and *miter limit*. They are editable by the **Stroke style** tab of the **Fill and Stroke** dialog, right below the stroke width control. The three possible join types, represented by the three toggle buttons, are **Miter join** (default), **Round join**, and **Bevel join**:

Miter join

In this join, the outer outline of the stroke at the cusp point is continued by two straight line fragments, tangential to the stroke on both sides of the joint, until these straight lines cross. As a result, the joint is adorned by a sharp peak, called a *miter*, which becomes longer and sharper as the angle at the joint decreases, reaching far beyond the position of the cusp node.

This leads us to a problem, however. How long can the miter become? It is easy to see that when the angle at the joint becomes zero (which is perfectly legal), the miter should be infinitely long. This is obviously infeasible. To handle this situation, the **Miter limit** control allows you to set the maximum length of a miter in units of stroke width. For example, for the default miter limit of 4, any miter shorter than 4 stroke widths remains sharp-tipped, but as soon as you decrease the angle to make the miter longer than that, it will be cut (beveled) at the distance of 4 stroke widths from the joint.

Bevel join

This join is basically the same as a **Miter join** but with the miter limit set to 0. This means that for any angle, the miter is cut off by a *bevel*—a straight line perpendicular to the bisector of the cusp angle.

Round join

This simulates the effect of tracing the join with a perfectly round pen. It is similar to the **Bevel join**, but instead of a straight bevel, the miter is cut by a circular arc whose center is at the cusp point. This option is the most natural for largely curvilinear paths where occasional cusps might look out of character if not rounded.

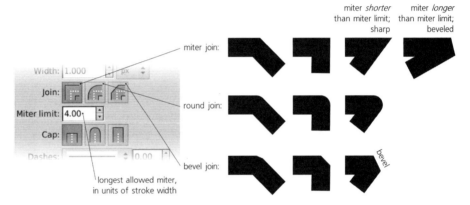

Figure 9-2: Stroke join controls in the Fill and Stroke dialog

Perhaps the most dramatic effect of different stroke join settings are on a stroked text object:

MITER
BEVEL
ROUND

Figure 9-3: The effect of join settings on stroked text

SVG *In SVG, the joins are controlled by the* stroke-linejoin *CSS property, which can take values of* miter, bevel, *and* round. *The miter limit is stored in a separate property,* stroke-miterlimit.

9.3 Caps

Open paths need to know how to draw the ends of the stroke. For caps, again, there are three options available, which are somewhat similar to the three join types:

Butt cap
Bluntly cuts the stroke, perpendicular to the stroke direction, right at the end node of the path.

Round cap
Adds a semicircular blob that smoothly rounds the end of the stroke.

Square cap
Adds a half-square blob to the end of the stroke.

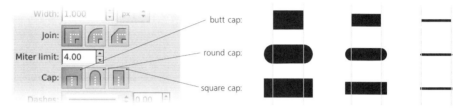

Figure 9-4: Stroke cap options in the Fill and Stroke dialog

Both round and square caps make the open path longer by its full width, with a half-stroke-width cap added to each end. Only with butt caps (which essentially means no caps), the path is as long as the distance between its end nodes.

The effect of join and cap options is most visible on wide strokes; for strokes that render at 1 px or narrower, they make very little visual difference (except possibly for long miters).

SVG *In SVG, the stroke caps of a path are controlled by the* `stroke-linecap` *property, which can take values of* `butt`, `round`, *and* `square`.

9.4 Dash Patterns

A stroke does not need to run solidly from end to end of a path. SVG allows you to stroke a path with a regular pattern of dashes separated by empty intervals of any length. If you know how to edit raw SVG (for example, using Inkscape's XML Editor, 4.7), you can create any pattern you like. Otherwise, you can choose one of the many predefined patterns provided by the **Fill and Stroke** dialog, as shown in Figure 9-5.

Ordered roughly from the most common to the most exotic, these patterns include:

- Dotted patterns that consist of dots (i.e., stroked segments whose length is equal to stroke width) with intervals equal to 1, 2, 3, 4, 6, and so on up to 48 stroke widths (this means the pattern scales up or down proportionally when you make your stroke wider or narrower).

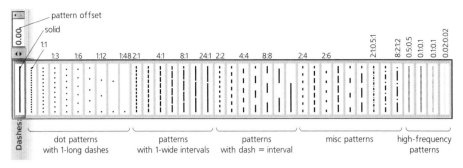

Figure 9-5: Dash patterns in the Fill and Stroke dialog

- Patterns with long dashes (1, 2, 3, and so on up to 24 stroke widths) and single-stroke width intervals.

- Patterns with equal dash and interval lengths, from 2 to 24 stroke widths.

- Patterns with varying dash and interval widths: 2:4, 4:2, 2:6, 6:2, 2:8, and 8:2.

- Patterns where a long dash is followed by a short one.

- Patterns with equal dash and interval lengths that are shorter than stroke width, from 0.5 down to 0.02 stroke widths (for example, a "square" path which is as long as it is wide will have 25 repetitions of the 0.02:0.02 pattern). Note that using such high-frequency patterns may slow Inkscape down considerably.

The editable field next to the dash pattern selector allows you to shift the chosen pattern along the path, again in units of stroke width.

SVG *In SVG, the dash pattern of a stroke is specified in the* `stroke-dasharray` *property. It can take values of* none *(solid line) or a comma-separated list of values where each odd value gives the length of a dash and each even value gives the length of an interval. For example, a specification of* `stroke-dasharray:2,1,0.5,1` *means that the dash of length 2 is followed by an interval of length 1, which is followed by a short dash of 0.5 and another interval of 1 (all lengths are in the units of stroke width).*

*The list of the predefined dash patterns available in the **Fill and Stroke** dialog is stored in your* preferences.xml *file, inside the* group *element with* id="dashes"*. By editing the children of this element you can add, remove, or change the patterns available in the Inkscape UI.*

Note that the stroke caps (9.3) affect dashes, too. If you set a path to use round or square caps, they will be added to both ends of each dash. As a result, each dash will become longer by one full stroke width compared to its length when using the default butt caps. For example, the 1:1 pattern with round caps loses all its intervals; the round caps of adjacent dashes, each cap 0.5 stroke widths in length, now touch each other, as shown in Figure 9-6.

As a consequence, to create a pattern of round dots following a path, you need to create a dash pattern with zero-length dashes and round caps. Unfortunately, Inkscape does not list such a pattern in the **Fill and Stroke** dialog; you will need to create it manually by first assigning a pattern with the interval length you need and then editing the `stroke-dasharray` property in the style attribute of the corresponding path element to set its dash length (first value) to 0. Note,

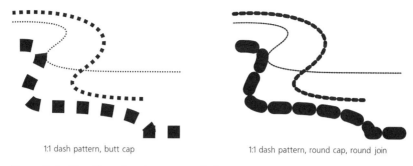

1:1 dash pattern, butt cap   1:1 dash pattern, round cap, round join

Figure 9-6: The effect of stroke caps on dashes

however, that without round or square caps, such a pattern will render the path completely invisible (which is the main reason it is not among the standard patterns—remember that the default caps setting is butt).

One interesting use of dot patterns with very wide intervals (such as 1:48) is quickly creating a random scattering of dots. Draw a quick spiral-like doodle with the Pencil tool (**14.2**) and assign a 1:48 dash pattern to it to turn it into a cloud of seemingly unconnected dots.

1 px wide solid stroke   Same, with 1:48 dash pattern

Figure 9-7: Using a dash array with large intervals to imitate a random scattering of dots

Also, the regularity of dash patterns plays nicely with spirals—a shape which is also regular but consists of progressively longer and longer turns (**11.6**). An interplay of the equidistant dashes and gradually devolving paths can produce interesting patterns:

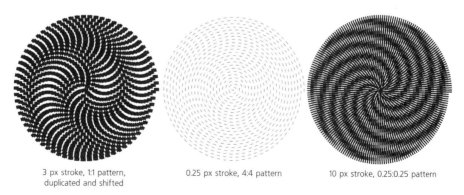

3 px stroke, 1:1 pattern, duplicated and shifted   0.25 px stroke, 4:4 pattern   10 px stroke, 0.25:0.25 pattern

Figure 9-8: Dashed spirals are a form of art.

9.5 Markers

Markers are arbitrary objects (or even groups of objects) that are attached to a path and are displayed as part of that path at some of its nodes (12.1). A path can have three different types of markers on its start node, intermediate (mid) nodes, and the end node. Each copy of the marker is positioned at the node and rotated so as to follow the direction of the path at this node. The most common use of markers is for creating arrowheads in diagrams and flowcharts.

The bottom of the **Stroke style** tab in the **Fill and Stroke** dialog contains three large drop-down lists where you can select start, mid, and end markers for the selected paths.

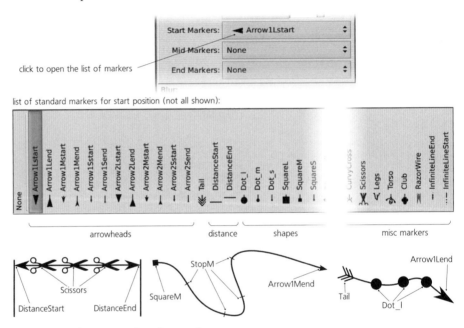

Figure 9-9: Choosing markers for a path

These three lists show all the same markers (in other words, you can use any marker in any position), but the preview thumbnails show them applied to the start, mid, and end of a horizontal straight line path, so you can get an idea of how the marker will look on the actual path.

Let's look at what markers are in Inkscape's standard list:

Arrowheads

There are two types of arrowheads: One is dart-like with straight lines on the back, and the other is delta-shaped with a circular concave arc at the back of the arrow. Each type of arrowhead comes in three sizes: large, medium, and small; and each size has two orientations: start and end.

For example, if you want your arrowhead to point away from the path, you should choose **Arrow1Mstart** (first type, medium size, start orientation) as the start marker and **Arrow1Mend** as the end marker; you can, however, reverse this choice and have your arrowheads point inward from both ends of the path. Or, you can choose **Arrow1Mend** for all three positions and have all arrowheads on your path point in one direction towards the end of the path (see 12.1.1 for how to tell the start of a path from its end).

Arrow tail

An arrow tail marker is available only in one size (matching the large arrowheads) and one orientation (making sense as an end marker—that is, oriented toward the path start).

Distance measurement markers

Distance measurement markers are just arrowheads (same shape and slightly smaller than **Arrow1M**) with an added perpendicular straight line at the tip. There are two orientations: **DistanceStart** as a start marker and **DistanceEnd** as an end marker is what you need most of the time.

Geometric shapes

There is a collection of geometric shape markers: round dots, squares, diamonds (squares rotated by 45 degrees), equilateral triangles, straight line stops, filled and empty half-circle marks. Most of them have solid black and white-filled variants. Just as arrowheads, these markers come in three sizes (large, medium, and small); some also have start and end orientations (although for symmetric markers such as diamonds, the orientations only differ in the position of the marker relative to its node). The start and end variants of triangle markers can be used as just another arrowhead shape.

Misc markers

There are several fancy markers, of which the most notable are the **Scissors** (assign it to mid markers to create a typical "cut-off line") and the "infinite line" ellipsis endings.

If your document already uses some markers, these markers will be added to the top of the drop-down marker menus, separated from the standard Inkscape-provided markers below. To remove markers from a path, select **None** from the list.

SVG *When you assign a marker to a path, Inkscape places a copy of the marker into the document's* defs *(A.4) and makes the path refer to the marker in* defs. *The list of the markers above the separator in the marker menus is simply that of the markers in* defs; *if you want to remove some markers you no longer use, use the **File ▸ Vacuum Defs** command.*

9.5.1 Mid Markers and Nodes

Start and end markers are simple: Their position on the path is never a surprise (although their orientation may sometimes be, if the end node has a very short Bézier handle, which has very little effect on the shape of the curve but may rotate the marker at this node in some unexpected direction). Mid markers are more interesting: They are located at the middle nodes (12.1) of a path, and the positions of these nodes may not be what you need or even expect.

A simple use case is a path consisting of straight line fragments (with no Bézier curves). On such a path, mid markers will be displayed at the corners. Use markers which don't have end or start variants and are thus positioned symmetrically around the node—for example, dots or squares:

SquareM   DotM

Figure 9-10: Mid markers at the path joints

Sometimes, you may want to evenly "fill" a path with mid markers, similar to the way the dash pattern is evenly repeated along the path. This is trivial for a simple straight line path, where you can add or remove as many mid nodes as necessary without changing the straight line shape. In a more complex path, however, some nodes may be necessary for the path to have the shape it already has, and you cannot move these nodes along the path without distorting that shape. On the other hand, you also cannot choose to not apply markers to these nodes; in SVG, mid markers apply to all mid nodes without exception. As a result, it may be impossible to distribute markers along a path perfectly evenly; however, the shorter your desired interval between markers and the simpler the path, the less noticeable this inevitable unevenness.

How can you add nodes to a path without changing its shape, for the purpose of using mid markers? A single new node can be added in the Node tool (12.5.3) by double-clicking or Ctrl-Alt-clicking anywhere on the path. For even distribution of nodes, however, another shortcut is more useful: Insert creates a new node in the middle of each segment between selected nodes and adds the new node to the node selection.

For example, selecting both nodes of a two-node path and hitting Insert adds one new node in the middle; now you have three nodes selected with two segments between them, so pressing Insert again adds two more nodes; another Insert adds four more nodes, and so on. In this simple case, all nodes will be distributed evenly at all times; however, if your path already had some mid nodes, selecting all nodes and hitting Insert repeatedly will add nodes more profusely in areas that had more nodes to begin with, as shown in Figure 9-11.

Another approach to creating evenly distributed nodes is the **Add Nodes** extension (13.3). In it, you specify the maximum distance (in px units) between nodes along the path. In the result, the existing nodes may happen be closer to their neighbors than this distance, but no nodes cannot be farther apart; segments between nodes will be filled by new nodes equally spaced at the specified distance.

To delete an individual node, in the Node tool Ctrl-Alt-click it, or select it and press Delete (12.5.3). A good method to delete all nonessential nodes (those that were added only for the sake of mid markers and do not affect the shape of the path) is to use the **Simplify** command (12.3). Of course **Simplify** cannot really *know* which nodes are essential and which are not; it tries to guess it—and usually performs acceptably well, although undesired nodes and some shape distortion are impossible to avoid.

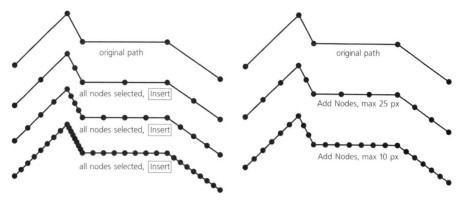

Figure 9-11: Adding mid nodes by pressing Insert repeatedly (left) and by using the Add Nodes extension (right)

9.5.2 Coloring Markers

Typically, connector lines in diagrams and flowcharts are black. Therefore, all standard markers provided by Inkscape are either solid black or black with white filling. Unfortunately, even if you assign a different stroke color to a path with markers, this color will only apply to the stroke itself and won't affect the markers. A red stroke with a black arrowhead is rarely what you had in mind.

SVG *This problem is rooted in SVG itself. In SVG 1.1, there's no way to force markers to inherit style parameters from the path they are applied to. However, a workaround for this is planned in SVG 1.2, so adding support for it to Inkscape will eventually resolve this issue.*

The easiest (although still clumsy) workaround for this is the extension called **Color Markers to Match Stroke** in the **Extensions** menu. Simply call it with your path selected, and it will paint the markers with the current stroke color of the path. (If you want a more complex paint job to be done on your markers, see the next section on how to turn a marker into a regular editable object and back.)

The desynchronization of stroke style and marker style has its advantages, too. Sometimes you may want to use a path only as an invisible string for a rosary of mid markers—in other words, to see the markers but to hide the stroke itself. This is easy: First assign the markers to a stroked path, and then remove the stroke (by middle-clicking the stroke swatch in the selected style indicator, 8.4).

Note that markers are always drawn on top of their stroke in z-order. So, if your stroke has a different color than markers, it will only show through from underneath markers if they are transparent.

9.5.3 Creating New Markers

A marker does not necessarily need to be a single object painted by a solid color. It can consist of any number of objects, grouped or not, with any paint, opacity, or even blur properties—in other words, anything Inkscape can draw can be a marker on a path. Applying such complex markers to paths with many added nodes (9.5.1) can produce amazing compositions. To make use of this versatility, however, you need to know how to create markers out of objects.

Generally, it's as easy as selecting the object or objects and choosing **Objects to Marker** from the **Object** menu. Selected objects disappear, but if you now select any path, open the **Fill and Stroke** dialog, go to the **Stroke style** tab, and open the list of markers, you will see your new marker at the top, in the section listing this document's markers. (You may need to close and reopen the **Fill and Stroke** dialog to refresh the marker list.)

When creating the new marker, Inkscape assumes that the original objects are oriented as they should be on a horizontal path that goes from left to right. For example, if you create a new arrowhead that you plan to use as an end marker, make it point horizontally to the right before converting it to a marker.

Similar to standard markers, the user-created marker will scale up and down as you change the stroke width. Its initial size (the size of the object that you have turned into a marker) corresponds to the 1 px stroke.

Each marker has an *anchor point*—the point which will coincide with the node to which that marker is attached. When you create a new marker, Inkscape uses the rotation center of the (first) selected object as that anchor point. By default, the rotation center is in the center of the object's bounding box (**4.2**), which means the newly created marker will be centered around its node. If you move the rotation center, for example, to one of the corners of the object, the new marker will touch its node by that corner.

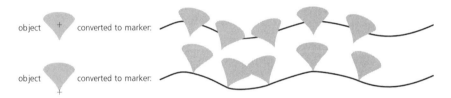

Figure 9-12: Creating a new marker from a selected object

Can we do the opposite and convert a path marker to an editable object (perhaps with the intention to make it a marker again after editing)? Yes, although this involves destroying the path that the marker was applied to (so you may want to make a copy of the path first). This is done by choosing the command **Stroke to Path** from the **Path** menu. It turns the stroke into a filled path and, if the original path had markers, groups the converted path with objects that represent former markers. Just ungroup, choose one of the former markers, rotate it into the default orientation, and edit it as necessary.

NOTE   *You can turn a clone (Chapter 16) into a marker and then continue to edit the original object, with markers being updated live.*

9.5.4 Markers Miscellany

SVG markers have a few other options that are not yet available via the Inkscape UI but can be accessed by manually editing SVG, best of all in Inkscape's XML Editor (**4.7**). You will need to locate the marker object in the document's defs first. Select an object that uses this marker and, in its style attribute, find the corresponding marker property—for example, `marker-start:url(#Arrow1Lstart)`. Note the URL it refers to (in our case, `Arrow1Lstart`). Now go to the defs element under root svg and find the marker element with id="Arrow1Lstart". Here's what you can do by editing that marker element:

- By default, markers rotate to orient themselves along the path direction. If you want your marker to always have the same orientation regardless of how the path goes in this point, remove the orient="auto" attribute.

- If you don't want a marker to scale up and down when the stroke width is changed, add the attribute markerUnits with the value userSpaceOnUse to the marker element.

10

GRADIENTS AND PATTERNS

Using gradients is the easiest way to depart from the lifeless flat look of solid color fills, and as such, gradients are one of the most important features of vector graphics.

Designers can create amazingly complex and photorealistic art using nothing but carefully laid out gradients. For all their versatility, gradients are relatively simple to create and edit, render quickly, and are almost universally supported in SVG software—none of which is quite true, for example, for SVG filters such as blur (17.1).

Basically, a gradient is a smooth transition between two or more colors. *Color* also includes a level of opacity; this means that you can, for example, make a gradient from opaque red to transparent red, with semitransparent red shades in between. SVG supports two types of gradients: *linear* (along a line) and *elliptic*, or *radial* (away from a center, with possibly unequal *axes* and a noncentral *focus point*).

10.1 The Gradient Tool

The Gradient tool (g or Ctrl-F1) is where you create new gradients on objects. It is also the best environment for *editing* existing gradients—even though, once created, a gradient on a selected object can be edited (by dragging handles and assigning colors to them) not only in the Gradient tool but also in the Node tool (**12.5**), all shape tools (Chapter **11**), and in the Dropper tool (**8.6**). Still, the Gradient tool has a number of gradient-specific editing conveniences.

Creating a new gradient is very simple: Make sure you have the necessary object or objects selected and drag on the canvas. You will see an actual gradient appearing and following your mouse as you drag, and you will also see a system of *handles* (small on-canvas controls) connected by lines.

You don't need to drag *on* the selected objects—gradient handles can very well lie completely outside the object they apply to. You can have any number of objects selected and get them all painted by the same gradient (more precisely, by multiple but coinciding gradients) with a single drag. Another method to quickly create a gradient that spans the entire object is to double-click that object with the Gradient tool.

To use the most common object selection shortcuts, you don't need to switch to the Selector tool; click to select, Alt-click to select under, and Shift-click to add to selection all work in the Gradient tool as well.

Gradients can be applied to the *fill* of objects, their *stroke*, or both (**8.1.1**). In Inkscape, stroke gradients use greenish connecting lines between the handles, while fill gradients use blue lines:

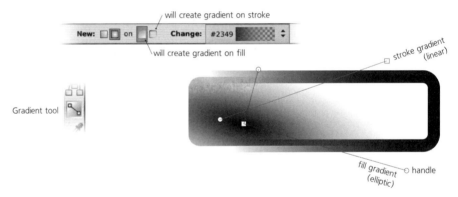

Figure 10-1: *Different gradients on the fill and stroke of an object*

If you are creating a gradient for an object that had flat color paint before, the gradient will go from the fully opaque to the fully transparent version of the color of the object *on which you started the drag*. For example, if you have a yellow rectangle selected and drag starting from that rectangle, you will fill the object with a gradient going from opaque yellow to transparent yellow. You can, however, fill it with an opaque-blue-to-transparent-blue gradient if you have a blue-filled object somewhere and start dragging from it. To put it another way, the gradient you create applies to selected objects, but the color it uses may come from any object, selected or not, from which you start your drag. (If that's not what you wanted, don't worry—it's very easy to change gradient colors once it's created.)

Similarly, if the object where you started your drag already had some gradient, the tool will just redraw it for the selected object, preserving the colors of that gradient (i.e., preserving the *gradient definition*, **10.2**). If you start dragging from an empty space and not from any object, the color or gradient of the *topmost selected* object will be used for the new gradient.

Of the many ways to *remove* gradients from an object, perhaps the easiest is to make sure none of the gradient handles are selected (all are white, not blue) and click any color on the palette. The object will be filled by the flat color, replacing any gradient it had before.

NOTE *Neither gradients nor any other paint (8.1.1) can be applied to bitmap objects (Chapter 18); if you want a transparency gradient applied to a bitmap, use a mask (18.4). The same is true for clones (Chapter 16), except where the paint of a clone's original is unset.*

Let's now look in more detail at the two types of gradients Inkscape can create: linear and elliptic.

10.1.1 Linear Gradients

A linear gradient goes along a straight line, where both ends (as well as, possibly, some points in the middle) have certain colors and opacities assigned to them. The transitions between color areas on the object are always perpendicular to the gradient line. This is the default kind of gradient that the Gradient tool creates; the linear gradient mode of the tool is set by the first toggle button in the tool's controls bar, as shown here:

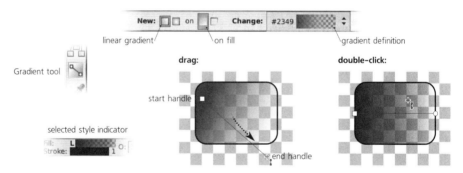

Figure 10-2: Creating linear gradients by dragging and double-clicking

NOTE *In the selected style indicator, linear gradients are marked with the letter L followed by the gradient swatch.*

A linear gradient has two freely draggable handles: a square one at the start and a circular one at the end of the gradient line. By dragging them around, you can change the direction and length of the gradient (note how the gradient repaints itself in real time as you drag a handle).

With Ctrl pressed, drawing a new gradient or dragging a handle of an existing one makes the gradient line *snap* to angle increments, by default every 15 degrees (this value is changeable in the **Steps** tab of the **Inkscape Preferences** dialog, compare 6.3). Double-clicking an object in linear gradient mode creates a horizontal linear gradient that goes through the center of the object's bounding box.

10.1.2 Elliptic Gradients

To switch the Gradient tool to creating *elliptic gradients* instead of linear, press the second toggle button in the tool's controls bar (above the canvas). Now, if you drag on canvas with some objects selected, an elliptic gradient for them will be created:

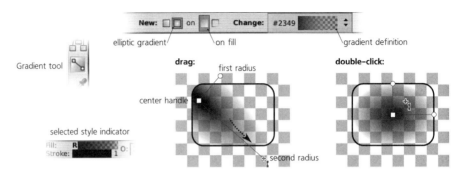

Figure 10-3: Creating elliptic gradients by dragging and double-clicking

NOTE *In the selected style indicator, elliptic gradients are marked with the letter* R *(for* Radial) *followed by the gradient swatch.*

An elliptic gradient has at least three draggable handles—the *center* (square handle) and the two perpendicular *radii* (round handles). This makes it possible to move, stretch, squeeze, or rotate such a gradient; you can make it into anything from a circle to a narrow ellipse, rotated at any angle. Moving the center handle moves the entire gradient (i.e., all handles); moving the radii stretches and rotates the gradient without moving the center. The two radii always remain perpendicular. As in the linear gradient mode, dragging a radius with Ctrl pressed *snaps* it to 15-degree angle increments.

When you start a drag creating a new gradient, you are dragging one of the radii; the other one gets created to be equal to half of the selected object's height. This means that if you start dragging from the center of the object and drag horizontally to the right edge of its bounding box, the ellipse will be neatly inscribed into the bounding box. The same effect can be achieved simply by double-clicking an object.

NOTE *If you need a symmetric "bilinear" gradient with a mountain-like profile, the easiest way to do this is via an elliptic gradient with one radius made very long, dragged far beyond the boundaries of the object. Then, the central part of the stretched ellipse will look almost indistinguishable from a couple of counter-directed linear gradients.*

An elliptic gradient also has a fourth, normally hidden, handle—the *focus.* This is the point with the color and opacity of the gradient's central stop. Normally, it is merged together with the central handle and moves with it, producing a perfectly symmetric gradient. You can, however, separate the focus—visualized by an X-shaped handle—from the center by dragging away from the central handle with Shift. This creates an asymmetric, eccentric gradient, shown in Figure 10-4. To merge the focus back, just drag it close enough to the central handle and it will snap.

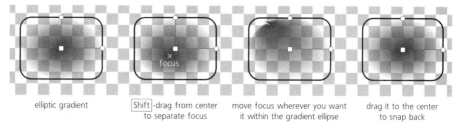

| elliptic gradient | Shift-drag from center to separate focus | move focus wherever you want it within the gradient ellipse | drag it to the center to snap back |

Figure 10-4: Creating an eccentric elliptic gradient by moving the focus

10.2 Gradient Definition

Every gradient has a set of *stops*, each with its own color and transparency value. The minimum number of stops is the two *end stops*, in which case they apply to the ends of the gradient line (linear) or to the center and edges of an ellipse (elliptic). However, a gradient can also have any number of *middle stops*, each one having, along with its own color and transparency, a certain position between the end stops (for example, a middle stop may be at 0.5 of the gradient—that is, exactly in the middle between the end stops). For each gradient, the full set of its stops with their colors, transparencies, and positions is called the *gradient definition*.

Gradient definitions are document-wide resources. This means that any gradient you create or edit adds its definition to the list of all gradient definitions in the document. After that, you can assign that definition not only to the original gradient but to any other gradient in this document. The drop-down list in the controls bar of the Gradient tool displays swatches for all gradient definitions in the document:

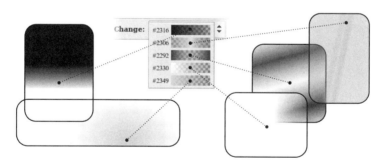

Figure 10-5: Choosing a gradient definition

The same list of gradient swatches is available in the **Fill and Stroke** dialog. When you have one or more objects with gradients selected, choosing a definition from the list will assign it to all selected gradients. This does not change the position of the end handles, but replaces the colors and may add or remove middle stops.

NOTE *As of this writing, there's no way to save and reuse gradient definitions across documents, but this is planned for a future release. Also, there is no way to rename a gradient from its default numeric name (other than by using the XML Editor).*

You can *reverse* the color definition of the selected object's gradient by pressing `Shift-R`. For example, if you have an elliptic gradient with opaque blue in the center and transparent yellow at the edge, after pressing `Shift-R` you will have transparent yellow in the center and opaque blue at the edge. (With a linear gradient, this is equivalent to rotating the gradient line by 180 degrees, but an elliptic gradient can't be reversed simply by moving its handles, which makes `Shift-R` especially useful.)

By the way, if you want to change the opacity of *all* stops in a gradient by the same amount, you don't need to tweak the opacity of each stop separately. Instead, simply adjust the master opacity of the object that is using the gradient (**8.1.2**).

10.2.1 *Sharing Gradient Definitions*

When copying and pasting or duplicating an object with gradient, the object's copy automatically gets a *copy of the original gradient*, so that modifying it does not affect the source object's gradient definition. This behavior is controlled by the **Prevent sharing of gradient definitions** checkbox on the **Misc** tab of the **Inkscape Preferences** dialog. It is checked by default; if you uncheck it, then copying and pasting, duplicating, pasting style, and explicit assignment of an existing gradient definition to an object via the Gradient tool controls will result in a *shared* gradient definition. When two objects share a gradient definition, changing the colors or middle stop positions of the gradient on one object (but not changing the coordinates of the end handles) affects all the other objects that use the same definition.

The **Vacuum Defs** command in the **File** menu removes, among other things, any leftover unused gradient definitions that may be lingering in your document. It's a good way to tidy things up and reduce the document size a bit.

10.3 Gradient Repeat

As we've seen, gradient handles don't need to coincide with the edges of the object they apply to; they can be positioned absolutely anywhere on the canvas, and the object will just display whatever part of the gradient happens to fall within its limits. This, however, invites the question: What will be used to paint those parts of the object that are not covered by the gradient—those parts that are beyond the ends of a linear or outside the edge of an elliptic?

By default, these areas are painted by the flat color and transparency of the first or last gradient end stop. For example, if you have a small elliptic gradient with semitransparent white at the radii, the rest of the object outside the gradient will also be semitransparent white. However, this is not the only possibility.

Select an object with a gradient (but make sure that none of the handles are selected) and in the **Repeat** list of the **Fill and Stroke** dialog, select either **reflected** or **direct** instead of the default **none**. These options force the gradient to repeat itself indefinitely, either unchanged (direct), or with inversion of every second copy (reflected). This is an easy way to create various striped patterns on objects, as shown in Figure 10-6.

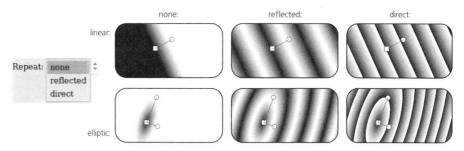

Figure 10-6: Using the gradient repeat option

10.4 Handles

Handles are the on-canvas controls that correspond to the gradient stops. In the Gradient tool, they can be not only freely dragged around, but also *selected* and *painted*, much the same as selected objects are painted.

10.4.1 Selecting

Selected handles are blue, unlike the unselected ones which are white. The simplest way to select a handle is by clicking it; you can also Shift-click to add a handle to selection or remove it from selection, or Shift-drag around multiple nodes to select them with a rubber band (compare 5.7). After you have created a new gradient by dragging, the handle you've been dragging remains selected.

Similar to the Selector tool, in the Gradient tool you can also select handles with the keyboard: Tab and Shift-Tab select the *next* and *previous* handle (or first and last, if none were selected before), Ctrl-A selects *all* handles in selected objects, and Esc deselects any handles (but leaves the objects selected; a second Esc deselects objects).

NOTE *Watch the status bar (2.6): It always displays useful information on the selected gradient handle(s) as well as the object(s) and gradient types they belong to.*

10.4.2 Painting

You can assign any color or level of transparency to the selected gradient handle or handles, using all the same methods you would use to change the style of an object (8.1). When a handle is selected, the palette, the **Fill and Stroke** dialog, the color gestures and commands in the selected style indicator (8.1.1), the **Paste Style** command, and even the Dropper tool all work on the selected handle, not on selected object. Figure 10-7 shows an example.

Unlike an object, a gradient stop does not have fill or stroke (even though the gradient itself can apply to fill or stroke). Therefore, when you have one or more stops selected, the style indicator in the status bar shows the color of the stop in *both* fill and stroke swatches; this may not be perfectly logical, but it is handy. The opacity of a gradient stop is reflected by the master opacity control (labeled **O:** in the status bar). The displayed stroke *width*, however, is always that of the object (if it has stroke), not a stop, since stops cannot have any strokes.

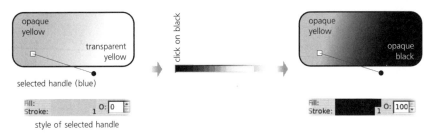

Figure 10-7: Assigning color to selected gradient handles

It is especially convenient to use the Dropper tool if you want one end of the gradient to blend smoothly into other objects; make sure the corresponding handle is selected, switch to Dropper, and click the area into which you want it to blend. (Note that by switching to the Dropper tool, you leave the Gradient tool, but this is not a problem; like many other tools, Dropper displays gradient handles and even preserves handle selection. You cannot select objects in Dropper, but you can switch gradient handle selection.)

When *multiple* gradient handles are selected, the selected style indicator displays the *averaged* color and opacity of the selected stops (this is the same behavior as for multiple selected objects, 8.2.1).

When at least one handle is selected, the **Copy** command (Ctrl-C) copies to the clipboard the style (both color and opacity) of the single selected handle, or the averaged style of several selected handles. This means you can copy and paste style between gradient stops—select a handle, copy, select some other handle(s), and paste style (Shift-Ctrl-V). If you select several handles, this allows you to quickly average their actual colors and opacities by copying and pasting their style back onto them.

10.4.3 Moving, Merging, and Snapping

You can *move* the selected gradient handles by directly dragging them with the mouse, or by the arrow keys with all the regular modifiers (Shift for ten times the standard 2 px displacement, Alt for pixel-size displacement, Shift-Alt for 10 pixels displacement; see 6.5.1). Naturally, the end stop handles (gradient ends in a linear, center and radii in an elliptic) can be moved arbitrarily, whereas the middle handles can only be moved along the gradient line. (Don't confuse *middle* handles with the *center* handle of an elliptic gradient; the latter, despite being in the center of an ellipse, represents an *end stop* of the gradient definition.)

If you selected multiple objects, all those that have gradients will display their handles (regardless of whether they are linear or elliptic, on fill or on stroke) and allow you to edit any of them simultaneously. This opens up interesting possibilities. For example, you can select ends of all linear gradients and move them all in parallel. Or, you can press Ctrl-A to select all stops in all gradients and use arrow keys to move the entire ensemble of gradients as a whole.

What's more, any number of end stop handles (but not middle stops) can be *merged.* Just move one handle close enough to another, and it will snap to it and merge. (The status bar will report the merged status of such a handle, for example *handle merging 2 stops.*) Now, when you drag such a merged handle, it will affect all gradients it belongs to at once. To separate merged handles, drag away from a merged handle with Shift.

For example, you can merge the centers of two objects' elliptic gradients, merge an elliptic handle with another object's linear handle, merge all three elliptic handles of multiple objects, or merge the gradients on fill and stroke of the same object:

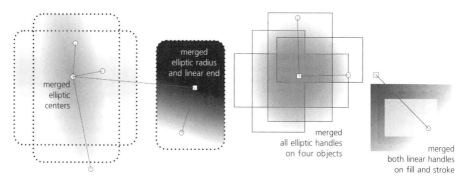

Figure 10-8: Merging gradient handles

When you drag to create a new gradient with several objects selected, you get what looks and acts like a single gradient applied to multiple objects but is in fact many gradients with their handles merged together.

If two handles have different colors or opacities, they will remain different after you merge them. However, if you assign a color or opacity to a merged handle, it will apply to all gradient stops sharing this merged handle, equalizing their styles. If you want to change the style of one of the merged handles without unmerging it, this is possible if the merged handles belong to different objects: Simply deselect everything (both handles and objects) and select only the object whose handle you want to repaint.

When being dragged by the mouse, all handles of an object's gradient *snap* to the edges of the object's bounding box, its central axes, and their continuations (apart from snapping to the regular snap destinations such as guidelines or grid, 7.3). This makes it easy, for example, to place a gradient handle exactly in the center of the object. Also, when dragging a handle or when creating a gradient, holding Ctrl snaps the gradient angle to horizontal, vertical, and 15-degree increments in between:

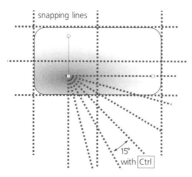

Figure 10-9: Snapping gradient handles

10.5 Multistage Gradients

A gradient that has at least one middle stop between the end stops is called *multistage* because it contains more than one color transition. In such a gradient, each middle stop has its own color and transparency, but its position is limited to somewhere in the middle between the end stops. In Inkscape, a middle stop is represented by a diamond-shaped handle, as shown in Figure 7 on the color insert.

10.5.1 Creating Middle Stops

To add a middle stop in a gradient, double-click or Ctrl-Alt-click anywhere on the gradient line. The new stop will automatically get the color and transparency of the clicked point, so that the look of the gradient remains unchanged.

Also, you can *drag and drop* a color from the palette onto the gradient line. Dropping a color on an existing handle changes the color of that stop; dropping it anywhere else on the gradient line *creates* a new stop with this color. Also, when two or more adjacent handles are selected, pressing Insert adds new stops in the middles of all selected stop intervals (much the same as it does for nodes in the Node tool, 12.5.3). New handles added by Insert are included in the handle selection, so pressing Insert repeatedly adds more and more handles; if you start with two handles selected and press Insert n times, you will end up with a total of 2^n handles.

To delete all selected stops, just press Delete. Individual stops (selected or not) can also be deleted by Ctrl-Alt-clicking them.

Deleting is not limited to middle stops; you can delete an end stop as well, so that the nearest intermediate stop becomes the new end stop of the gradient. If you delete an end handle in a linear gradient or a radii handle in an elliptic gradient, the remaining handles do not move, so the gradient span becomes shorter as a result. If you delete the central handle of an elliptic, its nearest handle moves to become the new center. Finally, if you delete an end handle in a two-stop gradient, the gradient disappears and the object gets painted with the flat color and opacity of the last remaining stop.

Pressing Ctrl-L with some intermediate stops selected *simplifies* the selected portion of the gradient, removing those stops that can be removed without noticeable change in the look of the gradient (compare 12.3). In particular, new stops created by double-clicking or pressing Insert initially do not change the appearance of the gradient, and simplifying will delete all redundant stops that weren't moved or repainted since creation. (You may have to press Ctrl-L repeatedly to delete all unneeded stops.)

10.5.2 Moving Middle Stops

Naturally, a middle stop's handle can only be dragged or moved with arrow keys along the gradient line no further than its neighboring handles. Dragging a middle handle with Ctrl snaps it to 1/10 fractions of the available range—that is, it will snap to 1/10, 2/10, 3/10, and so on of the span between its neighbors.

Two or more middle stops may *coincide*. If they have different colors, the gradient in that point will have a sharp color boundary. For example, add two middle stops, paint one green and the other blue, and then drag the green one all the way to the blue one to create a sharp green-blue boundary in the gradient.

Dragging multiple selected handles with Alt pressed moves each one by a distance which depends on how close that handle is to the one that is being dragged. The handle which you grab and drag moves all the way, but all other selected handles lag behind, the more so the farther they are from the handle you drag (these distances are calculated using a smooth bell-like curve, similar to the node sculpting feature in the Node tool, 12.5.7.2).

Why is this useful? One gradient feature Inkscape (and SVG in general) lacks is *profiles*, which means you cannot make the transition between colors accelerating or decelerating (i.e., shifted towards one of the two neighboring stops) instead of linear. Yet, Alt-dragging of middle stops makes it easy to *approximate* such nonlinear profiles. For example, if you have a two-stop gradient that you want to shape according to a curve profile, select both ends of the gradient, press Insert several times to add a number of intermediate handles, then Alt-drag a handle in the middle to smoothly reshape the gradient:

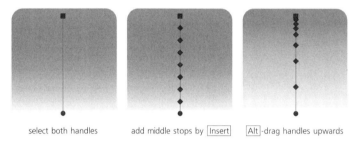

select both handles   add middle stops by Insert   Alt-drag handles upwards

Figure 10-10: Approximating a profiled gradient by dragging middle stops with Alt

10.6 Transforming Objects with Gradients

Normally, when you transform (i.e., move, scale, rotate, or skew, see Chapter 6) an object that uses gradient on fill or stroke, the gradient handles are transformed along with the object, so the gradient stays firmly put in place. However, the third **Affect** button on the Selector tool controls bar (6.10) can change that.

If you uncheck this button (checked by default), gradients will remain fixed relative to the canvas, no matter how you transform the objects that use them. This can be useful, for example, if you want to scale an object up or down so its size matches that of the elliptic gradient it uses.

10.7 Gradient Tips and Examples

If you want to "fade out" or "feather" the edge of an object, you don't have to (indeed, often you *can't*) apply a color-to-transparent gradient to it. One way to address this need is by using a mask (18.4); however, in many cases, if the background under the object is a solid color, an overlay object—a *shader*—of the same color as the background with opaque-to-transparent gradient would be easier to create and maintain. This method works equally well for multiple objects that need to be feathered as a group, for feathering more than one side, for objects that already have different gradient fills, or for bitmaps or pattern-filled objects.

In this example, four gradient shaders are put over the edges of a bitmap to feather it out on a white background:

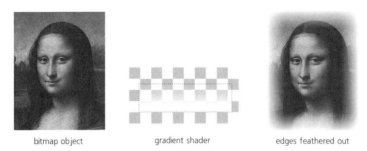

bitmap object   gradient shader   edges feathered out

Figure 10-11: Feathering the edge of a rectangular object with linear gradient shaders

When using shaders, normally you don't need to move the gradient handles to put the gradient where you need it. Instead, just transform the entire shader object with that gradient. In Figure 10-12, the Gradient tool was only used twice: to create opaque-to-transparent elliptic gradients on two ellipses, one white and one black. Then, a total of 29 clones (linked copies) of these shader ellipses, variously scaled and rotated, all with various reduced master opacity levels, were used to add depth to the cartoon face.

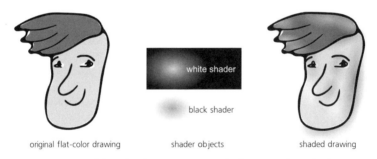

original flat-color drawing   shader objects   shaded drawing

Figure 10-12: Adding depth to a cartoon with elliptic gradient shaders

One problem with black (or any other dark-colored) shaders is that they often look too blunt at the edges, too definite, especially if you make them opaque enough. This is the result of the default gradient profile being linear, and therefore it can be fixed by adding mid stops and "profiling" them by Alt-dragging (10.5.2). Another useful approach is blurring the shader a bit so that its edges become less pronounced (17.1).

However, perhaps the simplest workaround for this problem is drawing a gradient not from opaque black to transparent black (which is the default), but from opaque black to transparent *white* (or, if you will be using the shader on some other light color, to the transparent version of that light color). This changes the perceived gradient profile drastically, making its edges a lot smoother and more natural. On the downside, this may make the center of the elliptic gradient a little too sharp, which can often be fixed simply by scaling the shader object up somewhat.

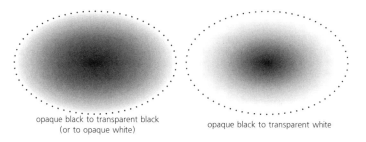

opaque black to transparent black
(or to opaque white)

opaque black to transparent white

Figure 10-13: Changing the gradient profile in a dark shader by using a fully transparent light color at the edge

Using gradients in design often involves *overlaying* several objects with semitransparent gradients. Figure 8 on the color insert demonstrates a colored water drop or a glass button which is in fact a group of six objects with various elliptic gradients.

The color modes of the Tweak tool (**8.7**) can paint or randomize colors not only in flat color fill or stroke but in gradients, too. For gradients, the tool takes into account not only the position of the object with the gradient, but also the position of *each gradient stop* relative to the brush.

For example, you can recolor only the blue end of an object filled with blue-red gradient simply by painting over that blue end with a brush small enough to not touch the red. Color tweaking does not *create* gradients on objects that used flat color before, nor does it add stops, but only paints the stops of the existing gradients in the drawing.

As an illustration, let's take a simple opaque-black to transparent-black gradient, add a lot of middle stops by repeatedly pressing ⌈Insert⌉, and randomize the lightness of the stop by stroking over the objects with a Tweak brush in Jitter Colors mode, with only the L channel enabled. Then, repeat the same for two more copies of the smooth original gradient, and overlay them all on top of each other with a little rotation. The resulting texture is a quite believable seascape in a mist:

opaque black to transparent white

32 middle stops added by ⌈Insert⌉,
opacity randomized by the Tweak tool

3 copies overlaid,
75% opacity, with rotation

Figure 10-14: Randomizing a gradient with the Tweak tool

10.8 Patterns

A *pattern* is a paint type (8.1.1) where an object's fill or stroke consists of repeated copies of a *tile*. The tile can be anything: a single object (e.g., a bitmap) or a group of objects, using any style properties or Inkscape techniques. In this regard, patterns are a very rich and flexible feature. In another respect, however, patterns in SVG are quite limited: They can only use a simple rectangular grid of tiles with no rotations or reflections (compare, e.g., with the clone tiler which implements 17 different symmetry types, 16.6).

You cannot have both a gradient and a pattern on an object; they are two alternative paint types. If you want a transparency gradient on an object with pattern, read 10.7 on shaders or 18.4 on masks.

10.8.1 Creating Patterns

Unlike gradients, patterns don't have a dedicated creation tool in Inkscape. Instead, just select the objects that you want to turn into a tile and choose **Pattern ▶ Objects to Pattern** (Alt-I) from the **Object** menu.

The selected objects do not disappear and apparently don't change; however, it's easy to see that instead of the original object you now have a single *rectangle* selected. This rectangle is filled with the pattern made out of your objects, and it has exactly the size and position of their bounding box, which means that exactly one copy of the pattern fits into the rectangle. If you now drag the rectangle sizing handle (using the Rectangle or Node tool), you will see the other tiles as well:

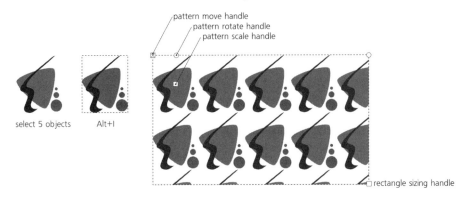

Figure 10-15: Creating a pattern from objects

Now you can easily assign the new pattern to any object by choosing **Copy** and **Paste Style** from this rectangle (which you can then delete if no longer needed), or by choosing it from the pattern list in the **Fill and Stroke** dialog, as shown in Figure 10-16.

SVG allows you to set margins around tiles in a pattern to space them apart. Unfortunately, Inkscape does not yet support doing this via the UI. While you can do this in the XML Editor if you know how, a simpler approach is to add to the objects from which you create your pattern a transparent rectangle extending

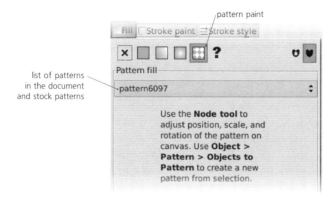

Figure 10-16: The pattern paint in the Fill and Stroke dialog

beyond the edges of the other objects and thus adding separation between the pattern's tiles.

If you want to extract the tile objects back from a pattern in order to edit them, select an object with that pattern and use the **Object ▸ Pattern ▸ Pattern to Objects** command.

10.8.2 Editing Patterns

When you are in the Node tool or a shape tool, each object with a pattern fill displays three editing handles that allow you to move, scale, and rotate the pattern within the object. As with gradients, these handles can be anywhere on the canvas, not necessarily on the object itself. Unlike gradients, however, these handles are not connected by lines and cannot be selected nor moved by keys, but only dragged by the mouse.

Also, unlike the Gradient tool, currently only a single selected object can display its pattern handles. Patterns on stroke, while correctly rendered, are not yet editable by handles at all.

X-shaped handle

Positioned in the top-left corner of one of the tiles (the "origin" tile). Dragging this handle *moves* the pattern in any direction.

Square handle

Positioned in the center of the origin tile. Dragging this handle *scales* the pattern. To make the scaling uniform (i.e., preserve the width/height ratio of the tiles), drag it with Ctrl.

Round handle

Positioned in the middle of the top side of the origin tile. Dragging this handle *rotates* the pattern around the X-shaped handle as an axis. Drag with Ctrl to snap rotation angle to 15 degree steps.

From an aesthetic viewpoint, the major problem with patterns is the same as their main advantage: *repetitiveness*. While necessary or at least acceptable in technical illustrations, artistic drawings are rarely improved by an overly repetitive rectangular pattern (even though they can sometimes use to a great effect some more complex pattern types). Two simple things that often help are to *scale the pattern up* as much as possible (so that fewer copies of it fit into the object) and *rotate it* so it's no longer horizontal/vertical and therefore does not look as regular.

10.8.3 Stock Patterns

The **Objects to Pattern** command is not the only way to add patterns to your document. Inkscape comes with a selection of simple *stock patterns* which you can reuse in your documents.

Select some object and switch it to pattern paint by clicking the **Pattern** button in the corresponding tab of the **Fill and Stroke** dialog. You will see a drop-down list (Figure 10-16) which contains your document's patterns, if any, at the top, and a set of stock patterns at bottom, after a separator. To use one of the patterns, simply select it from the list.

- There is a selection of plain **Stripes** with different ratios of stripe width to gap width, in the range from 4:1 to 1:64. For example, the **Stripes 1:2** pattern has gaps twice as wide as stripes. All stripes patterns exist in two versions: with black stripes and with white stripes (gaps are always transparent).

- There are two **Checkerboard** patterns with black and white odd squares (even squares are transparent).

- The **Packed Circles** option is a dense hexagonal pattern of black circles with transparent gaps.

- **Polka Dots** is a scattering of dots, designed to appear randomly but evenly distributed to mask the regularity of the repeating pattern. There are three size variants of this pattern (small, medium, and large dots) and two color variants (black and white dots).

- **Wavy** is a pattern of wavy lines with transparent gaps between them.

- **Camouflage** is a green-toned protective pattern such as that used by the military.

- **Ermine** is the traditional heraldic pattern, originating from a stylized representation of stoat furs with black tails.

- The three bitmap patterns, **Sand**, **Cloth**, and **Old Paint**, are based on seamless photographic tiles and allow you to add some natural texture to your drawing. All of them are grayscale, so you can make objects with these textures semi-transparent and overlay them over other colored objects to "texturize" them.

Stock patterns are stored in the file *patterns/patterns.svg* in Inkscape's *share* directory (typically */usr/share/inkscape* on Linux, *<inkscape-dir>\share* on Windows). You can add your own patterns to this file or replace it with any other SVG file containing the stock patterns you need.

11

SHAPES

The freedom to do anything, any time, the way you like is one thing that a good vector editor prides itself on. With a small vocabulary of generic object types and generic tools for manipulating them, you can render, or at least approximate, any graphic imaginable.

However, absolute freedom is not always a good thing. For example, a path (Chapter 12) can represent any possible two-dimensional shape. But often, what you need is not "any" shape but some very simple and well-defined geometric entity, such as a rectangle. Of course, a four-node path will give you a perfect rectangle—but isn't there a faster and more convenient way to do that, specifically for rectangles?

To respond to this need, Inkscape has several object types for commonly used geometric shapes: rectangles, 3D boxes, ellipses, polygons, stars, and spirals. Each shape type has a corresponding creation tool; it also provides an array of numeric parameters, draggable handles, and shortcuts for manipulating these shapes. You cannot do "everything" to such a shape object, but what you *can* do to it makes perfect sense for that specific shape type.

You can always press Shift-Ctrl-C to convert a shape to a path (or, in the case of a 3D box, to a group). The reverse conversion, however, is not possible (at least, not automatically). This means that a shape is a *higher level of abstraction* than a path; converting a shape to a path loses some information and is therefore a one-way, destructive operation.

AI   *Surprisingly, shape tools in Inkscape have no direct equivalent in Adobe Illustrator. All AI has in this department is a number of "quick shape" tools that can create some basic shapes—but, once created, the objects forget how they were born and become plain paths without any shape-specific capabilities. The convenience of Inkscape's "self-conscious" shapes is one of its important advantages over Illustrator.*

SVG   *Inkscape's ellipses and stars are significantly more versatile than the shape elements defined by the SVG standard. Therefore, Inkscape uses the generic* path *element for these shapes, instead of the* ellipse *and* polygon *elements provided by SVG (although it can read and display these SVG shape elements too). For spirals, there's no SVG element at all, so they are also represented by a* path *element internally. The only shape that uses a non-*path *element is the rectangle which uses the* rect *element.*

11.1   Shape Tools

A new shape object is created by dragging on the canvas with the corresponding tool—for example, dragging with the Rectangle tool creates a new rectangle. The newly created shape remains selected, and any selected shape displays its editing *handles* (similar to the gradient handles). By dragging those handles, you can immediately edit what you have created.

Most handles work differently when you drag them with or without various keyboard modifiers (Ctrl, Shift, Alt). When you hover your mouse over a handle, the status bar tells you what this handle will do when dragged or clicked with different modifiers.

Like most other tools, shape tools have certain object selection capabilities. In any shape tool, you can select an object by clicking, which works as Ctrl-clicking does with the Selector tool (i.e., ignores any grouping, **5.10**). Alt-click (select under, **5.9**) also works; Esc deselects.

Shift-click (add to selection or remove from selection) also works in shape tools, but is less useful because, currently, shape editing handles are only shown when a *single* shape is selected; multiple selected shapes are not editable by handles. This may be fixed in future versions of Inkscape.

It's not that you can only edit, for example, a rectangle in the Rectangle tool. *All* types of shapes display, and let you drag, their shape-specific handles in *any* shape tool, as well as in the Node tool (F2).

11.1.1   Shape Parameters

Numeric parameters of the selected shape—or, if none is selected, the parameters that will be used for newly created shapes—are accessible in the controls bar (**2.3**) of each shape tool. Usually, there are a few numeric entry fields and toggle buttons there, as well as a button to reset the values to the defaults (this button is placed after all other controls on the right).

Any changes made to these controls are remembered and used for the next object you draw with that tool, in the same way that the style properties you assign to an object are typically used for the next created object (**11.1.2**). For example, after you change the number of corners of a star, new stars you're drawing will have the same number of corners.

Moreover, even simply selecting a shape sends its parameters to the controls bar, where these parameters are remembered and later used for newly created shapes of this type. This makes it easy to reuse the shape parameters in a way similar to pasting styles from object to object (8.1), but without using copy and paste at all. For example, if you have in your drawing a slightly rounded star with nine corners and no randomization, simply selecting that star is sufficient for subsequent stars to be created with exactly the same parameters.

11.1.2 The Style of New Shapes

What *style* will be used for the next shape you create? You can always get an answer to this question by looking at the far right end of the controls bar. All shape tools—and, in fact, all object-creating tools—have a style swatch there displaying the fill, stroke, and opacity that will be used for the newly created objects:

Figure 11-1: This style will be used for newly created shapes.

By default, all shape tools except Spiral use the *last set style* as the style of new objects they create. This means that every time you change some style property in an object, Inkscape remembers this property and will use it for new shapes. For example, after you paint something green, all new rectangles, ellipses, stars, and so on will come up the same shade of green. Or, if you assigned 3 px stroke width with 1:1 dash pattern to some path or shape, new shapes will also have this stroke style. (This behavior becomes more complex for 3D boxes, which use not one but six different styles for the six sides of a box; see 11.3.5 for details.)

If you don't like the idea of using the most recently set style for new objects, you can change that. Double-click a shape tool's button in the toolbox on the left; this opens that tool's page in the **Inkscape Preferences** dialog (3.1.1). There, a two-way switch for the style of new objects can be either the *last used style* or a fixed *tool style* specific to this tool. In the latter case, you can press the **Take from selection** button to remember the style of the current selection as the tool's fixed style.

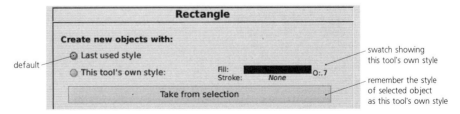

Figure 11-2: A shape tool's preferences page

For example, if you want all your rectangles to always come up black without stroke, select some black strokeless object, go to **Inkscape Preferences**, switch the **Rectangle** tool to using its **own style**, and click **Take from selection**.

11.2 Rectangles

Rectangles, boring as they may sound, are the most commonly used type of shape; you'll be hard pressed to find a design not dominated by rectangles. Inkscape strives to make creating and editing rectangles as easy and versatile as possible.

Switch to the Rectangle tool (by clicking the toolbar button on the left, or by pressing r or F4) and drag anywhere on the canvas. Drag with Ctrl to get a square or an integer-ratio (2:1, 3:1, and so on) rectangle; drag with Shift to make the starting point the rectangle's center instead of one of the corners. Ctrl and Shift can be combined.

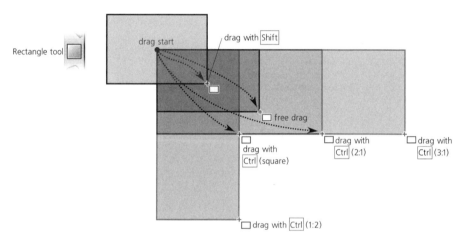

Figure 11-3: Drawing rectangles

The new rectangle displays four handles. Two are little squares, in the top-left and bottom-right corners; these are the *sizing handles*. The two others, which appear as little circles, are *rounding handles*; they are both in the top-right corner and therefore look like one handle until you drag one of them off.

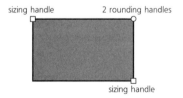

Figure 11-4: Rectangle handles

11.2.1 Sizing

With sizing handles, you can resize the rectangle simply by *dragging* any of the sides in any direction. Dragging with Ctrl, naturally, locks the rectangle's width, height, or width/height ratio by snapping the handle to its sides or to the diagonal.

NOTE *Unlike with the Selector tool, you cannot move, for example, the bottom-right sizing handle further up or further to the left than the top-left handle. The most you can do is make the rectangle zero width, zero height, or both (and therefore invisible).*

In the controls bar, a couple of numeric controls labeled **W** and **H** also control the width and height of the selected rectangle. They use the measurement unit chosen in the unit selector on the right.

Why use the sizing handles when you can just as well resize the rectangle with the Selector tool? The problem with the Selector tool is that it always scales things horizontally or vertically in the document coordinate system (i.e., along the edges of the page). In contrast, a rectangle's sizing handles scale it *along the sides* of that rectangle, even if the rectangle was rotated or skewed. The **W** and **H** values also always reflect a rectangle's intrinsic width and height, instead of the dimensions of its bounding box (which may be quite different if the rectangle is rotated or skewed).

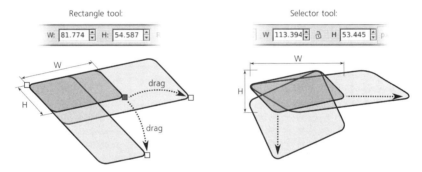

Figure 11-5: Rectangle sizing handles vs. scaling with the Selector tool

Another advantage of the sizing handles is that they always preserve the rounding radii of the rectangle (although, as we'll see shortly, this is possible with the Selector as well).

As with any other shape type, handles of rectangles can be made to snap to grids, guides, and other objects. If you start from a particularly rotated and/or skewed rectangle and enable snapping of nodes to paths, nodes, and intersections (**7.3**), it's easy to use duplication (Ctrl-D) and sizing handles to create snugly fitting, gapless compositions of axonometric rectangles, as shown in Figure 11-6.

NOTE *What snaps is the* mouse point, *not necessarily the handle itself. These two may diverge quite far if, for example, you are resizing a rectangle with Ctrl to lock its width or height. In Figure 11-6, I wanted to make the leftmost rectangle narrower but keep its height, so I moved the handle with Ctrl from A to B. However, I also wanted this rectangle to abut* *the left edge (marked by a bold line) of rectangle D. So, while dragging and without letting go of* Ctrl, *I moved the mouse cursor to point C so it snapped to the edge I needed (the actual handle was then at B), and there I released the mouse. To make this possible, enable nodes and handles as snappables and paths as snap targets (7.3).*

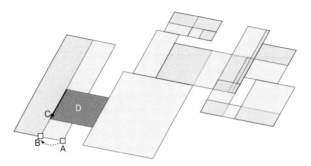

Figure 11-6: Snapping slanted rectangles to each other

11.2.2 Rounding

Now, grab one of the circular rounding handles and drag it along the side of the rectangle. All four corners of the rectangle become rounded by circular arcs; also, now you can see the second rounding handle—it remains in its original position in the corner. If *circular* rounded corners are what you need, you can leave it at that. If you want *elliptic* corners instead, move that other handle away from the corner along the other side of the rectangle:

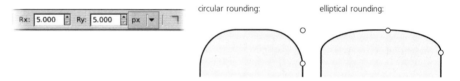

Figure 11-7: Rectangle rounding handles

NOTE *Even the circular rounding can look elliptic if the rectangle is skewed (see 23.3).*

Using the **Rx** and **Ry** numeric fields in the controls bar, you can explicitly specify both rounding radii in absolute units (chosen with the unit selector to the right). If multiple rectangles are selected, the value you type will apply to all of them (if any non-rectangles are selected, they will be ignored). The button with a corner icon on the right removes any rounding from the selected rectangles.

The maximum distance you can move the rounding handles is half the length of the corresponding rectangle size. Reaching this maximum with both rounding handles effectively turns a square into a circle and a non-square into an ellipse.

Often, in technical drawings such as schemes and diagrams, the size and shape of the rounded corners must be the same in the entire composition, even if the sizes of the rectangles are different. Inkscape makes this easy. The second of the four **Affect** buttons on the Selector toolbar (6.10), displaying two concentric rounded corners, controls whether the rounded corners are scaled when a rectangle is scaled or not. For comparison, Figure 11-8 shows a bunch of rounded rectangles scaled with this button on and off.

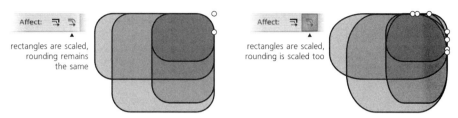

Figure 11-8: Scaling a rectangle may or may not affect the size of the rounding radii.

Here are the shortcuts for the rounding handles of a rectangle:

- Drag with Ctrl to make the rounding circular (i.e., make the other radius the same).
- Ctrl-click a handle to make the rounding circular without dragging.
- Shift-click a handle to remove rounding.

11.3 3D Boxes

A *3D box* is an object which represents a projection of a three-dimensional box (rectangular prism) onto the plane of the drawing. As such, it consists of six *sides*, and from the pure SVG viewpoint it is simply a group of six paths, each with four nodes. Inkscape, however, treats these objects in a special way, allowing you to resize and move them in their own 3D space, reposition their vanishing points, and so on.

Apart from the 3D Box tool, most other tools and commands treat a 3D box as a group. In particular, you can Ctrl-click and Ctrl-Alt-click using the Selector tool to select any side within the box (most often for changing its style), just as you select objects inside a group. Selecting inside does not destroy the box; however, you can also easily "unbox" it with the **Ungroup** (Ctrl-U) or **Object to Path** (Shift-Ctrl-C) commands. This removes any 3D-specific capabilities and leaves you with a regular group with paths inside.

11.3.1 Why Use 3D Boxes?

What makes such an apparently limited construct as a 3D box useful?

Inkscape is not planning to become a full-featured 3D application—it does not model a "true" three-dimensional space in which you would place your 3D objects. Inkscape is and always will be a two-dimensional drawing tool. However, it is often used to draw three-dimensional objects. So, to assist in such tasks, Inkscape implements a simple, 2D-oriented system of *perspective drawing*, which has remained basically unchanged since being perfected by the Renaissance artists six hundred years ago.

In Inkscape, you don't "build a 3D world"; you just create a flat drawing that represents a three-dimensional scene in a certain perspective. Inkscape's 3D Box tool is mostly a helper that makes creating such perspective drawings easier. In perspective drawing, a box is almost as important as a rectangle is for two-dimensional drawing and layout; drawing anything in correct perspective usually starts with drawing its enclosing box. So, Inkscape's 3D boxes are most often used not for their own sake, but as quick and 3D-accurate guides to lay out your perspective drawing—something to align your objects against and to inscribe them into (see Chapter 21 for an example).

On the other hand, the ease of creating and reshaping 3D boxes in Inkscape is an inspiration in itself. A style of art dominated by 3D boxes is exemplified by the About box (**Help ▶ About**) of Inkscape 0.46 in which this tool made its debut:

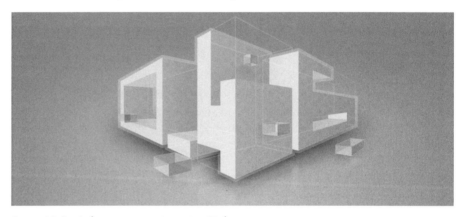

Figure 11-9: A design composition using 3D boxes

11.3.2 Drawing

To draw a 3D box, switch to the 3D Box tool (x or Shift-F4) and drag on the canvas. This draws the front side of the box in the X/Y plane; the depth of the box along the Z axis remains fixed. To switch to the Z axis, drag with Shift; this leaves the X/Y side fixed but lets you adjust the depth:

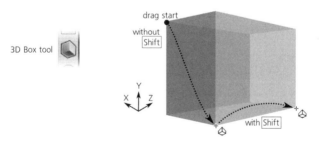

Figure 11-10: Drawing a 3D box

Once a box is created, it displays a handle in each of the eight corners as well as in the center. Also, colored lines go from the edges of the box to the vanishing points. Let's look at these controls in detail.

11.3.3 Perspective and Vanishing Points

Each 3D box exists in a certain *perspective* which is defined by three *vanishing points*, corresponding to the three spatial dimensions: X (red guides), Y (blue guides), and Z (yellow guides). Each vanishing point may be either *finite* (in which case it is an actual handle that you can drag around) or *infinite* (in which case it is just a direction toward the point which is at infinity; you can change the angle of this direction).

By default, the X and Z vanishing points are finite, located in the middle of the left and right edges of your document's page. The Y vanishing point is infinite, its direction being vertical:

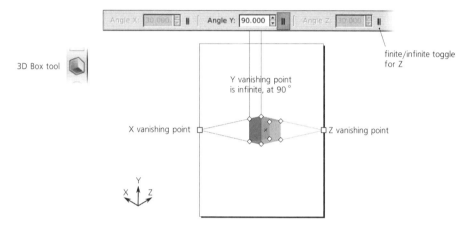

Figure 11-11: The default perspective

The finite/infinite status of the vanishing points in any dimension can be toggled by the three buttons in the controls bar of the tool. The finite vanishing points can be simply dragged freely on the canvas. The angles of the infinite ones can be adjusted numerically in the controls bar or by the shortcuts:

- [and] rotate X vanishing point directions.
- (and) rotate Y vanishing point directions.
- { and } rotate Z vanishing point directions.
- Shift-X, Shift-Y, and Shift-Z toggle the corresponding vanishing points from finite to infinite and back.

Without modifiers, these keys rotate by the angle step (the default is 15 degrees, 6.3). With Alt, they rotate so that the perspective lines are displaced by at most 1 screen pixel at the current zoom.

For example, you can make all three vanishing points infinite and rotate them at the angles of 150 (X), 90 (Y), and 30 (Z) degrees for drawing isometric boxes without any perspective foreshortening. Also, while boxes look most natural when they are located somewhere in between the three vanishing points, they are not obliged to be there; moving a box away from the sweet spot of a "natural" perspective makes it look curiously distorted which, sometimes, may be exactly what you want.

For a newly created 3D box, Inkscape will reuse the perspective of the last selected 3D box. As a result, usually multiple boxes will *share* the same perspective. The important thing to be aware of is that when you change a perspective, *all* boxes using this perspective—whether selected or not—will respond to the change:

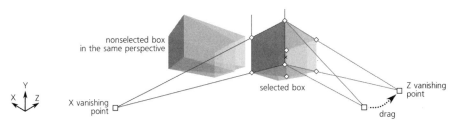

Figure 11-12: Changing a perspective by dragging a vanishing point affects all the boxes in this perspective.

If several boxes share a perspective, you can *unmerge* any one of them by dragging its finite vanishing point (with only that box selected) while holding Shift. Unlike dragging without Shift, this will affect only the selected box. Another way to unmerge a box's perspective is by moving the box object in Selector; this will drag its own set of vanishing points along with the box, without affecting any other boxes. After unmerging a box, changing the perspective of the box will only affect that box.

On the other hand, it is just as easy to *merge* two different perspectives together so they become one. To do this, select two boxes with different perspectives and move the finite vanishing points of one perspective to those of the other—they will snap and join (similar to how the gradient handles join when dragged close enough, **10.4.3**), and the boxes will now have the same perspective. (If the perspectives had any infinite vanishing points, their direction angles must be the same for perspective merging to work.)

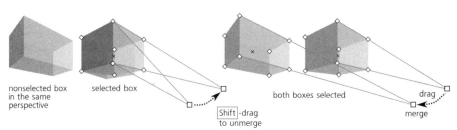

Figure 11-13: Merging and unmerging vanishing points

11.3.4 Handles

Each 3D box, when selected in any of the shape tools or the Node tool, displays eight diamond-shaped *corner handles* and an X-shaped *center handle*. Without modifiers, the four handles on the front X/Y side reshape that side, while the four others change the Z depth of the box. With Shift, however, their roles are exchanged, as shown in Figure 11-14.

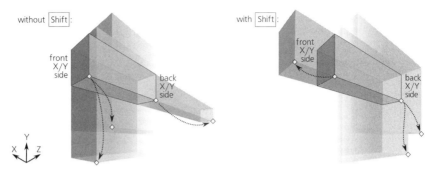

Figure 11-14: Dragging a box's corner handles with and without Shift

With Ctrl, the side-resizing handles snap to the continuations of that side's edges and its diagonal. (For depth-changing handles, Ctrl has no effect.)

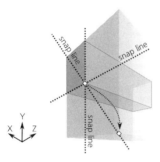

Figure 11-15: Dragging a box's corner handles with Ctrl

Similarly, dragging the central handle without modifiers moves the box in the X/Y plane, and with Ctrl it snaps it to the directions of its X and Y vanishing points as well as the bisector between them. With Shift (with or without Ctrl), the central handle moves the box along the direction toward its Z vanishing point:

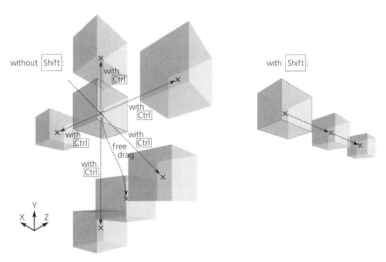

Figure 11-16: Dragging a box's center handle with and without Shift

As with rectangles, if you enable snapping of nodes to paths, nodes, and intersections (**7.3.3**), your 3D scene will feel very snappy—everything you draw or resize will eagerly join and line up, making it a pleasure to build solid gapless constructions out of many boxes. As a simple example, to build a multi-story building, draw a single-story box, then duplicate it by Ctrl-D and Ctrl-drag the central handle of the copy upward to raise it to the next level until it snaps into place:

Figure 11-17: Using Ctrl *and snapping handles to paths makes building complex scenes easy.*

11.3.5 Styling

From the viewpoint of styling, a 3D box is no different from a group of paths. By default, all six sides of a new box have different shades of blue; you can paint the entire box with some color (thereby removing any difference between the sides), or you can Ctrl-click and Ctrl-Alt-click to select any single side in it to paint it separately.

Moreover, you can even *enter* the box just as you would enter a group (**5.10**) by selecting it and pressing Ctrl-Enter; after that, you will be able to select single sides by simple clicking or by Tab and Shift-Tab. After any of these operations, the box remains a box—to remove its 3D box functionality, you would need to ungroup it (Ctrl-U) or convert it to paths (Shift-Ctrl-C, which in this case actually converts it to a *group* of paths).

Apart from color, you can apply blur (**17.1**), clips, and masks (**18.4**) to an entire box or to any of its sides individually. If you lower the opacity of a 3D box, it behaves exactly as a semitransparent group (**4.5.1**): You can see what's beneath the box, but you cannot see the hidden sides of the box itself. To be able to see the hidden sides, you need to lower the opacity of individual sides by selecting them separately, as shown in Figure 11-18.

The *z-order* of sides within a box is always automatically correct from the 3D viewpoint—that is, the sides that are supposed to be farther away from you are at the bottom, and the front sides are at the top of the z-order. However, the z-order of different boxes is not enforced by Inkscape in any way; as all other shape tools do, the 3D Box tool creates new boxes on top of the current layer's z-order (**4.3**). This means that after drawing a box, you may need to move it in the z-order stack relative to other boxes for the composition to look correct.

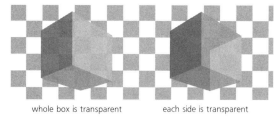

whole box is transparent   each side is transparent

Figure 11-18: Comparison of opacity on the whole box and on individual sides

For the newly created boxes, the choice between the last set style and the tool's own style (11.1.2) applies as well, but with a twist. By default, the 3D Box tool uses the last set style, but its definition of the last set is different: Unlike all other tools, it remembers the style last set on *the same side of a 3D box*, not on any object. For example, if you paint the top side of any box red, all new boxes you create after that will have their top sides (but not other sides) red.

Since a 3D scene typically assumes a single light source, this behavior makes sense: draw a single box and paint its sides as they would look when lit from, for example, the top-left corner. After that, all new boxes you create will be "lit" in a similar way.

NOTE   *The last set style is only remembered by this tool when you assign it to individual sides, not the entire box. For example, if you just select a box and paint it all red, new boxes will* not *honor this. So, supposing you want all new boxes to have stroke but no fill ("wireframe"), the easiest way to achieve this is to enter a box as a group (Ctrl-Enter), select all its sides (Ctrl-A), and assign the stroke and remove fill on all of them at once.*

The Tweak tool works on 3D boxes exactly as you would expect it to work on a bunch of paths (grouped or not). With path tweaking modes (12.6), once you distort the sides of a box, it ceases to be a 3D box and becomes a simple group. The Color Paint and Color Jitter modes, however, paint over boxes without destroying their 3D capability. It often makes sense to only enable the hue and possibly saturation channels but not lightness (8.7.3), so that you can change the colors of boxes but preserve the relative lightness and darkness of their sides for the 3D effect, as shown in Figure 9 on the color insert.

11.4 Ellipses

An ellipse is a shape that can represent not only an *ellipse* or a *circle* but also an *arc* (unclosed) or a *segment* (closed, an arc plus two radii going from the ends of the arc and meeting in the center):

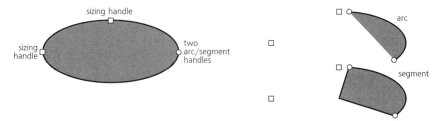

Figure 11-19: Handles on an ellipse, arc, and segment

11.4.1 Drawing

To switch to the Ellipse tool, press e or F5. Here are the ellipse drawing shortcuts:

- Dragging on the canvas creates an ellipse inscribed into the (imaginary) rectangle that your drag creates.

- With Ctrl pressed, that imaginary rectangle is first restrained to a square or an integer ratio (1:2, 2:1, and so on) and then the ellipse is inscribed into it.

- With Shift pressed, drawing starts from the center, so *one quarter* of an ellipse is inscribed into this rectangle instead of the whole ellipse. With both Ctrl and Shift pressed, you get a circle or integer-ratio ellipse starting from the center.

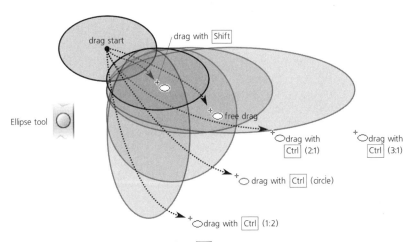

Figure 11-20: Drawing ellipses without Alt

- When Alt is pressed, the behavior of the tool changes (see Figure 11-21). Now it draws an ellipse whose *diagonal* goes from the start to the end points of your mouse drag. In other words, you may start your drag in the 10:30 o'clock point on the ellipse and end at the 4:30 point, and the ellipse is squeezed as needed to fit this diagonal.

- With Ctrl-Alt, the tool always draws a perfect circle, with its diameter stretching from the drag start to drag end. This is convenient if you need a circle with the given diameter.

- Adding Shift to Alt and Ctrl-Alt works the same as without Shift, but it will begin drawing from the center. You'll just need to replace the word "diameter" by "radius" in the above descriptions.

One way to quickly create circles of a fixed size is by Ctrl-click in the Pen tool in the Straight lines or Paraxial mode (14.1.4). The size of these circles can be set in the **Inkscape Preferences** pages for the Pen tool. Add Shift to make them twice that size, or Alt to make their size randomized.

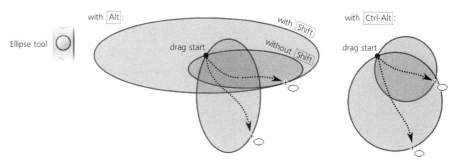

Figure 11-21: Drawing ellipses with Alt

11.4.2 Handles

Upon creation, an ellipse displays three handles: two square ones and a round one. Just like with rectangles, the square handles are the sizing handles, and the round handle is in fact two handles sitting on top of one another. In ellipses, however, the round handles are not for rounding but for turning an ellipse into an arc or segment, as we'll see shortly.

As with rectangles, the sizing handles of an ellipse change the ellipse's width and height *in ellipse's own coordinates* instead of the document coordinates. No matter how you rotate or skew your ellipse, these handles remember the position of both axes of the ellipse and let you stretch or squeeze the ellipse with respect to these intrinsic axes, always preserving the position of the center:

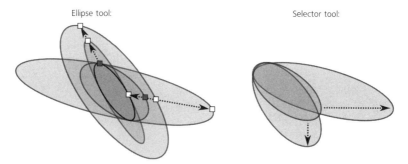

Figure 11-22: Transforming ellipses in Selector and by the sizing handles

Here are the shortcuts of the ellipse sizing handles:

- Drag with Ctrl to turn an ellipse into a circle by making the other radius the same.

- Ctrl-click a handle to turn an ellipse into a circle without dragging. (Note that the circle may appear elliptic due to skewing.)

Now let's look at the arc/segment handles (the round ones). To make a segment (an arc plus two radii), drag one or both of these handles *outside* the ellipse; to make an *arc*, drag while remaining *inside* it. Of course the handle itself always remains neither inside or outside but exactly on the edge of an ellipse;

the phrase "drag inside" refers to where your mouse goes while you have that handle grabbed. Note that the sizing handles remain functional and in the same positions as for a whole ellipse, which may be outside your arc or segment.

The controls bar of the Ellipse tool lets you specify the exact angles of an arc, turn it into a segment, and make the ellipse whole:

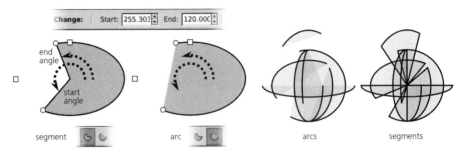

Figure 11-23: Segments and arcs

Note that unlike segments, arcs are *unclosed* shapes; in other words, the stroke only goes along the ellipse's edge but does not connect the ends of the arc. You can make this obvious if you remove the fill, leaving only stroke.

Here are the arc/segment handle shortcuts:

- With [Ctrl] pressed, snap the handle to angle increments (15 degrees by default, **6.3**) when dragging.
- [Shift]-click a handle to turn an arc or segment into a whole ellipse.

Remember that like all other shape parameters, start and end angles of an ellipse are remembered and reused for newly created shapes. It may sometimes be a surprise when you intend to draw an ellipse and get a narrow pie slice instead.

11.5 Stars and Polygons

The Star tool (the [*] key or [Shift-F9]) creates two slightly different kinds of centrally symmetric shapes—polygons and stars. Despite the simplicity of the idea, this is one of the most complex tools in Inkscape, endlessly entertaining and perfect for wowing your friends.

A *polygon* is just a number of points located equidistant on an imaginary circle and connected by straight line segments. An Inkscape polygon has one diamond-shaped handle used to scale and rotate it.

A *star* is a much more interesting object: It contains two sets of equidistant points on two imaginary concentric circles, with the outline of the star zig-zagging back and forth between points on the inner and outer circles. Using a star's two handles, you can vary the diameters of the circles and rotate the circles relative to one another around their common center, which produces a fascinating variety of intricate symmetric shapes.

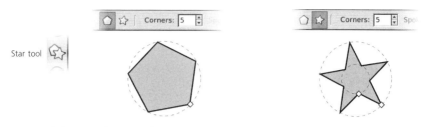

Figure 11-24: A polygon and a star

11.5.1 Drawing

Before you draw a new shape, decide whether you want it to be a polygon or a star by pressing one of the toggle buttons on the controls bar, and choose the number of corners (convex vertices) in the numeric control. For example, a polygon with three corners is an equilateral triangle, and will have three nodes if converted to path; a star with three corners, however, will have six nodes. You can always change the polygon/star type and the number of corners in an existing shape, too—just select it and edit the values.

NOTE   *The number of corners can range from 3 to 1000, but setting this too high may slow down Inkscape considerably unless you use the Outline mode (3.11).*

Drawing a shape is, again, as simple as dragging your mouse upon the canvas. A star or polygon is always drawn starting from its center. There's only one keyboard shortcut: Dragging with Ctrl snaps the angle of one of the shape's corners relative to its center to 15-degree increments.

11.5.2 Handles

A polygon's single handle can only be used to scale and rotate the polygon—something you can do just as well by transforming it in Selector. The two handles of a star are much more interesting.

First, by moving one of them to or from the center of the star, you are changing the ratio of the diameters of the two circles on which the corners of the star lie. This ratio is called the *spoke ratio* and is also adjustable as a numeric parameter (disabled for polygons) in the controls bar:

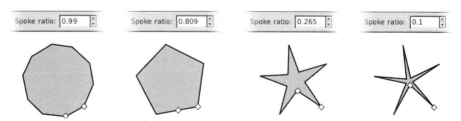

Figure 11-25: Adjusting the spoke ratio of a 5-vertex star

You can even move what was originally the inner handle farther away from the center than the outer one. The control will still show a ratio less than 1 because it always divides the smaller radius by the larger, regardless of which of them was initially inner and which was outer.

Second, the inner handle (initially on the inner circle) can be moved *tangentially* (i.e., along an arc around the star center) to skew the star's vertices. (Rotating the outer handle simply rotates the entire star.)

Figure 11-26: Moving the inner handle of a star tangentially

Drag the inner handle with Ctrl if you want to keep the vertices strictly radial (no tangential displacement), or Ctrl-click it to remove any existing tangential skew without dragging.

11.5.3 Rounding

Many fascinating effects with stars and polygons can be achieved by *rounding* them. A star's rounding is different from the rounded corners of a rectangle; with a star or polygon, not only the corners lose sharpness but all of the the star's sides bend into elegant Bézier curves:

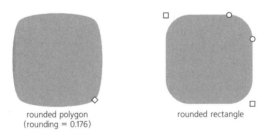

rounded polygon
(rounding = 0.176)

rounded rectangle

Figure 11-27: A rounded 4-sided polygon compared to a rounded rectangle

As you can see, a rounded square has straight line segments between circular or elliptic rounded corners, whereas a rounded polygon or star has no straight lines at all—all its segments become Bézier curves.

The **Rounded** numeric control of the Star tool is the ratio of the length of the Bézier handles (12.1.4) to the length of the polygon/star side which these handles affect. This parameter can be negative, which reverses the direction of tangents. Typically, values between 0.2 and 0.4 give the most natural-looking results. Negative or too high positive values tend to result in twisting, looping, and self-intersections. By playing with handle positions in variously rounded stars, you can get an infinite variety of beautiful shapes:

Figure 11-28: Fun with rounded stars

Apart from setting the numeric rounding parameter on the controls bar, rounding can be done by Shift-dragging any of the handles tangentially. Counterclockwise rotation of a handle around the star's center results in positive rounding; clockwise rotation makes it negative. Shift-clicking a handle removes any rounding.

If you want the outer corners of a star to be sharp but the inner ones smoothed, or vice versa, try creating an offset path (12.4) from the star.

11.5.4 Randomizing

Yet another way to make a star more interesting is by *randomizing* it. Randomization moves all vertices of a star or polygon in random directions and by random distances. If the star was rounded, randomization preserves the smoothness of all vertices.

The overall force of the effect is controlled by the **Randomized** parameter in the controls bar, which can take positive and negative values. As you change this value—or simply Alt-drag a star's handle tangentially—the direction of random displacement for each node remains the same, and only the distance changes; negative values simply move the vertices in the opposite directions. In other words, the star remains randomized in the same way but to a different extent.

On the contrary, when you simply drag a randomized star's handle to scale or reshape it, or when you draw a new star with nonzero randomization, the shape trembles and jitters, abruptly changing the random displacements for all nodes (in mathematical terms, *reseeding* the randomization) on every slightest move of your mouse. So, if you want your star to get randomized differently by with the same overall amplitude, simply drag any of its handles slightly:

same randomization seed, different levels:

same randomization levels, different seeds:

Figure 11-29: Randomizing stars

What are randomized stars good for? Randomness is one of the fundamental forces of nature, and randomness in design is a great way to make shapes livelier and less rigid. Your artistic sense and experience will tell you where and how much randomness is appropriate. In Inkscape, there are many sources of artistic randomness; you can easily shuffle the positions of objects (**7.5.1**), create patterns with random placement, scaling, and rotation (**10.8.2**), as well as randomly displace nodes in paths to distort them (**12.6.6**). Still, randomized stars are unique in how fast and easy it is to draw a shape where intrinsic symmetry emphasizes its randomness.

Slight randomization makes a star more humane, sometimes outright funny; strong randomization produces a variety of wild and unpredictable shapes. Messy hairballs, rounded amoeba-like ink blotches, fantastic landscapes at the edge of a large star with many vertices and spoke ratio close to 1—all this and more is possible with star randomization. As an example, Figure 11-30 shows a star with 500 vertices, not randomized (left) and randomized by just 0.005 (right) to look more naturally hairy and to get rid of the moire pattern that mars the star without randomization.

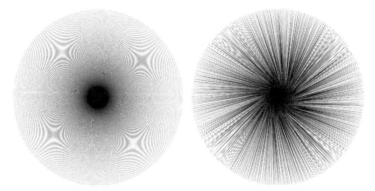

Figure 11-30: A 500-vertex star without randomization (left) and randomized by 0.005 (right)

As another example, here are randomly scattered and unclumped pentagons, rounded at 0.28 and randomized at 0.15, looking very much like pebbles on a beach:

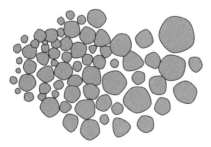

*Figure 11-31: Pebbles: an unclumped (**7.5.1**) scattering of rounded and randomized pentagons*

11.6 Spirals

The Spiral tool (the $\boxed{\text{i}}$ key or $\boxed{\text{F9}}$) creates another simple but versatile shape—a *concentric spiral*. While not quite as exciting as the star, it is sometimes very useful.

A spiral, like a star, is drawn from the center. Dragging with $\boxed{\text{Ctrl}}$, as usual, snaps the drag point (the outer end of the spiral) to 15-degree increments (**6.3**).

Unlike all other shape tools, the Spiral tool by default uses its own style for new spirals—no fill, black stroke—instead of the last used style (**11.1.2**).

Once drawn, a spiral displays two handles on both ends of the line. Simply dragging these handles circularly rolls the spiral in or out, from the inside or from the outside. In this way, you can, for example, create a spiral with only one turn.

The **Turns** parameter in the controls bar reflects how many full circles you will need to do to reach the outer end of the spiral. The maximum number of spiral turns is 1000. The inner end is controlled by the **Inner radius** value, which shows the percentage of the total turns at which the spiral starts (Figure 11-32). For example, an **Inner radius** of 0 means that the spiral starts right from the center; 0.5 means that it starts half-way between the center and the outer end.

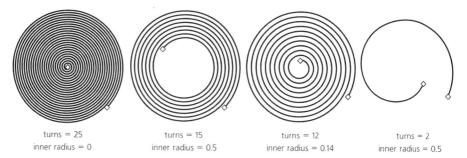

| turns = 25 | turns = 15 | turns = 12 | turns = 2 |
| inner radius = 0 | inner radius = 0.5 | inner radius = 0.14 | inner radius = 0.5 |

Figure 11-32: Adjusting turns and inner radius

The **Divergence** of a spiral is the parameter controlling whether a spiral's winding is equispaced throughout (divergence = 1), becomes denser towards its center (divergence > 1), or becomes denser towards its periphery (divergence < 1). You can change this parameter either numerically at the controls bar, or by $\boxed{\text{Alt}}$-dragging the inner handle up or down:

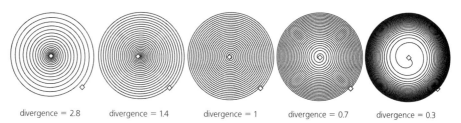

| divergence = 2.8 | divergence = 1.4 | divergence = 1 | divergence = 0.7 | divergence = 0.3 |

Figure 11-33: Adjusting divergence

Other shortcuts for the outer handle:

- Shift-drag to scale or rotate around the center (no rolling on unrolling, same behavior as when drawing the spiral).
- Alt-drag to lock radius while rolling or unrolling (i.e., the entire spiral becomes denser or sparser without changing its overall size).

Inner handle shortcuts:

- Alt-drag vertically to adjust divergence.
- Alt-click to reset divergence to the default of 1.
- Shift-click to reset the inner radius to 0 (i.e., move the inner handle all the way to the center).

When does it make sense to use spirals? A spiral fills in a given space with uniform concentric pattern—something that may not be easy to achieve manually or by any other tools. As such, it may well become a carrier or guide for other objects, such as markers (9.5.1), dash patterns (9.4), text on path (15.2.3), or live path effects (13.1). Also, like the Ellipse tool, the Spiral tool can be convenient for creating curves with smoothly varying curvature; unlike a plain Bézier curve, an arc or a spiral can be made shorter or longer by dragging a handle *along* the curve without affecting its shape.

12

EDITING PATHS

In most vector drawings, paths constitute an overwhelming majority of all objects. That's why a familiarity with paths is so important—without it, you cannot really say you know how to work in a vector editor.

Inkscape provides a versatile selection of tools, commands, and effects that work on paths. We will start with the basics of SVG paths and the traditional path tools whose analogs you may have already seen in other software. Then, in the second half of this chapter and in the next one, we will look at the advanced Inkscape techniques for path editing that are often more efficient—and almost always a lot more fun to use. You may find, for example, the Tweak tool (12.6) so easy and natural that you will rarely want to resort to the more technical and low-level Node tool (12.5). Still, it is important that you know what a path consists of and are able, when necessary, to directly manipulate path nodes, as this is one of the cornerstones of vector graphics of any kind.

12.1 The Anatomy of a Path

A path is a sequence of *nodes* (points) connected by straight or curved *segments* (Figure 12-1). Each node may have either one neighboring segment (if it's an end node) or two (if it's a middle node); SVG does not allow you to have branching paths with more than two segments joined at the same node.

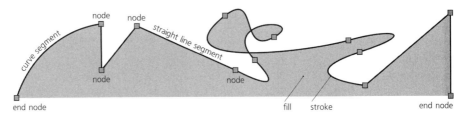

Figure 12-1: Path = nodes + segments

The length of a path is not limited; it may have anywhere from two to many thousands of nodes (although paths that are too complex are slow to render and therefore should be avoided).

NOTE *It is legal to have a path with one or even zero nodes, but such a path is invisible.*

With a path, you can at least approximate (and in many cases, reproduce exactly) any conceivable shape, form, or figure. Depending on the shape you need and the required precision, in the worst case you'll just have to use many densely positioned nodes.

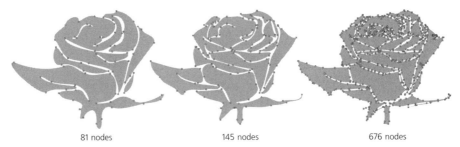

Figure 12-2: The same figure can be roughly approximated with a few nodes or reproduced more precisely with more nodes.

12.1.1 Subpaths

In a path, a pair of nodes that are adjacent in sequence may not be connected by a segment. This produces a gap in the path, and each such gap divides the path into disconnected parts called *subpaths*, as shown in Figure 12-3.

A path without any gaps is said to consist of a single subpath. Any subpath, just like a piece of rope, can be *open* (with two loose ends, called *end nodes*) or *closed* (tied into a loop, so that its end nodes are one and the same node).

In many respects, subpaths look and behave just like separate paths. You can always convert subpaths of a path into independent path objects by using the **Break Apart** command in the **Path** menu. The opposite command, **Combine**, converts several selected paths into subpaths of a single path.

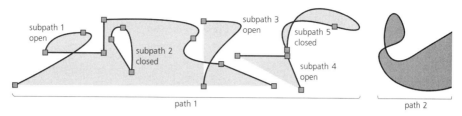

Figure 12-3: Subpaths are groups of connected nodes within a path.

When combining paths with different styles, you will lose the styles of all but the topmost (in z-order) selected path—because a single path, with no matter how many subpaths, can only have a single style. However, no path data will be lost or added: If you combine and then break apart any number of paths, their nodes will be exactly the same as before.

Every subpath has a *direction*—that is, its nodes are always ordered from start to end. In a closed subpath, the start node and the end node are the same node; in an open subpath, start and end nodes are different. Usually, the direction of a subpath does not matter, but it determines positioning of the start and end markers (**9.5**) and text on a path (**15.2.3**). The direction may also affect the fill of the path via the winding rule (**12.1.2**). Use **Path ▸ Reverse** (Shift-R) to flip the direction of the selected path or paths.

12.1.2 Filling Paths

No matter what you use to fill your path—solid color, gradient, or pattern (**8.1.1**)—there are several important things to be aware of.

Fill always stops at the path itself—that is, at the center line of the path's stroke, if it has any. Closed subpaths that do not intersect themselves or other subpaths are simply filled on the inside. Open subpaths are filled as if there's a straight line segment between the end nodes of the subpath:

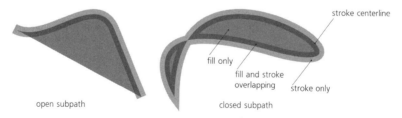

Figure 12-4: Filling open and closed subpaths

NOTE *Remember that this straight line is not part of the path; it is not stroked and you cannot, for example, bend it with the Node tool. If, when editing an open nonstroked path, you run into a straight line segment that refuses to be edited as you expect it to, most likely it's not really a segment but simply an edge of the fill. Close the subpath (12.5.4) to edit it without limitations.*

When a path intersects itself or when one subpath is completely inside another, the decision on whether to fill some area depends on two factors: the *directions* of the subpaths surrounding the area and the *fill rule* of the path. The fill rule is a style property that can take one of two values, nonzero or evenodd, as set by one of the two toggle buttons in the **Fill and Stroke** dialog (see Figure 8-2):

- With the fill rule value of evenodd, holes and loops are always left unfilled, except when you have a hole within a hole; then the inner hole becomes an island of fill.

- The fill rule value of nonzero means that a loop or hole is filled only if its boundary is counterdirected relative to the outer path and is empty if they go in the same direction.

With the fill rule of nonzero, those loops and holes that are filled are therefore invisible unless the path is stroked. Usually they are not a problem, but sometimes you may want to get rid of them. The easiest way to do that is to select that one path and use the **Path ▸ Union** command (Ctrl-+). Unioning a path with itself removes all subpaths that do not affect its fill.

There's no way to reverse the direction of a single subpath inside a path. If you need to do that, you'll have to **Break Apart** the path (**12.1.1**), reverse one of the resulting paths, and **Combine** them back into a single path.

12.1.3 Stroking Paths

The *stroke* of a path is a strip of paint that goes along the path itself, so that the path marks the *centerline* of the stroke. The stroke is painted on top of the fill, if there is any. There are many style properties that affect the look of a stroke; they are covered in great detail in Chapter **9**.

The **Path ▸ Stroke to Path** command (Ctrl-Alt-C) converts the stroke of the selected path into fill. In other words, it replaces it with a new path whose *fill* looks exactly the same as the original path's *stroke*, honoring all the join, cap, miter, and dash properties of that stroke. The stroke paint of the original becomes the fill paint of the new path, whereas the original path's fill is discarded. If the original path had markers (**9.5**), the result will be a group where the stroke converted to path is grouped with markers that are now separate objects.

7 nodes   49 nodes

Figure 12-5: Converting stroke to path

12.1.4 Bézier Curves

As already mentioned, segments—parts of paths between the nodes—can be either straight or curved. Now, let's have a closer look at those curved segments, called *Bézier curves* after Pierre Bézier (1910–1999), a French engineer who was the first to use them in design.

A Bézier curve is completely determined by the position of four points, two of which are the *nodes* and two of which are the *handles,* or controls. The curve itself is always completely inside the quadrilateral of these four points. In the Node tool (12.5), each of the handles is connected with its node by a straight line. These *handle lines* are always tangential to the curve at the corresponding node:

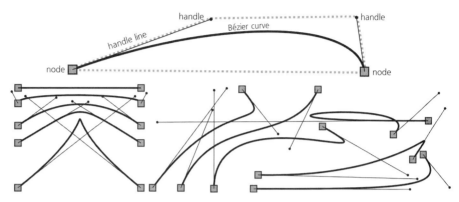

Figure 12-6: Bézier curves

Note that in a path, if a node is between two Bézier curve segments, it will have two handles connected to it, one for each adjacent segment.

The way a Bézier curve reacts to moving its handles is hard to verbalize, but you will quickly get a feel for it once you experiment a little. A Bézier curve may be indistinguishably close to a circular arc, but it may also have sharp bends, almost cusps; it may self-intersect or be perfectly straight when the handles are fully retracted (i.e., coincide with their nodes).

Of course, for all its versatility, not many shapes are possible with a *single* Bézier curve. When building a path to approximate something (e.g., when manually tracing over a bitmap, 18.8.2), experience will tell you how far you can reach with the next Bézier curve and where best to place the next node. Forcing a path to more closely approximate some real-life shape usually involves subdividing its Béziers by adding nodes and adjusting their handles. In contrast, simplifying a path, either manually or with the **Simplify** command (12.3), usually reduces the number of nodes and results in longer Bézier curves.

12.2 Boolean Operations

British mathematician George Boole (1815–1864) didn't specialize in geometry. He invented his *Boolean algebra* for dealing with the logical values of "true" and "false." However, it was later discovered that the same concepts make perfect sense for various other mathematical objects—such as sets or arbitrary geometric shapes.

All Boolean operations are listed in the **Path** menu; they can also be accessed by keyboard shortcuts derived from the symbols of the corresponding mathematical operations. Some of them require exactly two objects to be selected; others will work on any number of selected shapes. All of them will accept not only paths but also text objects and shapes (except 3D boxes), automatically converting them to paths. If a Boolean operation fails (for example, due to a wrong number or type of selected operands), it will explain the reason for its failure in the status bar.

Union (Ctrl-+)

The *union* of two or more paths creates a path that covers with its fill every point that any of the original paths covered. As such, it joins any number of paths into a single path, giving it the style of the bottommost selected object:

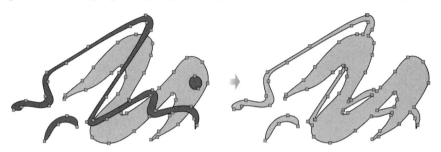

Figure 12-7: Unioning paths

If the paths do not overlap at all, the result will be exactly the same as for **Path ▸ Combine** (12.1.1). However, if the paths do overlap, this command, unlike **Combine**, will never create any holes; it will create new nodes where the paths intersect and remove any parts of the path that would end up inside the fill of the resulting path.

For example, if a small circle is completely inside a bigger circle, a **Union** of these two circles will simply remove the smaller inner circle. If you want the smaller circle to become a hole in the larger one, use either **Difference** or **Combine**. The **Union** command makes sense even for a single selected path, as it allows you to quickly clean up the path of any inner parts that do not affect the fill.

Difference (Ctrl--)

The *difference* of two paths creates a path whose fill covers all points that were covered by the bottom (in z-order) path but not the top one—in other words, it *subtracts* the top from the bottom. The result has the style of the bottom object:

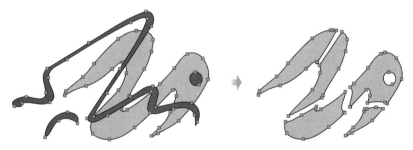

Figure 12-8: Subtracting a path from another path

If the paths do not overlap, **Path ▸ Difference** simply deletes the top path; if the top path completely overlays the bottom path, the result will be empty (objects get deleted and nothing is selected). This command is the primary tool for creating holes and erasing the parts of paths that you don't need.

NOTE *The Calligraphic pen (14.3) unions the new path it creates with the selected one when you draw with* Shift *and subtracts from it when you draw with* Alt.

Intersection (Ctrl-*)

The *intersection* of two or more paths creates a path whose fill covers only those points that were covered by *all* original paths. It uses the style of the bottommost selected object for its resulting path:

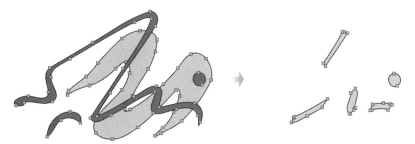

Figure 12-9: Intersecting paths

If at least two of the selected paths do not overlap (i.e., their intersection is empty), **Path ▸ Intersection** deletes all paths without creating anything. This command works similarly to setting a clipping path (18.4), except that a clipping path is nondestructive and works on any object, not just on paths. On the other hand, **Intersection** allows you to intersect any number of paths at once.

Exclusion (Ctrl-^)

The exclusion of two overlapping paths creates a path whose fill covers the points that were covered by *only one* of the original paths. It uses the style of the bottom object for its resulting path:

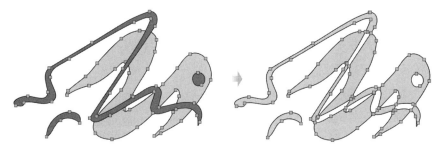

Figure 12-10: Excluding a path from another path

When the two paths do not overlap, the result of **Path ▸ Exclusion** is exactly the same as that of **Path ▸ Combine**. When they do overlap, the result *looks* exactly like a **Combine**, but the actual path is different: It has new nodes in the points where the outlines of the original paths intersect, whereas **Combine** creates no new nodes.

Division (⌃Ctrl-/)

A *division* of two paths cuts the bottom path into separate pieces by the edges of the top path, deleting the top path:

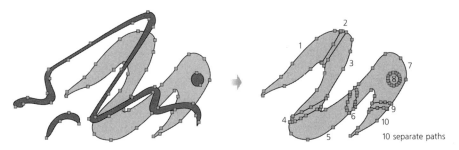

Figure 12-11: *Dividing a path by another path*

AI *This is the closest Inkscape has to the Knife tool in Adobe Illustrator: Use the Pen or Pencil tools (Chapter 14) to draw a cut line over the path you want to cut, Shift-click that path, and select* **Path ▸ Division** *to cut it.*

Cut Path (Ctrl-Alt-/)

This operation is similar to **Division**. The main difference is that **Cut Path** does not create any new nodes or segments along the cut line, thus leaving the resulting paths unclosed. It also removes any fill of the path being cut. It is natural to use **Division** for slicing filled paths and **Cut Path** for cutting stroked paths without fill:

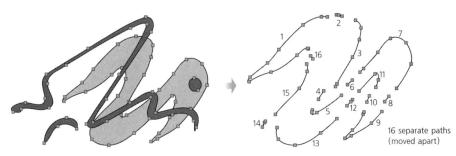

Figure 12-12: *Cut Path is similar to Division.*

12.3 Simplifying

A very important operation on paths is *simplifying*. When you simplify a path (**Path ▸ Simplify** or Ctrl-L), Inkscape attempts to redraw that path using fewer nodes, ironing out smaller details but preserving the large-scale features and the overall shape. If this description sounds a bit vague, it's because the operation itself is not entirely deterministic; usually, it is difficult to accurately predict the result of simplifying before you actually try it. Even the reduction of the number of nodes is not guaranteed, although common.

Despite that, it is a very common operation and a true lifesaver for certain styles of artistic drawing. In technical drawing, on the other hand, it is rarely useful, if only because it considers any sharp corners in a path to be "defects" that should be smoothed out.

One effect that you can almost always count on is that if your path has nodes that can be deleted without *any* change in the shape of the path, they *will* get deleted by simplifying. This includes any nodes you have added with the Node tool (12.5.3) or by the **Add Nodes** extension (13.3) but never moved from their initial positions.

Path simplification is similar to gradient simplification in the Gradient tool, also accessible by Ctrl-L (10.5.1). Gradient simplification, too, removes any gradient stops that you added but didn't yet move from their initial positions.

Any simplification operation uses a certain *force*. Weak simplification changes the path just a little, removing only the most obviously redundant nodes. Stronger simplification will change the path more and smooth out larger bumps in it.

The default force used when you press Ctrl-L *once* can be set in the **Simplification threshold** value on the **Misc** tab of the **Inkscape Preferences** dialog. The default is 0.002; anything greater than 0.01 is probably too strong for most cases. If you change it at all, consider lowering this value, because it is actually the *minimum* simplification force; you can always temporarily strengthen your **Simplify** command, raising this value without going into the **Inkscape Preferences** dialog.

How to make **Simplify** stronger? Just press Ctrl-L several times in quick succession. Each invocation of the command will increase the force a little, provided it happened less than half a second after the previous invocation. With such *accelerated simplification*, you can apply exactly the amount of simplification you need for each path. If the first keystroke didn't smooth the path enough, just keep pressing Ctrl-L, and it will gradually pick up. If you wait more than half a second, though, the simplification force is reset back to the default value from **Inkscape Preferences**.

Figure 12-13: Simplifying paths

Figure 12-13 shows some examples of how simplification affects paths (see also Figure 12-2, which was produced by gradual simplification of the most node-rich rose silhouette). As you can see, apart from reducing the number of nodes and ironing out small details, this operation melts sharp corners and curves straight lines, producing a natural and often artistically engaging kind of distortion.

12.4   Offsetting

Offsetting a path means expanding or contracting it in such a way that each point moves perpendicular to the path in that point. Offsetting inward is called *insetting*, and offsetting outward is called *outsetting*. Imagine that your path is an island; then, outsetting means enlarging it by moving every point of the shoreline the same number of steps seaward, and insetting makes it smaller by allowing the sea to encroach inland by the same number of steps everywhere:

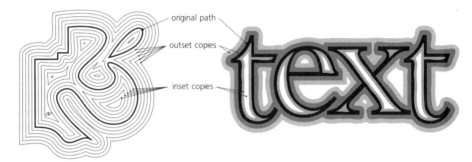

Figure 12-14: Offsetting paths

To inset the selected path or paths, press either Ctrl-((inset by 2 px), or Alt-((inset by 1 screen pixel at the current zoom), or Shift-Alt-((inset by 10 screen pixels). To outset a path, use the) key with the same modifiers. On most keyboards, the 9 and 0 are on the same keys as (and), so the digits will work the same as the parentheses.

Offsetting is used in situations where you want to make a path "bolder" or "thinner" without changing its overall shape. This is useful for shadows, outlines, halos, bevels, and the like. (Sometimes, instead of outsetting you can simply set a wide enough stroke on the path, colored the same as its fill.)

If you outset and inset a path several times, it becomes distorted in a characteristic way, similar but distinct from the distortion of simplification (12.3). Such distortion welds together parts of a path, rounding corners, smoothing the intersections, and fusing together close brush strokes within a path. For example, try to union all brush strokes of a drawing, and do a few inset/outset cycles on it to make it appear more natural and worn-down, as shown in Figure 12-15.

Offsetting, just like simplification, is a destructive operation: You cannot restore the exact original path except by undoing it. (For one thing, offsetting an open path always closes it.) However, Inkscape also has two dynamic object types, *linked offset* and *dynamic offset*, which store the exact original path and let you adjust the amount of offsetting without accumulating distortion (13.2).

Figure 12-15: Melting complex paths with repeated offsetting

Also, while the **Inset** and **Outset** commands apply the same offset distance to the entire path, it is also possible to inset or outset just one part of a path (for example, one tip of a calligraphic brush stroke) using the Grow and Shrink modes of the Tweak tool (12.6.4).

12.5   The Node Tool

Like all of Inkscape, the Node tool—the second button from the top in the main toolbar, also accessible by pressing [n] or [F2]—strives to make simple things easy and hard things possible. This is probably the most complex of all the Inkscape tools; in any event, the number of keyboard and mouse shortcuts available in the Node tool is bigger than in any other tool. You certainly don't have to know all of its tricks in order to use Inkscape efficiently, but you do have to know the basics.

12.5.1   Path Display

After you switch to the Node tool any single selected path displays its *nodes* as little gray squares, diamonds, or circles (depending on the type of each node, 12.5.5).

NOTE   *As of version 0.47, the biggest limitation of the Node tool is that it can only edit one selected path at a time. If you select two or more paths, they don't display their nodes and are not editable. You can, however, edit multiple subpaths of a path simultaneously.*

Some or all of the nodes can be selected, in which case they become blue and slightly larger. *Handles* of the Bézier curves (12.1.4) are only visible for selected nodes and their neighbors. Even then, these handles, when not needed, can be suppressed by a button on the controls bar, as shown in Figure 12-16.

The selected path itself is not, by default, visualized in any special way when in the Node tool. Normally, you just watch the path's stroke and/or fill, which update live in response to editing the nodes. Sometimes, however, your path is too transparent, or blurred, or has some path effect applied; in that case, you can ask Inkscape to highlight the actual path with a red line by toggling another button on the controls bar (Figure 12-17).

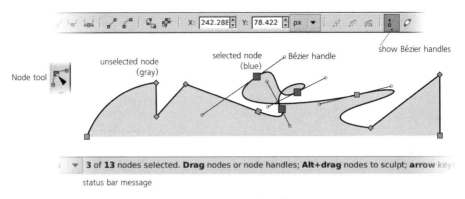

Figure 12-16: Nodes and Bézier handles in the Node tool

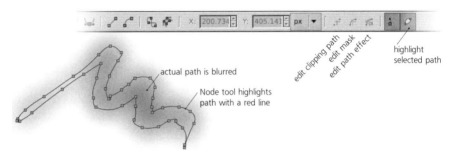

Figure 12-17: Path highlighting in the Node tool

Apart from the path itself, some objects may have other paths associated with them that are invisible but affect the way the path looks. You can edit them with the Node tool, too. There are three toggle buttons that switch the tool to editing the clipping path (green, **18.4**), mask path (blue, **18.4**), and a path associated with a path effect (dark green, **13.1.2**).

While the Node tool is specifically for editing paths, every object that has some kind of editing handles will display them when selected in this tool. This means you can use the Node tool to, for example, round your rectangles (**11.2.2**), reshape your stars (**11.5.2**), edit gradients (**10.4**), or change the dimensions of a flowed text (**15.2.2**).

12.5.2 Selecting Nodes

Like so many other things in Inkscape, the nodes of a path can be *selected* when in the Node tool. Not surprisingly, most methods of node selection are quite similar to those for object selection (Chapter **5**).

NOTE   *Unlike selected gradient handles (10.4.2), selected path nodes cannot be styled. Only the path as a whole can have a style, not its nodes.*

Before we look into selecting nodes in a path, it is worth noting that the tool can also select *objects* (remember that object selection is common to all tools and commands in Inkscape). So, in the Node tool you can use some of the shortcuts you know from the Selector tool: Clicking selects an object (ignoring grouping),

Shift-clicking adds to selection, and Alt-clicking selects under just as the Selector does (5.9).

To select a *single node*, just click on it. The node becomes blue and slightly larger than a gray unselected node. Shift-click *adds* a node to the node selection; selected nodes need not be adjacent or be all on the same subpath. *Rubber band* selection (dragging a rectangle around nodes, compare 5.7) also works; dragging with Shift adds nodes inside the rubber band to the selection.

If you click a path segment between two nodes, both nodes get selected. Clicking an empty space away from the path deselects any nodes, as does pressing Esc.

The convenient Tab and Shift-Tab keys, which in the Selector tool go to the next or previous object, here go to the next or previous node on the path. When the last node is reached, pressing Tab jumps to the first node; when the first node is reached, pressing Shift-Tab jumps to the last node. (Among other things, pressing Tab a couple times is a quick way to find out the direction of a (sub)path without changing the document in any way.)

Also like in the Selector tool, Ctrl-A selects all nodes in the path. However, if you already have some nodes selected in one of the subpaths, then Ctrl-A selects all nodes *in that subpath only* (much like in Selector, where Ctrl-A selects objects within the current layer only). To always select all nodes in all subpaths, use Ctrl-Alt-A. The ! key *inverts* selection (selects what was not selected and vice versa) within the subpaths with selected nodes; Alt-! does the same in the entire path.

Yet another method of selecting nodes is unique to the Node tool. As you hover your mouse over a node, you can *expand* or *contract* the selection by rotating your mouse wheel or pressing the Page Up and Page Down keys. Rotating the wheel *up* one notch or pressing Page Up adds the *closest* unselected node to the selection; rotating the wheel *down* one notch or pressing Page Down deselects the *farthest* selected node.

To determine the "closest" and "farthest" nodes, Inkscape measures the direct spatial distance from each node to the mouse pointer. However, if you press Ctrl while rotating the wheel or pressing Page Up or Page Down, the distance will be calculated *along the path* and the selection will be limited to the subpath over which you are hovering.

12.5.3 Deleting and Creating Nodes

Deleting any number of selected nodes is as easy as pressing Delete or Backspace or clicking the "minus" button on the controls bar.

Deleting an end node of a subpath makes the subpath shorter, but you cannot open a closed subpath by deleting nodes; you'll need to *break* it as described in 12.5.4.

When deleting mid nodes (those between other nodes), Inkscape replaces each group of adjacent nodes being deleted with a single Bézier curve segment. In most cases, this is not possible to do without distortion, although Inkscape will try to minimize that distortion: It will adjust the handles on the remaining nodes so that the new Bézier segment runs as close as possible to the part of the path it replaces. So, deleting some nodes in a path often works like a local **Simplify** command (**12.3**).

Sometimes, however, you don't want a new Bézier to bulge out all the way to replace the nodes you're deleting, or you want to avoid any change to the handles of the remaining nodes. In that case, simply press Ctrl-Delete or Ctrl-Backspace:

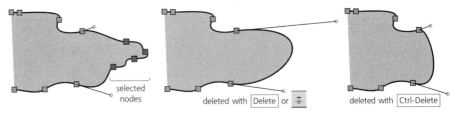

Figure 12-18: Deleting nodes

Unlike deletion, *inserting* new nodes is always possible at any point of a path without changing its shape. Simply double-click or Ctrl-Alt-click on the path (i.e., on the center line of stroke or the edge of fill) where you want the new node to be. A new node is inserted, and the handles of its neighbor nodes are automatically adjusted so that the shape of the path remains unchanged:

Figure 12-19: Creating a node by clicking

There is another node creation method which does not require mouse clicks. Simply select two or more adjacent nodes and press Insert (or click the "plus" button on the controls bar) to insert a new node in the *middle* of each adjacent pair (see Figure 9-11). Since the new nodes are then added to the selection, this is a quick way to multiply the number of nodes on a path; for example, if you start with two nodes and press Insert 8 times, your path will have 257 nodes ($2^8 + 1$). This is very similar to creating new gradient stops by pressing Insert (**10.5.1**).

Yet another approach is *duplicating* nodes. With any number of nodes selected, press Shift-D; for each selected node, this will create and select a duplicate node at the same point. Here's how it will look if you now move away the duplicated nodes by pressing →:

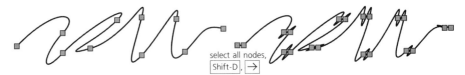

Figure 12-20: Duplicating nodes

The $\boxed{\text{Shift-D}}$ method is especially useful for continuing an open subpath by duplicating and moving away its end node. For example, if you select an end node adjacent to a straight line segment (i.e., without a Bézier handle), you can easily "draw" with line segments by multiple $\boxed{\text{Shift-D}}$ followed by arrow keys.

12.5.4 Joining and Breaking

Often, you will switch to the Node tool in order to join or break subpaths or to make an open subpath closed or vice versa. (Since the Node tool cannot yet edit more than one path, you cannot use it to join different paths unless you first combine them, 12.1.1.)

To *join* two end nodes, first select them. These can be the end nodes of the same open subpath, in which case joining them will close that subpath; or, they can belong to different subpaths, in which case you will join these subpaths into a single subpath.

There are two ways to join, corresponding to the two join buttons on the Node controls bar. The first method, available by the **Join Nodes** button or by pressing $\boxed{\text{Shift-J}}$, actually moves and joins the two end nodes into a single node located half-way between their original positions. The second method—the **Join with Segment** button—leaves the end nodes where they are but adds a new path segment between them. If you want to use the first method but don't want one of the end nodes to move, hover your mouse over it to lock its position while pressing $\boxed{\text{Shift-J}}$:

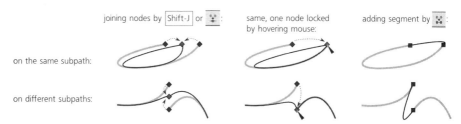

Figure 12-21: Joining nodes and inserting segments

Similarly, there are two ways to *break* a path. For the first method, select one or more nonend nodes and click the **Break Nodes** button or press $\boxed{\text{Shift-B}}$. This will duplicate each selected node but without connecting it to the original node, so the path will be broken at each selected node point. For the second method, select two adjacent nonend nodes, and click the **Delete Segment** button to delete the segment between them:

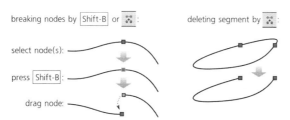

Figure 12-22: Breaking nodes and deleting segments

12.5.5 Node Types

A mid node may have one or two handles attached to it, one for each side. Inkscape supports several *node types* which behave differently when you drag one of these handles or the node itself.

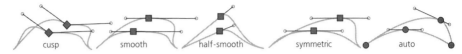

Figure 12-23: Node types: cusp, smooth, half-smooth, symmetric, and auto

- If a node has no handles (they are both *retracted*), or one handle noncollinear with the opposite segment, or one handle remains unmoved when you drag the other one, such a node is called *cusp*, because when its two controls are at an angle, the node represents a sharp turn (cusp) in the path. Cusp nodes are shown as little diamond shapes.

- If the other handle rotates so as to always be collinear (on the same straight line) with the control you're moving, such a node is called *smooth*, because it keeps the path flowing smoothly. Smooth nodes are shown as squares.

- The node may have only one handle—that is, it may have a Bézier curve on one side but a straight line segment on the other hand—and the only handle of the node may be locked to be always collinear with the line segment. Such a node, called *half-smooth*, is also shown as a square. If you drag a half-smooth node, its handle automatically rotates so as to always remain collinear with the line segment.

- The other handle may both rotate and scale so as to always be both collinear and have the same length as the control you're moving. Such a node is called *symmetric*, because its handles are always symmetric around it. Symmetric nodes are also shown as squares.

- Auto nodes, shown as circles, are special: They are smooth nodes that move their handles automatically when you move them. You should not try to adjust the handles of an auto node manually; if you do, the node will at once convert itself from auto to smooth. Therefore, if you use auto nodes, it is better to hide the handles using the controls bar button, so they don't get in the way (see Figure 12-16).

    An auto node adjusts both angle and length of its handles so as to make the adjacent path segments as smooth as possible. If the adjacent nodes are also auto, their handles will also be adjusted accordingly. For example, when you move an auto node A closer to auto node B, both will make their handles progressively shorter and rotate them toward each other so as to keep the curvature of the segment between them, as well as the adjacent segments on both sides, as low as possible without breaking the smoothness of the nodes. The result of this behavior is reminiscent of the **Spiro Spline** path effect (13.1.7).

To change the type of node in a cycle (cusp to smooth to symmetric to auto and back to cusp), Ctrl-click it. With one or several nodes selected, you can click one of the node type buttons on the controls bar, or use the keyboard shortcuts:

- Press Shift-C to make the selected nodes cusp. The first Shift-C just changes the node type but does not change the handles; a second Shift-C will retract all handles of selected nodes.

- Press Shift-S to make the selected nodes smooth. If a node is adjacent to a straight line segment, the first Shift-S will make it half-smooth, locking the single handle to the direction of the line segment; another Shift-S will extend the second handle, making the node fully smooth.

- Press Shift-Y to make the selected nodes symmetric.

- Press Shift-A to make the selected nodes auto.

Switching all nodes of a path from cusp to smooth or auto distorts the path in a characteristic way, removing straight lines and sharp corners:

Figure 12-24: Converting node types in an entire path

12.5.6 Moving Handles

Perhaps the easiest way to edit the shape of a Bézier curve segment is by dragging not any node or handle but the curve itself. This does not require any nodes to be selected nor moves any nodes. Inkscape simply adjusts the Bézier handles of the two adjacent nodes, so that the curve always follows your mouse:

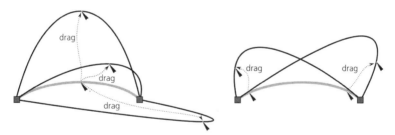

Figure 12-25: Curve dragging

NOTE *If a node is smooth or symmetric, dragging the curve on one side of that node will also change the curve on its other side, because the movement of one of the node's handles will be mirrored by its other handle. Curve dragging next to an auto node converts the node to smooth.*

Of course, you can also simply drag the Bézier handles of any selected node (if you don't see the handles, check if you have the **Show Handles** button pressed on the controls bar, Figure 12-16). Note that unlike nodes, handles *cannot be selected*, although they are shown only for selected nodes and their neighbors on the path.

With Ctrl pressed, the handle you're rotating snaps to 15-degree increments. With Shift pressed, the other handle of the same node rotates by the same angle (this is also the case for smooth nodes even without Shift). Finally, with Alt you

lock the length of the handle, changing only its angle. These modifiers work
in any combination.

NOTE   *As you drag a handle, Inkscape's status bar reports the current length and angle of
that handle.*

It is also possible to move node handles using keyboard shortcuts. In 12.5.7.3,
we'll see that the < and > keys scale and [and] rotate several selected nodes
as if they were an object. Quite naturally, when you have a *single* node selected,
these same keys rotate and scale (i.e., change the length of) the Bézier handles
of that node without moving the node itself:

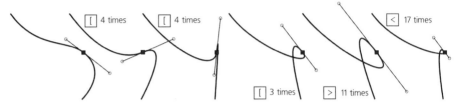

Figure 12-26: Adjusting node handles with keyboard shortcuts

What if you have a Bézier curve but need a straight line segment or vice
versa? Actually, a straight line is just a special case of a Bézier curve with both its
handles *retracted*, that is, coinciding with the corresponding nodes. To retract
a handle, Ctrl-click it; to pull out a retracted handle out of a node, Shift-drag it
away from that node.

Another way to convert Bézier curves to lines and back is by using the two
segment type buttons on the controls bar. These buttons require that at least
two adjacent nodes are selected, but they will also work on any number of segments between selected nodes. The **Make Segment Line** button (or Shift-L) retracts
any pulled-out handles; the **Make Segment Curve** button (or Shift-U) does not
by itself make the segment curvilinear, but pulls out the handles and puts them
along the segment, following which you can convert them to smooth:

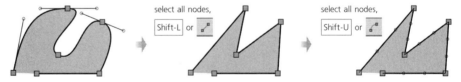

Figure 12-27: Changing the types of segments

12.5.7 Moving Nodes

The easiest way to reshape a path is by selecting some of its nodes and moving
them. The Bézier handles belonging to those nodes move parallel with them
(except for half-smooth and auto nodes, which may rotate their handles as you
drag them).

As in Selector, simple click-and-drag works as expected for moving a single
unselected node; if you drag a selected node, you're dragging *all* selected nodes
with it. With Ctrl pressed, mouse dragging is restricted to moving horizontally

and vertically. If you press Space while dragging, the path you're editing is duplicated (compare stamping with the Selector tool, 4.4).

Arrow keys move selected nodes exactly in the same way and by the same distance as the Selector tool does (6.5.1): by 2 px (default value) without modifiers, by 10 times that distance with Shift pressed, by 1 screen pixel with Alt pressed, and by 10 screen pixels with Shift-Alt pressed.

A more interesting technique is dragging nodes with the mouse while pressing Ctrl-Alt. This restricts the movement to the directions of the dragged node's Bézier handles and perpendiculars to them. If a node has a straight line segment on one side, then the direction of that segment is taken instead of a handle. So, if the node's two handles or adjacent segments are collinear, you can Ctrl-Alt-drag it in one of four directions; otherwise, one of eight:

Figure 12-28: Directions of dragging nodes with Ctrl-Alt pressed

You can Ctrl-Alt-drag more than one selected node; in that case, the movement will be restricted to the handles and segments of the node that you actually drag with your mouse.

Depending on the document settings, the nodes being dragged by the mouse may snap (7.3.3) to guides, grids, and other objects or nodes. (By default, snapping to guides and grid is enabled, but snapping to objects is not.) You can, however, temporarily disable snapping if you drag with Shift.

12.5.7.1 Aligning Nodes

The coordinates of a single selected node are displayed in the **X** and **Y** fields in the Node tool's controls bar; editing these values moves the selected node to the new coordinates:

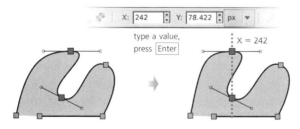

Figure 12-29: Using the X and Y editable fields to align nodes

If you have more than one node selected, these fields show their *average* coordinates—or, to put it another way, the coordinates of the geometric center of the selected nodes. In this case, typing a value in one of these fields assigns this coordinate to all selected nodes, which has the effect of *aligning* all selected nodes horizontally (if you edit **Y**) or vertically (if you edit **X**).

Another approach to lining up nodes uses a tool that you have probably used for objects: the **Align and Distribute** dialog (**7.4**). When you switch to the Node tool, this dialog hides all its object alignment and distribution buttons and instead displays the four buttons that allow you to align and distribute the selected nodes horizontally and vertically.

12.5.7.2 Node Sculpting

All the methods we've seen so far move all selected nodes the same distance. Often, this is what you need. For example, in a simple schematic face profile as in Figure 12-30 on the left, you can easily make the nose longer by selecting two nodes and pulling them to the right; the result is acceptable for this style of drawing. However, what to do if you have a more complex and realistic drawing with a lot of nodes, such as that on the right? No matter how many nodes you select, dragging them will introduce discontinuities and break the natural silhouette of the face.

Figure 12-30: Pulling two noses

In such cases, it would be nice to be able to move different nodes different distances so that the tip of the nose moves farthest, and the other nodes move less and less as you go along the path away from the tip. That is exactly what Inkscape does when you select all nodes of the nose and drag one of them with Alt. This technique is called *node sculpting*.

In the simplest case, when all selected nodes are on the same straight line, Alt-dragging the middle selected node bends the path into a smooth bell-like curve. Farthest selected nodes stay put; the dragged node moves all the way; and all other selected nodes move by some intermediate distance. Now, if your selected nodes formed a wiggly line, text converted to path, or a realistic nose, Alt-dragging will smoothly bend them while preserving their features:

Figure 12-31: Sculpting nodes with Alt

NOTE *When determining what nodes to move by what distances while Alt-dragging, the distance to the node being dragged is calculated along a straight line (spatially), not along the path.*

If you have a pressure-sensitive tablet, you will notice that node sculpting is affected by the pen pressure while you drag. The profile of the bend is always bell-shaped, but with low pen pressure this bell is is narrow and pointy; most selected nodes remain closer to their initial positions. As you increase pressure, the bell becomes wider and more blunt as more nodes shift farther in the direction of the drag. To avoid losing the pressure when you lift your pen, release `Alt` first and only then lift the pen.

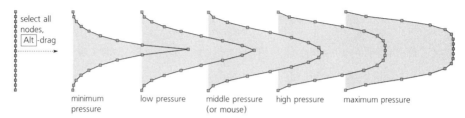

Figure 12-32: The effect of pen pressure on node sculpting

If you don't have enough nodes on the part of a path that you want to sculpt, just select the nodes you have there, and press `Insert` a few times to populate this part of the path with nodes. When sculpting complex shapes with many densely packed nodes, such as bitmap tracings (18.8), hide their Bézier handles (by unpressing the toggle button on the controls bar) so they don't get in the way, and select nodes by expanding selection from a node (12.5.2).

Node sculpting is comparable to the Tweak tool (12.6) in that it makes path editing more natural and lets you develop complex shapes out of simple ones. However, unlike the Tweak tool, this technique does not create or delete nodes and is more deterministic overall. Thus, repeated applications of the Tweak tool to a complex path will eventually simplify and degrade all of it, melting away small details even if you don't touch them with the tool. With node sculpting, only selected nodes are affected, and no degradation occurs no matter how many times you `Alt`-drag the selected nodes back and forth.

12.5.7.3 Transforming Nodes

What does *transforming nodes* mean? We already know many ways to move nodes around and even sculpt them. How is this different?

Remember that with the Selector tool, "transforming" includes not only moving but also scaling and rotating (Chapter 6). These kinds of transformations make perfect sense for a group of nodes in a path as well—if you think of such a group as an "object." Currently, this feature is only available via keyboard shortcuts.

Just as in Selector, the `<` and `>` keys scale the selected nodes, and the `[` and `]` keys rotate them as a whole (Figure 12-33). Without modifiers, rotation is by 15-degree increments and scaling is by 2 px; the same keys with `Alt` pressed rotate and scale by 1 screen pixel at the current zoom. The `h` and `v` keys for flipping (reflecting) horizontally and vertically also work.

By default, scaling, rotation, and flipping are performed around the geometric center of the selected nodes. However, if you hover your mouse cursor over one of the nodes, it will remain fixed, and all other selected nodes will scale or rotate around it as center. For example, you can select all nodes of an object by pressing Ctrl-A and then rotate the entire object around any of its nodes with [and].

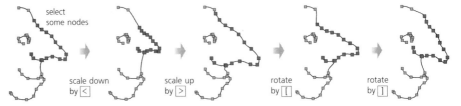

Figure 12-33: Transforming selected nodes

12.6   Path Tweaking

We've already seen in **8.7** how the Tweak tool (w, Shift-F2) can be used to paint and jitter colors in objects, and in **6.9**, how it can be used to move and transform objects. Several other modes of this versatile tool—*Push, Shrink/Grow, Attract/Repel,* and *Roughen*—are for editing the shape of paths.

AI   *The Tweak tool's path editing modes are somewhat similar to the Pucker and Bloat tools in the latest versions of Adobe Illustrator.*

The Tweak tool's approach to editing paths is fundamentally different from that of the Node tool. The Node tool, true to its name, allows you to edit nodes, and you need to have a good working knowledge of how nodes define the shape of the path. With the Tweak tool, you can forget everything you ever knew about nodes; just interact with your path as a pliable body, like a lump of modeling clay, bending and sculpting it at any point and in any direction. While hardly useful for technical drawing, tweaking paths is extremely handy for creating artistic images such as cartoons.

The Tweak tool will work on any number of selected objects. For example, you can select all (Ctrl-A) and "smear" your entire drawing in Push mode. You can also apply tweaking to groups of objects; the tool will go into groups and act on individual paths inside groups. If you're trying to use it without selecting something, it will remind you to select some objects first with a status bar message.

NOTE   *As of version 0.47, the Tweak tool won't correctly work on open paths—an open path becomes closed if you tweak it.*

12.6.1   *Width and Force*

In any of the Tweak tool's modes, what you have at your disposal is a circular *brush* (the orange-edged circle centered on the cursor) with which you "paint" over the selected objects to change them. The size of the brush is controlled by the **Width** parameter, and the amount of action it applies depends on the **Force** parameter (as well as pen pressure if you have a pressure-sensitive tablet). See **6.9** for more details on these parameters.

It takes practice to learn to apply the right amount of drag at the right place, with the proper force (including pen pressure), and with the correct brush size to get the result you need. However, this skill is very rewarding—with the Tweak tool, you are fully in control of the paths in your drawing; what used to be awkward and time consuming with the Node tool is now quick and natural.

12.6.2 Fidelity

Any tweaking of a path slightly distorts—more precisely, *simplifies*, just like the **Simplify** command—the entire path, including even those parts that you didn't touch with the brush.

The **Fidelity** value allows you to control the amount of this parasite simplification. The tradeoff here is the number of nodes in the resulting path; with low fidelity, the resulting path will be node-poor but probably distorted more than you would find acceptable, whereas high fidelity minimizes distortions but the path may end up having a lot of nodes, which inflates the SVG size and slows down Inkscape.

The best value for fidelity depends on the nature of your artwork. If you're sculpting an amorphous blob, you can work with a low fidelity of about 20. If, however, you are pushing or growing a text string converted to path and want the letters outside the distorted area to remain as clean and legible as possible, you will need to raise fidelity to 80 or more.

NOTE *The Tweak tool works by recasting the path into an "approximating polygon" with thousands of tiny straight line sides, tweaks the vertices of that polygon, and then recasts it back into an approximating path with Bézier segments. The fidelity controls the precision of this transformation and thus the number of the nodes in the result, but no fidelity setting will give you the exact nodes of the original—they will always move somewhat, just like they do after a **Simplify**.*

12.6.3 Push Mode

Push is the default mode of the Tweak tool. To switch to Push mode from any other mode, press Shift-P, or click its button on the controls bar.

Push is a general-purpose sculpting mode. When you drag in this mode, the parts of the selected paths covered by the brush get shifted in the direction of your drag, for as long as the mouse button or pen is held down:

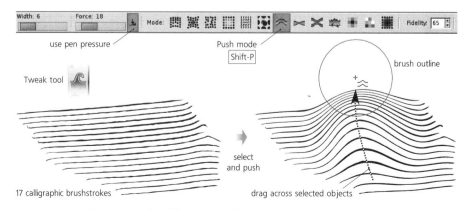

Figure 12-34: The Push mode of the Tweak tool

Varying brush width as necessary, you can push any path into almost any other—but you can also use it for small tweaks, such as flattening a bump, bending an appendix, or curving an engraving grid. Thanks to the bell-like profile of the brush, the paths you're pushing respond by curving softly and smoothly:

Figure 12-35: Sculpting paths in Push mode

12.6.4 Shrink/Grow Mode

The Shrink/Grow mode (Shift-S) moves each point of a path in a direction perpendicular to the path's edge in that point, either inward (shrink, plain drag) or outward (grow, drag with Shift). To quickly access this mode from any other mode of the tool, Ctrl-drag to shrink and Shift-Ctrl-drag to grow.

The Shrink/Grow mode is very similar to the **Inset** and **Outset** commands (**12.4**), except that the Tweak tool, as always, acts softly on a part of a path instead of the whole path. Most often, this mode is used to lighten or darken parts of drawings composed of many details, such as engravings, freehand scribbles, or even text (converted to paths):

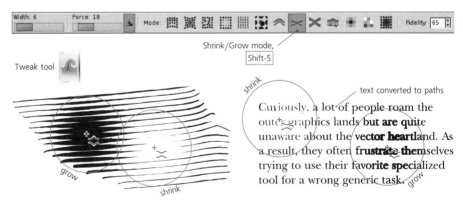

Figure 12-36: The Shrink/Grow mode of the Tweak tool

Unlike Push, the Shrink/Grow mode does not require you to actually *drag*; you can just click and hold while the path keeps bulging or retracting under your brush. However, you can just as well drag to chase the moving edge of the path; this way, using a small-sized brush, you can grow appendages and branches of any length out of a path. (Such growing can also be done in Push mode, but Grow is somewhat easier for this task.) Also, the Shrink mode can act as a quick eraser. Cutting through paths, evaporating small crumbs and bits, and trimming long brush strokes is very easy in this mode:

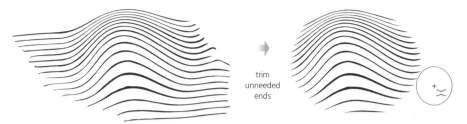

Figure 12-37: Using Shrink mode as an eraser

12.6.5 Attract/Repel Mode

The Attract/Repel mode (Shift-A) works by moving each affected point on a path toward (attract, plain drag) or from (repel, drag with Shift) the cursor point, pinching and exploding whatever paths fall under the brush. In some cases, this may look similar to Shrink/Grow, but the difference is that Attract/Repel doesn't care about the direction of the path being tweaked. This mode moves everything symmetrically, relative to the center of the brush:

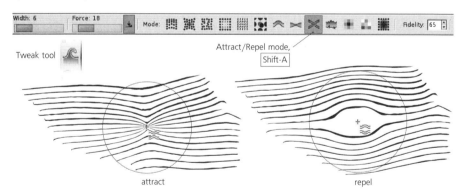

Figure 12-38: The Attract/Repel mode of the Tweak tool

12.6.6 Roughen Mode

The Roughen mode (Shift-R) randomly distorts the edge of the path where you apply your brush, without changing the overall shape of the path, as shown in Figure 12-39. Slight roughening simply makes the edge crooked and uneven, while strong roughening tears and explodes the edge into random blobs and splotches.

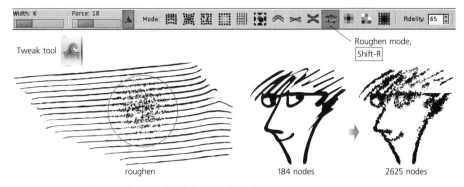

Figure 12-39: The Roughen mode of the Tweak tool

NOTE *This operation, especially with high fidelity, adds a lot of nodes. Such a roughened path is always hard to edit—it's awkward to handle with the Node tool and may be painfully slow with the Tweak tool. For this reason, you should finalize the overall shape of a path with pushing, growing, and shrinking first, and only roughen it, if necessary, as the final step.*

Figure 1: An example of a complex vector drawing created in Inkscape; it contains 280 objects, mostly paths and groups (page 4).

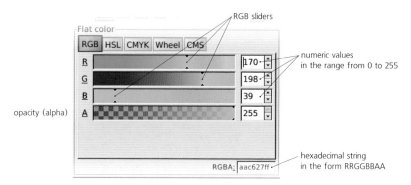

Figure 2: Edit a fill or stroke color by dragging the RGB (Red, Green, Blue) sliders in the Fill and Stroke dialog (page 122).

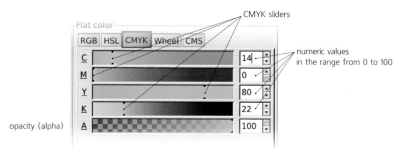

Figure 3: Edit a fill or stroke color by dragging the CMYK (Cyan, Magenta, Yellow, blacK) sliders in the Fill and Stroke dialog (page 122).

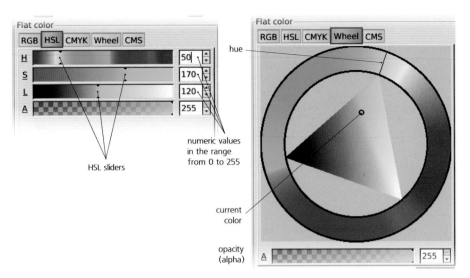

Figure 4: Edit a fill or stroke color by dragging the HSL (Hue, Saturation, Lightness) sliders or the color wheel in the Fill and Stroke dialog (page 123).

Figure 5: Inkscape's default color palette at the bottom of the window; here it is wrapped to show all colors without scrolling. You can choose from about 20 palettes that come with Inkscape, or create your own (page 124).

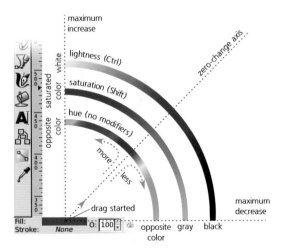

Figure 6: Using color gestures to adjust the fill or stroke color of a selection: Start dragging from the selected style indicator at the left of the status bar, then drag around the NE line with various keyboard modifiers to adjust hue, saturation, or lightness (page 126).

Figure 7: A linear gradient with middle stops, setting arbitrary color/opacity values at arbitrary points along the gradient line; in the Gradient tool, double-click the gradient line to create a middle stop, then assign style to it as you would to an object (page 158).

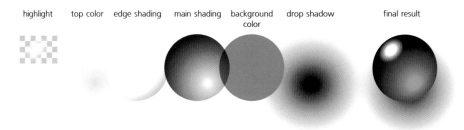

Figure 8: Creating a translucent glass effect with various elliptic gradients (page 161).

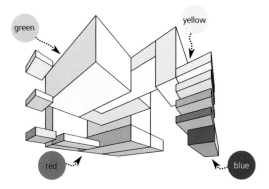

Figure 9: A composition of 3D boxes is painted different colors using a wide brush in the Tweak tool, Color Paint mode. This tool allows you to smoothly adjust the color of multiple objects in one stroke, partly preserving their original differences—in this case, the lightness differences in the sides of the boxes (page 177).

Figure 10: A rainbow pattern created by the Create Tiled Clones dialog, Color tab; you start with a single rectangle with unset color and set the original color as well as the amount of change for each color channel per row and per column (page 283).

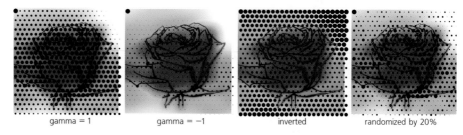

gamma = 1   gamma = −1   inverted   randomized by 20%

Figure 11: The Create Tiled Clones dialog can trace an image by a pattern. Here, a rose image is traced by a pattern of black dots, converting picked lightness to dot size. The color value picked from the image is modified by gamma correction, inversion, and randomization (page 284).

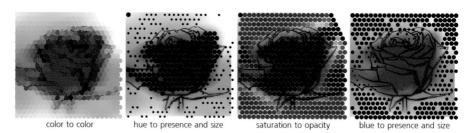

color to color   hue to presence and size   saturation to opacity   blue to presence and size

Figure 12: A rose image is traced by a pattern of black dots using the Create Tiled Clones dialog (page 284). Here, we try various combinations of what value to pick (color, hue, saturation, blue channel) and to what aspect of the pattern to apply it (to color, to presence, to size, to opacity).

original bitmap   Darken   Multiply   Lighten   Screen

Figure 13: A bitmap image can be tinted if you overlay it with colored rectangles residing in layers with various blend modes set (page 289). All rectangles have 100% opacity.

original bitmap   traced to 16 color steps

Figure 14: A bitmap image (left) and a group of colored vector paths (right) created by the Trace Bitmap dialog in Multiple scans mode with 12 colors (page 313).

13

PATH EFFECTS AND EXTENSIONS

As comprehensive as the last chapter was, it didn't cover everything there is to know about paths in Inkscape. This chapter is smaller, but it has the potential to grow much larger in later editions as Inkscape continues to evolve. Path effects (**13.1**) first appeared in version 0.46; they are really taking off in version 0.47 and will likely grow even more in future versions. Extensions dealing with paths (**13.3**) are another area of continuing growth; in the future, some of them may be turned into path effects to improve interactivity and integration with the rest of the program.

13.1 Path Effects

Path effects are an easy-to-use (for the end user) yet powerful (for the developer) mechanism for implementing modifications of the visible shape of the path—for example, rounding all corners, roughening it, blowing or pinching it. No matter which path effect you apply to a path, the *original* path before the effect can still be viewed and edited—and after you edit the original path, the *visible* path is automatically recalculated from it and from the effect parameters.

Thus, path effects in Inkscape are another example of the basic principle of vector graphics: Instead of making some permanent and destructive change, leave the original object unchanged and just record the way this change is to be applied. After that, both the original object and the parameters of the change applied to it can be edited separately at any time.

13.1.1 How Path Effects Work

Path effects, despite the name, apply not only to paths but also to shapes (Chapter 11) which remain shapes and are still editable as such, using the handles or numeric parameters in their shape tools. Path effects don't, however, apply to text objects, clones, or bitmaps. A path effect can be applied to a group, which gives the same result as if the effect was applied to all paths and shapes in the group *combined* (i.e., made subpaths of a single path).

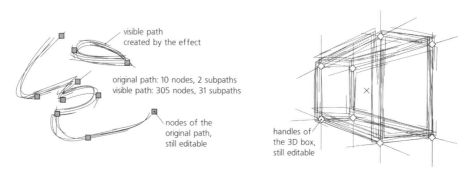

Figure 13-1: The Sketch effect (13.1.6) applied to a path (left) and to a 3D box (right)

When a path effect is applied to an object, the only aspect that changes is the *visible shape* of the object; if you want to change its *style* in a nondestructive way, try filters instead (Chapter 17). Path effects can be stacked on top of one another, so that the output of one effect is an input for the next one.

SVG *Live path effects are an Inkscape-only feature; unlike, for example, filters, path effects are not part of the SVG standard. However, they are implemented in an SVG-compatible way: If you load an SVG file using a path effect into an SVG viewer (or into an old version of Inkscape that did not support this effect), you will see the same* visible *path that you see in Inkscape, but without access to the* original *path and the effect parameters. There's a caveat: If you try to edit that visible path in a version of Inkscape that does not support the effect and then reload the changed file into a newer version that does support it, your changes will be lost because the new visible path will be generated from the unchanged original one and the effect parameters.*

In a path *element with a path effect applied, the original path data is stored in the* inkscape:original-d *attribute. The path's effect is specified in the* inkscape:path-effect *attribute, which refers to an element with the same name stored, along with its parameters, in the* defs *of the document (A.4). The result of the effect is automatically recalculated and stored in the standard* d *attribute of the path object. All Inkscape tools and commands know that, in a path with a path effect applied, they should not edit or change the* d *but work on, or display, the* inkscape:original-d *instead.*

To assign one object's path effect to any number of other paths or shapes, copy the source object (Ctrl-C), select the target, and use the **Paste Path Effect** command (Ctrl-7). Inkscape comes with a number of sample SVG files (in */usr/share/inkscape/examples* on Linux, *<inkscape-dir>\share\examples* on Windows), some of which demonstrate various path effects; you can use this copy/paste trick to reuse the effects from any of these sample files in your documents.

When you combine (12.1.1) shapes or paths, the result will have the path effect of the topmost object, if any. Breaking apart a path with a path effect causes the effect to be applied to all resulting new paths.

To clear away the path effect and return to the original path, use the **Remove Path Effect** command in the **Path** menu. If, however, you want to preserve the result of the effect and forget the original path, use the **Object to Path** command (Shift-Ctrl-C); this will not change the way the path looks, but the effect will be gone.

SVG *The **Object to Path** command is also the best way to ensure that your file is not only correctly rendered but also editable in older versions of Inkscape and in SVG editors other than Inkscape.*

With the Node tool, you are editing the original path, not the visible path after the effect. Since the path you're editing is not visible by itself, it is convenient to highlight it using the corresponding toolbar button (Figure 12-17); most effects will enable this highlighting automatically for you.

13.1.2 The Path Effect Editor Dialog

The **Path Effect Editor** dialog (Shift-Ctrl-7, see Figure 13-2) is the main control hub of path effects. It lists all path effects supported by Inkscape (this list expands with each new Inkscape version) and lets you choose those to apply to your selected path, shape, or group. When an object with one or more path effects is selected, you can use this dialog to view its stack of effects, add or remove effects, and adjust the parameters of the selected effect.

NOTE *If you have applied some path effects to a group, you can edit those effects' parameters only when you select that group, not when you select any of the paths in it.*

The **Effect list** in the dialog lists all the effects applied to the selected object. They are listed top to bottom; that is, the first effect applied to the source path is the topmost one, its output is passed to the second one, and so on until the last listed effect whose output is displayed.

A new effect you add is placed at the end of the stack. You can move any effect in the stack up or down by the arrow buttons below the list. The eye icon before each effect's name allows you to disable an effect, forcing Inkscape to bypass it (the **Is visible?** checkbox in an effect's parameters has the same function). To delete an effect from the stack, use the button with the minus sign.

Parameters of an effect can belong to several types:

- *Numbers* can be either integers or fractional, depending on the nature of the parameter. When a number denotes a distance, it is usually in px units (A.6).

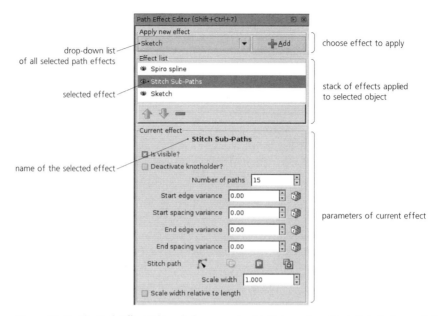

Figure 13-2: The Path Effect Editor dialog; a path with Spiro spline, Stitch Sub-Paths, and Sketch effects is selected.

- In *random number parameters*, the editable number specifies the range in which the random values must fall, and the dice button reshuffles the random values controlled by this parameter:

Figure 13-3: A random number parameter of a path effect

- *Link parameters* are used when one path's effect uses some other path as one of its parameters. That *linked path* can be a separate object located somewhere on the canvas (in the same document), or it can be a path stored entirely within the path effect and not visible in the document.

Figure 13-4: A link parameter of a path effect

A link parameter displays a row of four buttons:

Edit button

Switches Inkscape to the Node tool and lets you edit that linked path, regardless of whether it's a separate object or a path stored inside the effect (Figure 13-5). In the latter case, that path is shown as a green outline.

This is the same as if you switch manually to the Node tool and click the **Edit path effect parameter** button on the controls bar.

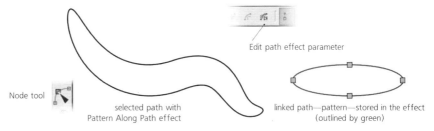

Node tool

selected path with
Pattern Along Path effect

Edit path effect parameter

linked path—pattern—stored in the effect
(outlined by green)

Figure 13-5: Editing a path effect's linked path

Copy button

Copies the linked path to the clipboard.

Paste button

Pastes the path from the clipboard into the effect, making a copy of the
clipboard path and storing it in the effect.

Link button

Takes the path copied to the clipboard and links the effect to its original
in the document. Now, editing the object you had copied will change
this path's effect.

Apart from the numeric controls in the dialog, some path effects allow you
to edit their parameters visually by on-canvas handles accessible in the Node or
shape tools. We will see examples of this as we discuss specific effects.

13.1.3 Pattern Along Path and Bend

The **Pattern Along Path** and **Bend** effects are very similar. They both take one
path (called the *pattern*) and bend and/or stretch it along another path (called
the *skeleton*). This is very similar to "skeletal paths" in software such as Microsoft
Expression, typically used for freehand drawings (see Figure 14-11).

As usual with path effects, both the skeleton path and the pattern remain
editable at any time, with the result updated live. This is a great way to create
easily editable vector brushes—for example, you can start by creating a drawing
with the Pen or Pencil tools, and then try applying various patterns to all its
paths, adjusting the widths for the best result.

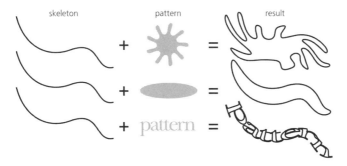

Figure 13-6: Bending a pattern along a skeleton

Aside from the ability to repeat a pattern, the main difference between the **Pattern Along Path** and **Bend** effects is which path is the skeleton and which is the pattern:

- In **Pattern Along Path**, the path you're applying the effect to becomes the skeleton, and the pattern is linked up using a link parameter. This effect is ideal for simple, possibly repeated patterns applied to arbitrary skeletons. The linked pattern path can be either an independent path object in the document, or a path stored inside the effect itself. The result gets the style of the skeleton. This is the effect used by the **Shape** option in the Pen and Pencil tools (14.1.5).

  Once you apply **Pattern Along Path** to a skeleton path, you need to supply the pattern using the **Pattern source** link parameter. The **Edit** button does not work unless you paste or link some pattern path first, so the usual sequence of operations is this: Select a pattern path, copy it (Ctrl-C), select a skeleton path, assign **Pattern Along Path** to it, and paste or link the pattern to it. Or, you can quickly draw skeletons with the copied pattern applied to them automatically if you choose **From clipboard** in the **Shape** list in the Pen or Pencil tools.

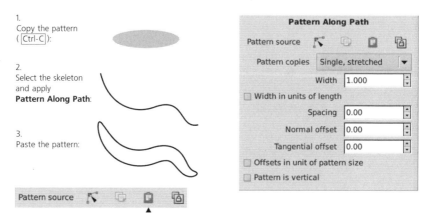

Figure 13-7: The Pattern Along Path effect

- In **Bend**, the path you're applying the effect to becomes the pattern, whereas the skeleton is linked up using a link parameter. This is more convenient when you have a complex pattern that you want to lightly curve along a simple, possibly shared skeleton path. Similarly, the linked skeleton path can be either an independent path in the document or a path stored inside the effect itself. The result gets the style of the pattern.

  For this effect, you start with the pattern and use the **Bend** link parameter to link to a skeleton. Unlike **Pattern Along Path**, however, **Bend** provides a default two-node skeleton path that stretches along the horizontal axis of your pattern—so you can at once use the **Edit** button to edit that skeleton. If you prefer, however, you can still paste a skeleton from the clipboard or link to the copied path.

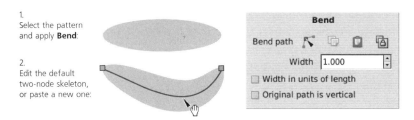

1.
Select the pattern
and apply **Bend**:

2.
Edit the default
two-node skeleton,
or paste a new one:

Figure 13-8: The Bend effect

NOTE *You can use any path for an external linked skeleton with* **Bend**, *including a path with some other path effect applied to it.*

Both effects allow you to change the *width* of the pattern. This width can be measured either in the units of the original width of the pattern or in the units of the skeleton length:

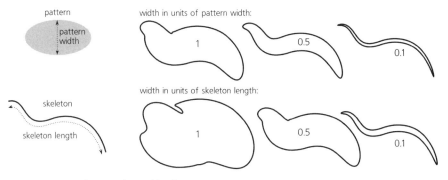

Figure 13-9: Adjusting the width of a pattern

The **Pattern Along Path** effect can use one of the following *repeat modes*:

Single

Places a single copy of the pattern along the skeleton, from start node, without stretching it. So, if the pattern is shorter than the skeleton, it will only cover part of the skeleton length; if the pattern is longer (i.e., does not fit even once), it will not be applied.

Single, stretched (default)

Also places a single copy of the pattern along the skeleton, but always stretches or squeezes it so it exactly fits the skeleton length. The **Bend** effect always uses this mode; unlike **Pattern Along Path**, in **Bend** the repeat mode is not changeable.

Repeated

Places as many copies of the pattern along the skeleton as fits the skeleton length, but does not stretch them, so the remainder of the skeleton length less than one pattern length remains unfilled. (However, this does not mean that the copies of the pattern are identical; the curvature of the skeleton may noticeably distort them, as Figure 13-10 demonstrates.)

Repeated, stretched

Places as many copies of the pattern along the skeleton as would fit and stretches them evenly, so that they exactly fill the entire skeleton length.

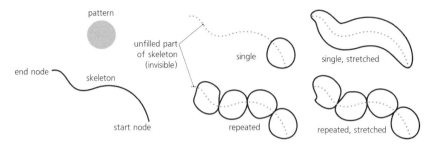

Figure 13-10: Repeat modes of Pattern Along Path

The pattern always starts from the start of the path; if you want it to go the other way, use **Path ▸ Reverse**.

Also, the **Pattern Along Path** effect allows you to adjust some *distance parameters*:

Spacing (only for repeated modes)

Sets the spacing between copies of the pattern on the path.

Normal offset

Moves all copies of the pattern *perpendicular* to the skeleton path at each point.

Tangential offset

Moves all copies of the pattern *along* the skeleton path, starting the first pattern not at the start of the skeleton but this specified distance from it.

These offsets and spacing parameters are, by default, in absolute px units. By checking the **Offset in units of pattern size** checkbox, you can express them as multipliers of the pattern size—for example, a tangential offset of 0.5 will shift the pattern along the skeleton by half of the pattern's width.

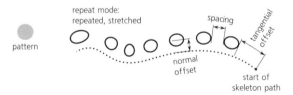

Figure 13-11: Spacing and offsets in Pattern Along Path

By default, the original of the pattern is considered to be horizontal—that is, the pattern is aligned on the skeleton by the pattern's horizontal axis. By checking the **Pattern is vertical** (for **Pattern Along Path**) or **Original path is vertical** (for **Bend**) checkboxes, you can rotate the pattern by 90 degrees so that it's aligned on its vertical axis, as shown in Figure 13-12.

pattern   pattern is horizontal (default)   pattern is vertical

Figure 13-12: Orientation of pattern in Pattern Along Path

13.1.4 Stitch Sub-Paths

The surprisingly useful **Stitch Sub-Paths** effect works only for paths with two or more subpaths (12.1.1). It replaces the source path with a lattice of paths connecting equispaced points on the subpaths; you can set the number of the connecting paths via a parameter. With this effect, you can create all kinds of hair, fur, lattices, moiré patterns, or "power fields":

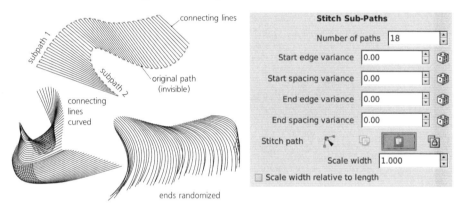

Figure 13-13: Stitching subpaths

NOTE   *If the path has three or more subpaths, each pair of subpaths gets its own connecting lattice. This means that the number of connecting lines literally explodes as you increase the number of subpaths in the original—so don't try this effect on a path with more than a few subpaths, or you will easily bog Inkscape down to a halt!*

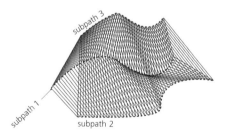

Figure 13-14: Stitching three or more subpaths

The connecting lines need not be straight, although that is the default. You can use the **Stitch path** link parameter to paste or link any existing open path to serve as the stitches, or you can edit the lines with the Node tool. The **Scale width** parameter scales the stitch path in the direction perpendicular to its start-end direction (the value of 1 gives it its natural width). The **Scale width relative to length** makes the width of each stitch depend on the length of this stitch, as shown in Figure 13-15.

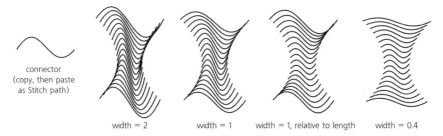

connector
(copy, then paste
as Stitch path)

width = 2   width = 1   width = 1, relative to length   width = 0.4

Figure 13-15: Adjusting the width of curved stitch path

Finally, a group of randomization (**variance**) parameters allows you to shuffle the attachment points of the stitches, both along the path (**spacing**) and perpendicular to it (**edge**), separately for the beginning and end of each stitch:

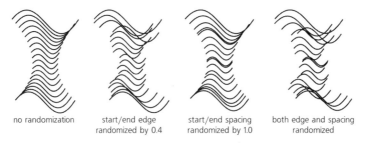

no randomization   start/end edge   start/end spacing   both edge and spacing
                          randomized by 0.4   randomized by 1.0   randomized

Figure 13-16: Randomizing the stitched subpaths

13.1.5 Knot

This effect breaks a path into subpaths, creating gaps between them where the path (or a group of paths) self-intersect. It can turn a stroked path with self-intersections into a Celtic knot:

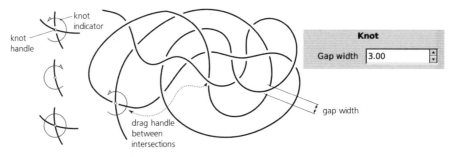

Figure 13-17: The Knot effect on a path with self-intersections

The only numeric parameter for this effect specifies the width of each gap in px units. On canvas, you can control each intersection individually. Select a path with the **Knot** effect, switch to the Node tool, and notice that one of its self-intersections has a diamond-shaped handle and a green circular indicator which is open on one side. Click that handle; the indicator flips to the other side and the gap now affects the other line at the intersection. Click it again and you close the intersection removing any gaps; the indicator is now a solid circle.

You can cycle through these three states of an intersection by clicking the handle. To control another intersection on your path, just drag the handle and drop near the intersection you need.

13.1.6 Sketch

Sketch is a complex artistic effect that turns a path into a sketch-like drawing with multiple strokes, as if hand-drawn by an artist who was trying to find the best shape:

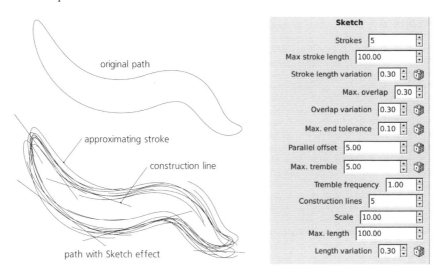

Figure 13-18: The Sketch effect

To make sense of the plethora of parameters of this complex effect, remember that the sketch consists of two types of artifacts: approximating strokes and construction lines. The *approximating strokes* cover the entire path; they are typically curvilinear, more or less parallel to the original path (with certain tremor), and travel at some distance from it. The *construction lines*, on the other hand, identify and emphasize straight or almost straight parts of the path by drawing straight lines that extend on both sides.

For the approximating strokes, you can change:

- The average **number** of parallel strokes at each point of the path (the default is five). Set this parameter to 0 to hide approximating strokes (leaving only construction lines); low values make the sketch airy and tentative, increasing the number makes it bolder and noisier:

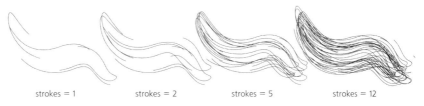

Figure 13-19: Changing the number of approximating strokes (construction lines are off)

- The maximum **length** of strokes (in px units) and the range of the random length **variation** (relative to the maximum length).

- The maximum **overlapping** of subsequent strokes (in px units) and the range of the random **variation** of this parameter (relative to the maximum overlap value).

- The **end tolerance** affecting how close the approximating strokes follow the original path.

- The average **offset** of the approximating strokes from the original path; by varying this parameter, you can make the sketch either neat and tight or wide and ruffled.

- The maximum **tremble** and its **frequency**; these control how the strokes oscillate around the original path. Increasing the maximum tremble ruffles the sketch, similar to increasing offset but more randomly; increasing the frequency makes the sketch lines look rougher by making them tremble on a smaller scale.

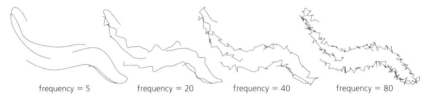

frequency = 5   frequency = 20   frequency = 40   frequency = 80

Figure 13-20: Changing the tremble frequency of approximating strokes

For the construction lines, you can change:

- The total (not average) **number** of the lines in the sketch (the default is five). Set this to 0 to suppress construction lines, leaving only approximating strokes.

- The **scale** parameter tells how far the ends of the construction lines can go beyond the ends of the straight (or approximately straight) parts of the path.

- The maximum **length** and its random **variation** set the upper limit on the length of construction lines:

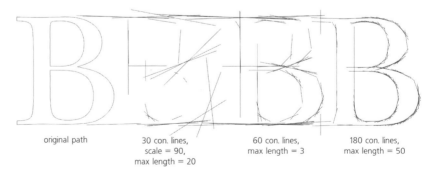

original path   30 con. lines,   60 con. lines,   180 con. lines,
                 scale = 90,   max length = 3   max length = 50
                 max length = 20

Figure 13-21: Playing with construction lines (approximating strokes are off)

13.1.7 Spiro Spline

Building paths with Bézier curves (12.1.4) has many years of tradition behind it. All modern graphics software worth its salt supports it in much the same way, and millions of users are familiar with it. The Bézier paradigm is, undoubtedly, extremely flexible and powerful. I think most people who have ever used it will find it difficult to name any major disadvantages specific to it.

And yet, once you try something better, these disadvantages become painfully obvious.

Spiro splines are a novel way of defining curvilinear paths, developed by Raph Levien. They take some getting used to, but for certain tasks (such as lettershape design) Spiros have a clear advantage over Bézier curves. Since version 0.47, Spiro splines are available as a path effect in Inkscape, which means you can use all the convenient Inkscape path tools (such as moving and transforming groups of nodes, node sculpting, etc.) on Spiro paths. The Pen and Pencil tools can produce Spiro paths directly (14.1.4).

A Spiro path is defined by a sequence of nodes. However, unlike a regular path consisting of Bézier curves, all Spiro nodes lie on the path, and there are no off-path handles. The curvature of the path is defined entirely by the positions of the nodes and their types. The path behaves very similar to a springy rod that is forced to pass through the given points and which uses the minimum possible curvature to satisfy the requirement:

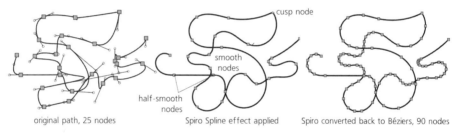

Figure 13-22: Converting a regular path to a Spiro path and back

Once you get the basic idea, the Spiro behavior will feel more and more natural as you're getting used to it. More importantly, the resulting path is always very smooth—not just superficially smooth, as in having no cusps, but smooth at a deeper level, which you can only achieve with Béziers after a lot of laborious tweaking.

After a Spiro experience, it becomes clear that the main problem with Béziers is each node having not only a position but also its own intrinsic "direction" and "curvature," as defined by its handles. So, whenever you move a Bézier node around, you also need to carefully adjust its handles so the curve still looks smooth and natural. With Spiros, you are freed of this requirement; just move the node wherever you want the curve to go, and the smoothness of the curve is taken care of automatically.

NOTE   *After a Spiro path is converted to a regular path, it gets two to three times as many nodes; now, consider that each of these Bézier nodes are actually three points (the node itself and its handles) compared to just a single point of a Spiro node—and you will get an idea of how much faster and easier Spiro path editing can be.*

Figure 13-23: Lettershapes created with Spiro paths

To create a Spiro path, select any path and assign the **Spiro spline** path effect to it. There are no parameters. Each node of your path becomes a point of a Spiro path, depending on the type of node (**12.5.5**):

- **Smooth nodes** (those with two collinear Bézier handles) are smooth points on the Spiro path. Note that the length and direction of the Bézier handles on the source path are ignored; the only thing that matters is their collinearity (i.e., smoothness). Press Shift-S to line up the handles of the selected node to make it smooth.

- **Half-smooth nodes** (those with one Bézier handle collinear with a straight line segment on the other side) behave exactly the same on a Spiro path: They sit between a straight line and a curve and enforce that these two segments join smoothly without a cusp. If you have a straight line segment on one side of a node, the first Shift-S will make it half-smooth.

- **Cusp nodes** on the source path become corner points of the Spiro path. They behave like free hinges on the springy rod, allowing it to bend at any angle. Between two corner points, the Spiro path is always a straight line. To make a node cusp, press Shift-C twice (the first Shift-C just changes the type of the node and the second actually retracts the handles).

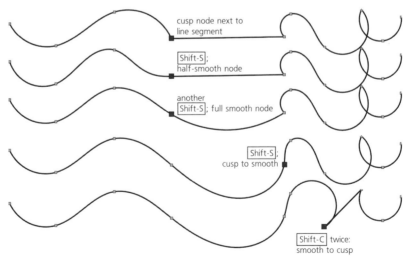

Figure 13-24: Playing with node types in a Spiro path

NOTE
What matters for Spiro is the actual collinearity of a node's handles, regardless of the node type that the node has in the Node tool. For example, if a node designated as cusp (diamond-shaped) has collinear handles, it will still be a smooth curve point on the Spiro path.

Probably the biggest problem with Spiro splines is that some configurations of points are unstable and produce wild loops and spirals instead of a smooth curve. Still, sensible sequences of points usually work fine; you just need to avoid sharp changes in direction between points to prevent such instability. Hopefully, the robustness of the algorithm will be improved in future releases.

Figure 13-25: A divergent Spiro path with five nodes

When editing Spiro paths with the Node tool, the red highlight of the source path may be a distraction; you can turn it off with a toggle button in the controls bar.

13.1.8 Envelope Deformation

This effect distorts a path or a group of paths by fitting them into a curvilinear envelope. After you apply the effect, the envelope is rectangular, and you can curve its sides one by one by the Node tool. The effect treats all four sides as separate helper paths ("bend paths"), which is slightly inconvenient: You need to click the **Edit** buttons for each side in turn to curve all four sides. The **Copy** and **Paste** buttons allow you to transfer the exact shape of the envelope from one object to another.

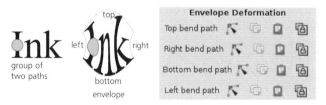

Figure 13-26: Envelope distortion of a group of paths

13.1.9 VonKoch

This fractal-like recursive effect takes the original path and repeats it twice (as subpaths) with shifting, scaling, and rotating; it then repeats the same operation on these copies, and so on for the specified number of *generations*. The transforming of the copies is determined by the configuration of three helper paths: a *reference segment* (initially, horizontally across the source path) and two *generating paths* (initially, horizontally across the two first-generation copies). These helper paths are two-node straight line segments (i.e., their curvature is disregarded); to edit them, you can use the Node tool and click the **Edit path effect parameter** button on its control bar once or twice; or, you can click the **Edit** button in the effect's parameters for the corresponding helper path. Here are some examples:

Figure 13-27: A number of VonKoch fractals for the same source path and different helper segments

13.2 Dynamic and Linked Offsets

We've already seen the regular offset commands (**12.4**) that expand (*outset*) or contract (*inset*) a path perpendicular to its direction at each point. Those commands are destructive—once you offset a path, you lose the original. There exist, however, nondestructive versions of the same commands: *dynamic offsets* and *linked offsets*.

NOTE   *Dynamic offsets and linked offsets are conceptually very similar to path effects—they, too, have an invisible original path, the visible offset path, and the parameter specifying how much to offset. However, for historical reasons, offsets are not implemented as path effects and therefore are not available in the **Path Effect Editor** dialog. It appears likely, however, that in a future version offsets will be reimplemented as path effects.*

With a *dynamic offset*, the original path is not visible anywhere on canvas—it is *stored* inside the dynamic offset object, which displays only the offset path. To create such an object, select a path and press Ctrl-J or choose **Path ▶ Dynamic Offset**. A *linked offset* is different only in that it *links* to an existing path as its source. In this way, you can create multiple offsets from a single source path, and all of them will be updated when the source path is edited. To create a linked offset, select the source path and press Ctrl-Alt-J, choose **Path ▶ Linked Offset**, or simply duplicate (Ctrl-D) an existing linked offset of the same original.

Both kinds of offsets display a single, diamond-shaped handle on the offset path. You can drag that handle anywhere; its distance from the original path determines how much the path is inset or outset, but you can also move it along the path to where it's most convenient for you:

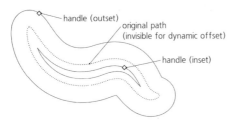

Figure 13-28: Dynamic and linked offsets: offsetting with handles

As with path effects, to convert a dynamic or linked offset to a regular path, choose **Path ▸ Object to Path** (Shift-Ctrl-C).

13.3   Path Extensions

Extensions are simple external programs that perform some actions on the selected objects in the document. They are represented by the commands in the submenus of the **Extensions** menu. However, they should not be confused with path effects; they are one-off, destructive operations that change objects without preserving the originals. The only way to reverse the effect of an extension command is by using **Edit ▸ Undo**.

A typical extension has a number of *parameters* you can set in a dialog before running the extension. Most extension dialogs have the **Live preview** checkbox which, when checked, lets you preview the effect of various parameters in the document without having to undo and call the extension again. Note that while the **Live preview** is off, the extension dialog is not modal, which means you can pan the canvas and select different objects; as soon as you turn **Live preview** on, the dialog locks the rest of Inkscape so you can only change the parameters in the dialog and see their effect on the current selection. (There's usually a pause between changing the parameters and updating the canvas with **Live preview**.) To apply the changes as final, click the **Apply** button; to cancel without applying, click **Close**.

Not all extensions deal with paths; some extensions were already mentioned where it was relevant, and others will be covered throughout the book. In this chapter, we will look only at the extensions that modify or create path objects.

In the **Generate from Path** submenu, there are several extensions that take the selected path and generate some new path or paths from it:

Inset/Outset Halo

Adds to the selected path a specified number of inset or outset paths, spaced by a given distance, each further offset having lower and lower opacity. This may be an acceptable choice if you want to blur the edge of your object but don't want to use the **Gaussian Blur** filter (**17.1**):

Figure 13-29: The Halo extension creates a "poor man's Gaussian blur."

Extrude

Creates a primitive 3D effect by extruding the selected path at a given angle to a given distance. The result of the effect is a group of two objects, one being the original path and the other its extrusion skirt, which you can style differently, as shown in Figure 13-30.

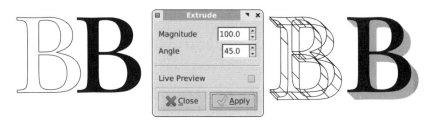

Figure 13-30: Extruding creates a simple 3D-like effect.

Interpolate

Creates an interpolation, or *blend*, between two paths—a sequence of intermediate paths that smoothly transition between the two paths. You can specify the number of the **Interpolation steps** and the **Exponent**, which, if different from the default 0, shifts the blend toward one of the ends:

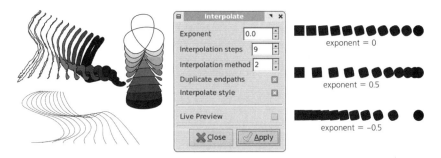

Figure 13-31: Interpolating paths

The **Interpolate style** option, although marked "experimental," worked well enough in my tests. The two interpolation **methods** differ slightly in the way they generate intermediate steps. The extension generates all the intermediate steps as a group of paths; the **Duplicate endpaths** option adds copies of the original paths to this group as well. Since interpolation always connects beginnings and ends of the two paths, you may need to reverse one of the paths (**Path ▶ Reverse**) in order to get the result you want.

Pattern Along Path

This is similar to the path effect of the same name (**13.1.3**) and, in fact, is the first version of this functionality, introduced before path effects became possible. Currently, the extension has one advantage compared to the path effect: It can use a group of objects (each with its own style) as the pattern, whereas in the path effect you are limited to a single-pattern path. To use the extension, select the pattern path or group and the skeleton path (the pattern must be on top of the skeleton in z-order) and choose the extension from the menu. Its options are similar to those for the corresponding path effect.

The **Modify Path** submenu contains extensions that change the selected path directly:

Add Nodes

This useful extension creates more nodes in the path without changing its shape. You can specify either the maximum allowed distance between adjacent nodes or the number of segments into which each segment will be divided. We've seen this extension in action in Figure 9-11.

Envelope and Perspective

Both of these extensions require that you select two paths, the second being exactly four nodes long. This second path is treated as a deformation envelope into which the first path is inscribed (only the coordinates of the corners matter; curvature of the sides, if any, is ignored). These extensions have no parameters. The only difference between the two extensions is that **Perspective**, unlike **Envelope**, interprets the four-node envelope as a perspective plane, performing foreshortening so that parts "farther away" are made smaller:

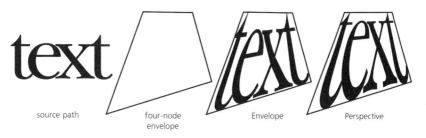

Figure 13-32: Envelope and Perspective

Flatten Béziers and Straighten Segments

The **Flatten Béziers** extension approximates each Bézier curve in the selected path with a sequence of straight line segments (the higher **Flatness** is, the rougher the approximation), whereas **Straighten Segments** simply shortens all Bézier handles by the given percent, so that setting this to 100 percent turns each Bézier curve into a straight line segment:

Figure 13-33: Flattening Béziers and straightening segments

Jitter Nodes

This extension randomizes the selected path by displacing all nodes in random directions and at random distances, limited by the **Maximum displacement** parameters, which can be set separately for X and Y (for example, set maximum displacement for X to 0 if you want the nodes to be jittered only vertically). Also, you can separately enable jittering for nodes themselves and for their Bézier handles. Turn **Use normal distribution** on to make smaller displacements more probable than large ones; without it, any displacement within the **Maximum displacement** limits is equally probable.

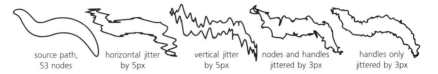

Figure 13-34: Jittering nodes

Fractalize

This is another way to randomize a path. Unlike **Jitter Nodes**, it creates new nodes between existing nodes itself, and then moves these new nodes (any Bézier handles in the original path are discarded) leaving all the original nodes in place. The **Subdivisions** parameter determines how many times each segment will be subdivided in two (caution: Increasing this value makes the node count grow exponentially—for example, 10 subdivisions turn a two-node path into one with 1,025 nodes), whereas **Smoothness** changes how far the new nodes can move (lower **Smoothness** produces a rougher path). This effect is perfect for creating coastal lines in fantasy maps:

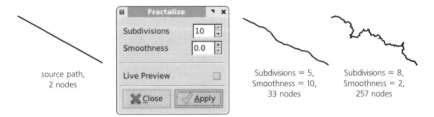

Figure 13-35: Fractalizing a path

Rubber Stretch

This extension stretches the object vertically (rotate it before and after applying the extension if you want a different stretch direction) while blowing it horizontally on the sides, making it behave in a nonlinear way as if made of rubber:

Figure 13-36: Rubber Stretch pulls a path vertically.

Whirl

This distorts the selected path into a whirl, its center being in the center of view in Inkscape when you start the extension. You can always place the center of view at the geometric center of selection by pressing 3 or choosing **View ▸ Zoom ▸ Selection** (3.9). This extension gives better results if you add more nodes to the source path, either by Insert in the Node tool (12.5.3) or via the **Add Nodes** extension:

Figure 13-37: Whirling paths

The **Render** submenu contains extensions that generate entirely new objects not based on anything in your document:

Grid

This extension generates a rectangular grid as a single path, each line being a subpath (such as the grid in Figure 13-36). You can set the number of horizontal and vertical lines and the spacing.

Barcode

This is a universal barcode generator supporting a number of common barcode standards (EAN8, EAN13, Code39, and others).

Function Plotter

This is a complex extension that draws a graph of an arbitrary function in Cartesian (rectangular) or polar coordinates. Before calling this extension, draw or select a rectangle that will define the scale of the graph; the first four numeric parameters define the ranges of the X and Y coordinates. The **Multiply X range by 2*pi** checkbox is convenient for trigonometric functions; when it's checked, the X range of, for example, 0 to 2 is treated as 0 to $2 \times \pi$. The **Use polar coordinates** checkbox transforms the graph into a circle, centered at the center of the original rectangle, with the X range mapped to the angle and Y to the radius.

The **Samples** parameter sets the total number of times the function will be sampled, at points equidistant on the X axis; since each sampling produces a node, this is also the total number of nodes in the generated path. The higher this number, the more precise the graph. The optimum number of samples, however, depends on the nature of your function; for example, if you're using a periodic function with n periods in the X range, you will need at least several samples per period to reproduce it with any fidelity.

The function itself must be written using the syntax of the Python programming language. It can use a number of built-in mathematical functions such as sin(x), log(x), or sqrt(x); refer to the **Functions** tab for a full list.

Each sampling of the function creates a smooth Bézier node; the *first derivative* of the function at that point is what determines the angle of the handles of that node. You can ask the extension to **Calculate first derivative numerically**, or you can uncheck that checkbox and provide the derivative function analytically, using the same Python syntax and built-in functions as for the function itself (for example, the first derivative of sin(x) is cos(x)).

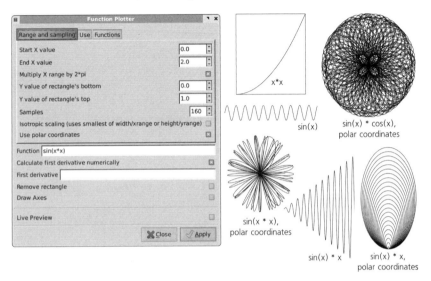

Figure 13-38: Function Plotter examples

L-system

This extension implements *Lindenmeyer systems*—a simple graphic language with recursion that can produce complex sequential or tree-like structures:

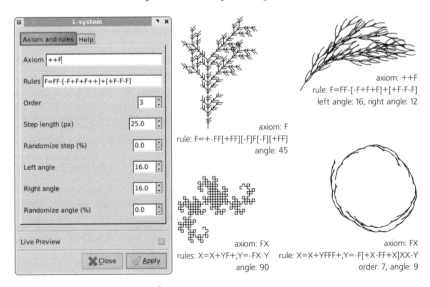

Figure 13-39: L-system examples

The "program" in this language, built of simple commands like "draw one step forward" or "turn left," contains two parts: the **Axiom** and the **Rules** for substitution. The rules are applied to the axiom as many times as specified by the **Order**. The rest of the parameters determine the length and angles produced by the primitive commands in the axiom and rules and allow you to randomize these values to render the result more natural. For a complete list of the commands recognized in the axiom and rules, refer to the **Help** tab.

Random Tree

This is similar to the **L-system** extension but is much more primitive; all it does is draw a randomly branching tree, where the first segment of the trunk is **Initial size** long, and each subsequent branch is progressively shorter, until the **Minimum size** is reached and the drawing terminates. Thus, the bigger the difference between the initial and minimum sizes, the more complex the tree.

Spirograph

This is an implementation of the popular toy of the same name, in which a small circle rolls along the edge of a larger circular hole. In the extension, you can vary the diameters of these two circles and some other parameters.

Finally, the **Visualize Path** submenu collects extensions that, in one way or another, visualize the selected path:

Number Nodes

This replaces a path with a group of dots, each dot corresponding to the node of the original path, numbered sequentially. You can change the size of the dots and the font size of the text objects that represent the numbers.

Draw Handles

This extension adds lines that correspond to the Bézier handles of the selected path, as a new path with separate subpaths.

Dimensions

This creates a frame and dimension lines around the selected object (not necessarily a path), such as those used on plans or technical drafts. After creating dimension lines, you can use the **Measure Path** extension to add the actual length measurements.

Measure Path

This extension calculates the length of the path, from start to finish, and adds this value as a text-on-path object put on the source path (**15.7**). You can specify the **Precision** and the **Length Unit** of the value and adjust the **Font size** and the distance from the path (**Offset**).

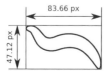

Figure 13-40: The combined effect of Dimensions and Measure Path

14

DRAWING

Historically, one of the names of vector editors was *vector drawing*—or even simply *drawing*—applications. Bitmap editors, on the other hand, are sometimes called *paint programs.* The difference between drawing and painting, established in traditional media (such as paper and canvas), is thus carried on into the digital realm. Even though vector programs are now used—perhaps even preferentially—for more high-level tasks such as composition and layout, "simply drawing" is still the most basic application of this kind of tool.

It is true that vector drawings can never be as naturalistic and "painterly" as bitmaps; even the best vector art has that recognizable smooth, computer-generated look. Often, however, this look is not a problem; it can even be an advantage. Also, vector editors have something that no bitmap editors can match: the ability to treat each stroke as a separate object that never merges or "flattens" into others (unless you tell it to). As it turns out, this infinite tweakability is sometimes more important for producing a good freehand drawing than the ability to imitate pastel strokes or wet-on-wet watercolor.

Inkscape has three major drawing tools to choose from, depending on the type of art you want to create. If you need strict geometric or Bézier-shaped paths with precise placement of nodes, use the Pen tool (14.1). For freehand paths, smoothed to some degree, use the Pencil tool (14.2). Finally, for complex, naturalistic, pressure-sensitive filled strokes imitating various physical effects such as trembling or inertia, use the Calligraphic pen (14.3). We will also discuss the Paint bucket tool (14.4) for filling bounded areas, most often used in cartoons and freehand drawings.

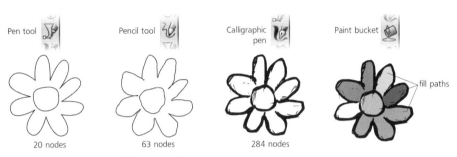

Figure 14-1: Inkscape's drawing tools

14.1   The Pen Tool

The Pen tool is for those situations where you know more or less exactly where you want to place the nodes of your path. It can be thought of as a sibling of the Node tool (12.5), except it is optimized for creating and connecting nodes instead of editing them.

Switch to the Pen tool (Shift-F6 or b), click and drag on the canvas. The first *node* of a new path appears where you clicked; the gray straight line between that point and your current mouse position is the *handle* of this node (12.1.4). As soon as you release the mouse button, the handle is fixed—but the path is not finished; it now expects you to click or click-and-drag for a second node. In this mode, just moving the mouse around (without clicking) displays a red Bézier segment that shows you how the path would look if you create the next node at this point.

Figure 14-2: Pen: first node set, ready for the second

Now, click and drag for the second node (Figure 14-3). After you release, the part of the path between the two defined nodes becomes green, and you once again have a red segment between the last created node and the current mouse point. This can be repeated indefinitely—just keep clicking and dragging (for smooth symmetric nodes) or just clicking (for cusp nodes); on each step, the path you have created so far is green, and the segment you are about to create is red.

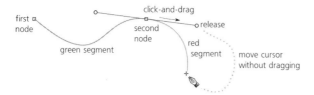

Figure 14-3: Pen: two nodes set, ready for the third

To finish the path, double-click or right-click (this adds one more node and finishes the path) or press Enter (this cancels the red segment without adding any more nodes and finishes the path). It is only at this point that the entire path is actually created as an object; what you saw until now was just a virtual scaffold. Another way to finish a path is to *close* it; if you create the next node exactly over the first node of the path (which is marked by a little square anchor), the path will be closed and finalized.

To cancel creating a path at any time, press Esc or simply switch to another tool.

NOTE *Most key and mouse shortcuts for zooming, scrolling, and panning (Chapter 3) work in the Pen tool without disrupting path creation. For example, you can middle-drag the canvas and middle-click to zoom in so you can better position your next node.*

14.1.1 Node Types

As you've just seen, click-and-drag creates a smooth node with two symmetric handles (unless this is a first node of a path which only has one handle). A simple click creates a cusp node without any handles. You can also create cusp nodes with noncollinear handles; for this, click-and-drag but press Shift while dragging. This fixes the opposite handle and lets you move the near handle independently:

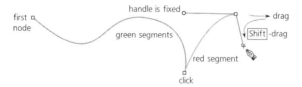

Figure 14-4: Creating cusp nodes with Pen

You can also press Ctrl while dragging a handle to snap it to 15 degree increments (compare 6.3; you can choose another snap value in **Inkscape Preferences**). Pressing Ctrl while moving the mouse around between creating nodes will similarly snap the direction between the last created node and the mouse point; this is an easy way to create strictly horizontal or vertical lines:

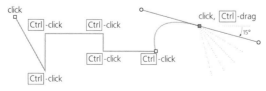

Figure 14-5: Pen: snapping with Ctrl

14.1.2 Going Back

You can always step back in your path creation process; to cancel the last added green segment, press Backspace. You can press Backspace repeatedly to remove several segments; removing the last remaining node cancels the entire path.

It is not always easy to click exactly where you want the node to appear on the first attempt. Inkscape allows you to move the last created node (i.e., the end of the green segment) without finalizing the path; just use the arrow keys with the same convenient modifiers as in other tools: Alt to move by 1 screen pixel, Shift to move by 10 times the distance (6.5.1).

14.1.3 Continuing a Path

With the Pen tool, any single selected path displays its end nodes, if it has any (i.e., is open), as little squares called *anchors*. (This applies to any path you just created with this tool itself—after finalizing, it remains selected.) These anchors allow you to continue adding to the selected path (by placing your first node in the anchor) or to close it (by penning from one anchor to the other).

You can also add a new subpath (12.1.1) to the selected path. To do this, just hold down Shift *while* you click to create the first node. After that, create and finalize the path as usual; your path will be added as a subpath to the selected path. All open subpaths of the selected path show anchors, which means you can close them or connect them to one another:

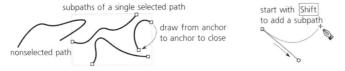

Figure 14-6: Pen: adding or closing a subpath

14.1.4 Modes

Now, let's have a look at the controls bar of the Pen tool (above the canvas). Notice the four **Mode** buttons:

Figure 14-7: The Pen tool modes

These buttons control the type of path Inkscape is creating. So far we have worked in the first (default) mode, which creates regular paths out of straight lines and Bézier curves.

The second mode creates Spiro paths (13.1.7), that is, paths with the **Spiro Spline** path effect applied. In a Spiro path, the exact positions of the node's handles are not important; the only thing that matters is whether the node is smooth (with collinear handles) or cusp (without any handles or with non-collinear handles). Therefore, in this mode it makes no difference where or how far you drag the handle of a node you create; all that matters is whether you drag it at all (this creates a smooth Spiro node) or just click (this creates a cusp Spiro node).

NOTE *Unfortunately, in Spiro mode the green and red segments you see while creating a path do not correspond to how the finalized path will look—they show you the path without the **Spiro Spline** effect applied.*

The two other modes are restrictions of the regular mode. The Straight lines mode disables creation of smooth nodes (i.e., it makes sure that even a drag works as a click, creating a cusp node without handles). The Paraxial mode additionally restricts the segments to horizontal and vertical, ensuring that each segment is perpendicular to the one that precedes it.

Also, in the Straight lines and Paraxial modes, Ctrl-click creates a single *dot* (a little circle) instead of starting a path. This is convenient for creating geometric and technical drawings. The size of Ctrl-click dots can be set in the units of stroke width in the Pen tool's preferences (double-click the tool icon in the toolbox to access its tab in the **Inkscape Preferences** dialog). If you use Shift-Ctrl, the dot is twice as big.

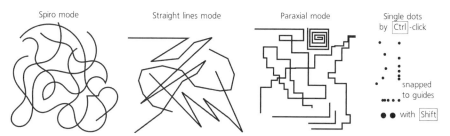

Figure 14-8: Pen: Spiros, straight lines, paraxial lines, and single dots

14.1.5 Stroke Shapes

The **Shape** drop-down menu on the Pen tool's controls bar lets you choose the *stroke shape* for the path you are creating.

By itself, SVG does not support shaped strokes; in SVG, a stroke is always a constant-width strip (Chapter 9). This is why there's a difference in behavior between the default **None** and the rest of the stroke shapes in this list.

With **None**, you get the barebones SVG path with a plain, constant-width stroke; the path may or may not have a fill inside it, depending on the style the tool uses (14.1.6). With any other **Shape** option, the tool applies the **Pattern Along Path** effect to your path (13.1.3) so as to imitate a shaped stroke by the fill of the path. Therefore, you cannot have any other fill inside the path when using these options, and the tool automatically applies the style of stroke to the fill and discards the original stroke style so the result looks as expected (see Figure 14-9).

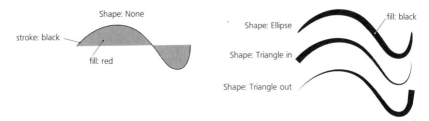

Figure 14-9: Shaped strokes with the Pen tool

The available stroke shapes include **Ellipse**, two triangles (**Triangle in** means the width *decreases* from the beginning to the end of the path, **Triangle out** means the width *increases* from beginning to end), and any other shape you placed on the clipboard if you select the **From clipboard** option.

To adjust the width of the shaped stroke, open the **Path Effect Editor** dialog (**13.1.2**) and use the **Width** control of the **Pattern Along Path** effect. This parameter can be set either as a multiple of the shape's natural width (which for all three standard shapes is 10 px) or as a multiple of the path length.

In the Node tool, normally, it is the original skeleton path that is editable, not the shape applied to it, but you can also use the **Edit path effect parameter** button to edit the applied shape (Figure 13-5).

Path shapes work with any of the modes of the Pen tool, including Spiro. For example, you can draw a Spiro path with the Ellipse shape, then switch to the Node tool and adjust the Spiro nodes—and the entire elliptical shape will bend and curl exactly as a Spiro does. In the **Path Effect Editor** dialog for this path, you will find both **Spiro Spline** and **Pattern Along Path** effects stacked on top of one another.

To turn a path with a shape and/or **Spiro Spline** applied into a regular path, use the **Object to Path** command (Shift-Ctrl-C).

14.1.6 Style

Like all object-creating tools, the Pen and Pencil tools can either use the last set style or their own tool style (**11.1.2**). By default, they use their own style, which is initially set to no fill, 1 px black stroke. This is because more often than not, the last set style has fill and no stroke, whereas when drawing with these tools, you would probably expect the result to have stroke but not necessarily fill. Refer to Figure 11-2 for how to change the tool style. As usual, the style that will be used for the next path you create is displayed on the right end of the controls bar (Figure 11-1).

NOTE *When using a **Shape** other than **None**, Inkscape does what you'd expect: It applies the* stroke *properties of the tool's style to the* fill. *Thus, if **None** creates a black stroke with no fill, **Triangle in** will create a shaped stroke with black fill but no stroke (Figure 14-9). However, if no stroke is set, it will use the fill properties, if there are any, for the shaped path.*

14.2 The Pencil Tool

The Pencil tool (F6 or p) is very similar to the Pen tool and shares most of the same controls. Its primary difference is that with the Pencil, you don't have to worry about nodes or handles; you just draw a freehand line and Inkscape approximates it with a path.

The most important setting in the Pencil tool's controls bar is **Smoothing**, which specifies, in a range from 1 to 100, how precise this approximation is going to be. With small values of smoothing, Inkscape tries to precisely trace every tiny movement of your mouse; the resulting path will be quite uneven and contain a lot of nodes. Conversely, large smoothing produces generic, approximate paths with few nodes—and, at the maximum of 100, most mouse drags will create just a single Bézier segment between two nodes:

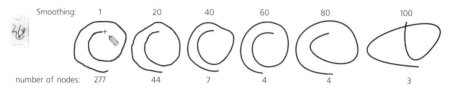

Figure 14-10: Pencil strokes at various smoothing levels

NOTE   *The **Smoothing** control only affects the newly created paths in the Pencil tool. If you want to change the evenness and the number of nodes of an existing path, you can only make the path more loose by using the **Path ▸ Simplify** command (12.3).*

Similar to the Pen tool, in the Pencil tool any selected path displays anchors on the open end nodes of all its subpaths. You can continue, close, and connect subpaths by drawing from one such anchor to another, and you can add new subpaths to the selected shape by beginning to draw with Shift held down.

Also like the Pen tool, the Pencil tool has a **Mode** switch, but it only has two options: regular path and Spiro path. The **Shape** menu is exactly analogous to that of Pen, allowing you to draw freehand shaped strokes. Here are some examples of Pencil paths created with Spiro and/or stroke shapes:

Figure 14-11: Shaped strokes with the Pencil tool

Drawing with Alt enables the "sketch mode" of the Pencil tool. In this mode, any number of drags that you perform while holding Alt will be *averaged*; the actual path is only created after you release Alt. This allows you to "feel your way" when drawing and distill the best outline without leaving a thicket of tentative lines. On Pencil's **Inkscape Preferences** page, the **Average all sketches** setting (on by default) averages *all* sketches made while you hold Alt with equal weight; if you turn it off, it will average between the latest stroke and the previous average, thus giving the latest strokes more weight.

14.3   The Calligraphic Pen Tool

The name *Inkscape* is a quite apt one: The most sophisticated drawing tool in the program, the Calligraphic pen, indeed feels very *inky*. This tool, as its name implies, was initially intended for calligraphy—that is, beautiful handcrafted lettering. But over time, it grew versatile enough for general artistic sketching, drawing, and inking.

Switch to the Calligraphic pen (Ctrl-F6 or c) and drag on the canvas. You will see a filled path being created as you draw, the width and shape of which depend on the angle of the stroke, the speed of dragging, and the pressure of your pen (if you are using a tablet). The result is similar to the Pencil tool with a stroke shape (Figure 14-11), but the calligraphic stroke looks much more natural. The result of this tool is always a plain, filled path without any path effects.

14.3.1   Width

Let's see how we can change the output of the Calligraphic pen. The most important setting on the tool's controls bar is **Width**, specifying the width of the stroke (or more precisely, its *maximum* width; many other factors may also affect width, but it will never exceed the value you set here). This width value can be adjusted by the ← and → keys at any time while using the Calligraphic pen tool.

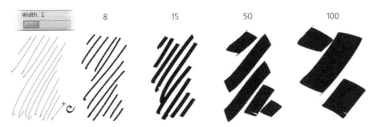

Figure 14-12: *Varying width (pressure sensitivity is off)*

By default, width is measured *in relative units* from 1 to 100. This means that this value of width is relative to the size of your document window, not to any objects or measurements in the document. In other words, if you zoom out, your stroke will be wider in absolute units but will *look* exactly the same to you. The value of 1 always gives hairline, and 100 always gives a stroke about 2 centimeters wide, as measured on your screen.

This allows you to have always the same feel for the tool, regardless of the current zoom level, and provides for intuitive workflow: First, while zoomed out, sketch out the broad strokes; then, zoom in to add finer and finer patches—all without shifting the **Width** back and forth. If you don't like this approach, go to the **Inkscape Preferences** for the tool (as with any tool, you can access it by double-clicking the tool icon on the toolbar) and check the **Width in absolute units** checkbox; now the **Width** control will set the absolute width of the stroke in px units.

14.3.1.1 Pressure Sensitivity

If you have a pressure-sensitive tablet as your input device, Inkscape allows yo
to use the pressure information to change the width of the stroke—press lightly
for a thin line, press harder for a wider brush:

Figure 14-13: Drawing with or without pressure sensitivity at the same width

To enable pressure sensitivity, click the toggle button to the right of the
Width control. Without pressure sensitivity, the tool draws as if maximum pressure
is applied.

NOTE *Before you can use pressure sensitivity, you may need to configure your tablet as your
input device. Usually, all you have to do is choose* **Input Devices** *from the* **File** *menu,
then choose the* **Screen** *mode for each of the available* **Devices**. *The rest of controls in this
dialog can be left in their default state.*

14.3.1.2 Tracing Background

Another factor that can affect the width of the Calligraphic pen stroke (if you
enable this feature) is the darkness of the color of the background objects over
which you are drawing. That is, your brush is thinnest when you draw over white
and broadest when you draw over black. This is most useful when you use *guide
tracking* (14.3.7) to create hatching in a background drawing or bitmap and want
to achieve a shading effect with strokes of smoothly varying width:

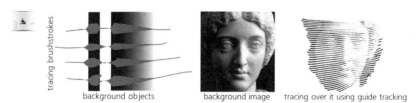

Figure 14-14: Tracking background by width

To enable tracing the background, click the second toggle button to the
right of the **Width** control. This setting can be combined with pressure sensitivity
though it usually makes sense to turn pressure sensitivity off when you are tracing.

14.3.1.3 Thinning by Speed

Finally, the speed of your drawing—how fast you're dragging the mouse or
pen—may also affect the width of your stroke. This is controlled by the **Thinning**
value, which takes values from –100 to 100 (Figure 14-15). Positive values make
your stroke wider as you go faster; negative values make it thinner. If you set this
parameter to 0, thinning by speed is disabled.

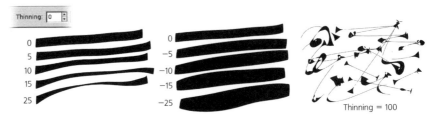

Figure 14-15: Thinning by speed (pressure sensitivity is off)

Since a stroking movement is usually faster in the middle of a drag, the result is a shape with the fixed width at the ends and a "breathing" middle, thinner for positive values of this parameter. Pressure sensitivity usually has the opposite effect, as pressure in the middle of a stroke is typically higher than at the ends. An interplay of these two factors gives a very natural feel to the stroke.

A real-world felt pen or pencil usually leaves a thinner trail when you move it faster; the default value for this parameter is set to 10 to emulate this behavior. However, you can also push it all the way to –100 or to 100, which produces curious effects of an "exploding" or "imploding" brush very much unlike anything in the real world!

14.3.2 Angle

The **Angle** and **Fixation** parameters treat the Calligraphic pen according to its name—that is, as a flat-tipped calligraphic pen that can be held at varying angles. The **Angle** sets the angle of the pen's tip to the horizontal: 0 means the tip is horizontal, +90 means it is rotated all the way to the vertical counterclockwise, and –90 means it is rotated clockwise. This value can be also be changed by pressing the ⬆ (increase) or ⬇ (decrease) arrow keys.

Figure 14-16: The Angle and Fixation of the Calligraphic pen

Setting an angle with a nonzero fixation is most useful for producing calligraphic lettering. For most styles of calligraphy, the angle should be somewhere between 30 and 60 degrees.

NOTE *If your tablet supports pen angle detection, you can, for extra realism, bind the **Angle** parameter of the tool to the actual physical angle of your pen. For this, just press the toggle button next to the **Angle** slider.*

The **Fixation** (in the range of 0 to 100) controls how strictly this angle is enforced. When fixation is at its maximum, the tip is always rotated at the set angle, regardless of the direction in which you draw, so that drawing in parallel to the pen angle always gives a hairline stroke, whereas drawing perpendicular to it produces maximum width. With zero fixation, the direction of the pen is always perpendicular to the direction of movement, which makes angle irrelevant and gives you the effect of a felt-tip pen or a round brush. Intermediate values of fixation produce a stroke that is affected by *both* angle and the direction of movement, in varying proportions.

14.3.3 Caps

By default, Calligraphic pen strokes are cut blunt at the ends. This is appropriate for calligraphy work, but at other times you may want a more rounded appearance. Increase the **Caps** parameter to about 0.5 for slight bulges at the ends, to 1.3 for approximately round caps, and up to 5 for long, protruding caps:

Figure 14-17: Caps of a calligraphic brush stroke

14.3.4 Tremor, Wiggle, and Mass

What we've seen so far of the Calligraphic pen tool is useful, even if maybe a little boring. Now it's time to add some fun! The last three parameters—**Tremor**, **Wiggle**, and **Mass** (all in the range of 0 to 100)—modify the behavior of the tool in some wild ways.

Even when using a graphics tablet with pressure sensitivity, the Calligraphy pen's brush strokes often look too smooth and computer-ish. Increasing tremor adds small-scale disturbances to the stroke for a more natural look—rough, trembling, or even splotchy. The frequency of the tremor is temporal, rather than spatial, which means that if you draw faster, the roughness will be stretched along the stroke and therefore look smoother.

The **Wiggle** parameter also disturbs the stroke but at a larger scale, making it waver in wavy or loopy patterns, departing sometimes quite far from the actual position of the cursor, especially at sharp turns:

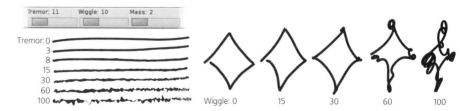

Figure 14-18: Effects of tremor (left) and wiggle (right)

Mass makes the brush lag behind the cursor, as if slowed down by inertia, resulting in smoothing of sharp corners and shortening of the fast flights of your pen. The default settings for tremor and wiggle are 0, but mass has a small nonzero default value (0.02) so that the Calligraphic pen feels light and responsive but not entirely weightless.

14.3.5 Calligraphic Presets

The Calligraphic pen is the most settings-rich tool in Inkscape—and at times, it can be overwhelming. Even if you know all of its controls by heart, tweaking several sliders and buttons every time you want to switch from a smooth marker pen to a wiggly brush is time-consuming. Presets are a solution to this problem: By choosing one of the presets from a drop-down menu on the left end of the bar, you can set multiple parameters at once. Several presets come with the program:

- **Dip pen** is an imitation of a soft calligraphy pen: smooth (no tremor or wiggle), pressure-sensitive, angle fixed at 30 degrees, no caps rounding.

- **Marker** is a plain, constant-width, felt-tip marker: smooth, no pressure sensitivity, no speed thinning, no angle fixation, round caps.

- **Brush**, compared to **Marker**, adds pressure sensitivity, negative thinning (i.e., the stroke is wider when you move faster), and some wiggle.

- **Wiggly**, as its name implies, features high wiggle and some tremor for a characteristic "dirty" look.

- **Splotchy** is a very wide brush with high tremor and high negative thinning, which can produce a series of "splotches" connected by thin streaks (see Figure 14-15, right).

- **Tracing** is similar to **Marker** but with the background tracing feature turned on (14.3.1.2).

NOTE   *Unfortunately, as of version 0.47 there's no way to add more presets to the list via the GUI—but if you really need to, you can add them by editing your* preferences.xml *file (3.1.1). In the* group *element with* id="preset"*, add something like this:*

```
<group name="My style" width="50" mass="0" wiggle="25" angle="30"
  thinning="-40" tremor="10" flatness="50" cap_rounding="1"
  tracebackground="1" usepressure="1"/>
```

14.3.6 Adding and Subtracting

If a single path was selected before you started drawing, and you had Shift pressed when you released the mouse button or lifted the pen, the new object you have created will automatically be *added* (via the **Union** path operation, 12.2) to the selected path, forming a new single path.

Analogously, if you had Alt pressed, the new object will be *subtracted* (via the **Difference** operation) from the selected path. (The Cut mode of the Eraser tool works the same, if you want to use this functionality as a separate tool without having to hold Alt.) This makes it easy to quickly "patch" or "carve" any path.

14.3.7 Tracking a Guide Path

Drawing in Calligraphic pen with Ctrl pressed activates the *guide tracking* feature, which causes your pen to "slide" at some constant distance from the edge of a selected "guide" path and lets you trace around or along that guide.

The inspiration for this feature came from the traditional line e techniques that were, for a long time, the only practical way of repr lifelike images in black-and-white print; about a century ago, line ε were almost completely displaced by automatic halftone screens. *Hatcnu*. space with many parallel straight or variously curved lines of varying width to represent gradual shading—is a very labor-intensive process. Inkscape's guide tracking, along with background tracing (14.3.1.2) and the Tweak tool (12.6), take the pain and boredom out of this ancient art. While you still need a keen eye and assiduousness, with Inkscape it is at least possible to create authentic-looking line engravings, entirely in vector, in a reasonable amount of time.

One way to approximate a hatching grid is by using path interpolation (blending, 17.2), but this method is not too flexible and produces too obviously computer-generated output without the "human touch." Manual drawing of hatch lines, on the other hand, is tedious and nearly impossible to do uniformly. However, the guide tracking capability allows you to hatch quickly and uniformly, at the same time giving you sufficient manual control over the process.

Here's how to do it. First, select the *guide path* that you will track. It may be another calligraphic stroke, any path or shape, or even a letter of a text object. Then switch to the Calligraphic pen tool (if you haven't already) and, before starting to draw, press Ctrl. You will see a gray *track circle* centered at your mouse pointer and touching the closest point on the selected guide path. (If you have no guide path selected, a status bar message will tell you to select it.)

Now move your mouse closer to the guide path, so that the track circle radius is equal to the desired spacing of your hatch pattern, and start drawing along the guide path. As soon as you start drawing, the radius of the circle locks and the circle turns green; now the circle slides along the guide path—and the actual stroke is drawn by the center of the tracking circle, *not* by your mouse point. As a result, you are getting a smooth stroke going parallel to the guide path, always at the same distance from it.

Figure 14-19: Tracking a guide path

When the stroke is ready, release your mouse button (or lift your tablet pen). However, do not let go of Ctrl yet, because as long as you have it pressed, the tool remembers the hatch spacing you set when you started drawing. Since you have just created a new stroke, that stroke object is selected instead of what was selected before—which means it now becomes the new guide path. Next, draw a second stroke along the first one, then a third one along the second, and so on. Eventually, you can fill any desired space with nice uniform hatching, as shown in Figure 14-20.

The attachment to the guide path is not absolute. If you stray your mouse pointer far enough from the guide path, you will be able to tear it off (the track circle will turn from green to red) and move away (but not quite freely: The pen

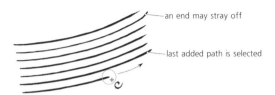

an end may stray off

last added path is selected

Figure 14-20: Creating uniform hatching

will have a heavy inertia from the guide tracking). This is intentional; for example, in this way you can continue drawing a stroke *past the end* of a guide path, in order to cover a wider area than the initial guide path would allow. With inertia, this tearing off is usually pretty smooth, but it is not possible to completely suppress jerks. If jerking and unintended tear-offs still bother you, try increasing the **Mass** parameter.

NOTE *Since tracking is designed for smooth engraving patterns, it does not work on guide tracks with too sharp turns or those that are too uneven (e.g., calligraphic strokes with high tremor).*

Tracking a guide also allows for some feedback by gradually changing the tracking distance in response to your drawing behavior. If you're consistently trying to draw closer or farther from the guide than the current tracking distance, the distance will decrease or increase a bit, so you will get a hatching that is spaced slightly closer or wider. Also, note that since tracking follows the *edge* of the stroke, strokes of varying width (such as those tracing background, see below) will result in gradual bending of the hatching pattern as you proceed.

If you've accidentally deselected your last created stroke (e.g., by performing an undo of a bad stroke), you can reselect it without leaving the Calligraphic pen tool by pressing Shift-Tab (5.11). Guide tracking can be combined with adding or subtracting (i.e., you can press Shift-Ctrl to add the new stroke to the selected guide path or Alt-Shift to subtract from it).

It is natural to combine guide tracking in the Calligraphic pen tool with the Tweak tool. A hatching rarely comes out perfectly; loose stray-off ends, the wrong slant or curvature, and incorrect stroke widths (i.e., too dark or too light hatching) are the most common problems. The Tweak tool can fix all of these problems so you don't have to redo the hatching. Use the Shrink/Grow mode to clear the loose ends as if with an eraser and to adjust stroke widths, and the Push mode to bend or shape the hatching. With these powerful tools, it is possible to create a complex and believable hatching by tracing a bitmap original:

Figure 14-21: Take a bitmap (top), hatch over it with the Calligraphic pen tool, and tweak the resulting hatching with the Tweak tool (bottom).

14.4   The Paint Bucket Tool

The concept of a "paint bucket" or "flood fill" tool is probably familiar to you from bitmap editors. In Inkscape, the Paint bucket tool works exactly as you would expect: Click in any area bounded on all sides, and it will fill the area with color. Being a vector tool, however, Inkscape's Paint bucket just creates a new *path* that "fills in" the area in which you have clicked:

Figure 14-22: The Paint bucket filling a bounded area

It is important to remember that the Paint bucket tool is *perceptual*, not *geometric*. That is, when looking for the boundaries around the point you clicked, it identifies as boundaries any *visible* color nonuniformities. Thus, filling will stop at gradients, blurs, and color boundaries in bitmap objects, but it will ignore any paths or other objects that are fully (or almost) transparent or for any other reason do not stand out from the background.

For example, you can scan a pencil sketch, import the bitmap into Inkscape, and quickly "trace" it by filling all its cells with colors. This is a very convenient and interactive way of digitizing your paper drawings, and it makes the traditional bitmap tracing (the **Trace Bitmap** dialog, 18.8.2) unnecessary in many cases.

NOTE   *Internally, the tool works by performing a bitmap-based flood fill on a screen-resolution rendition of the visible canvas and then tracing the resulting fill into a vector path. The resolution of the rendition used to perform the trace is defined by your current zoom; the closer you are zoomed in to an area, the higher the resolution of the flood fill. So, if the result of the Paint bucket fill is too imprecise, has rounded corners, or doesn't go into small nooks and crannies where it is supposed to go—just undo it, zoom in closer (but so that the entire area to fill is still visible), and repeat filling from the same point. Conversely, if the fill leaks out through a small gap, zoom out to make the gap less visible and fill again (or use the automatic gap closing parameter, 14.4.5).*

14.4.1   Filling Techniques

Filling a bounded area is as easy as switching to the Paint bucket tool (F7 or u) and clicking inside the area. If you click with Shift, the resulting path will be unioned (12.2) with the selected path; this way, if your first attempt did not fill in all of the desired area, just Shift-click the remaining corner to finish it off, as shown in Figure 14-23.

If you click-and-drag, you will fill from *all of the points* that you pass while dragging (you will see your path visualized by a red line). From each point, the fill spreads to its neighbors with colors similar to that point—in other words, it's like clicking with this tool at each point of the drag path and combining the

Figure 14-23: Adding a Paint bucket fill to an existing path

results. This lets you easily fill an area occupied by a gradient or blur—just drag from the darkest to the lightest points in the area you want to fill:

Figure 14-24: With one click, only a narrow strip of a gradient is filled; drag across an area to fill the entire gradient.

Alt-click and drag works similarly to simple drag, except from each point of the drag path, the fill spreads to the neighbors (if any) whose colors are similar to the color of the *initial point* (the point where you started the drag), not the point through which you're dragging. This lets you fill a series of similarly colored yet separated areas (for example, multiple cells in a cartoon) by starting the drag in one of those areas and Alt-dragging through all the other areas.

14.4.2 Filling by Channel

When looking for color boundaries to stop at, the Paint bucket looks by default at the colors as they are seen on the canvas. However, you can also restrict its vision to a specific color channel. The **Fill by** drop-down menu, apart from the default **Visible Colors**, allows you to choose any of the three RGB channels (**Red**, **Green**, **Blue**), any of the HSL channels (**Hue**, **Saturation**, **Lightness**), or the **Alpha** channel (opacity).

For example, if you select the **Red** channel, even the sharpest green/blue color boundaries won't stop the fill. Choosing the **Alpha** channel makes the tool ignore any colors and only look at where opacity changes; for example, if you have a complex, multicolored, but fully opaque object over a transparent background, clicking this object in **Alpha** mode will fill up to the outline of the entire object.

14.4.3 Threshold

The **Threshold** parameter, with a range from 0 to 100, controls how different a point's color must be, compared to the initial click point, in order to stop the propagation of the fill. Zero tolerance means only the area of strictly the same color will be filled; the larger the tolerance, the larger the filled area will be, and the easier it will be for the fill to leak away into adjacent color areas. The default value is 10.

14.4.4 Growing and Shrinking

Using the **Grow/shrink by** parameter, you can control the amount of inset or outset (12.4) to be applied to the created fill path. It works much the same as the **Outset** and **Inset** path commands, except it's done automatically after every fill.

A positive **Grow/shrink** value causes the fill path to be larger than the filled bitmap area it represents; this is often useful for eliminating anti-aliasing gaps between the fill and its boundary. A negative value makes the path smaller, ensuring a constant-width gap between the fill and the boundary.

14.4.5 Closing Gaps

With the **Close gaps** parameter, you can make the Paint bucket tool ignore any gaps in the area boundaries that would normally cause the fill to spill out of the desired area. There are four levels of automatic gap closing:

- **None**
- **Small** (gaps up to 2 screen pixels in size are closed)
- **Medium** (gaps up to 4 screen pixels in size are closed)
- **Large** (gaps up to 6 screen pixels in size are closed)

NOTE   *Setting this parameter to anything other than **None** may slow Inkscape down noticeably when filling large areas.*

14.4.6 Style

Like all object-creating tools, the Paint bucket can use the last set style (11.1.2) for the objects it creates (this is the default), or it can use its own fixed style. You can switch between these modes in the tool's **Inkscape Preferences** (double-click the tool icon to access it). As with other tools, the style swatch on the far right of the controls bar shows the style that will be used for the next fill object you create. To change the last set color without affecting any object, just deselect (Esc) and click a color on the palette.

Clicking with Ctrl turns the Paint bucket tool into a "single click styling" tool: Instead of filling an area, Ctrl-clicking an object simply changes that object's fill to the current fill color of the tool, and Shift-Ctrl-clicking changes the stroke to the current stroke color of the tool. If no stroke is set, then Shift-Ctrl-clicking behaves as Ctrl-clicking.

15

TEXT

As can be expected in a vector editor, any text you add to your Inkscape drawing remains fully editable *as text* at any time, despite any styling, filters, or transformations you apply to it. Creating and editing text objects is the domain of the Text tool where you can type or delete words, rewrap the text column (manually or automatically), apply style to parts of text, adjust kerning and spacing, and so on.

Of course, Inkscape is hardly competitive with programs that are specially designed for text, such as text editors or word processors. It is not too convenient for handling large pieces of text; since it is more visually oriented, Inkscape has no structural formatting tools such as automatic headings, footnotes, and so on—all this has to be emulated by manual styling and formatting.

15.1 Basic Editing

To start editing an existing text object, select it and switch to the Text tool (F8); this places the text editing cursor (a blinking vertical line) at the end of the object. You can now click anywhere within the text to position the cursor where you want to edit it, or move the cursor with the arrow keys. Or, in the Selector tool, you can just double-click a text object—this will switch tools, select the object, and place the cursor where you clicked, all at the same time.

*Clicking or double-clicking a text object is only possible when your cursor is over a char-
acter body. For example, if your text has its characters widely spaced, you need to click
exactly on a character, not in the empty space between characters (clicking in empty space
will create a new text object instead). Watch for the mouse cursor to change into an I
shape and a blue frame to appear around the text—these are indications that you are
over a clickable text object.*

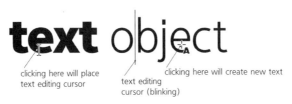

clicking here will place
text editing cursor

text editing
cursor (blinking)

clicking here will create new text

Figure 15-1: Placing the text editing cursor by clicking

Typing and editing text works the same way in Inkscape as it does in any
word processing application. Press `Enter` to start a new line, and use `Delete` or
`Backspace` to erase characters, including newlines. The text cursor can be moved
by the arrow keys (using `Ctrl` to jump by words), the `Home` and `End` keys (using
`Ctrl` to move to the beginning or end of the text object), and the `Page Up` and
`Page Down` keys. The canvas will automatically scroll, if necessary, so that the text
cursor is always visible.

*If, for some reason, editing text on the canvas is inconvenient, you can open the **Text
and Font** dialog (15.4.2) and, on the **Text** tab, edit the selected text object in a standard
text area. Unfortunately, clicking **Apply** loses any formatting you may have applied to
spans within your text (15.4.1); however, if you just open the window to read the text or
copy it to the clipboard without making any changes, it is perfectly safe.*

15.1.1 Selecting

You can select inside a text object by dragging *over* some characters (as with
clicking, you must start with a character body, not empty space) or by moving
the text editing cursor with the `Shift`-arrow keys. This *text selection*, visualized by a
greenish-blue rectangle overlay, is not to be confused with the program-wide
object selection (Chapter 5); text selection is unique to the Text tool and allows
you to style, kern, or delete spans inside the selected text object. When editing
text with the Text tool, pressing `Ctrl-A`, instead of selecting all objects, selects
all text inside this text object.

text selection

text editing cursor (always at the end of selection)

Figure 15-2: Text selection with the Text tool

Copying a text selection with `Ctrl-C` (or cutting with `Ctrl-X`) and pasting at the
cursor location with `Ctrl-V` is an easy way to move pieces of text around—be it
within the same text object, among text objects in the same document, across

documents, or even between Inkscape and other applications. For example, you can copy a piece of text in a word processor and insert it into a text object in Inkscape. Copy/paste does not transfer formatting, only the textual content.

15.2 Text Object Types

How do you create a new text object? This depends on what type of text you want to create, as we will discuss in the following sections.

15.2.1 Regular Text

To create a regular text object, switch to the Text tool (F8), click on the canvas (not on an existing text object!) to place a text cursor, and start typing. (If you drag instead of click, you will create a flowed text object, which is different in several important ways, as we will see shortly.)

Once you have typed at least a single character, the new text object is added to the document. At that point, you can switch to any other tool to deal with the newly created object (as long as it remains selected) as you would with any other object—for example, transform it with the Selector tool, paint it by clicking a palette color (this can be done in any tool), or draw a gradient across it with the Gradient tool.

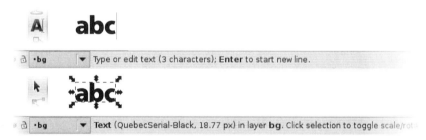

Figure 15-3: The status bar description of a text object in the Text and Selector tools

In regular text, there's no automatic line wrapping; you need to press Enter to go to the next line. If you don't do that and just keep typing into the same line, it can reach any length.

SVG *The text object is SVG's standard* text *element type. Each line in a multiline object is a* span *with a* sodipodi:role="line" *attribute and explicit* x *and* y *attributes that Inkscape calculates automatically, based on the coordinates of the root text object and line spacing (15.3.4).*

15.2.2 Flowed Text

Flowed text is different from regular text in that it has its own intrinsic width (or, more generally, *frame*), and it automatically *wraps* the text to fill this width (or frame). In other words, when typing in flowed text, you don't have to press Enter to go to the next line (but you press it to start a new paragraph).

15.2.2.1 Internal Frame

The easiest way to create a flowed text is by *dragging*, not clicking, over the canvas using the Text tool. This creates a rectangular frame, much like dragging with the Rectangle tool creates a rectangle. After releasing the mouse, you can type or paste your text, which will wrap upon reaching the edge of the frame. You can also drag the handle in the bottom-right corner to resize the frame and see the text automatically reflow to the new width.

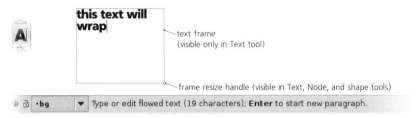

Figure 15-4: Flowed text with an internal frame

Text is wrapped at word boundaries; automatic hyphenation is not supported. If there's more text than fits the frame, extra text (starting with a word boundary) will be hidden (but it is still there; if you delete some text at the start, the end will move in and become visible). This kind of flowed text is said to have an *internal frame*, because its rectangular frame is part of the object itself, not a separate object; for example, when you transform the text, both the text itself and its frame are transformed as a whole.

NOTE *The bounding box (4.2) of a flowed text object only covers the visible characters of the text itself, regardless of the size of its frame.*

15.2.2.2 External Frame

There is another variant of flowed text which, instead of using its own internal rectangular frame, can be linked to any external path to shape its text. To create such an object, select two objects—any text (regular or flowed) and a path—and choose **Text ▸ Flow into Frame**:

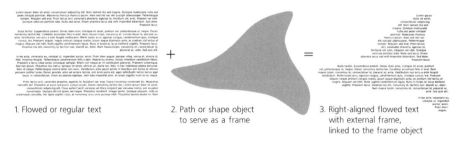

1. Flowed or regular text   2. Path or shape object to serve as a frame   3. Right-aligned flowed text with external frame, linked to the frame object

Figure 15-5: Flowed text with an external frame

This command does not remove or hide the frame object; the text and the frame remain separate objects, and the text is said to be *linked* to its frame, much like a clone is linked to its original (Chapter 16). Editing the shape of frame object forces the linked flowed text to reflow to the changed shape, but styling the frame (for example, hiding it by making fully transparent) does not affect the text.

You can move or transform the linked flowed text separately from the frame, but moving or transforming the frame affects the text as well (compare with the **Move according to transform** clone compensation mode, 16.2). Selecting a linked flowed text and pressing Shift-D will select its frame, just as it does with a clone and its original (16.4).

15.2.2.3 SVG Compatibility

The biggest problem with flowed text is that it is not a standard SVG feature but an Inkscape extension, which for historical reasons was implemented in a way that was incompatible with other SVG viewers. Therefore, if your file may be viewed in programs other than Inkscape, it must not contain any flowed texts.

How do you get rid of flowed text? One way is to use the **Unflow** command in the **Text** menu, which deletes the flowed text's internal frame (or breaks the link with its external frame) and converts it into a single line of regular text, which you can then rewrap manually.

Usually, it is more convenient to use the **Convert to Text** command (**Text ▶ Convert to Text**), which also turns flowed text into regular text, but does so while fully preserving its multiline appearance, removing only the autowrap capability. Of course you can also use the **Path ▶ Object to Path** command (15.7) to get a group of paths; you won't be able to edit the text anymore, but it will preserve the appearance.

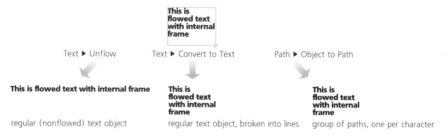

Figure 15-6: Three ways to get rid of a flowed text

15.2.3 Text on a Path

A single-line text object in Inkscape can link to a path to use the path not as a frame, but as a guide to bend the text's baseline. Just select both the text and the path and choose **Text ▶ Put on Path**:

Figure 15-7: Putting text on a path

This connection is live: Both the text and the path remain fully editable, and reshaping the path forces the text to bend correspondingly. If the text is longer than the path, its end is hidden (but it is still there; if you delete some text at the beginning, the end will move in and become visible). If the path consists of more than one subpath (**12.1.1**), the text will continue from one subpath to the next at character boundaries (but not word boundaries).

It makes no difference if the path has any stroke or fill; the only thing that matters for text is its geometric shape. Path direction also matters; if you want to put text on the other side of the path and in the reverse direction, just choose **Path ▸ Reverse** on the path:

Figure 15-8: Path direction affects the text on the path.

You can easily hide the guide path by making it fully transparent or removing both its fill and stroke. Moreover, as with flowed text, you can move the text object away from its path or transform it without breaking the link, whereas transforming the path moves or refits the text correspondingly.

More than one text object can be linked to the same path. Use **Text ▸ Remove from Path** to convert text on a path into a regular linear text, cutting its link to the path.

SVG *Text on a path is a standard SVG feature. In SVG, it has a* textPath *child element that contains the actual text and links to the path object by a* xlink:href *attribute (compare* **16.1**).

15.3   Text Layout

15.3.1   Direction

The two buttons on the Text tool's controls bar allow you to set the direction of the text flow—either horizontal (default) or vertical. This feature is primarily intended for writing in languages that prefer vertical direction (such as Japanese), but it can be used for text objects in any language, if necessary:

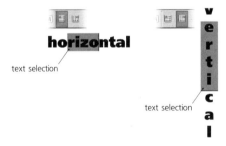

Figure 15-9: Text direction

NOTE *Inkscape's vertical text mode currently has a number of deficiencies if used for writing Japanese tategaki; for instance, choonpu are not rotated, and punctuation is often strangely positioned.*

15.3.2 Alignment

Each text object has a certain alignment: *left* (default), *right*, or *center*, which you can choose with the buttons on the Text tool's controls bar. For example, when editing left-aligned text, pressing Enter moves the cursor horizontally to the *beginning* of the next line, and the text you type grows to the right of this alignment edge, moving the cursor with it. In contrast, in a right-aligned text, Enter moves the cursor under the *end* of the previous line, and the text you type shifts to the left while the cursor remains in place.

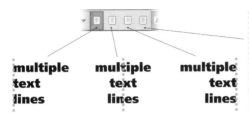

Figure 15-10: Text alignment and justification

For flowed text, there's an additional alignment option: *justify*, which expands spaces in each line to make both edges of the text column line up.

15.3.3 Kerning

What sets Inkscape apart from most other text-capable software is the freedom of moving each individual character and adjusting the spacing between letters. Unfortunately, most of this functionality is somewhat "hidden," as it is only available via keyboard shortcuts.

Position your cursor before a character, and press Alt-→. The rest of the line to the right of the cursor will move slightly to the right (by 1 screen pixel at the current zoom; pressing arrow keys with Shift-Alt moves 10 times the distance of an Alt-→, compare 6.5.1). What you have done is adjust the *kerning interval* between the two characters; it is easy to kern any pair of characters closer together or further apart to achieve the best overall balance and visual rythm in a line of text. Spaces can also be kerned to move *words* closer together or farther apart as needed.

To visualize the kerning you have added, simply select the text (e.g., via Ctrl-A). Whenever two letters were manually kerned closer together, their selection rectangles will overlap, and you will see a darker band; contrastingly, a kerned-out pair of characters will have a gap in the selection overlay between them (Figure 15-11). The width of the darker bands and gaps correspond exactly to the amount of kerning you have added at that point.

By zooming in closer, you can make finer kerning adjustments. Don't get carried away, however; always zoom out to see how your interval looks in the context of the entire text line.

Horizontal kerning is especially useful for text on a path. As you can see in Figure 15-7, letters tend to be too close together in concave bends and too far apart on convex arcs. With manual kerning, it is easy to counteract this effect and make the characters spread evenly along the curve.

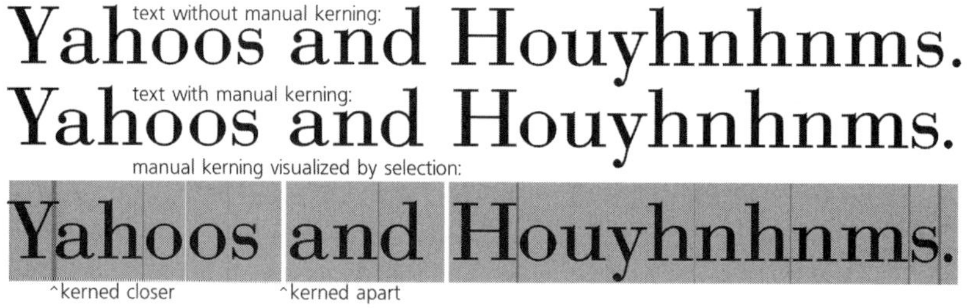

text without manual kerning:
Yahoos and Houyhnhnms.

text with manual kerning:
Yahoos and Houyhnhnms.

manual kerning visualized by selection:
Yahoos and Houyhnhnms.

^kerned closer   ^kerned apart

Figure 15-11: Adjusting kerning intervals in a string

NOTE *Many fonts contain built-in kerning instructions; for example, a font may specify that whenever Y and a are next to each other, they are kerned together by 0.03 of the font size. Inkscape honors these automatic font kerning instructions. However, if you try to manually adjust kerning in such a pair of characters, you will disable the automatic kern. This is why the first* Alt-← *to kern Y and a closer together may result in these two letters jumping, unexpectedly, further apart. Don't worry; just keep pressing* Alt-← *to achieve the kerning interval you need.*

You can also kern characters *vertically* by pressing Alt-↑ and Alt-↓. A combination of horizontal and vertical kerning gives you an absolute freedom in positioning individual letters in a text string:

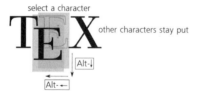

Figure 15-12: Combining horizontal and vertical kerning

If you select one or more characters by mouse drag or pressing Shift-arrows, applying kerning shortcuts will effectively move the selected fragment relative to the rest of the text by inserting two opposite kerns before and after it:

select a character

other characters stay put

Alt-↓

Alt-←

Figure 15-13: Moving a selection by kerning shortcuts

Finally, you can *rotate* any character in a text object by pressing Alt-[or Alt-] when the cursor is before that character:

Alt-[

baseline

baseline origin of X

kerns visualized by selection:

Figure 15-14: Rotating characters

This rotation is around the character's *baseline origin*—its leftmost point on the *baseline* (the line on which lie the bottoms of most letters without extenders, such as *i* or *m*). (By the way, the baseline origin of the first character of each text object is shown on the canvas as a little square when you select that text with the Selector tool.)

NOTE *For historical reasons, horizontal and vertical kerning as well as rotation are not available in flowed text, but only in regular text and text on a path.*

SVG *In SVG, kerning information is stored in the* dx *(horizontal),* dy *(vertical), and* rot *(rotation) attributes of the* text *element. Each attribute contains a list of space-separated numbers, each number corresponding to the character at the same position. For example,* dx="0 0 -2" *means that the third character in this text is moved by 2 px to the left.*

15.3.4 Letter Spacing and Line Spacing

What if you want to kern all characters in your text closer together or farther apart, not just some particular pair? This kind of adjustment is called *letter spacing* (in other software, it is sometimes called *tracking*); select all or part of the text and press Alt-> to space the characters apart or Alt-< to move them closer together (these are the same shortcuts that scale an object in the Selector tool).

The ideal amount of letter spacing depends on the final viewing size of your text. Usually, a smaller font size requires more airy spacing, while larger text should be tighter:

Houyhnhnms

Houyhnhnms

Figure 15-15: Spacing letters further apart (top) or squeezing them together (bottom)

Similarly, you can adjust the spacing between lines in a regular or flowed text object by pressing Ctrl-Alt-> and Ctrl-Alt-<. This adjustment affects the entire text object, disregarding any text that is selected. A numeric **Line spacing** control, measurable as a percentage of the natural line height for this font size, is also available in the **Text and Font** dialog (Shift-Ctrl-T).

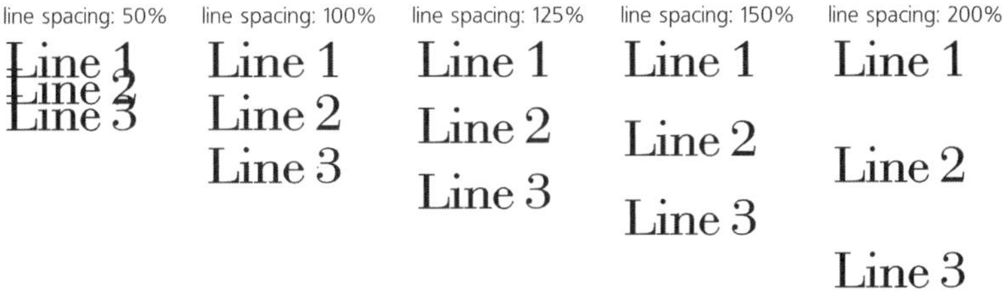

line spacing: 50%   line spacing: 100%   line spacing: 125%   line spacing: 150%   line spacing: 200%

Line 1
Line 2
Line 3

Line 1
Line 2
Line 3

Line 1
Line 2
Line 3

Line 1
Line 2
Line 3

Line 1
Line 2
Line 3

Figure 15-16: Adjusting line spacing

Consistent with other shortcuts, both letter spacing and line spacing shortcuts can be accompanied by Shift for 10 times the effect.

15.4   Styling Text

From most viewpoints, text objects are no different from any other object type; you can not only transform but also style (choose fill or stroke, adjust opacity, apply filters, etc.) a text object as a whole without even going into the Text tool (and, of course, without losing the ability to edit the text). However, only the Text tool allows you to change style properties specific to text (such as font family and font size) as well as apply style to *spans* (fragments) of a text in an object.

SVG   *To have a different style, a span of text must be enclosed within a* span *element. You don't need to think about it, of course; for any overlapping or nested spans you create or delete, Inkscape manages the* span *elements automatically.*

The two places where you can change text styles are the controls bar of the Text tool (above the canvas) and the **Text and Font** dialog. The former is faster and more convenient, while the latter provides access to more options.

15.4.1   Non-Text Style Properties

When you have a text span selected in the Text tool, most (but not all) style-changing commands and style-reporting UI elements apply to that text span, not to the entire text object. For example, you can easily change the color of a span of text by selecting it and clicking a color swatch in the palette, using the **Fill and Stroke** dialog (8.1.1), or color gestures (8.5). Similarly, you can assign or remove a stroke or adjust opacity of the span. However, blur or other filters cannot be applied to a span; if you try this, the entire text object will be blurred or filtered.

Assigning a gradient or pattern fill to a span is possible, though it is a bit tricky. You need to create a separate object with the gradient or pattern you need, copy it (Ctrl-C), then select a text span with the Text tool, and paste the style (Shift-Ctrl-V) onto it. Unfortunately, you cannot then edit such a gradient on a span by dragging the handles in the Gradient tool.

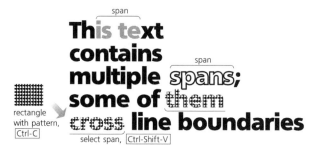

Figure 15-17: Styling text spans

In general, the paste style trick is very handy when styling text spans—it allows you to quickly transfer styles (including not only color but also font, size, letter spacing, etc.) between objects and parts of your text. To copy a style from a text span, you don't even need to select it; just place the text editing cursor anywhere inside the span and press Ctrl-C .

15.4.2 Fonts and Variants

With regard to fonts, Inkscape behaves as could be expected from a modern graphic application: It allows you to use any outline fonts (TrueType, OpenType, Type 1) that are installed in your operating system.

The list of all font families (not individual fonts), with graphic samples for each family, opens from the controls bar of the Text tool. You can choose a family by scrolling through the list; if you know the name of the font you need, you can click to place the cursor in the editing field and start typing; a dropdown list of possible completions will appear.

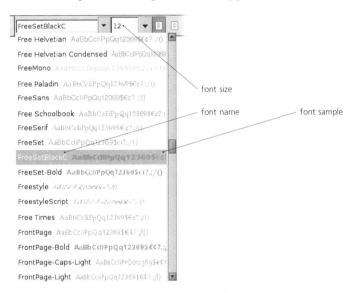

Figure 15-18: Choosing a font in the Text tool

The same list of font families is also available in the **Text and Font** dialog (Shift-Ctrl-T), as shown in Figure 15-19. Here, instead of a small generic sample, you can see a preview of the selected text object in the chosen font with the chosen font size.

Many fonts contain variants within the same families. In the controls bar, you can set bold, italic (oblique), or bold italic variants for your selected span, using the two toggle buttons; the Ctrl-I and Ctrl-B shortcuts, expectedly, work the same as these two buttons. In the **Text and Font** dialog, you have a complete list of all variants available in the family, which apart from italic and various weights (light, medium, bold, heavy, etc.) may include variations along the width axis (condensed, stretched, etc.). Once you choose a style you need in the dialog, click **Apply** for the changes to take effect.

NOTE *When you have a text object selected, the font you choose is applied to that object; if you select a span inside that text, only that span will be styled. With nothing selected, choosing a font style in the controls bar changes the default style of the Text tool which will be applied to newly created text objects; in the **Text and Font** dialog, click the **Set as default** button to make the style selected in the dialog the default style.*

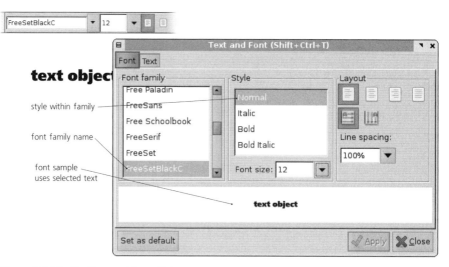

Figure 15-19: The Text and Font dialog

15.4.3 Font Size

Both in the controls bar and in the dialog, font size may only be set in px units
(**A.6**). However, in many cases you don't even need to use that numeric control;
you can simply scale an entire text object instead, for example, with the Selector
tool (**6.2**) or keyboard shortcuts. Both font size controls will then take this scaling
into account when displaying font sizes; for example, if you set a text object
to 12 px font size but then scale it up twice, you will see its font size reported
as 24 px.

15.5 Text Extensions

A number of extensions in **Extensions ▶ Text** are useful for dealing with text
objects. They include:

- A group of case manipulation extensions: converting text to **UPPERCASE**,
  lowercase, **Sentence case** (capitalize first letter of each sentence), **Title Case**
  (capitalize first letter of each word), **fLIP cASE** (convert lowercase to uppercase and vice versa), and **rANdOm CasE**. All these extensions work only on
  selected objects.

- A simple **Replace Text** extension that you can use to search and replace a
  text substring in a number of text objects (which must be selected).

- **Lorem ipsum**: a generator of pseudo-Latin gibberish traditionally used to
  fill in text in design mock-ups. You can choose the number of paragraphs,
  their length, and their variation; this extension will fill in the selected flowed
  text object with text or, if there's no text object, it will create a new one to
  fill the entire page (for an example output, see Figure 15-10).

15.6 Spellcheck

Inkscape's built-in spellchecker can use up to three dictionaries at the same time. To set it up, open the **Inkscape Preferences** dialog, and choose the **Spellcheck** tab. For example, you can use French as your primary language but add English and Russian as second and third languages. This way, you can check texts in any of these languages or in a combination of the languages, and only the words that are missing in all three languages will be flagged as misspelled. If you only need a single language, leave the second and third options set to **None**.

Figure 15-20: Setting up the Inkscape spellchecker in Inkscape Preferences

NOTE *On Linux, you need to install Aspell dictionaries for the languages you want to check; use your distribution's standard software installer for this. On Windows, Inkscape comes prepackaged with dictionaries for several languages (English, French, German, Russian, Spanish, and others).*

NOTE *Many languages have more than one dictionary. For example, English (en) has variants for USA (en_US), UK (en_GB), Canada (en_CA), and Australia (en_AU); the UK variant additionally breaks into subvariants by the preferred verb suffix (en_GB-ise or en_GB-ize), and so on.*

Once you invoke the spellchecker with Ctrl-Alt-K (or **Text ▸ Check Spelling**), it checks all the visible text objects in your document (they need not be selected) in turn, going top-to-bottom and left-to-right. Having found a misspelled word, it displays a red frame around the word and pops up a dialog:

Figure 15-21: Spellchecking a document

The object with the misspelling is selected; if you are using the Text tool, the editing cursor is placed at the beginning of the misspelled word. In the dialog, you can do any of the following:

- Choose one of the listed suggestions (they come from all active dictionaries) and **Accept** it; this button is disabled unless you choose something in the list.

- **Ignore once**; the next time this word is encountered, the spellchecker will flag it again.

- **Ignore** the word *for the rest of this session*; it will ignore any other instances of the word during this check, but the next time you run the spellchecker, it will flag it again.

- **Add** the word to one of the active dictionaries so that it is never flagged as misspelled again in this or subsequent sessions.

Also, since the dialog does not lock the Inkscape window, you can simply edit the word with the Text tool, as you would normally do. Once you edit it to something acceptable, the spellchecker will automatically turn off the red frame and continue checking the document.

You can stop the spellcheck at any time by clicking **Stop** or simply closing the **Check Spelling** dialog. When it is stopped, you can click **Start** at any time to restart the check.

15.6.1 Special Characters

To enter a character that does not appear on your keyboard, you need to know its Unicode number. *Unicode* is a worldwide standard that covers all existing and most historical alphabets, as well as a plethora of other special characters; the best place to look up the Unicode number for a character is *http://unicode.org*.

Once you know the hexadecimal Unicode number of the character you need, press Ctrl-U while editing a text object, type the number (watch the status bar for feedback), and press Enter. The character will be inserted at the text cursor. Here are a few commonly used special characters:

Name	Character	Hexadecimal number
em dash	—	2014
en dash	–	2013
left curly double quote	"	201C
right curly double quote	"	201D
left curly single quote	'	2018
right curly single quote	'	2019
left double guillemet	«	00AB
right double guillemet	»	00BB
ellipsis	…	2026
multiplication	×	00D7
copyright	©	00A9
registered sign	®	00AE
trademark	™	2122
round bullet	•	2022

If the character you requested exists in the current font, it will be used; otherwise, Inkscape will attempt to find any font on your system that has this character. If that fails, you will see a space inserted instead.

15.7 Converting Text to Path

Despite Inkscape's powerful text-editing capabilities, sometimes you will still want to convert text to path—for example, to edit the outlines of the letters, to clip something with your text (that requires a path), or to be able to send your SVG document to someone who may not have the font you're using. The command **Path ▸ Object to Path** (Shift-Ctrl-C) will work on text objects just as it does on shapes (13.1.1).

Unlike a shape, a text object becomes not a single path but a *group* of paths, one for each glyph (character) of the original text. This allows Inkscape to fully preserve the appearance of the text, including any styling applied to spans inside it. Now you can select any individual letter with Ctrl-click in the Selector tool or with a simple click in the Node tool. If you prefer to have a single path corresponding to the entire text object, choose **Path ▸ Object to Path** as above, then use **Path ▸ Combine** (Ctrl-K) to combine all of the characters into a single path object with a uniform style.

16

CLONES

The idea of a *clone*—a linked copy of an object that updates itself when the original changes—comes naturally from the vector way of thinking about graphics. You might say that a clone is not a real object—rather, it is just a command: "Display a copy of the object here." The document stores that command, not an actual copy of the object. An actual cloned object exists only in the memory of an SVG application such as Inkscape when it loads the document.

There are both artistic and technical reasons to use clones. Watching several objects change live when you edit only one is in itself an exciting experience, opening many creative possibilities. On the other hand, using clones instead of duplicates makes the SVG document smaller and faster to display. Map symbols, repeated design elements such as bullets or icons, various symmetric designs or patterns—all these are easy to do with clones. Few other vector editors allow you to create live linked copies of objects with such directness and ease as Inkscape.

16.1   Creating a Clone

To clone one or several objects, just select them and press $\boxed{\text{Alt-D}}$ (or use **Edit ▸ Clone ▸ Create Clone**). The visible result of this is exactly the same as that of duplicating ($\boxed{\text{Ctrl-D}}$): A copy of each selected object is created and placed on top of the original. If you need to get a clone of several objects as a whole, just group them together and clone the group.

A clone is a *linked* copy of an object. What constitutes this link?

Most importantly, a clone copies the original's *content*. If it is a clone of a path (Chapter 12) or a shape (Chapter 11), then it exactly reproduces the form of the original, and it updates automatically when you edit the original in the Node tool or in a shape tool. If it is a clone of the text, it has the same textual content and is also updated live when you edit the original with the Text tool. Finally, if you clone a group, you can then enter that group (5.10) to add, delete, or edit objects within the group—and the group's clone will update immediately. On the other hand, since a clone has no content of its own, you cannot edit its content—no node editing, text editing, or ungrouping is possible on a clone so long as it remains a clone.

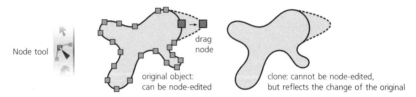

Figure 16-1:   A clone is a linked copy of an object.

What about *transforms*? If you scale, rotate, or skew the original, all its clones will do the same. However, if you just move the original object, by default the clone will *not* be affected (although that can be changed, see below). Of course if you select *both* the original and its clone, you can transform them together in any way, by moving or otherwise.

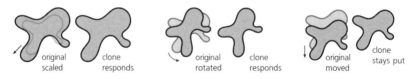

Figure 16-2:   Clones respond to the original's transforms, except for moving.

You can also move, scale, rotate, or skew the clone completely independently of its original. The clone's own transform is applied *on top* of the transform inherited from the original. For example, if you squeeze a clone vertically and then rotate its original, the clone will be both rotated and squeezed—but the vertical squeeze will be applied to the shape *after* it is rotated, resulting in a skew, as shown in Figure 16-3.

The *style* of the original is also passed on to its clones. If you paint the original a different fill or stroke color, all its clones will take the same color at once.

Figure 16-3: A clone's own transform is applied on top of the transform inherited from the original.

Conversely, if you try to paint a clone, it will simply refuse to change its color, remaining true to its original. (Again, this rule has exceptions, as we will see below.)

To summarize, here's a table that lists various things you can and cannot do on a clone and its original and how those changes affect one another:

	Move	Scale, rotate, skew	Node or shape edit	Style
applied to **original**	does *not* affect clones (by default)	does affect clones	does affect clones	does affect clones
applied to **clone**	is possible	is possible (on top of original's transformation)	is impossible	is impossible (unless unset in the original)

SVG *In SVG source, a clone is represented by an* svg:use *element. Its* xlink:href *attribute contains a URL pointing to the original of this clone. Per the SVG standard, this URL can point to any element, be it within the same document or in a different document anywhere on the Internet. However, Inkscape does not yet support cross-document references, so any clone created in Inkscape must have its original in the same document.*

16.2 Transforming Clones

In general, as we have seen, a clone can be transformed in any way you want; this transform is applied on top of the transform it inherits from its original. You can use any transformation method: Dragging by mouse, transforming by keys (**6.5**), aligning, distributing, and snapping all work on clones exactly as they do on regular objects.

On the other hand, transforms of the original are classified—by how they affect the clones of that original—into two groups: simple moves and everything else. For "everything else" (scales, rotates, and skews) the transform is passed directly on to all clones. Simple moves, however, are treated differently.

By default, Inkscape tries to isolate clones from the moves of the original, so that they remain in place when the original is moved. Under the hood, this is done by moving the clone in the opposite direction, cancelling out the move. This works pretty intuitively and is generally convenient; this way, for example, you can take the original of a large pattern of clones and move it away without disturbing the pattern. You can also grab both the original and its clones and move them anywhere; they would behave as expected, that is, move in parallel, even if the clone has a transform of its own.

This compensating behavior can be adjusted by the user. The **Clones** tab of the **Inkscape Preferences** dialog (Figure 16-4) contains the following options:

- The first option, **Move in parallel**, forces all clones, including those rotated or scaled, to always move in parallel with the original, as if they were always selected together with it (even if in fact they are not).

- The second option, **Stay unmoved** (this is the default), forces those clones that were not selected to stay unmoved (but those that *are* selected are moved as usual).

- The final option, **Move according to transform**, turns off any clone movement compensation; now each clone, selected or not, moves according to the transform inherited from its original, without any compensation. When there are complex transformations in effect, the resulting behavior may seem surprising and unpredictable, but from SVG's viewpoint, it is the least intrusive, since the inherited clone transformations are not tampered with in any way.

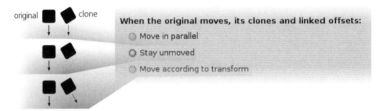

Figure 16-4: Setting up movement compensation of clones

It is also important to remember that transforming clones does not honor the **Affect** buttons on the Selector controls bar (**6.10**); it always behaves as if all these buttons were pressed. You cannot scale a clone in such a way as to leave its stroke width unchanged or its gradient unaffected—because what you're transforming is, in effect, an image of the original, and that image cannot have a different stroke width or gradient position compared to the original.

16.3 Styling Clones

In the beginning of this chapter, I mentioned that clones inherit their style from their originals. That is true: A clone of a red rectangle will be red. There are, however, several important exceptions and workarounds for this limitation.

First of all, opacity (**8.1.2**) and blur (**17.1**) are not subject to this limitation at all: You can easily blur a clone or make it semitransparent. This is because these properties *accumulate*—that is, if you blur something and then blur its parent, these blurs add up, and the result will be more fuzzy than from either of these blurs taken alone. This also means that if your original is *already* blurred or has less than 100% opacity, you can make its clone *more* blurred or *more* transparent, but not less.

The same applies to filter effects (Chapter **17**; actually, blur is just one of the filters). You can apply any filter to a clone, and it will work on top of any filters that the original of this clone has. For example, you can make the clone of a red rectangle green or gray by applying the **Color Matrix** filter primitive (**8.8**).

But what about plain fill or stroke colors? Even they can be changed in a clone, but only if the original cooperates. Namely, any style property that you want to change in a clone must be *unset* in the original. Unsetting (**8.1.1**) is not the same as setting to none; a property is unset when it is simply *not specified* for an object, which allows its clone's property to take effect instead.

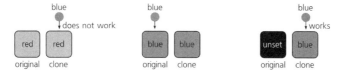

Figure 16-5: A clone can be painted if its original has the paint unset.

Inkscape has a special button in the **Fill and Stroke** dialog, as well as a command in the selected style indicator (**8.4**), for unsetting the fill or stroke properties of an object. An object with an unset stroke simply has no visible stroke, but if you unset its fill, the object is shown as black. If you want to unset some other style property, you will need to use the XML Editor (**4.7**) and manually edit the style attribute of the object, removing the property you want to override in the clones.

If you have a group as the original object, then you can unset fill or stroke in only some of the members of that group, leaving others colored. Then, if you clone that group and paint the clone, only the objects with unset properties will take on that color, whereas everything else will remain true to the original.

16.4   Chaining Clones

Duplicating (**4.4**) or copying and pasting a clone gives you another clone *of the same original.* (You can copy and then paste a clone into a different document but only together with its original; if you try to paste a clone alone, it will end up being *orphaned* and invisible.) Duplicating an existing clone is often convenient, as this duplicate will also get the first clone's own transform and style, if it had any. Of course, you can also get another clone simply by cloning the original again.

Moreover, nothing prevents you from cloning a clone object itself. The resulting object—a *clone of a clone*—will still display the content of its ultimate original, but its link to it is no longer direct; it is now a grandchild of the original, while the child (the first-order clone) stands between them. This means that the grandchild clone inherits transforms and style first from the original, then from its parent clone, and finally, it has its own transform and style on top of all that. Such clone-of-clone chains (they can be of any length) are rarely useful and not recommended, if only because long chains of clones can be bad for rendering performance; in almost all cases, multiple clones of the same original can be used instead, as shown in Figure 16-6.

To figure out if the object you selected is a clone—and if so, what it is a clone of—look at the status bar. It will describe your selected object as, for example, *Clone of: Group* or *Clone of: Clone of: Path.* If you want to know exactly which object is the parent of the selected clone, press Shift-D: Inkscape will draw a dashed line from the clone to its original (that line will disappear after one second) and select the original object (Figure 16-7).

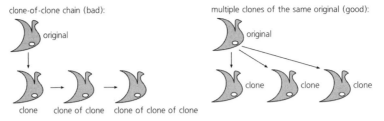

Figure 16-6: Instead of clones of clones, use multiple clones of the same object.

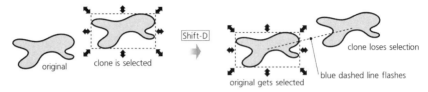

Figure 16-7: Find the original of a clone by pressing Shift-D.

16.5   Unlinking and Relinking Clones

A clone's link to its original is its main characteristic feature; that is, after all, why we use clones. This link facilitates a lot of tasks in complex designs—for example, you can use clones for identical buttons or bullets on a website mockup, with the ability to change all such elements at once by changing their common original. However, sometimes this link becomes an obstacle, and you want to edit your object independently of its former original. For this, you need to *unlink* the clone.

Select a clone and press Shift-Alt-D (or select **Edit ▸ Clone ▸ Unlink Clone**). Visibly, nothing changes; but the clone ceases to be clone and becomes a regular object—a full copy of the original, with all its additional transforms and style preserved, now totally independent and independently editable. You can unlink many clones at once.

What happens if you delete the original of a clone? By default, its clones are automatically unlinked—that is, they are turned into full copies of the object being killed. On the same **Clones** tab of the **Inkscape Preferences** dialog you can, however, choose a different behavior and force all clones to commit mass suicide when their original goes under:

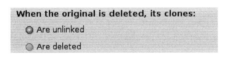

Figure 16-8: Setting up the behavior of clones being orphaned

When you *relink* a clone, it remains a clone, but its original changes. Manual relinking is done as follows: Suppose you have a clone C of an object A, but want it to be a clone of B instead. Select B and copy it to the clipboard (Ctrl-C), then select the clone C and do **Edit ▸ Clone ▸ Relink to Copied**. After that, C becomes a clone of B—which, depending on what is B, may result in C changing shape, style, position, transform, or any combination of these (Figure 16-9).

Figure 16-9: Relinking a clone to a different original

Manual relinking is a rarely needed operation. More useful is *automatic relinking on duplication*. Imagine that you have a complex group of objects, some of which are clones of others—for example, a 3D-like graphic button where the shadow is a blurred clone of the main shape. Now, you select this entire group and duplicate it. What happens?

Within the group, each regular object will duplicate to a regular object, and each clone will duplicate to a clone. However, the clones will still be linked to the originals in the source group—which is most likely not what you wanted! It would be more natural for the shadow in the duplicated group to be a clone of the shape *in the same group*, instead of some other group far away. To ensure this, go to the same **Clones** tab and check **When duplicating original+clones: Relink duplicated clones**. Now, after duplication you will have two independent buttons, each with an independently editable shape and a shadow linked to its own shape:

Figure 16-10: Automatically relinking clones on duplication

16.6   Tiling Clones

The huge and powerful **Create Tiled Clones** dialog (**Edit ▸ Clone ▸ Create Tiled Clones**) is basically a tool for creating many clones at once. These created clones can be placed into many kinds of spatial and color patterns, ranging from absolutely regular to totally randomized. Moreover, you can also make these clones trace the image underneath them.

16.6.1   Size and Bounding Box

The first thing to do, before you can create a tiled clone pattern, is to select the object you will be cloning. I recommend using a group for that; even if you have a single object, group it (Ctrl-G). This way, you will later be able to add more objects to the original group and the clones will reflect that. Place the original into the top-left corner of the area you want to fill with the pattern.

In the **Create Tiled Clones** dialog, start by specifying the size of the tiling (Figure 16-11). You can either give the number of rows and columns in the pattern, or if you have some specific area to fill, you can type or paste its width and height. Note that too-large patterns—with more than a few thousands of clones—can slow Inkscape down considerably.

Figure 16-11: Setting the size of a pattern

To create a tile (after you set all other parameters as described below, or if you just trusted the defaults), click the **Create** button. The pattern appears on the canvas, but you still have the original object selected. The **Remove** button deletes any previously tiled clones of the selected object. Note that **Create** implies **Remove**—that is, once you click **Create**, any existing tiled clones (but not regular clones created by Alt-D) are removed and replaced by a new pattern.

The **Unclump** button works exactly as the same-name button in the **Align and Distribute** dialog (7.5.1), except that it moves all the tiled clones of the selected object rather than all selected objects. Unclumping is especially useful for making randomized patterns more uniform without regularizing them. The **Reset** button changes all parameters of the dialog back to the defaults.

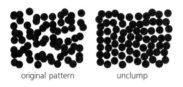

Figure 16-12: Unclumping a randomized pattern

The **Use saved size and position of the tile** checkbox has no effect when you create a pattern for the first time. However, if you modify the object you're tiling and create the pattern again, normally Inkscape will use the altered size of the object, which may result in the pattern changing its overall size and the alignment of the tiles. To make Inkscape use the same tile size as the last time you created a pattern from that object, even if the object's size has changed, check this checkbox. For example, you can create a pattern from a rectangle, fine-tune all the parameters, then remove the pattern, scale up the original rectangle, and recreate the pattern with this checkbox checked. You will now have the exact same pattern as last time, but with its tiles larger and overlapping each other. (Of course, you can also simply edit the original without removing and regenerating the pattern.) Every object may thus remember its last "tiled size."

NOTE *Note that all patterns include a clone that exactly (except when randomized) overlays the original object. This means that if you lose the selection of the original, simply clicking the original's location will select the overlying clone and not the original. Use* Alt*-click (5.9) or select any of the clones and press* Shift-D *to jump to the original.*

16.6.2 Symmetry

The first tab in the dialog is titled **Symmetry**. All it has is a list of *symmetry groups* from which you select one to use for your pattern. Each symmetry group is a specific way to transform the clones to form the pattern. It is not by a whim of Inkscape's programmers that the number of these groups is exactly 17; mathematicians have proved that any possible regular pattern on a plane can be classified into one of these 17 types. For a complete description of each symmetry, see the Wikipedia article on "wallpaper group." Here is an overview of the types:

P1

This is the simplest possible symmetry: The pattern tile is simply repeated in a rectangular grid without any rotations or flips.

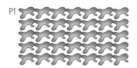

Figure 16-13: The basic symmetry: P1

P2, PM, PG, CM, PMM, PMG, PGG, and CMM

These symmetries use rotations by 180 degrees as well as vertical and horizontal flips in various combinations. However, all of these symmetries use the same rectangular grid placement as P1, with the width and height of the unit of grid being the same as width and height of the original object.

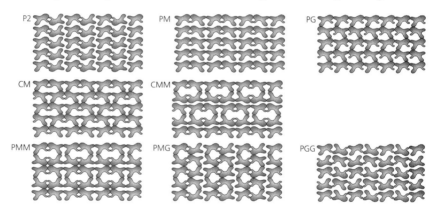

Figure 16-14: Symmetries with flips and 180-degree rotations

P4, P4M, and P4G

These symmetries involve rotations by 90 degrees, so they produce square-based patterns. The P4M symmetry results in partial overlapping of rectangular tiles; with it, use triangular tiles to avoid overlapping and fill the plane (Figure 16-15).

Figure 16-15: Symmetries with 90-degree rotations

P3, P31M, and P3M1

These symmetries involve rotations by 120 degrees and are thus roughly triangular in appearance. Again, P31M creates a more dense pattern with partially overlapping tiles, so you can use a "pie slice" shape to fill the plane with this symmetry without overlapping.

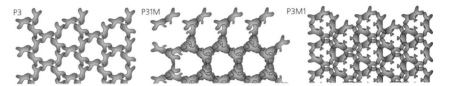

Figure 16-16: Symmetries with 120-degree rotations

P6 and P6M

These symmetries rotate the tiles by 60 degrees, forming snowflake-like hexagonal patterns. Of them, P6M again overlaps the tiles and requires a "pie slice" shape to fill the plane without overlapping.

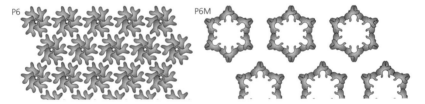

Figure 16-17: Symmetries with 60-degree rotations

For "dense" patterns (P4M, P31M, P6M) that overlap the tiles, the following trick may be useful: Create the pattern and then scale the original down. This will make the pattern more sparse, and its characterisic logic will be easier to understand.

When working on a tessellation (a pattern that completely fills the plane without gaps or overlapping), it would be very difficult to create a tile of the proper shape in isolation, even if you understand well how your chosen symmetry works. Instead, just start with any random shape, create the pattern from it using the desired symmetry, and then node-edit the original path watching how the pattern's clones repeat its changes. In this way, a surprisingly sophisticated tessellation can be produced very quickly (see 24.2).

16.6.3 Shift, Scale, and Rotation

The next three tabs in the dialog allow you to specify the *additional* transforms to be applied to the pattern's tiles—that is, transforms on top of those shifts, rotations, and flips implied by the chosen symmetry group.

All of these additional transform components can be specified separately per row and per column, and each value can include a degree of randomness. You can specify, for example, an equivalent of "Make tiles in each next row 20 percent taller, rotate tiles in each next column by 5 degrees, and make the rotation angle vary randomly by 50 percent." All shifts, scales, and randomization values are measured as percentages of the original object's dimensions.

Figure 16-18: The Shift, Scale, and Rotation tabs

Here's how it works for shifts:

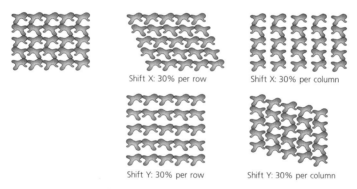

Figure 16-19: Specifying shifts per row and per column (PG symmetry)

Negative shifts are possible, too. Naturally, to get all the clones to overlay the original, you need to specify **Shift X: −100%** per column and **Shift Y: −100%** per row. In combination with rotation per row, this makes it possible to easily create a flower or a clock face:

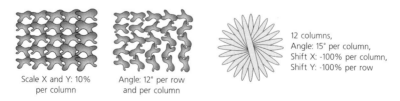

Figure 16-20: Specifying scale and rotation per row and per column

You can make the values **Alternate** (for example, scale clones in every second row). The **Cumulate** checkbox forces the values of shift or scale to accumulate;

for example, normally a shift of 10 px per column means that each column is shifted by 10 px relative to the previous column. If you check **Cumulate**, the same value would mean every column being shifted 10 px further than was its predecessor—that is, the second column is 10 px from the first, the third is 20 px from the second, and so on.

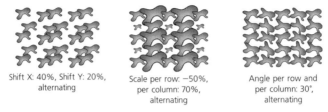

Shift X: 40%, Shift Y: 20%, alternating

Scale per row: −50%, per column: 70%, alternating

Angle per row and per column: 30°, alternating

Figure 16-21: Alternating transforms

For complex symmetries, a natural question is: What should be considered a "row" and a "column" when calculating transform values? Inkscape draws complex patterns by symmetric clusters (of 3, 4, 6, or 12 clones, depending on the symmetry), going from one cluster to the next horizontally within a row. In other words, clones that belong to one cluster are considered to be in the same row but in different columns. This means that the **Per row** shift values work by shifting rows of clusters or scaling clones in each cluster uniformly, whereas **Per column** values affect each clone independently, and as a result clusters lose their symmetry. If you want to space out symmetric clusters in both dimensions, just create a single cluster with your chosen symmetry, then group it, and tile the group with a simple P1 symmetry, possibly with alternating shifts.

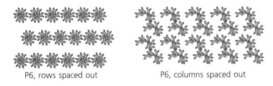

P6, rows spaced out

P6, columns spaced out

Figure 16-22: Transforming complex symmetries

16.6.4 Blur and Opacity

This tab of the dialog looks and acts very similar to the transform tabs; here, you can adjust the blur and the opacity (the **Fade out** value) of the clones in the pattern, per row or per column, with optional alternating or randomization. Remember that you can only make a clone more blurred or more transparent than its original, but not less.

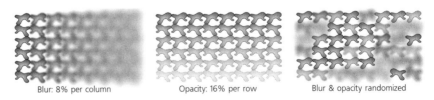

Blur: 8% per column

Opacity: 16% per row

Blur & opacity randomized

Figure 16-23: Varying blur and opacity in a pattern

16.6.5 Color

As we've seen in 16.3, if you want to paint a clone with its own color, you need to unset the corresponding property in the original. Once you've done that for the paint you're going to change (fill, stroke, or both), the **Create Tiled Clones** dialog allows you to create a wide variety of color patterns.

The **Color** tab of the dialog looks very similar to all the tabs we already know. Here, you can vary any of the three components of the clone color in the HSL model—hue, saturation, and lightness (8.2.3)—per row or per column, as well as alternate or randomize the changes. You also need to specify the **Initial color** from which all these variations will start; just click the color swatch and use the color selector dialog. Remember that the original must have unset fill or stroke, otherwise this tab will have no effect!

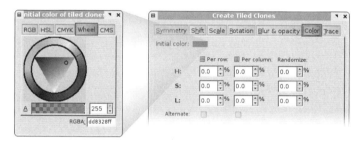

Figure 16-24: Setting an initial color for the Color tab

For example, by starting with red and varying the hue by 5 percent per row and per column, you get a slanted rainbow, as shown in Figure 10 on the color insert.

16.6.6 Tracing

The last tab of the **Create Tiled Clones** dialog (Figure 16-25) is quite different from the rest. Here, you can make the pattern *trace* any kind of image on top of which it is built—that is, make it so that some of the aspects of each clone will depend on what is below it. The background image you're tracing can be anything—for example, you can cover with the pattern an imported bitmap such as a photo, or you can draw anything with vector objects; it makes no difference to the tracer what it picks its values from.

The tab contains three main areas that correspond to the three main steps of the tracing algorithm. First, you pick some value at the location of each clone; second, you do some optional processing with that value; and third, you apply the result to some aspect of the clone. Enable the controls of the tab by checking the **Trace the drawing under the tiles** checkbox.

- For the input value, you have the option of picking the **Color**, **Opacity**, or any single component of the color in RGB or HSL models. The value you pick for each clone is averaged over the entire rectangular area that will be covered by that clone's bounding box. Of these options, all produce a single numeric value in the range from 0 to 1, except **Color**, which picks all three components of the color as a composite value.

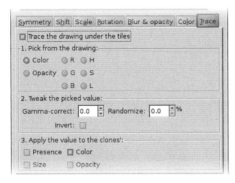

Figure 16-25: The Trace tab

- The possible ways to process the value include:

gamma correction
Positive gamma shifts the picked value up, negative shifts it down.

randomization by a given percentage
The value will have a random component of the given size; 0% randomization means the value is exactly as picked, 100% randomization means it is totally random and does not depend on the picked value at all.

inversion
Turns high values into low and vice versa.

If a color is picked, this processing is applied to each of its components independently, as shown in Figure 11 on the color insert.

- Finally, the resulting value can be applied to the clone's probability of presence (0 translates into absence of the clone at this location, 1 into presence, and intermediate values make it appear with this given probability); color (this can directly reuse the background color if it was picked; otherwise, it translates single values to shades of gray), size (from disappearance at 0 to its full size at 1), and opacity (smaller values make the clone more transparent). Any number of these options can be enabled at the same time; for example, you can pick lightness, invert it, and apply it to both the opacity and size of the clones (see Figure 12 on the color insert).

17

FILTERS

Inkscape filters are a way to apply complex bitmap processing algorithms to the objects in your drawing. True to the vector spirit, filters are nondestructive: You can always change the parameters of any filter, and the original vector object remains fully editable. Examples of what filters can do include blurring, sharpening, color adjustments, adding texture, various distortions, 3D-like effects such as bevels, and many others. Moreover, you can combine filters into arbitrarily complex *filter stacks*.

SVG filters (as defined by the SVG standard and implemented by Inkscape) are extremely powerful; a whole book could be written on their uses and capabilities. Unfortunately, they can also be quite technical, especially if you're trying to compose your own filter stacks. Therefore, in this chapter, we will start by looking at some simple ways to use filters, such as the **Blur** control (17.1) and preset filter effects (17.3). Then, for those who seek more flexibility and are not afraid to go technical, we will discuss the powerful **Filter Editor** dialog (17.4), which enables you to create your own filter stacks from standard filter primitives.

17.1 Blur

We have seen blurring used many times throughout this book. Properly called *Gaussian blur* (named after Carl Friedrich Gauss, a German mathematician), this effect smoothly "dissolves" the object, as if viewing it through an out-of-focus lens. **Blur** is only one of the 14 filter primitives that Inkscape supports—but of all these primitives, **Blur** has by far the most user-friendly interface: You can adjust it, for any object at any time, with a simple slider in the **Fill and Stroke** dialog:

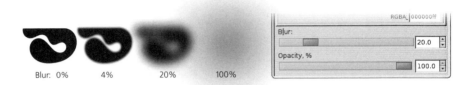

Figure 17-1: The Blur slider in the Fill and Stroke dialog

One might thus say that Inkscape treats blur as a fundamental property of an object, just like its opacity. Why this special treatment? On one hand, it is because blurring an object is such a natural, basic operation. Blurring is everywhere in the physical world: Non-crisp shadows, glows, and things viewed out of focus or in motion are all renderable with blur. This filter is therefore absolutely essential if you want to draw anything photorealistic. On the other hand, blur is not something you can easily imitate with regular vector shapes or gradients. So, by adding just one easily accessible slider, Inkscape's capabilities expand enormously.

The **Blur** slider controls the *amount* of blur in a range from 0 to 100 percent; the setting of 1 percent barely changes the appearance of an object, and 100 percent turns any object into a shapeless puff. The percentage makes sure that this scale works the same for objects of any size; in other words, a large object blurred by 10% has a larger *absolute* amount of blur (larger *blur radius*), but it looks exactly proportional to a small object that is also blurred by 10 percent. If you want to get the same blur radius in objects of different sizes, you need to use different blur amounts.

Figure 17-2: Blur amount (same in A and B) and blur radius (same in A and C)

As you will notice, blurring an object affects its bounding box (only if the visual bounding box type is used, **4.2**). The expanded bounding box will cover all of the blurred fringe of the object.

Each blurred object is processed separately, as if on its own, fully transparent layer, and thus it never "smears" any adjacent nonblurred objects. Since that per-object layer is by itself transparent, the edges of a blurred object become partially translucent. However, you can blur a group, and in that case, all members of the group are blurred together, as if placed on a single layer that is blurred as a whole. In Figure 17-3, on the left there are two adjacent rectangles with no gap between them and no blur. In the middle, each rectangle is blurred by 20 percent separately; as you can see, the striped background can be seen through the blurry gap between the objects. On the right, however, the same two rectangles are first grouped and then the group is blurred by 20 percent; now there is no gap—blurring only adds transparency at the edges, but it cannot reveal what was completely covered by the center of the opaque group.

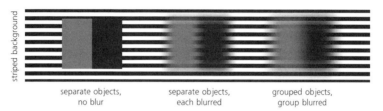

Figure 17-3: Blurring separate objects vs. blurring a group

Also, grouping allows you to apply several layers of blurring to the same object. For example, you can blur the object itself, then group it (possibly even just with itself, that is, placing a single object into the group) and blur the group. Naturally, by blurring a group, you can make any member objects *more* blurred than they were before, but not *less*. (Similarly, as we saw in **16.3**, you can blur a clone more than its original object was blurred, but not less.)

NOTE   *Blur is not the same as* feathering. *Blur affects all of the object; in particular, the lines on a bitmap object or the object boundaries inside a complex group are all blurred. Feathering, on the other hand, is simply blurred transparency that masks out the outermost edges of an object (such as a photo). Inkscape can do feathering as well, using a predefined composite filter (17.3).*

Object ▸ Fill and Stroke ▸ Blur   Filters ▸ ABCs ▸ Feather

Figure 17-4: Blurring vs. feathering

17.1.1   Blur and Transformations

What happens if you transform a blurred object?

Moving a blurred object is not very interesting: The object just moves as a whole, remaining as blurred as ever. Proportional (uniform) scaling also scales the object as a whole, including the blur radius, so that the amount of blur stays the same as it is relative to the object size (i.e., the percentage indicator in the **Fill and Stroke** dialog does not change).

Nonuniform scaling is more interesting. For example, if you squeeze a blurred object vertically, its blur will squeeze with it and become *nonuniform*—now the object is more blurred horizontally than vertically. Such nonuniform blur is sometimes called *motion blur* because it approximates the way the object would look on a photo when captured in fast motion (in this case, horizontal). So, if you want to apply a motion blur to the original nonsqueezed object, simply start by stretching it in the opposite direction, then blur it, and squeeze it back into shape (this only works for paths and bitmaps):

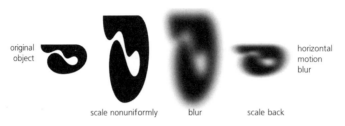

Figure 17-5: Motion blur, step-by-step

Another way to create nonuniform motion blur is by adjusting the parameters of the **Gaussian Blur** filter in the **Filter Editor** dialog (**17.4**), but the stretch/squeeze method described here is usually easier.

SVG   *If you're interested in how this works at the SVG level, the trick is to make sure the blur is applied to an object with a* transform *attribute (A.7), which assures that the blur will be affected by that transform as well. When you stretch a path object without blur, this stretching is by default embedded into the points of the path (12.5.7.3); but once you apply the blur, reverse squeezing will instead add the* transform *attribute, affecting the blur as well.*

To create motion blur on a group or text object (i.e., not a path or bitmap), use this trick: Stretch the object, then group it (Ctrl-G, **4.5**), apply a blur to the group, and squeeze it back. The grouping step makes sure that in the end, you get an object with the correct proportions but also with the squeezing transform attribute affecting the blur.

Similar remarks apply to the way many other filters behave when transformed. For example, squeezing and/or rotating objects allows you to create perspective-distorted variants of the texture filters (**17.3**) for applying to walls and floors in 3D scenes (**11.3**). Of course, transforming filters by stretching and squeezing objects is not as convenient as dragging handles on canvas would be—but it works.

NOTE   *Filters work on the rendered image of the object on your screen—that is, they are always given as input a bitmap that is created for the current zoom level. This is why filters may be so slow: Every time you zoom in or out, the filter is reapplied to the new rendering of the object. This also explains why some filters may look somewhat different depending on zoom. For example, a sharpening filter, when applied to a bitmap object at 100 percent zoom, works on the image features as you would expect it to. However, if you zoom in close enough, you will see the pixels of the bitmap object as rectangles (1.1), and the sharpening will now apply to the borders of these pixel rectangles!*

17.1.2 Tweaking for Blur

The Blur mode of the Tweak tool blurs the selected objects under the brush more (by default) or less (with Shift pressed). The amount of blur added or removed depends on **Force**, pen pressure (if you're using a tablet pen), the closeness of the object to the center of brush, and how long you apply the brush.

17.2 Blend Modes

Blend modes are another type of filter for which Inkscape has a dedicated control. Choosing a blend mode affects how the colors of an object *blend* (i.e., mix) with those of the background objects beneath it.

However, unlike blur, which can be applied to any single object, Inkscape allows you to assign blend modes only to layers (4.6); the corresponding control is in the **Layers** dialog. This has its reasons in the way SVG treats these filters; for you, this means that you can only change the blending mode of all objects in a layer at once, and that blending mode will affect how the objects in this layer blend with those in layers below, not between themselves.

The five blend modes are: Normal (default; switch to this option to remove any unusual blending), Multiply, Screen, Darken, and Lighten. In Normal mode, only non-100 percent opacity allows the objects in the top layer to be translucent; in all other modes, bottom-layer objects can "show through" even without any transparency. Here is a demonstration:

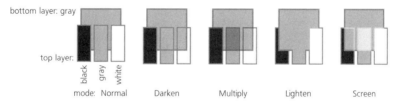

Figure 17-6: All large rectangles are in the background layer, all small rectangles are in foreground layers with various blend modes set; opacity is 100% everywhere.

Perhaps the most common application of blend modes is for tinting bitmaps. For example, imagine you have a color photo but want to render it completely or nearly monochrome, for example, in sepia or blue tones, to match the color scheme of your composition.

Of course, you can just overlay a semi-transparent rectangle of the target color over your bitmap, but that does not entirely get rid of the bitmap's own color; worse, the bitmap fades out and loses contrast. You can also adjust the colors of the bitmap in an external bitmap editor (if it's not yet embedded into your SVG, 18.2), or you can use a predefined composite filter such as Sepia, but these options are not as flexible. Instead, place the photo on one layer and the colored rectangle on its own layer above, and change the blend mode of that top layer (see Figure 13 on the color insert).

- The **Multiply** and **Darken** modes apply tinting primarily to the *light* areas of the photo. Therefore, if the tint color is itself light, it will nicely color your photo while preserving its contrast; if the tint color is dark, the result will likely be too dark.

The difference between Multiply and Darken is that for each pixel, Darken just chooses whichever of the background and foreground colors is darker, whereas Multiply actually combines the two colors. Try both and choose whichever suits your photo.

- The **Screen** and **Lighten** modes apply tinting primarily to the *dark* areas of the photo. Therefore, if the tint color is itself dark, it will nicely color the photo while preserving its contrast; if the tint color is light, it will just "bleach out" the photo, making it too light overall.

  Again, the difference between Screen and Lighten is that for each pixel, Lighten just chooses whichever of the background and foreground colors is lighter, whereas Screen actually combines the two colors. Try both and choose whichever suits your photo.

Summarizing, if your tint color is dark, use the Screen or Lighten modes; if it is light, use Multiply or Darken. Change the opacity of the tint layer object to adjust the amount of tinting.

17.3   Preset Filters

Inkscape comes with an extensive collection of preset composite filters. To apply a preset filter to any number of selected objects, just choose a command from the submenus of the **Filters** menu. Most filters will apply immediately; a few will first display a simple dialog where you can adjust their parameters, similar to any other extension effects (see **13.3**; such filters have an " . . . " at the end of their names in the menu):

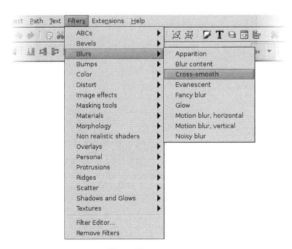

Figure 17-7: Preset filter effects

To get a brief description of an individual preset filter (or of any menu command, for that matter), just hover the mouse over its command in the menu and read the status bar. I will not describe all preset filters here; there are dozens of them, and more are added with each Inkscape version. Instead, here is a brief description of the submenus that group together similar filters:

- The **ABCs** submenu collects the most used, simple, basic filters that typically contain just one or two primitives. They include:

  - Smoke-like "fractal noise" texture applied either to fill (**Noise Fill**) or to transparency (**Noise Transparency**).
  - 3D bevel with gloss (**Specular Light**) or without gloss (**Diffuse Light**).
  - **Feather** (Figure 17-4) applies a blurred opacity mask to the edges of the object.
  - **Roughen** randomly distorts the shape of the object.
  - **Simple Blur** adds a small amount of Gaussian blur (17.1).

  Most often, these filters are used not on their own but as components in more complex filters that you can build just by layering multiple preset filters on top of one another. You can even roughly adjust the amount of a filter by applying it multiple times to the same object (for more precise adjustments of filter parameters, you will need to visit the **Filter Editor**, 17.4).

Roughen   Feather   Specular Light   Diffuse Light   Simple Blur   Noise Transparency

Figure 17-8: Filters from the ABCs submenu

- The **Bevels** submenu presents many variations on the theme of bevels (pseudo-3D raised edges): Here you will find opaque and translucent materials, glossy and matte finishes, bevels lit by multiple sources of light, with and without shadows, with depressions in the middle and with raised border, and so on. All these filters mostly preserve the original color of the object, though they may make it lighter or darker in places for the 3D effect.

Metal Casting   Bloom   Ridged Border   Button   Translucent   Fat Oil

Figure 17-9: Filters from the Bevels submenu

NOTE   *If you want to change the direction of the light cast upon a bevelled object, open the **Filter Editor**, select the **Specular Light** or **Diffuse Light** primitive in the filter stack applied to the object, and adjust the **Azimuth** parameter.*

- The **Blurs** submenu offers horizontal and vertical motion blur, soft blurry glow behind an object, different approaches to blurring the inside color boundary of the object while keeping its outline crisp (**Evanescence**, **Blur Content**, and **Cross-Smooth**), **Noisy Blur** that combines shape distortion with blurring, and some other filters (Figure 17-10).

Motion, Horizontal   Motion, Vertical   Apparition   Fancy Blur   Blur Content   Noisy Blur

Figure 17-10: Filters from the Blurs submenu

- **Color** submenu contains filters that only modify the colors of the object they apply to. Here you will find **Desaturate** for turning any object to grayscale, **Sepia**, **Invert** and **Invert Hue**, various colorization filters (**Colorize**, **Solarize**, **Moonarize**), and others.

- **Distort** filters distort the shape of the object using horizontally stretched jitter, like a reflection in water (**Ripple**), random roughening of edges (**Torn Edges**), scattering of disconnected bits (**Chalk and Sponge**), or edge distortion in combination with uneven texture (**Pixel Smear**). The **Roughen Inside** filter leaves the outline intact but roughens any color boundaries inside the object.

Ripple   Pixel Smear   Pixel Smear, Glossy   Torn Edges   Roughen Inside   Chalk and Sponge

Figure 17-11: Filters from the Distort submenu

- **Image Effects** are the filters that largely make sense for bitmaps, such as **Sharpen**, **Edge Detect**, **Emboss**, or **Oil Painting**.

Age   Blueprint   Soft Bump   Dark Emboss   Film Grain   Drawing

Figure 17-12: Filters from the Image Effects submenu

- The **Masking Tools** submenu contains several effects that make parts of objects transparent. The most basic of these, **Eraser**, makes every white area in the object transparent. For example, if you overlay a small white circle over a black rectangle, group them together, and apply **Eraser** to the group, the white circle will turn into a hole through which the background will show.

- The **Materials** submenu presents a gallery of imitations of various materials: wood, gold splatter, marble, wax, leopard fur, and many others. Most these filters discard the original color of the object and use their own color.

Iridescent Beeswax   Eroded Metal   Lizard Skin   Gold Splatter   Enamel Jewelry   Wavy Tartan

Figure 17-13: Filters from the Materials submenu

- The **Morphology** submenu contains filters that deal with the shape of the object by cutting holes in it, adding outlines, and so on.

- The **Non Realistic Shaders** submenu filters take a flat-colored object and add soft or crisp shading to it, highlighting some areas and darkening others, as may be useful for cartoons. This is a bit similar to thick bevels, but it goes deeper and produces more interesting and believable shapes.

- **Overlays** do not change the object itself, but treat it as a pad for displaying some kind of texture, adding it as an overlay on the object's original color.

Speckle   Zebra   Clouds   Barbed Wire   Swiss Cheese   People

Figure 17-14: Filters from the Overlays submenu

- The **Ridges** submenu filters turn an object into a narrow ridge along the edge and treat this ridge in various ways.

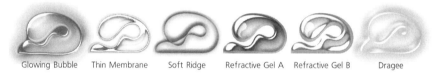

Glowing Bubble   Thin Membrane   Soft Ridge   Refractive Gel A   Refractive Gel B   Dragee

Figure 17-15: Filters from the Ridges submenu

- The **Scatter** submenu filters explode an object into variously shaped fragments—tree leaves, cubes (looking more like squares), random spray splotches—and scatter these fragments randomly around.

- The **Shadows and Glows** submenu filters treat the edges of the object in some way, usually making use of Gaussian blur. Perhaps the most widely used filters in this category are **Drop Shadow** and **Drop Glow**, which are identical except that the former creates a black shadow and the latter, a white glow (invisible unless you have dark background under your object). For these two filters, you can adjust the amount of blur, the opacity of the shadow or glow, and its offset.

Cutout   Inset   In and Out   Cutout Glow   Darken Edges   Dark and Glow

Figure 17-16: Filters from the Shadows and Glows submenu

- The **Textures** submenu contains all kinds of naturalistic textures: crumpled plastic, jam spread, bark, horizontally striped carpet, and many others (see Figure 17-17).

Organic   Jam Spread   Bark   Silk Carpet   Crumpled Plastic   Rough Paper

Figure 17-17: Filters from the Textures submenu

To remove any filters applied to the selected objects, use the **Filters ▶ Remove Filters** command. You can also combine preset filters in any order just by applying them on top of one another; for example, after you change the texture of an object, you can add a drop shadow to it. The **Remove Filters** command will remove all filters you have applied, not just the one you added last.

If the scale of the applied filter is not what you need (e.g., the bubbles or the feathered edges are too large or too small for your object) and the filter does not allow you to adjust that with a dialog, you can use this simple trick: Scale your object up (or down), for example by pressing Ctrl-< or Ctrl-> a few times, then apply the filter, and scale the result back down (or up) by the same multiplier.

The illustrations and descriptions here cover only a subset of the preset filters available. If you want to review all of the preset filters, load the file *filters.svg* from the *share/examples* directory of your Inkscape installation.

NOTE *You can easily add your own preset filters to the menu—no programming required! Once you have an SVG file with the filters you'd like to be able to reuse, simply place that file in the* Filters *subdirectory of your Inkscape's profile directory (~/.config/inkscape on Linux,* Documents and Settings\<your username>\Application Data\Inkscape *on Windows; create the* Filters *subdirectory there if it does not yet exist). After that, any filters defined in that file will be listed in a **Personal** submenu under **Filters**. (All these filters will apply immediately; unfortunately, you cannot at this time create a filter with an adjustment dialog without doing some programming.)*

NOTE *The preset filters that come with Inkscape are useful not only by themselves but also as starting points for your own derivative filters. Once you are familiar with filter primitives and the **Filter Editor** dialog, choosing one of the preset filters—closest to what you want to get—and working from it is usally much easier than starting from scratch.*

17.4 The Filter Editor Dialog

Now, let's have a look at the principal filter powerhouse of Inkscape: the **Filter Editor** dialog (shown in Figure 17-18). Open it with the **Filters ▶ Filter Editor . . .** command.

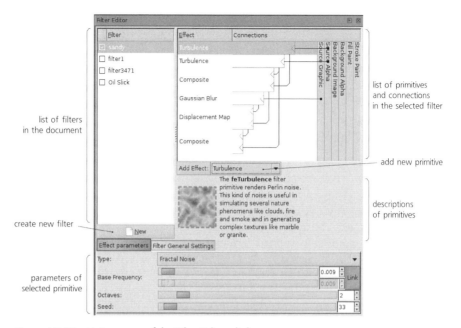

Figure 17-18: Major areas of the Filter Editor dialog

In the figure, the following labels appear:

- create new filter
- list of filters in the document
- parameters of selected primitive
- list of primitives and connections in the selected filter
- add new primitive
- descriptions of primitives

17.4.1 The Filters List

The list in the top-left corner of the dialog contains all filters defined in your document. You can highlight any filter and edit its structure and parameters in the dialog. If the currently selected object has a filter applied, that filter will have a checkmark in the list; so, by setting or removing the checkmark, you can apply or unapply any filter to any object. (Note that even unused filters remain in the list; to remove them from the document, use the **File ▶ Vacuum Defs** command.)

Under the list, there is a **New** button for adding a new filter. If you opened this dialog in an empty document, the list of filters is also empty; now, press **New** to create a new empty filter, usually called `filter1` (to rename it to something else, just click the selected name in the list and type). You can also duplicate or delete a filter in the list by right-clicking it and using the corresponding pop-up menu commands.

After that, you can create or select some object in the document and check the checkbox for your new filter. Nothing changes—an empty filter does not affect the rendering of an object. For the filter to actually do something, we need to add some primitives to it.

17.4.2 The Stack of Primitives

Turn your attention to the area to the right of the filter list. This is the main filter construction board where you list, arrange, and connect the stack of *primitives* that constitute a filter. Initially, it is empty because we haven't yet added any primitives to our filter.

The 14 different primitives supported by Inkscape are listed in a drop-down list below the construction board. When you choose a primitive in the list, it displays a brief description and illustration below. You can read the description in the dialog to get an initial idea of what each primitive does. A detailed explanation of all primitives is beyond the scope of this book; if you want all the gory technical details, refer to the SVG specification (*http://w3.org/TR/SVG11*).

Instead, let's go through the step-by-step process of creating a fairly complex filter that uses several different primitives to get an integral idea of how it all works. The filter we'll construct is called Sandy Blur; I designed it for the background coloring of the Rose image (see Figure 24-5). This filter aims to imitate blurry watercolor strokes on a rough paper.

Plain Gaussian blur is not satisfactory: It is too smooth, too computer-generated, too boring. For an acceptable watercolor imitation, we need to model both the small-scale roughness of the paper texture and the larger-scale "blotches" resulting from the watercolor paint flowing and sticking differently in different places. For both these sources of unevenness, we will use the **Turbulence** primitive, which creates random fractal "noise" at the given scale.

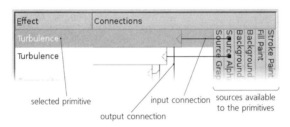

Figure 17-19: The two Turbulence primitives

The two **Turbulence** primitives are the first two components of our filter—the two topmost boxes in the stack. Each filter primitive has one or more *inputs* and one *output*; in the list, the input is depicted by a line coming into the primitive box horizontally from the right, and the output is the line going from the box vertically downward. As you can see, the outputs of some primitives are the inputs for others.

You can wire the connections yourself by dragging; start by dragging from the input triangle at the right-hand edge of a primitive's box. Generally, information flows from top to bottom in the stack of primitives; the output of the bottommost primitive is what you see rendered in the document window. You can also rearrange the primitives by dragging; a right-click menu allows you to duplicate or delete a primitive.

What are the vertically stacked boxes on the right? These are the predefined sources that any primitive can use as input. The most useful (and, as of version 0.47, the only ones fully implemented) are **Source Graphic** and **Source Alpha**. **Source Graphic**, as the name implies, supplies the original rendered image of the object we're filtering, at the current zoom's resolution. The **Source Alpha** is different in that it provides a grayscale representation of the original object's opacity (alpha) mask; so, points that are fully opaque (regardless of color) in the **Source Graphic** will be opaque black on the **Source Alpha** image, and points that are transparent will be transparent black.

17.4.3 The Parameters of a Primitive

Let's look again at the two **Turbulence** primitives at the top of the stack. They both take **Source Alpha** as input and pass their result—random noise—down to other primitives. What differentiates them are the parameters of these filters.

When you select a filter primitive in the stack, its parameters are displayed in the bottom area of the dialog. Here are the parameters of the two **Turbulence** primitives:

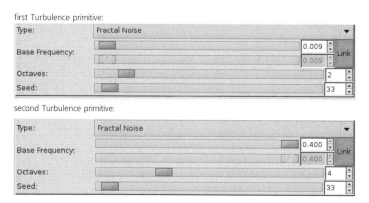

Figure 17-20: The parameters of the two Turbulence primitives

As you see, these two primitives have the same **Type** (**Fractal Noise**, which looks better in our case than the other option, **Turbulence**) but differ in **Base Frequency** and **Octaves**. The **Base Frequency** parameter determines the scale of the turbulence; higher frequency results in smaller, sand-like texture, while lower frequency produces larger clouds. The number of **Octaves** specifies, in fractal terminology, how deep is the recursion in the algorithm: Increasing **Octaves** produces sharper unevenness with more small details; decreasing this value gives a smoother, more nebulous image.

Now, we need to composite our turbulence outputs together. For this, we will use another primitive, aptly named **Composite**:

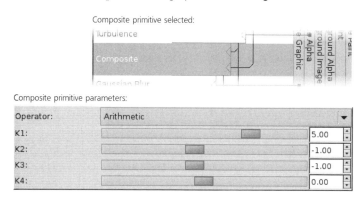

Figure 17-21: The Composite primitive

It has two inputs and combines them, pixel by pixel, using one of a number of methods. Here, I used the **Arithmetic** method; with the provided numeric values for the coefficients (**K1** to **K4**), it results in the large-scale wave and small-scale ripples being combined into a composite with somewhat increased contrast, as shown in Figure 17-22.

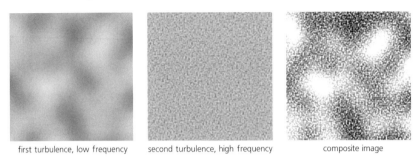

first turbulence, low frequency   second turbulence, high frequency   composite image

Figure 17-22: The result of compositing two turbulences

NOTE *Refer to the SVG specification* (http://w3.org/TR/SVG11) *for the detailed formulas used by the* ***Composite*** *filter in various modes.*

So far, we didn't use the image of the object itself to which we will apply the filter—that is, didn't use the **Source Graphic**. Supposedly, that object would be some kind of broad brush-like path, likely created with the Calligraphic pen tool (**14.3**). Of course, the first thing we need do to a flat-color, crisp-edged path to make it more like a watercolor stroke is to blur it:

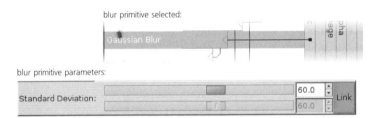

Figure 17-23: The Gaussian Blur primitive

The **Standard Deviation** parameter of **Gaussian Blur** is similar to the blur amount you would adjust in the **Fill and Stroke** dialog (Figure 17-1), except that here it is measured in absolute px units (**A.6**) instead of percentages of the object's size.

How do we combine the blurred stroke with the turbulence? **Composite** won't work here. Any of its modes will just result in a smooth blur being *overlaid* with the turbulent ripples, but the underlying smoothness will not go anywhere (try it). It won't look like watercolor on a rough paper at all—it will look more like computer-produced blur viewed through a spotted glass.

Let's consider what happens when you paint with a real brush on a real paper. The blurriness of your stroke results from the softness of the brush—you apply more pressure in the middle than on the edges of the brush. When a brush meets a dimple in the paper, that pressure is changed; if this area of the paper is a rise, it will get painted more intensively, as if it were closer to the maximum-pressure point of the brush; if it is a depression, it will get less paint. In other words, the roughness of the paper jitters the blurred stroke *in the plane of the drawing*, as if randomly displacing parts of the stroke sideways. How do we achieve this with filters?

The **Displacement Map** primitive is a perfect match for the job. It takes its first input and moves its pixels around according to its second input. You can choose which of the channels (Red, Green, Blue, or Alpha) of the second input will move the first in each of the two axis directions (X and Y), as well as scale this displacement. In our case, the first input is the blurred object, and the second input is the composite turbulence field, of which we take the Alpha channel for both axes:

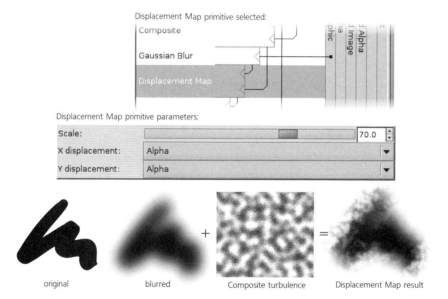

Figure 17-24: The Displacement Map primitive

As an added bonus, the result looks rougher in some areas and smoother in others. This is because in the smooth areas, the displacement map hits the almost-flat inner parts of the blurred stroke, and there, the high-frequency jitter just moves around pixels of almost the same color without disturbing the smoothness. On the edges of the stroke, however, different-color pixels are mixed and jittered, producing visible roughness. All this is additionally modulated by the low-frequency noise, producing a very convincing watercolor simulation.

However, if you apply this filter to a light-colored stroke (and not black as in Figure 17-24), the result is still not quite perfect. When you're looking at a real rough paper with watercolor strokes on it, what you see is not just the distribution of the paint; you also see the roughness itself, which looks like a pattern of shades. Without this shading, light-colored strokes with our filter still look too unnaturally flat. Fortunately, that is easy to fix; we already have the high-frequency turbulence source, which will work nicely as shading if we just compose it with our displacement-mapped blur, as shown in Figure 17-25.

Now the filter looks pretty decent, and we can declare it complete. You could continue working on it, adding various smears, water leaks, diffusion, and so on; however, since my demo image used this filter only for the background, I thought it was already good enough for the purpose.

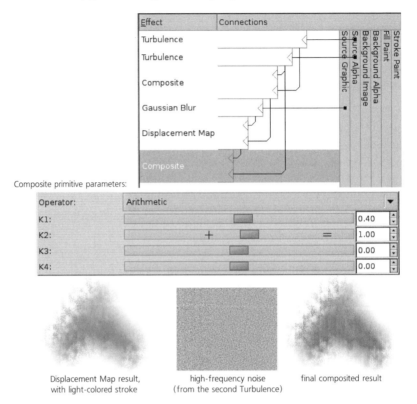

Figure 17-25: The final filter and the parameters of the last Composite primitive which overlays the shading

17.4.4 The Filter Area

The second tab in the filter parameter area in the **Filter Editor** dialog is called **Filter General Settings**. It contains parameters that apply to the entire filter stack, not any single primitive. Currently, the only thing you can change here is the *filter area*—the area which the filter will render into, measured in the units of the bounding box of the object to which the filter is applied.

The **Coordinates** line specifies the top-left corner of the area, and the **Dimensions** line specifies the bottom-right corner. For example, if you set the **Coordinates** to 0/0 in and the **Dimensions** to 1/1, the area will be exactly equal to the bounding box. This will work fine if your filter does not reach beyond the object in any way—for example, if you're just performing a color change with a **Color Matrix** primitive. However, if you are using something like blur in your filter, it will need to paint outside the bounding box, and you must provide sufficient margins for this to prevent cropping. When you apply blur via the **Fill and Stroke** dialog, these margins are set for you automatically; however, when creating a new filter stack from scratch, you must take care of it yourself. The default is 0.1/0.1 for **Coordinates** and 1.2/1.2 for **Dimensions**, which results in 10 percent margins on all sides of the object, as shown in Figure 17-26.

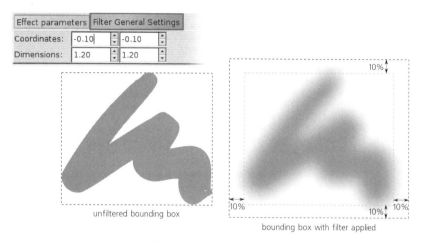

Figure 17-26: Specifying the filter area

If the visual bounding box option is used (which is the default, see 4.2), the bounding box of a filtered object—the frame you see when you select it in Selector—is the enlarged filter area. Among other things, this means that, when exporting a selected object to bitmap (18.9), Inkscape will make sure the bitmap contains the blurred edges without cropping.

17.5 Filter Rendering Options

As you may have noticed by now, for all their power, filters in Inkscape have a significant drawback: They are *slow*. Sometimes, very slow. While future versions of the program may to some extent address this (most likely, by enabling Inkscape to use the graphics card processor for filter calculations), there's something you can do right now.

First of all, recall that you can always switch to the Outline mode (3.11) to speed up rendering while working on a document. There is also the No Filters mode, which is the same as normal mode except that no filters are rendered; this is perhaps the best option if filters are the main source of slowness for you.

Also, the **Filters** tab of the **Inkscape Preferences** dialog (Figure 17-27) has some settings that you can try to tweak to speed up rendering. The first group of radio buttons applies to blur and allows you to choose your desired level of the speed/quality tradeoff. The default, **Average quality**, looks *almost* perfect and renders reasonably fast. At lower quality settings, visible defects appears, but rendering becomes even faster; the higher settings bring little quality improvement but are significantly slower.

NOTE   *Bitmap export (18.9) as well as rasterization of filters for PS/EPS/PDF export always use the highest quality of blur, which is why exporting is typically slower that rendering the same image on screen at the same resolution.*

The second set of radio buttons applies to all filters (including blur). It also offers to trade an improvement in rendering speed for worse rendering quality, but its speed advantage is less significant, so here the **Best quality** option is probably optimal.

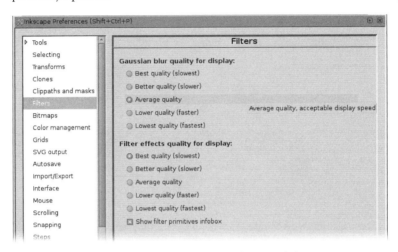

Figure 17-27: The Filters tab of the Inkscape Preferences dialog

17.6 Exporting Filters to PS and PDF

Since version 0.47, Inkscape no longer ignores filters when exporting to PostScript and PDF formats (which, while being vector, do not support anything like SVG's filters). Now, any object with a filter applied will be by default rasterized (i.e., converted into a bitmap object) in the exported file, fully preserving the appearance it had in Inkscape (but, potentially, increasing the file size). In the export options dialog, you can specify the resolution of the bitmaps, as well as turn rasterization off, in which case objects will remain vector but will lose any filtering.

Figure 17-28: Specifying the treatment of filters when exporting

When performing export via the command line (C.2), the corresponding options are --export-dpi to specify the resolution and --export-ignore-filters to turn off rasterization.

18

BITMAPS

Most vector images start or end (sometimes both) their lives as bitmaps (1.1), and Inkscape's SVG documents are no exception. Many vector drawings, artistic as well as technical, are developed from tracings of photos, scans, or other bitmap drawings; at the other end of its lifetime, almost all vector art is eventually exported into bitmap formats for viewing in software that cannot deal directly with vectors. Bitmaps are an important object type in Inkscape, and the techniques for dealing with them are sufficiently versatile to warrant a whole chapter to cover them.

18.1 Import

If you have a bitmap image file, you can insert it as a bitmap object into your Inkscape document by using the **File ▸ Import** command. Inkscape can deal with a large number of bitmap formats, including all of the major ones (PNG, JPG, TIFF, GIF, and BMP). Choose **All Bitmaps** for the type of the files in the **Import** dialog so that only the supported bitmap formats are in the list.

Also, you can use **File ▸ Open** to display any bitmap file as a document in its own right. In this case, Inkscape automatically creates a new SVG document, its page size (3.4.3) matching the pixel size of the bitmap, and places the bitmap on the canvas (into the document root—that is, not in any layer). You can now add vector objects to that document and save it as SVG (if you want to get a bitmap with the result, you need to export it, 18.9), or you can copy and paste the bitmap object from that document into any other.

In any case, what you now have in your document is a *bitmap object* displaying the bitmap's contents. In most aspects, this is a regular object that you can transform, duplicate, clone, apply filters to, and so on. In the status bar, it is described as *Image* with its pixel size, for example *640 × 480*.

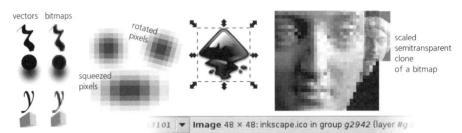

Figure 18-1: Bitmap objects in a document and the status bar display for a selected object

Bitmaps consist of pixels (1.1), and Inkscape does not attempt to conceal this fact. Just zoom in close enough, and you will easily see the separate pixels in a bitmap object as flat-color squares. By default, all bitmaps are imported at the resolution of 90 pixels per inch, which means the size of each pixel square is exactly 1×1 px (A.6). If you squeeze, skew, or rotate the bitmap, its pixels will be transformed correspondingly.

18.2   Linking vs. Embedding

By default, any bitmap you import into Inkscape is *linked* to the document. This means that the actual content of the bitmap is taken from the original bitmap file; what the SVG document contains is just a reference to that file—its filename, including path. This way, the SVG file size is kept to a minimum, and multiple SVG documents can reuse the same bitmap file. The status bar description of a linked bitmap object reports its filename (Figure 18-1).

This also means that any changes you do to that linked bitmap file outside of Inkscape (for example, color correction or cropping) will be immediately reflected in the Inkscape document. Moreover, you can run an external editor (such as GIMP or Photoshop) on your linked image from inside Inkscape by right-clicking the bitmap object and choosing **Edit externally**. On the **Bitmaps** page of **Inkscape Preferences** (3.1.1), you can disable the automatic reloading of changed bitmaps as well as choose which external editor you want to use.

The biggest disadvantage of linked bitmaps is how easy it is to disrupt this link. If the bitmap file is deleted or moved to a different location relative to the SVG document, the result is not pretty, as Figure 18-2 demonstrates.

Figure 18-2: This is what Inkscape shows when it cannot find a linked bitmap file.

This is a common problem when you send your art to someone but forget to include the linked images.

SVG *What matters for Inkscape is the relative location of the bitmap, because in the* xlink:href *attribute of the* svg:image *object, it stores a* relative path *from the SVG document location to the image file. For example, if the bitmap is in the* images *subfolder of the folder in which your SVG document resides, you can move that folder along with its* images *subfolder to any location on your computer without a problem.*

Moreover, Inkscape to some extent protects you against a situation where you move the SVG document to another location on the same computer but leave the linked image behind. Inkscape additionally stores the absolute path *to the image in the* sodipodi:absref *attribute and tries to use it if the relative link in* xlink:href *fails. This won't help, however, if you move your SVG onto a different computer without its associated images.*

There is a way to prevent these linking problems once and for all by *embedding* an image into your SVG document. An embedded image is stored right inside the SVG file and will never be lost. On the downside, this increases the file size of the SVG file (by about 1.4 times the file size of the bitmap file, which may be significant); also, embedded images cannot be edited in an external bitmap editor.

To embed one or more images into the document, use **Extensions ▶ Images ▶ Embed Images**. You have the choice of embedding only the selected bitmap object (leaving all others as they are) or embedding all the bitmap objects in the document:

Figure 18-3: Extensions ▶ Images ▶ Embed Images embeds either all or just selected images into SVG.

An embedded image is described in the status bar as, for example, *Image 64 × 64: embedded*. With **Extensions ▶ Images ▶ Extract Image**, you can reverse the embedding of a bitmap—that is, extract an embedded image into a separate linked file; you will be asked for the path to save the extracted file to.

18.3   Bitmap as Pattern

Usually, the first thing you'd want to do to an imported bitmap is *crop* it, removing the unnecessary margins and only leaving part of the image. In Inkscape, there are several ways to achieve this.

If you want the bitmap to remain a rectangle and you only want to shave off some margins, it is convenient to turn it into a *pattern* (10.8) by pressing Alt-I. This does not change the visible display but converts a rectangular bitmap (it must not be rotated or skewed for this to work properly) into a rectangle object (11.2) with a pattern fill displaying the bitmap.

Now you can resize the rectangle using its two corner handles, for example with the Node or Rectangle tool (11.2.1). This does not affect the fill, which means you can crop it by moving the rectangle handles inward. At the same time, you can also use the pattern's three handles to move, scale, and rotate the pattern, as described in 10.8.2. (Initially, the pattern handles coincide with the rectangle handles; drag the X-shaped handle in the top-left corner to separate them.)

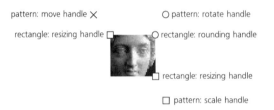

pattern: move handle ✕   ○ pattern: rotate handle

rectangle: resizing handle ☐   ○ rectangle: rounding handle

                                  ☐ rectangle: resizing handle

                          ☐ pattern: scale handle

Figure 18-4: A bitmap as a pattern in a rectangle

After you convert your bitmap to a patterned rectangle, you can turn the rectangle into any other path—for example, by converting it to path by Shift-Ctrl-C and node-editing the result, or by intersecting (12.2) the rectangle with a path. This method is convenient because you can edit the shape or path and its bitmap fill at the same time. Transforming, by default, affects both the shape/path and its pattern fill; see 6.10 for how to change that.

18.4   Clipping and Masking

Another approach to cropping images is to use *clipping* or *masking*. Although here, these techniques are illustrated by bitmap objects, you can in fact clip or mask any kind of object, including groups.

Inkscape allows any object to be clipped by a path, so that only the part of the object inside that path will be visible. Starting from a bitmap object, draw a clipping path or shape over it using any convenient tool—for example, Calligraphic pen or Pencil. Then, select both the bitmap and the path and choose **Object ▸ Clip ▸ Set**. The clipping path disappears (it now resides in defs, A.4) but the bottom object is now clipped by it. To edit the clipping path without unclipping, click the corresponding button in the Node tool's controls bar, as shown in Figure 18-5.

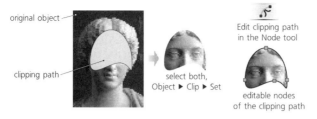

Figure 18-5: Applying clipping to a bitmap object

At any time, you can do **Object ▶ Clip ▶ Release** to remove the clipping and get the object and its clipping path as two separate objects again.

NOTE   *The clipping path needs not be a single path; it can just as well be a group of paths.*

Masking is very similar to clipping: You select the object and the mask and choose **Object ▶ Mask ▶ Set** to mask it, or **Object ▶ Mask ▶ Release** to remove the mask. The main difference between clipping and masking is that a clip limits the object to the interior of the clipping path, disregarding any embellishments such as fill color, stroke style, gradient, or blur. Clipping is *binary*; at any point, the clipped object is either visible or not. Masking, however, is *gradual*—it may make an object *partially* transparent.

The rule to remember is this: In a mask, *black* makes masked objects *transparent* (invisible) and *white* makes them *opaque* (visible). What's more, the "no color" fill or full transparency in a mask is considered "transparent black"—that is, areas of the object not covered by a mask at all or areas that fall into gaps or holes in a mask disappear. To make a part of an object visible, the mask over that part must be non-black; pure opaque white gives 100 percent opacity in the masked object, while anything darker or more transparent produces less than 100 percent opacity.

Obviously, masking is most useful when you use gradients or blurring. For example, you can easily blend a photo strip with the background (using linear gradient mask) or feather the irregular edges of a photo cutout (using blurred mask):

Figure 18-6: Applying masking to a bitmap object

Just as a clipping path, a mask can be a group of objects instead of a single object. The Node tool has another button for editing the mask of the selected object. Unfortunately, this button only allows you to node-edit the single path or shape of the mask—you can't change its color, gradient, or blur; for this, you need to release the mask and set it again after changing.

18.5   Retouching and Patching

Simple bitmap editing tasks, such as removing defects or suppressing unnecessary details, are entirely possible in Inkscape using its vector tools, without resorting to an external bitmap editor. While this approach is limited, it is often surprisingly useful and fast.

Imagine we need to remove a small blemish in a photo. Start by zooming in closely and drawing a calligraphic stroke over it; then, switch to the Dropper tool and pick a color from the photo nearby. In some cases, this may be all you really need—even such a primitive patch may blend well enough to not be noticeable once you zoom out. More likely, however, the edges of the patch will be painfully obvious on at least one side. Here, a gradient may help; switch to the Gradient tool (10.1), draw a linear or elliptic gradient trying to match the dominant direction of color change in the background, and use the Dropper tool again (8.6) to pick colors for the gradient stops. If the gradient failed to make the patch completely blend into the background, see if a little blurring helps:

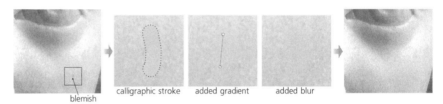

Figure 18-7: Covering a small blemish on the cheek with a vector patch path, made "invisible" by gradient and blur

When you're done retouching, don't forget to group the bitmap object with all its vector patches so the group can be moved as a single object.

18.6   Bitmap Filters

Some of the preset filters (17.3), collected in **Filters ▸ Image Effects**, are specifically designed for bitmaps (Figure 17-12). Of course, you can apply these filters to any other objects or apply any other filters to bitmaps; this submenu simply collects those filters that make sense *mostly* for bitmaps because they operate on the internal colors or textures of an object, not its overall shape.

18.7   Bitmap Effects

All of the techniques described so far, while essential for dealing with bitmaps, are equally applicable to any kind of object. However, Inkscape also has a number of "genuinely bitmap" extension effects, collected in the **Extensions ▸ Raster** submenu. (Refer to 13.3 for general tips on working with extension effects.)

Unlike the SVG filters we just saw, all these effects make permanent changes to the bitmap; they can be undone—but you cannot, for example, readjust the parameters of such an effect after it is applied. Also unlike filters, these effects can work *only* on bitmap objects; you cannot, for example, apply a bitmap effect to a clone of a bitmap. If the bitmap is linked, these effects embed it and work on the embedded copy, not on the external linked original.

There are over 30 raster effects; only those most useful (and not easily achievable via filters) are listed here:

original image　　Charcoal　　Contrast　　Median　　Resample down　　Swirl (41°)

Figure 18-8: Examples of extension effects from Extensions ▸ Raster

- **Add Noise** gives you a choice of various types of noise to overlay on your image; most types look more or less like scattered sand.

- **Channel** takes one channel from the bitmap (one of R/G/B, C/M/Y/K, opacity, or matte).

- **Charcoal** turns your image into an imitation of a charcoal drawing. Increasing **Radius** makes the strokes rougher, while raising **Sigma** makes the drawing darker overall.

- **Contrast** increases the contrast (difference between lights and darks). You can apply it several times for more effect.

- **Cycle Colormap** cycles the colormap of a bitmap.

- **Despeckle**, **Enhance**, and **Reduce Noise** implement various noise reduction algorithms.

- **Equalize** applies histogram equalization to the image.

- **Level** blackens pixels that are darker than the **Black Point**, whitens pixels brighter than the **White Point**, and scales those that fall within this range to the full color range. **Gamma Correction** specifies additional brightness correction (1 means no change).

- **Level (with Channel)** is the same as **Level** but for a single channel only.

- **Median** paints each pixel with the median color of its circular neighborhood, for an effect similar to blurring.

- **HSB Adjust** adjusts the hue (in the range of –360 to 360), saturation (–200 to 200), and brightness (–200 to 200).

- **Normalize** increases contrast by expanding the color range of pixels to the full range of color (for example, if the image has no reds, all colors will be stretched in the direction of the red to compensate for that).

- **Resample** is perhaps the most practically useful of all image effects: It allows you to change the pixel size of the bitmap without scaling it. Resampling *up* (i.e., making a bitmap larger than its current pixel size) does not change the appearance of an image but may be useful if you plan to apply some other effect and want it to work with higher resolution. Resampling *down* (to a smaller-than-current size) makes the image lose detail without changing its dimensions in the document; this is a good way to reduce the file size of an SVG document with an embedded bitmap.

- **Dither** randomly scatters pixels in a bitmap, with **Amount** specifying the radius of scattering.
- **Swirl** swirls the bitmap in a spiral around its center.
- **Unsharp Mask** sharpens the image using the popular "unsharp mask" algorithm.
- **Wave** warps the image along a horizontal sine wave with the given amplitude and wavelength.

18.8   Tracing

For a vector editor, one of the most important bitmap-related capabilities is converting bitmap objects to vectors (*tracing*) and vice versa (*bitmap export*). Inkscape offers rich and powerful tools for these conversions, which the rest of this chapter will cover in detail.

18.8.1   Manual Tracing

The most straightforward approach to creating vector art from a bitmap image does not involve any tools except those we already know. Just switch to the Pen tool (**14.1**), zoom in on your bitmap, and do a series of clicks around or along an area that you want to turn into a vector path, then double-click or press Enter to finish the path. Use click-and-release in a sharp corner to create a cusp node; for smooth curved edges, use a series of click-and-drags in critical nodes:

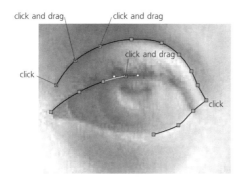

Figure 18-9: Manual tracing of a bitmap

You can vary the density of your clicks depending on how precisely you want to trace a specific area. If you want the shape to be extra smooth, switch to the Spiro mode (**13.1.7**); in this mode, it does not matter in which direction you drag after clicking, just as long as you drag a bit *somewhere* to create a smooth node. If you're tracing a polygon without any curves at all, it is convenient to use the Straight lines mode so that an accidental drag does not create an undesired smooth node.

While this technique may seem time-consuming at first, once you get the hang of it, you will be able to trace complex art very quickly. Like any manual technique, its main advantage is the complete creative control—you decide what parts to trace and what to ignore, how to simplify complex shapes, where to diverge from the bitmap blueprint, and where to place each node. Depending on your skill, the result will likely look much more satisfying than either an automatic trace or a fully manual drawing.

18.8.2 The Trace Bitmap Dialog

Inkscape's tool for automatic bitmap tracing is very powerful; based on the standalone Potrace open source tracer (*http://potrace.sourceforge.net*), it is acknowledged to be one of the best tools of its kind in modern vector editors. With it, you can trace anything from a simple black-and-white logo that needs just a few nodes to a complex photo that produces dozens of colored paths with thousands of nodes.

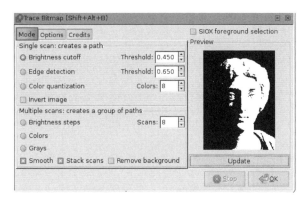

Figure 18-10: The Trace Bitmap dialog

The **Trace Bitmap** dialog (Shift-Alt-B) has two main areas: the options panel on the left and the preview panel on the right. Note, however, that the preview panel does not show you the traced vector path (that may be time-consuming to create); instead, you see the bitmap you're tracing with all the color reduction and filtering steps as specified in the options panel. To update the preview after the options have changed, click **Update**.

To perform the actual trace of the selected bitmap object, click **OK**. For a large bitmap, this may be slow; watch the status bar for progress messages. You can interrupt tracing at any time by clicking the **Stop** button.

The **Mode** tab of the dialog chooses the principal mode of operation of the tracing tool. The available modes are divided into two groups: the *single-scan modes* create a single path, while the *multiple-scan modes* create multiple paths (grouped together).

18.8.2.1 Brightness Cutoff

Brightness cutoff is the simplest and most common approach to tracing a path: The resulting path covers anything that is darker than the threshold you set. This trace path, while a single object, can consist of multiple nonoverlapping subpaths (**12.1.1**). The **Threshold** is set as a fraction of the entire brightness range of the image; for example, when set to 0.6, the trace path covers all the areas in the darkest 60 percent of the image. If you click **Invert**, the meaning of **Threshold** is inverted (i.e., the path will cover the brightest 40 percent of the image).

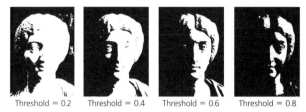

Threshold = 0.2   Threshold = 0.4   Threshold = 0.6   Threshold = 0.8

Figure 18-11: Brightness cutoff tracing for different threshold values

Usually, this is the best tracing mode for simple monochrome shapes such as logos, text, vignettes, and so on.

18.8.2.2 Tracing Quality

Even if the bitmap you're tracing is a rendition of a vector path, the trace will never exactly reproduce that original path. Rendering a vector into a bitmap always incurs some loss of information, and Inkscape's tracer cannot restore this lost information other than by guessing. Although it is generally pretty good at it, there will be cases where you will be disappointed by its failure to recognize some features (arcs, straight lines, corners) that you can easily "see" in the bitmap. This is especially evident when tracing low-resolution bitmaps or those containing text.

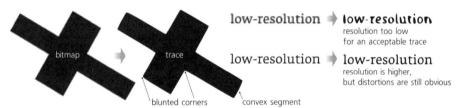

Figure 18-12: Some common quality problems with bitmap tracing

Perhaps the best piece of advice in this situation is to obtain the highest possible *resolution* bitmap. It is nearly impossible to get a decent trace from a bitmap where some crucial features are several pixels across; tracing a higher-resolution version of an image often makes a big difference. Also, you can try to adjust the **Threshold** and experiment with the contents of the **Options** page of the dialog (it applies to all modes, both single-scan and multiple-scan):

- The **Suppress speckles** option removes any color blobs that are smaller than the specified number of pixels across. This suppresses creating small superfluous subpaths when tracing dirty or "dithered" bitmaps.

- Increasing the **Smooth corners** parameter makes the trace algorithm less inclined to recognize sharp corners in the image. This may be useful when tracing a naturally smooth shape from a highly pixelated, low-resolution bitmap where you don't want accidental pixel cusps to become sharp corners in the traced path. Conversely, lowering this parameter is appropriate when you are tracing geometric shapes without any curved lines; when **Smooth corners** is zero, the resulting path almost entirely consists of straight line segments with cusp nodes between them.

- The **Optimize paths** parameter tries to reduce the number of nodes in the trace path, much like the **Simplify** command does (12.3). Raising this value decreases the number of nodes you get, but it also increases the chance of introducing visible distortions or losing some important details of the shape.

18.8.2.3 Other Single-Scan Modes

The **Edge detection** mode applies the edge detection filter to the bitmap before tracing it. As a result, the trace path will contain narrow strips that follow the color boundaries in the source bitmap. The lower the **Threshold** is, the more edges will be detected and traced.

The **Color quantization** mode first quantizes (divides) the image into the given number of areas (**Colors**), each with its own dominant color, much like when reducing a full-color image to a fixed palette using a bitmap editor. It then traces *every other* such area, which results in a stripped appearance for color gradients.

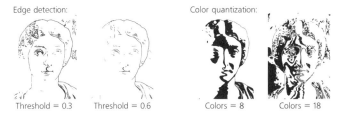

Figure 18-13: The Edge detection and Color quantization modes

18.8.2.4 Multiple-Scan Modes

Like the **Color quantization** mode we've just seen, each multiple-scan mode starts by quantizing the image into the given number of areas (specified by **Scans**). It then traces each area separately, assigns an appropriate color or gray level to the trace path, and groups all such paths together. With a sufficient number of quantization steps, the result may look very similar to the original bitmap, faithfully reproducing its color gradients, blur, natural textures, and so on.

The three multiple-scan modes differ only in the way the image is quantized. The **Brightness steps** option is the best one for grayscale images; it ignores any hue or saturation differences and groups pixels into areas based solely on their brightness (Figure 18-14). The **Colors** mode considers all aspects of the colors when performing quantization, which results in the most faithful reproduction of full-color images (see Figure 14 on the color insert). Finally, the **Grays** option works the same as **Colors**, except that the resulting paths are painted with approximating shades of gray instead of the original colors.

original bitmap | traced to 10 brightness steps, about 5000 nodes in total | same trace, all paths are stroked without fill

Figure 18-14: Multiple scans: 10 brightness steps

The **Smooth** option applies a certain amount of blur to the image before quantizing it; this may produce better results in complex photographic images. The **Stack scans** option is best kept on; it makes sure that each area's path covers not only that area but also all areas below it in z-order, which means there will be no gaps between the scans:

scans stacked, no gaps | scans abutted, gaps

Figure 18-15: Stacking scans vs. abutting them

The **Remove background** option simply removes the bottommost scan path from the group, which is useful when you are tracing a photo of something on a flat-color background and want the result to only contain the object itself, not the background.

18.9 Bitmap Export

In a bitmap-dominated world, a vector editor without a good rasterization and bitmap export capability is useless. Inkscape's bitmap export facilities are convenient and can be automated in numerous ways. On the downside, Inkscape lacks an export preview and supports only one bitmap format: PNG. Also, you can only create images with 8 bits per channel (no indexed color, no 16 bits per channel), and it is impossible to suppress antialiasing.

The lack of support for bitmap formats other than PNG is not as bad as it may sound. The PNG format faithfully preserves the maximum rendering quality Inkscape is capable of, including alpha transparency, antialiasing, filters, and so on. From a PNG file, you can easily create any other format (such as JPG or TIFF) using a bitmap editor or any image conversion utility such as ImageMagick (you can download it from *http://imagemagick.org*). During this conversion, you can optimize your image in various ways (e.g., to minimize the file size or palette).

If you think your PNG export has lost the transparency of the original SVG, the most likely source of the problem is not Inkscape but the image file viewer you're using to examine the PNG. Not all image viewers can handle alpha transparency in PNG; one program that is guaranteed to show your PNG correctly is the Firefox browser.

18.9.1   The Export Bitmap Dialog

With the **Export Bitmap** dialog ([Shift-Ctrl-E]), you can export your drawing or any part of it into a PNG file at any resolution. The dialog consists of three main areas, in which you configure the following:

- The canvas area you want to export
- The pixel size of the bitmap
- The filename of the export file

Figure 18-16:   The Export Bitmap dialog

For the **Export area**, you can choose either the *page* of your SVG document (anything beyond the edges of the page is not exported), the bounding box of the *drawing* (which can be smaller or larger than the page; the page rectangle is not in any way visible in the exported bitmap), or the bounding box of the *selection* (again, it can be inside or outside the page rectangle—this does not matter). These options correspond to the first three toggle buttons at the top of the dialog.

Alternatively, you can click the **Custom** toggle button and type your own values of the coordinates for the top-left corner (**x0, y0**), bottom-right corner (**x1, y1**), or width and height of the export area. You can also choose the measurement unit for these values (the default is px, **A.6**).

The **Export Bitmap** dialog is not modal—that is, you can keep working on the canvas as you normally do while it is open. Unless you choose **Custom**, the dialog responds to changing a selection on the canvas by switching to the **Selection** mode and updating the coordinates to match the bounding box of the new selection. If nothing is selected and you are not in **Custom**, the dialog defaults to the **Drawing** mode.

For the **Bitmap size**, you can type the width and height, in pixels, or you can adjust the resolution value (*dpi*, which stands for *dots*—that is, pixels—*per inch*). The default resolution of 90 dpi results in one SVG px unit corresponding exactly to one pixel of the rendered bitmap. The horizontal and vertical dpi values cannot differ; changing any one of the three editable values (**Width**, **Height**, **dpi**) changes the other two to match.

NOTE *If your drawing contains some px-sized objects (such as strokes a whole number of px wide) and you want them to export precisely into the pixels of the bitmap, it may not be sufficient to choose the 90 dpi resolution. For example, a 1×1 px square in SVG may fall on a boundary between pixels in an exported bitmap and this would end up "smeared" into four adjacent pixels instead of one. The easiest way to prevent such misalignment and ensure your export is as crisp as possible is to use the grid (7.2). Snap your objects to the default 1 px-sized grid, and make sure that your export area has integer x0 and y0 coordinates when measured in px—that is, is itself aligned to the px grid. After that, exporting at 90 dpi will give you a perfectly crisp image.*

For the **Filename**, you can type a complete path to the file (the *.png* extension will be added automatically) or click the **Browse** button to access your filesystem and choose a folder and a file.

18.9.1.1 Export Hints

When exporting a single selected object, the export filename and resolution of the export are remembered and stored in SVG document (so you may need to save it after performing the export) and restored into the **Export Bitmap** dialog when you select this object to export again. These *export hints* are one of the greatest time savers when using Inkscape to export multiple objects to multiple bitmap files—for example, slices of a web page graphic. Just as you select various objects with the **Export Bitmap** dialog open, you can see their saved export filenames popping up in the **Filename** field. For the same reason—to make it easier to export multiple objects one by one—the dialog stays open even after you click the **Export** button.

You can speed up the process even more if you select all objects that you want to export, each to its own file, and check the **Batch export all selected objects** checkbox. Now, clicking **Export** will create one bitmap file per each selected object. If an object has already been exported before—that is, has the filename and resolution hints saved—these values will be used for it; otherwise, a name for the bitmap file will be constructed from the ID of the object (for example, *text2402.png*, see **A.9**), and the file will be placed in the directory where your SVG document was last saved.

By default, even if you are exporting a selection, you are actually exporting an area—the bounding box of the selection—which may contain lots of other objects, all of which will be visible. Checking the **Hide all except selected** checkbox makes sure the exported bitmap will contain *only* the exported objects, while all others, even if they overlap the export area, will not be rendered.

18.9.2   Exporting via the Command Line

All of the capabilities of the **Export Bitmap** dialog are also available when you run Inkscape from the command line by using various switches and parameters. This way, Inkscape can be used as a GUI-less utility from scripts or programs to automate various SVG rendering jobs. For example, this is how you export an object with id="text2402" at 600 dpi:

```
$ inkscape document.svg --export-png=img/text.png --export-id=text2402 \
    --export-dpi=600
```

For a complete list of Inkscape's command-line switches, refer to Appendix C.

18.9.3   Icon Preview

While there's currently no preview pane in the **Export Bitmap** dialog, if you use Inkscape to create icons, one way to preview your work rendered to different icon sizes is via the **Icon Preview** dialog, which you can call from the **View** menu:

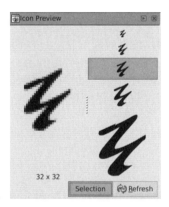

Figure 18-17: The Icon Preview dialog

This dialog contains previews of your document rasterized in a few typical icon sizes, from 16-by-16 to 128-by-128 pixels; on the left of the dialog, one of these renderings is additionally displayed scaled up so you can see how your vector objects translate to actual pixels. Click the **Selection** toggle button to switch the preview from the entire document to the current selection. The **Refresh** button updates the preview (there's no automatic update of the preview yet).

18.9.4   Make a Bitmap Copy

You can immediately import (18.1) the bitmap file you have exported back into the document to review how rasterization worked. If, however, you only need that bitmap in your document and not as a separate file, you can use Inkscape's shortcut: the **Edit ▶ Make a Bitmap Copy** command.

This command exports the selected objects and at once imports the resulting bitmap back to the document, overlaying it on top of the selection. The new bitmap object is not embedded (it is placed in the document's last save directory); use the embedding effect (18.2) to embed it. The resolution of the export can be set on the **Bitmaps** page of **Inkscape Preferences**; the default is 90 dpi, and for that value, the command will additionally snap the export area to the 1 px grid, making sure the pixels of the created bitmap align exactly with the boundaries of px squares.

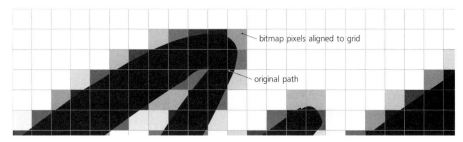

Figure 18-18: A 90-dpi bitmap copy of a path, aligned to the grid

This command can be used for a quick preview of how your art will rasterize (after which, the bitmap object can be deleted). It is also useful when you have some very slow-rendering filters (17.5) but do not want to work in the No Filters or Outline modes; in this case, just make a bitmap copy of the filtered object and delete or hide the slow-rendering original. Also, you can create a low-resolution bitmap copy of an object in order to trace it to achieve a characteristic distortion of its shape, which may have artistic value.

18.10   Color Management

The goal of color management tools is to ensure that the colors in your artwork are correctly translated between different output devices, most often from screen to print. The ranges of colors that can be reproduced are different for different devices, and some color distortions are unavoidable. Color management allows you to preview, control, and thereby minimize these distortions.

In Inkscape, color management is a developing area, and it is still in a quite primitive state. You can use screen proofing to preview output colors; however, using Inkscape alone, you cannot properly prepare a file for print (i.e., color-separate it and save it with a color profile embedded). However, in most cases you can get the result you need by using some tricks and employing some additional software, as described in this section.

However, before you go into it, consider if you really *need* color management. If you are going to print your art on a desktop color printer, chances are its quality is simply not good enough for color management to make a significant difference. A typical desktop printer will accept and print the same RGB data as is displayed on your screen, performing its own color conversion without bothering the user.

The need for color management arises when you are going to print your documents using a professional printer, e.g., by sending them to a print service provider. Even then, some providers will perform color management on your documents for you if you ask them to. If you have sufficient control over this process (for example, can review the print proofs), this is usually the best option because the print service staff knows what works best with their equipment.

18.10.1   ICC Color Profiles

An ICC color profile is a file that fully describes the color capabilities of an output device. If you want to prepare your document for outputting on a specific device, you must first obtain the ICC profile that exactly corresponds to this device and the output media (for example, paper type used for printing). Sometimes, you can find an appropriate profile file on the Internet (for example, on the web site of the printer hardware's manufacturer); sometimes, you can request them from the print service provider you will be using. A useful package of generic profiles can be obtained from Adobe at *http://www.adobe.com/downloads*.

Once you get the destination profile, put it into *~/.local/share/color/icc* on Linux and *system32\spool\drivers\color* inside the Windows folder on Windows.

18.10.2   Screen Proofing

Since the color range of a typical printer is narrower than that of a computer display, Inkscape can *preview* the printing output on screen by emulating the printer colors on your display. For this, you need to have two ICC color profiles: one for the printer you're going to use and another for your screen.

Ideally, you should have your display *calibrated* using a special hardware device called *colorimeter*; this calibration creates a custom ICC profile of your display. If you cannot do calibration, a generic RGB profile, such as "Adobe RGB" from Adobe's profile pack mentioned above, should work well enough unless your quality requirements are truly demanding.

In **Inkscape Preferences**, go to the **Color management** tab. Choose the display profile in the **Display adjustment** section. Then, in the **Proofing** section, check **Simulate output on screen** and choose the **Device profile** of your target device (i.e., printer).

For both screen and target device profiles, you can also choose **Device rendering intent**. The default **Perceptual** is the best choice in most cases; if you want the output to look as color-rich as possible (for example, when printing simple business graphics), try **Saturation**.

If a screen color is "out of gamut"—that is, cannot be rendered on the output device at all—it can be made immediately visible by converting it to a specially designated color. For example, if your design has no reds, check **Mark out of gamut colors** and choose red for **Out of gamut warning color**. Then, wherever you see red in your drawing, you know that you need to change the actual color of that object (it is of course shown correctly in the status bar or in the **Fill and Stroke** dialog, the red mark is only in the drawing) if you want it to print without gross distortions.

18.10.3 Separating and Embedding

Screen proofing is helpful, but sometimes it is not enough—you may be required to produce a file already converted to the target color system. Such files are often called *color-separated* because they contain the separate color channels (usually CMYK, 8.2.2) corresponding to the inks of the output device. Such a file may also have the target color profile embedded into it. The most commonly used formats are PDF (vector) and TIFF (bitmap); both can contain color-separated data and embed ICC profiles.

Although it can export PDF and render bitmaps, as of version 0.47 Inkscape cannot do color separation or profile embedding. You need some other software to do the job for you, such as Adobe Photoshop (for TIFF) or Illustrator (for PDF); both can import Inkscape's SVG format directly. You can also use open source software; the Scribus page layout program (*http://scribus.net*) will import SVG and create color-separated PDFs, and the Separate+ plugin for GIMP (*http://registry.gimp.org/node/471*) will take Inkscape-exported PNG bitmap and convert it into a color-separated TIFF with screen proofing for complete control.

19

TUTORIAL: DESIGNING A BUSINESS CARD

Even in this supposedly "electronic" age, business cards (or visiting cards, or address cards—if you don't want to sound too business-like) remain popular. This little piece of cardboard is a reflection of your—or your organization's—personality, a little presentation of what you consider most important about you. So, not surprisingly, the design aspect of this small item of stationery is very important. Like in a three-line haiku, you have a very limited space to make a clear, original, and memorable statement.

For the same reasons—simplicity, limited space, and the need for the design to stand out—a business card is a perfect test project for such an essential designer's tool as a vector editor. Inkscape's toolset makes it a great tool for the job; its only real weakness is the relative difficulty of creating print-ready output files with device colors.

The steps of this tutorial show two quite different sample designs, but I'm not inviting you to follow them exactly (unless you just want to learn the techniques). If you plan to design a real business card, try to find and analyze a lot more examples than these two, and play with Inkscape to come up with something that combines the best features you've seen with something completely original.

Creativity cannot be taught, but it can be inspired. My examples are both somewhat on the artsy side; perhaps what you have in mind for your own card would be more traditional—but the general approach would be the same.

19.1 Design 1: Template and Text

The first step is straightforward. Create a new document by choosing the template called **business_card_90x50mm** from the **File ▸ New** submenu. (If you need a different size, you can always change it in **Document Properties**, Shift-Ctrl-D.) Then switch to the Text tool and create text objects for all the text lines you will display on your card—name, position, address, phone, etc. Make them all independent objects (click and type each one separately) because you're going to move them around a lot, trying different layouts. If you will display a logo on your card, import the logo file (Appendix **B**) and, if you only have it in bitmap format, trace it (**18.8**) to convert it to paths.

Phone 123 4567

Dmitry Kirsanov
www.kirsanov.com

12 Address 27
City   dmitry@kirsanov.com
Country

Figure 19-1: Preparing the workspace and adding text objects

The next step is choosing font(s) for your text objects. A font you like will go a long way towards a design you like, too. If you're serious about design, you likely have a large library of your favorite fonts; otherwise, a few basic (but good) fonts usually come with your operating system. Many high-quality and free (or inexpensive) fonts can be found on the Web.

I have long liked the free font called Gentium;[1] its main feature is good Unicode support, but I also find it aesthetically pleasing, so I decided to use it for this design. After you assign the font to all the text strings, play with their relative sizes by resizing them in Selector (Figure 19-2). Do the different sizes of the same font look good together? Strangely, that is not a given—and if not, you will need to use different fonts for different elements. In any case, however, never use more than two fonts in such a small design—it will likely look too motley.

To make Inkscape see a new font, just install it as you usually do in your operating system and restart Inkscape. The new font will be listed in the **Text and Font** dialog as well as in the Text tool's drop-down list (**15.4.2**). Supported font formats include TrueType, Type 1, and OpenType.

---

[1] Available at *http://sil.org/~gaultney/gentium*

Figure 19-2: Fonts and sizes

19.2 Design 1: Layout

Designing a business card for a single person (as opposed to creating a template to be used by many cards with different names) has an important advantage: You can position and align your text objects precisely, without having to leave extra space for variable-length names and addresses. In this case, I was able to push all the address bits closely against the name, creating an asymmetric composition tightly bound together by its alignments (the address is aligned with the start of the last name, the email with the top of the name, etc.).

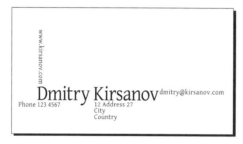

Figure 19-3: Laying out the text

This already looks interesting—but perhaps a little too rectangular. An obvious thing to try is to select all (Ctrl-A) and rotate a bit (press [once). Much better! The design now has a flair of constructivism—a short-lived but influential movement of the 1920s whose proponents loved bold contrasts and running texts at an angle (though they probably would not have approved of the Gentium font). Let's develop this style; add three black corners intruding into the composition from the edges and place a big red circle in the mass center of the composition, as shown in Figure 19-4. (Constructivists loved simple geometric forms in black and red!)

To look their best, most text objects require adjusting of letter spacing (uniform spacing between all letters in the text) and kerning (intervals between some particular letter pairs). In the Text tool, use Alt-<, Alt-> to change letter spacing and Alt-arrows to change kerning at the text cursor (15.3.3). Generally, large text objects look better with tighter letter spacing, while small type needs increased letter spacing for readability.

Figure 19-4: Rotating and adding shapes

19.3   Design 2: Graphic

Our first business card attempt was mostly inspired by a layout of the text lines, with graphic elements coming secondary to support and reinforce that layout. Could we go the other way around, starting from some piece of graphic and building the design around it?

Of course, if you're doing a company business card, the obvious starting point is the company's logo. If you're designing a card just for yourself and want it to be more personal, you can try tracing (**18.8**) an imported photo of yours. Finally, you can also use a piece of clipart, for example from *http://openclipart.org* (**1.3**), which has many decorations and abstract pieces that might become the centerpiece of your card.

For my second demo card, however, I chose another approach: artistic initials. I switched to the Calligraphic pen, set the **Angle** to 90 degrees with a **Fixation** of 100 and drew a couple of intertwined letters. After I finally got the lettershapes more or less right, the result was mildly interesting but far from exciting. I then tried to improve it by creating a union of the path objects and then simplifying, insetting, and outsetting it a few times:

original drawing (5 strokes)

unioned, inset/outset, simplified

Figure 19-5: Creating initials

Now the letters look more natural—but they can still be made much more interesting. The general rule of modern design seems to be: Don't be too neat! If you can dirty, distort, or damage your art in a creative way, go ahead and do it. So I selected a somewhat narrower pen nib, maximized **Tremor** to 100 and danced wildly around the letters with my tablet pen (though this could just as well be done with a mouse). At first the result may appear rather unattractive, but this is because I forgot to do the usual Simplify/Inset/Outset magic to it:

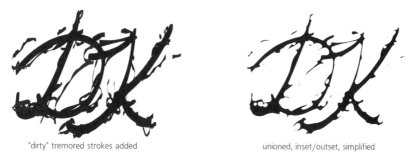

"dirty" tremored strokes added   unioned, inset/outset, simplified

Figure 19-6: Damaging the lettershapes creatively

19.4 Design 2: Layout

Naturally, such a piece of distortion art deserves the central place on the card, with the rest of the stuff being placed symmetrically around it. I used a plain, slanted, very light sans serif font (Helvetica Condensed Light) which does not distract from the artwork in the center. The horizontal layout may not be the best here—the card seems to be cramped. Rotating everything on its side (press Ctrl-[ ) gives ample space to the art and allows the text to float to the edges so it does not interfere:

Figure 19-7: Laying out the card around the initials

19.5 Design 2: Texture and Color

Something is starting to emerge here, but it's far from being ready. The card looks too empty, too flat, too hostile to the irregular blotch of ink in its center. Can we do something about it? Let's try adding some background gradients. As explained in 10.7, the default gradient from opacity 1 to opacity 0 of some color (for example, blue) looks crude and unnatural, its boundary clearly visible even if it uses a very pale color. To improve the look of a gradient over a white background, paint the transparent end of the gradient white, instead of the same color as the other end.

Here, I added four rectangles with irregularly slanted bluish green gradients at the edges of the card to achieve a naturally curly, softly blended, asymmetric look. The dashed lines are the bounding boxes of the four rectangles with gradients, and the gradient lines show the span and direction of each gradient. I painted the initials dark blue and added a blurred, 50% opaque drop shadow to the letters (**Filters ▸ Shadows and Glows ▸ Drop Shadow**).

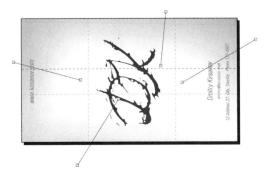

Figure 19-8: Adding gradients and shadows

Can it be still improved? A good way to add texture to the card is by overlaying a regular grid of semitransparent lines. Draw a rectangle over the entire card, open **Fill and Stroke** (Shift-Ctrl-F), switch the fill to pattern, and choose the **Stripes 1:1 white** stock pattern. Now, using pattern adjustment handles in the Node tool (10.8.1), rotate the strips and scale them down according to taste. Finally, move the rectangle over the gradients and the initials but below the text in z-order, and reduce its opacity to 20%.

Figure 19-9: Adding striped texture: The card is ready.

19.6 Export and Printing

We now have two decent business card designs—but how do we actually get them printed? The best course of action depends on the nature of the design, and you must understand the current limitations of Inkscape and the capabilities of various output formats (Appendix **B**) to identify the best approach.

19.6.1 PostScript

The first ("constructivist") design does not have any transparency or gradients; it is a collection of fully opaque shapes. This means it can be saved without any quality loss as PostScript or EPS, which most print service providers will accept. To be on the safe side, preview your PS or EPS output file using Ghostscript.[2] Or, you can directly print such a file to your local printer device by the **File ▸ Print** command, which sends the PostScript rendition of the document to the printer.

19.6.2 PDF

For more complex designs, the best output format is PDF (**B.3**). These days, nearly all print service providers accept PDF, often in preference to PostScript. PDF is a more powerful format by itself and it is better supported by Inkscape; with it, you don't have to worry about gradients or opacity. Filtered objects—such as the initials with a drop shadow in our second design—will be automatically rasterized on export to PDF if you enable this option in the PDF export options dialog.

Generally, the safest strategy for preparing your design for print is to separate the necessarily vector elements from those that can be rendered into a bitmap. For example, text (especially using small-size fonts), logos, and crisp foreground shapes must remain vector; avoid using filters on them, but separate them into a foreground layer and convert all texts to paths so they do not depend on the availability of the fonts. Anything else (background shapes with or without transparency, filtered objects, imported bitmaps, etc.) can be collectively pre-rendered into a single bitmap with **Make a Bitmap Copy**: Set the desired resolution in **Inkscape Preferences** (**Bitmaps** page), select all the objects to rasterize, and press Alt-B , after which you can delete or hide the vector originals. Thus, an "export-hardened" file—with best chances of being exported to PDF, imported into other programs, or printed without loss—would typically have just two layers: one with bitmap-like artwork rendered as one large bitmap and the other with vector-like artwork all in paths.

19.6.3 Bitmap Output

As a last resort, if even PDF doesn't cut it, you can always just export the entire design as a bitmap. Inkscape can only export as PNG, but any number of other programs, from expensive Photoshop to the free GIMP or command-line ImageMagick, will convert a PNG to another bitmap format, such as the old (but still popular in the print world) TIFF.

---

[2] *http://ghostscript.com*

19.6.4 Using Device Colors

Often, however, what you need to send to the print service provider is not just PDF or TIFF that faithfully reproduces the way your design looks on screen. Instead, you need your output to use device-specific CMYK or spot colors. While there's some limited support for using color-managed display, you can't export anything except the sRGB screen color space into any output format. Until this area is improved, you will need to use some other software to rectify this.

I have successfully imported Inkscape-produced SVG or PDF files into Adobe Illustrator in order to set a spot color for some objects, after which I resaved the file as PDF. With bitmap output, it is possible to create a device-specific CMYK file using only open source tools; first, convert the PNG exported from Inkscape to regular RGB TIFF, and then use the tifficc command-line utility from the LittleCMS library[3] to convert it to CMYK. You will need the ICC profile file of your target output device for this conversion.

19.6.5 Tiled Output

If you print your cards on an office or home printer, most likely you will use the A4 or Letter paper format instead of the business card format. In that case it makes sense to print multiple copies per sheet and then cut it into separate cards. To prepare a printable file, group all objects of your card, then use the **Create Tiled Clones** dialog to create a 2×5 grid of clones of the group that will exactly fit on your printable page.

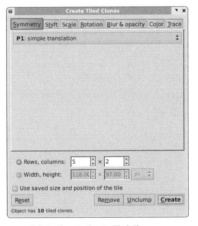

Edit ▶ Clone ▶ Create Tiled Clones…

Figure 19-10: Tiling the card to fill the output page

3 *http://littlecms.com*

20

TUTORIAL:
CREATING AN ANIMATION

From the start, SVG was designed as a language for both static and animated vector graphics. At one time dubbed "a Flash killer," it is indeed suitable for a wide variety of scripted and declarative animations. Unfortunately, even several years after the introduction of SVG, real SVG animations (as opposed to static SVG) are hard to find on the Web. There are several reasons for this, the most important being the lack of a single standard player that would offer a significant competitive advantage over Adobe's (formerly Macromedia's) Flash. Currently, almost all of the animations on the Web are either in Flash or in animated GIF formats—just as they were five years ago.

From Inkscape's perspective, however, this may be a good thing. Inkscape does not yet support creating animated SVG documents (except if you add animation attributes manually via XML Editor) and can only display SVG documents statically. But you still can use Inkscape to create static frames and then combine them into a GIF or Flash animation with some other software. This method may seem awkward at first, but it is in fact workable and may deliver very good results. Why is this worth the trouble, and what kinds of animations are best suited for this technique?

Any animation including complex natural or interacting movements is perhaps out of reach for the Inkscape-based animation technique described in this tutorial. Without a timeline control, it's difficult to work on anything but simple repeating animations several frames long. But then, many animations for the Web—banners, headings, blog avatars—fit this description perfectly.

20.1   Creating the Template

The most natural way to represent animation frames in Inkscape is by putting them on separate layers (**4.6**). You can easily toggle visibility of each layer to see how your frames stack up and control what changes from one frame to the next. However, creating many layers manually (**Layer ▸ Add Layer**) is very tedious. I wrote a simple Python script that creates a 200-by-200 px document with 100 empty layers:

```
print """<svg width="200" height="200"
  xmlns:svg="http://www.w3.org/2000/svg"
  xmlns:inkscape="http://www.inkscape.org/namespaces/inkscape">"""
for i in range(100):
  print '<g inkscape:groupmode="layer" display="none" id="%03d"/>' % (i + 1)
print '</svg>'
```

All layers are created hidden (that's what display="none" is for), so in Inkscape, you will need to unhide them one by one (**4.6.3**) to draw on them. You can vary the number of layers created by the script (range(100)) as well as the dimensions of the artboard (width="200" height="200"). Save the script into the file *generate-layers.py* and, in a command-line (or "terminal") window of your OS, run it and capture its output to an SVG file. (You will need the Python language interpreter to be installed on your computer; you can get it at *http://python.org*.) Then, run Inkscape on this file:

```
$ python generate-layers.py > ani.svg
$ inkscape ani.svg
```

You can also put the resulting file (*ani.svg*) into your *~/.inkscape/templates* folder where it will work as a template, so the next time you will be able to create an empty 100-layer file by choosing it from the **File ▸ New** list. Here is Inkscape's **Layers** dialog (**4.6.4**) which is essential for working with such a multilayer file:

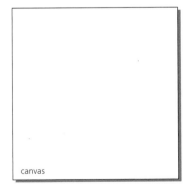

Figure 20-1: A 100-layer animation template loaded into Inkscape

20.2 First Frames

Let's make an animation of a dancing man—something catchy yet simple enough to not require much drawing skill and to fit the small format of the animation (and this brief tutorial). Our hero's claim to fame will be in his movements, so we don't need to make his countenance too sophisticated. Something as primitive as this stick figure will do:

Figure 20-2: The stick figure we're starting with, showing its nodes in the Node tool

It is made of three simple paths (hands, legs, and body) and one ellipse (head). Use the Pen tool (14.1) with Ctrl to draw horizontal/vertical straight lines; then use the Ellipse tool (11.4) to create the head. Then, to facilitate interpolation, do **Path ▶ Combine** on the body and limbs so they become one path, and use Ctrl-Alt-click in the Node tool (12.5.3) to add nodes in his elbow and knee joints.

20.3 Tweening

Now make a copy of the character by duplicating it (Ctrl-D with both head and body selected), move it to the right and play with its nodes (in the Node tool) to give our man a funky dancing pose. We thus get two *keyframes*, and the entire animation could be as simple as alternating between them.

Figure 20-3: Two keyframes

However, it would be much better to add intermediate frames to make the transition between the keyframes smoother. Animators call this *tweening* (derived from *between*), and Inkscape can to some extent automate this process: Select both bodies (i.e., two path objects) and do **Extensions ▶ Generate from Path ▶ Interpolate**. Specify the number of **Interpolation steps** (say, 4), select **Interpolation method 1**, and, if desired, use a nonzero **Exponent** value to make the movement speed up or slow down nonlinearly. Then, the head ellipses can be placed over the tweened bodies by another interpolation using the same number of steps and the same **Exponent** (Figure 20-4).

If the tweening steps don't look right to you, you can undo the interpolation, tweak the keyframes, and reinterpolate until you get what you like. **Interpolation method 1** (13.3) matches the nodes that are at the same position along the path, so it is preferable when one of the keyframe paths was created by tweaking the other one without adding or removing nodes (as in our case). If two paths are of different origin and have incompatible nodes, **method 2** is better.

Figure 20-4: Interpolating the keyframes

20.4 Compositing and Creating Frames

Now it's time to place our animation on its proper place on the canvas and distribute the frames across layers. Remove the tweening once again and place the second keyframe right over the first. (Note that the dancer's right foot coincides in both keyframes because it rests on the floor.) Select both overlapping figures and place them onto the canvas, scaling them if necessary and taking into account whatever other elements you plan to add (such as a text heading). Finally, interpolate the bodies and the heads again—right in place:

Figure 20-5: Interpolating in place

The next task to do in Inkscape is a bit boring (it may be automated in future versions). You need to ungroup the group of the interpolation paths and manually place each one on its layer from 002 to 005, with the keyframes occupying layers 001 and 006. Then, duplicate the frames in the reverse order: Frames 005 to 001 go into the range 007 to 011, to make the dancer smoothly return into the original position.

Use Shift-Page Up and Shift-Page Down to move the selected objects one layer up/down, and watch the status bar that tells you in which layer your selected objects are. Alternatively, you can cut (Ctrl-X) an object, switch to the destination layer, and paste it in place (Ctrl-Alt-V). Finally, make sure all the layers you've used are visible, and save the SVG file.

20.5   Export and Production

You can export the layers manually, but that would be rather frustrating—especially since you may need to do it more than once after viewing the result and making changes to the source. Since Inkscape offers a powerful set of command-line parameters, I wrote another Python script to automate the export. The script takes as parameters the name of source file, the numbers of the start and end layers to export, and the name of the resulting GIF; it then calls Inkscape to export each layer separately. After exporting, this script calls the convert utility from ImageMagick for combining the frames into an animated GIF file which can then be viewed in any graphic web browser.

```
import os, sys
for i in range(int(sys.argv[2]), int(sys.argv[3]) + 1):
  os.system("""inkscape --export-png=%s-%03d.png --export-id=%03d \
    --export-id-only --export-dpi=400 --export-area-canvas \
    --export-background-opacity=1 %s""" % (sys.argv[1], i, i, sys.argv[1]))
os.system("convert -loop 0 -delay 10 %s-*.png %s" % (sys.argv[1], sys.argv[4]))
```

Save it as *produce-gif.py* and run:

```
$ python produce-gif.py ani.svg 001 011 stick.gif
Exporting only object with id="001"; all other objects hidden
DPI: 400
Background RRGGBBAA: ffffffff
Area 0:0:100:100 exported to 444 x 444 pixels (400 dpi)
Bitmap saved as: ani.svg-001.png
Exporting only object with id="002"; all other objects hidden
...
Exporting only object with id="011"; all other objects hidden
...
```

Our output so far can be viewed online at *http://www.kirsanov.com/ inkscape-animation/stick.gif*.

NOTE   *Instead of the convert utility from ImageMagick, you can use the open source Gifsicle program* (http://www.lcdf.org/gifsicle) *for composing frames into an animated GIF file. Its advantage is that it can optimize the animation, reducing its file size.*

NOTE   *If you want your animation to be in Flash format instead of an animated GIF, a straightforward way to do it is to convert your SVG to static SWF frames (for example, using the svg2swf utility,* http://robla.net/1996/svg2swf) *and then combine the frames into an animation, for which I recommend the SWF Tools package* (http://swftools.org). *The resulting SWF file will not be very efficient but it will work.*

20.6   Hatching

Our stick-figure animation looks at most mildly engaging. This smooth, vectory style is good for technical animations, such as demonstrating the workings of a machine, but is not too inspiring for an animated dance. Can we do something about it?

Hide all layers except 001, select the figure and lower its opacity. Then arm yourself with the Calligraphic pen (**14.3**), select the **Width** of 20 with **Tremor** of 40, and draw over the stick figure trying to make it more random, funky, personalized. While at it, you can also add more pronounced feet and fists and more human-like body forms in general.

Figure 20-6: Hatching with Calligraphic pen

When done, delete the original skeleton figure—it's served its function of a blueprint and is no longer needed. The result is not bad, but it looks a bit foreign in its roughness upon the immaculate white background. To fix this, reduce the width of the pen to 1 and add some thin random strokes around the dancer, hinting at his limbs' motion and shadows on the floor. Don't worry if this looks *too* random to your taste—when you'll see him move, this randomness will come live and natural.

Figure 20-7: Skeleton removed, motion noise added

The main rule in this kind of the project is, *Don't copy*. Freehand roughness cannot be recycled; no matter how similar is one frame to another, you need to sketch each frame entirely from scratch, using nothing but the stick figure as your guide. Duplicating the freehand strokes (even if you move or scale them) will instantly kill the rough, natural feel and make your animation wooden and dull. Don't be lazy; the more you draw the easier it gets.

And the result is certainly worth the labor: See *http://www.kirsanov.com/ inkscape-animation/rough.gif* for the complete hand-drawn animation. Much more inspiring than the interpolated stick figure!

Using the same technique, you can manually trace with Calligraphic pen over any imported bitmap. Make the bitmap half-transparent and sketch on top of it, trying to highlight the most important features and ignore the rest. In an animation, the source bitmaps might be frames of a video, still photos, or rendered 3D images.

If necessary, you can move your entire animation—for example, to free up space for a heading above it—by unhiding all layers, selecting the whole bunch of shapes, and moving/transforming them as needed on the canvas.

20.7 Text

Now, let's add a textual banner to our animation—just a single word, "dance!". Can we do something more interesting than copying the same static text object into each frame?

Once again, we could use the Calligraphic pen to draw ruffled handwritten letters over some text object used as a guide, so that the entire animation is in a common style. However, for the purpose of demonstration, let's try another approach: Make the text banner smoothly billowing as if on a flag. To distort the text, you can use the **Envelope Deformation** path effect (13.1.8); however, it is probably faster to apply some node sculpting instead (12.5.7.2).

Create a text object using a nice-looking font, convert it to path (Shift-Ctrl-C), ungroup (Ctrl-U), union (Ctrl-+), switch to the Node tool (F2), select all nodes (Ctrl-A), and Alt-drag one of them. The entire shape will smoothly bend and stretch. If the lettershapes get too much distorted, undo the drag and press Insert a couple times, each time doubling the number of nodes—this usually helps make the path you're sculpting behave more naturally.

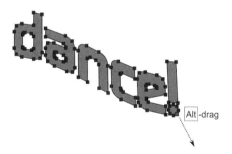

Alt-drag

Figure 20-8: Node sculpting on a text banner

Now make two copies of the text object, sculpt each one differently so they look like two shots of a banner floating in the wind, and interpolate between them. Then, just as we did for the dancer figure, distribute the interpolation steps into layers, placing them above the figure on the canvas (Figure 20-9). Don't worry about absolute precise placement; slight wobbling of the banner is not a problem (and will even add some character).

Figure 20-9: Interpolating the banner

To see where to place each object relative to the previous layer, use the **Opacity** control on the **Layers** dialog to make the previous layer temporarily half-transparent. Compose the animated GIF again using the *produce-gif.py* script. The result so far can be seen at *http://www.kirsanov.com/inkscape-animation/with-banner.gif*; here are the frames 001 to 005:

Figure 20-10: Half of the animation's frames (forward movement)

20.8 Background

The only thing not to like about our animation is its total lack of color. You can fix this by adding a different colored background to each frame, for a real stroboscopic dancefloor effect. Choosing these random colors can be automated, too: Create a rectangle with an unset color and use the **Create Tiled Clones** dialog (**16.6**) to multiply it with some hue variation.

Paint the "dance!" banner with a contrasting acid color, also varying from frame to frame. Finally, to make the dancing man stand out from the background, add an elliptic gradient "spotlight" behind him; randomly move, scale, and rotate the spotlight on each frame for an additional energizing effect. The very final version is at *http://www.kirsanov.com/inkscape-animation/final.gif*. Enjoy!

21

TUTORIAL: DRAWING A 3D-CORRECT CARTOON

As mentioned in **11.3.1**, Inkscape's 3D Box tool is not intended to be a replacement for specialized 3D design applications. Inkscape is a drawing program—and as such, its 3D Box tool is best used as a *drawing aid*. This is what we'll try to do in this simple tutorial.

A "3D-correct" drawing is simply one that satisfies the rules of perspective drawing which have been well known to artists for many centuries. It does not need to exhibit perfectly realistic shading and texturing; it just has to get its lines and objects approximately correct with regard to angles and dimensions.

Granted, some styles of drawing do not even need to have correct perspective; sometimes, intentional perspective distortions may have an artistic value of its own. Many artists have a knack for drawing 3D-correct art without using any technical aids. However, quite often you will notice perspective errors, ranging from barely noticeable to embarrassing, in pieces of art which would definitely do better without them. I think, therefore, that many artists—not only the beginners—would appreciate a quick and easy way to set up the perspective for a drawing without tedious manual measurements and helper lines. Let's see how this task can be approached in Inkscape.

21.1 The Room

Let's say we want to draw a simple scene of a meeting of two people in a room. Switch to the 3D Box tool (x) and drag in the middle of the canvas to draw the box for the room:

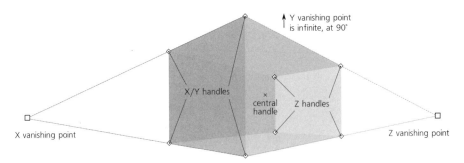

Figure 21-1: Creating the room

Don't try to get it right on the first try; instead, just drag the handles of the box and, if necessary, the vanishing points to adjust what you've drawn. The corner handles will let you resize your room; the four X/Y handles move in the X/Y plane by default and along the Z axis when Shift is pressed, whereas the four Z handles, conversely, will move along the Z axis without Shift and in the X/Y plane with Shift. The X-shaped central handle will move the entire room, again in the X/Y plane without Shift and along the Z axis with Shift. Whenever moving a handle in X/Y, press Ctrl to restrict its movement to only X or only Y axis. Finally, dragging the vanishing points will reslant and resize the room to fit the changed perspective (11.3.3).

You can create a third vanishing point on the Y axis in addition to the existing ones in X and Z (in other words, make Y vanishing point *finite*). Do this if you want your image to look "closer" and from a more emphatic perspective, as if viewed by a spider in the corner of the room instead of a human at a distance. Conversely, you can make two or three of the vanishing points infinite if what you're after is a more detached, technical look "from afar":

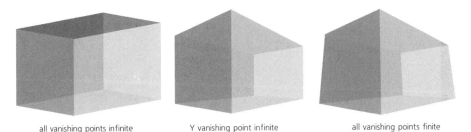

all vanishing points infinite   Y vanishing point infinite   all vanishing points finite

Figure 21-2: Different kinds of perspective

21.2   The Furniture

Next up, let's add some furniture—for example, a sofa.

In creating 3D box compositions, it is convenient to use snapping (**7.3**) so that boxes align precisely. Open the **Document Properties** dialog (Shift-Ctrl-D) and, on the **Snap** tab, enable both **Snap to paths** and **Snap to nodes**.

Now, draw a smaller box inside the larger one. (We don't need to worry about z-order of the boxes; their default style uses partial transparency so you can always see the edges of all boxes you created.) Note that the new box uses the same perspective (i.e., the same vanishing points) as the room box. Grab its lower left X/Y handle and drag it so it snaps to the lower left Z-edge of the room. That will be the foundation of the sofa; use the other corner handles to give it correct height, width, and depth:

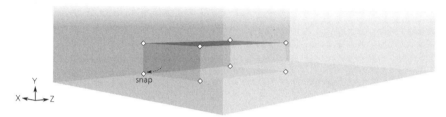

Figure 21-3: The foundation of the sofa

For the back of the sofa, you can draw a new box and snap it into alignment in a similar way; or, more easily, you can duplicate the sofa base (Ctrl-D) and drag its X/Y handles to resize it into the correct shape:

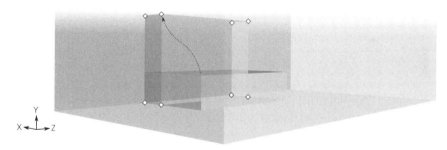

Figure 21-4: The back of the sofa

Now, assuming this is a basement, let's place two small basement windows on both sides of the sofa. A couple of boxes flattened in the X dimension will make perfect windows. However, how do we properly place them, given that no side of a window aligns with a side of any other box?

Again, the duplicate-then-resize trick is the easiest way to achieve this. Duplicate the largest box you have (i.e., the room itself); Ctrl-drag its front X/Y handle backward (along the X axis) to squeeze it into a thin layer; then, drag four handles on the X/Y plane to resize the window into place. For a second window, just duplicate the first one and Shift-drag its central handle in the Z direction; this way, the second window will be an exact perspective-aligned copy of the first one. Using the same duplicate and flatten trick, add a doorway box on the Z-most wall (i.e., the wall closest to the Z vanishing point), so that it protrudes outside of the room box:

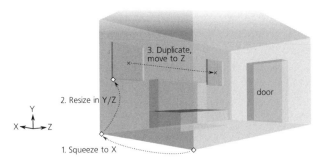

Figure 21-5: The windows and the door

21.3 People

Now, I want to draw two people, one standing by the sofa and the other in the doorway. What does the 3D Box tool have to do with drawing humans, you may ask? A lot! Although I'm not going to model robot-like constructions out of parallelepipeds, I still want to make sure the height and bulkiness of a figure are correct in the drawing's perspective, and an easy way to achieve this is with the 3D Box tool.

Here's what I do. First, I add a tall and narrow box in the doorway—this will be our human number 1. As before, I just duplicate the doorway box, squeeze it on the sides in the X/Y plane, and resize it so as to get a realistic proportion of the figure height and doorway height. (Ask someone to stand in a real doorway to get an idea.)

Then, I duplicate the first human box and, using its X-shaped handle in the middle, Shift-drag it to the front, then Ctrl-drag it horizontally a bit along the X axis. This will be our second human standing beside the sofa.

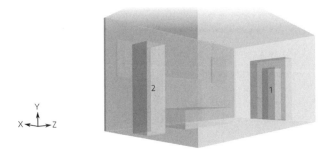

Figure 21-6: The two people

This way, both people boxes have the same perspective-adjusted height and will serve as useful guides for actually drawing the human figures. If I were trying to achieve even better anatomic fidelity, I could use a stack of three boxes for the legs, body, and head for each human (unfortunately, however, you cannot drag several selected boxes in 3D space at once. You can only drag them one-by-one in the current version of Inkscape).

21.4   Sketching and Coloring

Enough boxes; it is time to put away the 3D Box tool, arm yourself with the Calligraphic pen, and start sketching on top the 3D blueprint. Create a new layer so you can show and hide the 3D boxes and the actual drawing separately.

Of course you don't need to trace the edges of the boxes precisely. For nongeometric objects, such as the sofa and the humans, this is hardly possible, but even the walls and windows will benefit from some hand-drawn roughness and imperfections. Use the edges of the 3D boxes as general guides to keep an eye on, but otherwise draw as freely as you would draw without any guides at all, using your own manner and style of sketching. You also don't need to trace *all* of the lines; some can be omitted, and some just hinted at by short partial strokes.

Figure 21-7: Sketching over the 3D blueprint

You will discover that the 3D boxes make it much easier to keep in mind the overall composition and space relationships in your drawing while working on the details. I have described my own sketching style with the Calligraphic pen in another tutorial (20.6), so I won't go into much detail here; since the focus of this tutorial is the use of the 3D Box tool, in this drawing I am even more sketchy than usual. Don't try to copy me; you should try to work out a style which is most natural for you. After you're done with the basic outlines, you can turn off the 3D layer to see how your image stands on its own merits, as shown in Figure 21-8.

Figure 21-8: When sketching is complete, hide the 3D layer.

Finally, I colorize the drawing, again using my favorite approach with wide blurred colored strokes underneath the dark crisp outlines:

Figure 21-9: Adding color

22

TUTORIAL: ARTISTIC DRAWING

Among vector editors, Inkscape is one of the best choices for sketching and freehand drawing thanks to its wonderfully versatile Calligraphic pen tool (14.3). Far from being geometrically perfect (and boring) like other vector tools, the Calligraphic pen has character—and it produces always-editable vector objects.

In this tutorial, we'll go through the process of creating a simple drawing entirely in Inkscape—let's try drawing a funny, cartoon running horse which might be a mascot or a comic character. I've always found it challenging to draw anything from scratch (and I imagine many readers can sympathize). Yet with Inkscape, I was able to make a drawing that I actually liked.

22.1 The First Sketch

Let's start by switching to the Calligraphic pen tool and setting a **Width** of 0.05 and a **Thinning** of 0.2 in the tool's controls bar (14.3). If you have a graphics tablet, enable the pen pressure for varying the stroke width (14.3.1.1). The **Angle** and **Fixation** parameters only make sense for calligraphy, not freehand drawing, so we'll set the **Fixation** to 0, which effectively turns a fixed-angle pen into a round brush that has no orientation (14.3.2).

I've never drawn a horse before, and my first several strokes make this brutally obvious. With a beginning like this, I think many would be tempted, as I was, to give up right then and there. But patience and hard work pay off, especially in Inkscape. Just keep throwing strokes onto the canvas, undoing, tweaking, and throwing again. Sooner or later, something which is not entirely dreadful will flash through the tangle of bad lines.

Figure 22-1: The first strokes

For most people, drawing objects requires visual aids; you may find it hard to visualize on your own how a horse's body curves or which way the legs bend. I found that photos of real horses were of little help to me. Much more inspirational were stylized *drawings* of horses, where other, more capable artists have already done the hard work of abstracting and amplifying the core equestrian visual features. A Google image search will provide you with plenty of reference material. After much sketching, undoing, and emphasizing (by adding pen pressure), I arrived at this sketch:

Figure 22-2: The first sketch

22.2 Inking

The workflow of a comic or cartoon artist includes two main stages: *sketching* (typically with a pencil) and *inking* (with a pen) over the rough sketch. You can follow the same process in Inkscape. Now that the drawing looks more or less like a horse, it is time to start inking *over* it to develop it further. This way, you can see what was good in the original sketch and try to build on that without the risk of destroying it with too much tweaking. Select all strokes (Ctrl-A) and assign them an opacity of 0.05 so they become barely visible; this effectively hides the thin strokes, making it easier to concentrate on the bold ones. Then, lock this layer (using the lock toggle button in the status bar), create a new one (**Layer ▸ Add Layer**), and draw the same horse *again*, using the sketch as the guide:

Figure 22-3: Inking the sketch in a new layer

Is this the same horse? Not quite. The horse in the first sketch tried to look like a real horse—perhaps too real. Remember that what we want is a cartoon, not something realistic. This is typically achieved by enlarging, out of proportion, the head (especially the eyes) and the legs (or hands, or paws) of your creature. In the first inking layer, let's do just that: Keep the body the same but enlarge the hooves and the head, adding a pair of oversized, cartoonish eyes:

Figure 22-4: Getting cartoonish

22.3   Tweaking

The unique advantage of a vector editor is that all strokes remain independent objects. This makes it easy to nudge, scale, or rotate parts of your drawing. With the Selector tool, drag around the leg or the head to select all its objects and use either the mouse handles or the convenient keyboard shortcuts: Alt-arrows to move, Alt-< or Alt-> to scale, or Alt-[or Alt-] to rotate. It is fairly easy to produce a good stroke at a wrong scale or in the wrong location and then transform it to fit. Even if it already looks acceptable, playing with the limbs or facial features of your character can make it more expressive than you thought possible:

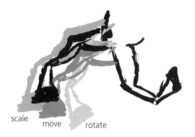

Figure 22-5: Adjusting elements of a drawing

Unlike on paper, you are not limited to just one inking layer. At any time, you can hide the previous sketch layer, fade out, lock your current layer to make it a new sketch, and create a new inking layer on top. Usually, with every such transition your drawing will look less and less like a pencil sketch and more like a real ink drawing with smoother strokes and more elaborate details. Here is my third inking attempt over the previous sketch layers (the head was especially difficult to sculpt—my horse originally looked more like a hippopotamus):

Figure 22-6: Another inking layer

22.4 Coloring and Smoothing

Now that the outline is almost done, it's time to start thinking about coloring the drawing. Inkscape can emulate many different styles of coloring. For example, you can imitate a painting by overlying many random calligraphic strokes and painting each one with a different color and opacity (you can use the Tweak tool for that, 8.7.1). Let's try a more traditional, smooth coloring, consisting of a flat color fill with some lighting and shading (white and black ellipses with elliptic opacity gradients, 10.1.2). Use the Paint bucket tool (14.4) to create the interior shape; you can apply a little blur to it (about 2 percent) for extra smoothness (Figure 22-7).

Figure 22-7: Coloring options

Let's get back to our outline (hide the coloring layer for now). It can be made much smoother and more attractive if you select all the strokes of some part of the figure (such as a leg or the head), union them (Ctrl-+), and simplify the result by pressing Ctrl-L a few times. This melts the sharp corners and welds the joints for a much more natural and integral look. Another very useful trick is making all strokes thicker by outsetting them (Alt-)) or thinner by insetting (Alt-(, 12.4). Multiple insets and outsets on a path have an effect similar to simplification. Too much insetting may make some parts of a stroke disappear altogether, but this is not necessarily bad—trust the overall impression and your artistic sense. Of course, the Node tool (12.5) can also be used for manual editing of strokes.

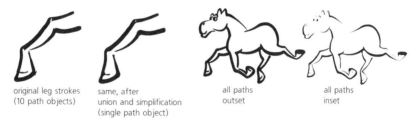

original leg strokes (10 path objects)

same, after union and simplification (single path object)

all paths outset

all paths inset

Figure 22-8: Welding and melting

22.5 Drawing Hair

For many beginning artists, drawing realistic-looking hair is especially difficult. Striking the right balance between regularity and chaos, between tidiness and untidiness is critical for the impression that your character will make. At this stage, the tail and especially the mane of my horse weren't impressive—I drew them over and over many times, but all my attempts looked either too lumpy or too bushy (or both). I was finally able to produce a decent wavy hair by using a high value of **Tremor** (14.3.4) in the Calligraphic pen, as shown in Figure 22-9. Maximizing this parameter makes the calligraphic brush strokes nicely blotchy and much more uniformly uneven than I was able to make them manually.

Figure 22-9: Drawing hair

22.6 Finalizing

The last touch is to try scaling, rotating, and skewing the entire drawing—this can sometimes improve it significantly without much work. Overall, the result turned out much better than I expected, and I'm pretty sure I would never be able to achieve this level of quality by drawing on paper. Of course, this is not the only style of drawing that you can do in Inkscape; experiment to find the techniques that are most natural for you. I have grown to especially like the Calligraphic pen with a high **Tremor** value, which gives you an almost "natural media" drawing tool.

Figure 22-10: Other freehand drawing examples

NOTE *While the best device for drawing on the computer is a graphics tablet (**14.3.1.1**), it is possible to do decent Inkscape drawings with a mouse only. A hand with a mouse cannot move quickly or naturally in any direction; horizontal strokes are usually easier than vertical and much easier than diagonal. Therefore, you may need to draw a few strokes stretched horizontally and then rotate them as needed, or even rotate the entire drawing so that the part you're working with is more convenient to stroke.*

23

TUTORIAL:
TECHNICAL DRAWING

In addition to everything we've seen so far, you can use Inkscape to create simple technical drawings. Let's try drawing an isometric image of a cross-section of an engine part (Figure 23-13). Inkscape does not intend to replace a real computer-aided design (CAD) application. It may be more straightforward to create such a technical drawing in a CAD program—but only if you have it and know how to use it. In most other cases, Inkscape is a natural choice due to its graphic power and versatility that can make your drawings not only precise but also visually impressive.

The key to creating such technical drawings in Inkscape is to use grids (7.2), snapping (7.3), transforming by numbers (6.6), and shapes, especially rectangles (11.2). As you will see in this tutorial, a combination of these functions makes it possible to create the entire drawing without ever once adjusting anything by hand or approximating shapes or positions: Every object, handle, and node just snaps into its place tightly and precisely. Once you get the hang of it, you will be able to produce similar drafts quickly and effortlessly.

23.1 Setting Up the Grid

We're going to make an *isometric* image, meaning all three coordinate axes are separated by equal angles (60 degrees) and have the same scale. This makes it much easier to use; for example, a cube remains the same length regardless of which axis you measure it along.

Open the **Document Properties** dialog (7.2.1), choose the **Grids** tab, and create the default axonometric grid with both X and Z angles set to 30 degrees (measured from the horizontal). You may want to set the spacing (it is called **Spacing Y** even though, the grid being isometric, it affects all three axes in the same way) to the minimum measurable distance in your drawing. For example, if all dimensions of the drawing elements must be in millimeters and precise to the first fractional digit, set the grid spacing to 0.1 mm so that you never have to put anything in between grid lines.

You can also change the spacing of the major (darker) grid lines; by default they appear every five regular lines. When you zoom out, minor grid lines disappear first to make the display less cluttered.

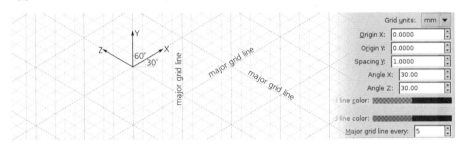

Figure 23-1: Setting up the isometric grid

23.2 Making the Box

With the grid (and, by default, snapping to grid) on, let's start by drawing the bottom box of our object. With the Rectangle tool, draw a rectangle of any size (we will resize and place it later). Notice that the corners of the rectangle readily snap to the grid line intersections (pay attention to the snap indicator and tips, 7.3.4), but the rectangle is not axonometric. What is the easiest way to skew it into the isometric projection so it fits the grid exactly?

Open the **Transform** dialog (Shift-Ctrl-M, 6.7) and, on the **Skew** tab, specify 60 degrees for the **Horizontal** skew and 30 degrees for the **Vertical** skew. After you click **Apply**, the rectangle is transformed so that it can serve as the top of the bottom plane of the box. Note that the rectangle resize handles now also move in the axonometric projection (11.2.1), so all you need to do is snap them into the corresponding grid intersections, as shown in Figure 23-2.

The other two sides of the box are even easier to create: For the front side, you only need 30 degrees of **Vertical** skew, with the **Horizontal** skew set at 0. The left side of the box is simply the front side duplicated (Ctrl-D) and flipped (h). After skewing and flipping, it takes less than a second to snap the corners of all

Figure 23-2: Creating, skewing, and snapping the top of the box

three rectangles to form a precise, solid, gapless 6-by-8-by-2 box (for our purposes, there should be an even number of units in X and Z, so that we have a grid line exactly across the center):

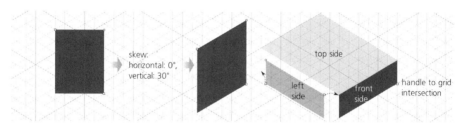

Figure 23-3: Creating the front and left sides of the box

Now that you have one box, you can quickly build up complex architectures just by duplicating its sides and re-snapping the corners to new positions. However, this is not exactly what we want to do. Our next step is to round the corners of the box.

23.3 Rounding Corners

To make rounded corners (11.2.2) in a rectangle, just grab the circular handle and drag it along the side. In the double-skewed top side of the box, rounding works entirely as expected—the rectangle becomes rounded in its plane with appropriate projective distortion. While Ctrl-dragging one of the rounding handles, snap it to the nearest intersection so that the rounding radius is equal to one grid unit. Then, move the sizing handles on the front and left sides to make them narrower by one grid unit on each side:

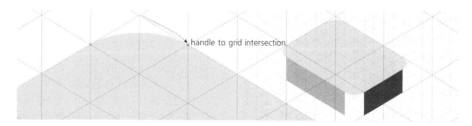

Figure 23-4: Rounding the corners on top of the box

Now we need something to fill the vertical gaps in the box's corners. For this, let's create a vertical cylinder whose copies (or clones) we will be able to put in all three visible corners of the box, as well as reuse them later for the large top cylinder of our engine part.

To make a cylinder, we need to start with an ellipse—but to make this ellipse, we do not even need the Ellipse tool. Instead, just duplicate the top side of the box and resize it to an isometric square of 2-by-2 grid units. Since such resizing preserves the rounded corners, which have the radius of one unit, this gives us a perfectly isometric ellipse:

Figure 23-5: Creating an ellipse out of a rectangle

To create a cylinder, we could duplicate this ellipse, move it down, and draw a flat non-isometric rectangle between them. While workable, this, however, would not be the "clean" way to do this, because we don't have any grid lines at the extremities of the ellipses to snap the left and right edges of the rectangle to. Such an approach would therefore require turning off snapping and using manual tweaking with its inevitable speed/precision tradeoff. Let's try another method.

Convert a copy of the ellipse-like rectangle to path (Shift-Ctrl-C) and switch to the Node tool (F2). Notice that there are no nodes at the left and right extremities of the ellipse where we will need them. Select all nodes (Ctrl-A) and insert new nodes between each of the two selected nodes by pressing Insert (12.5.3):

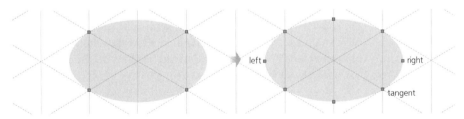

Figure 23-6: Adding nodes at the extremities of the ellipse

Now, select only the two nodes at the horizontal extremities (marked *left* and *right* above) and duplicate them (Shift-D). Add all the nodes in the bottom half of the ellipse to the selection by dragging around them with Shift. Grab the node that is tangent to the grid line (marked *tangent*) and Ctrl-drag it and the rest of the selected nodes downward until it all snaps at a level two units lower, creating the ideally precise cylinder shape. After that, all you need is to add a copy of the original ellipse back into its place on top, and draw a horizontal gradient (Figure 23-7).

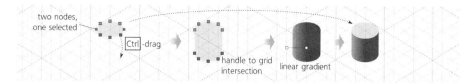

Figure 23-7: Pulling out, shading, and capping a cylinder

Now, just move three copies of the cylinder to fill in the gaps in the rounded box—they will fit snugly into their places. To make the box look like an integral whole, you just need to sort out the z-order and match the colors. Use the Dropper tool (8.6) to copy colors from the flat sides to the gradient stops on the cylinders or vice versa.

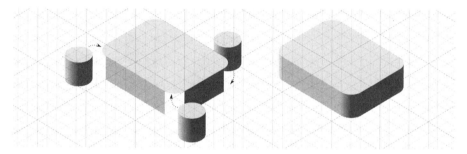

Figure 23-8: The box is ready.

23.4   Making the Top Cylinder

Make another copy of the corner cylinder and scale it up twice by pressing Ctrl->, then snap it into place on top of the center of the box.

Duplicate the top ellipse and scale it down to 50 percent in place (Ctrl-<). After that, you don't even need to move it anywhere—it is already precisely where it must be to imitate the hole in the top cylinder. All you need to do to make it *look* like a hole is add a horizontal linear gradient whose direction is opposite to that of the cylinder. While you're at it, make three more copies of the hole, snap each one into the corners of the base box, and scale down by pressing Ctrl-< again—these will be the holes for the bolts to fasten our detail in place:

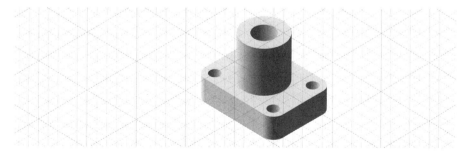

Figure 23-9: Adding the top cylinder and the holes

23.5 Making the Cutout

A full isometric view of the object is now ready. But, in order to demonstrate some additional techniques, I decided to create a cutout of the object showing its two perpendicular cross-sections.

Since everything we have done so far is snapped to the grid, adding the cutout shape is very easy. Switch to the Pen tool (14.1) and click near the corners of the left side of the cross-section. Then, starting with Shift pressed to create a second subpath of the same path, click through for the right side:

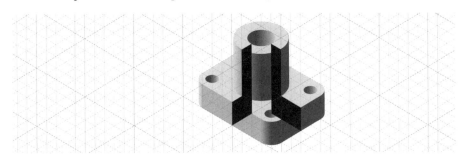

Figure 23-10: Adding the cutout shape

Often, cutouts in technical drawings are filled with a pattern that symbolizes the material of the object. Plain stripes are used for metals, and we can indicate that our object is metallic by using one of the preset patterns. Open the **Fill and Stroke** dialog (8.1.1), click the **Pattern** button on the **Fill** tab, and choose the **Stripes 1:8** pattern. The only problem with this pattern is that it shows black stripes on a transparent background, but we need black stripes on a white background. Just duplicate the shape, paint it white, and move the white copy under the striped one in the z-order.

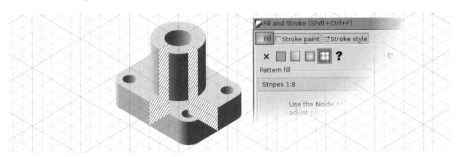

Figure 23-11: Painting the stripes

Now we need to remove the parts of the object in front of the cutout. Drag around and delete the frontmost rounding cylinder. Using rectangle resize handles, contract the top and left sides of the box to snap them to the edges of the cutout. As for the rest of the objects (the top of the box and the top ellipse of the cylinder), we need to actually *cut* them.

Again using the Pen tool, snap-draw a triangle and subtract this triangle from the shape (select both and press Ctrl--, 12.2), as shown in Figure 23-12.

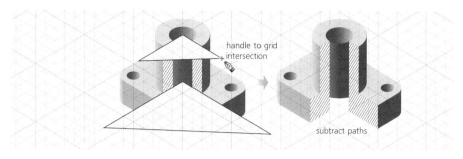

Figure 23-12: Cutting out unnecessary pieces

Finally, create the inside of the hole visible through the cutout: Duplicate the cylinder shape, scale it down (Ctrl-<), and step it down in the z-order so it's under the cutout shape and the hole ellipse; this will be the inner surface of the hole. Using the Node tool, select and pull down the bottom nodes of that shape. Then, duplicate the hole ellipse, paint it white, and move it down to represent the bottom edge of the hole. Select the ellipse at the top of the hole and copy it to the clipboard (Ctrl-C); then select the inner surface cylinder and paste the style (Shift-Ctrl-V) to spread the hole's horizontal gradient to the entire inner surface of the hole:

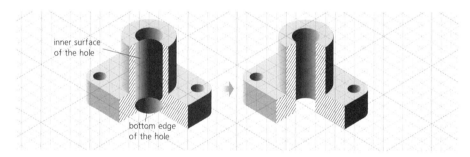

Figure 23-13: Creating the inner surface of the hole

24

TUTORIAL: THE ROSE

This complex image (see cover) was created to be a showcase of Inkscape's power and versatility. A single drawing of a rose is rendered in a different way in each of the five square windows as well as in the background. Thus, a single tutorial showing all stages of creating this image is equivalent to at least six different tutorials teaching you six different ways to draw a rose—or anything else, for that matter.

We will start with a photo. You don't have to, of course; if you can draw better than me, you can just draw anything you like on an empty canvas. Tracing a photo, however, is a useful technique by itself.

File ▸ Import (Ctrl-I) the photo, scale and position it as convenient. Rename the layer where the image is background and create a new layer, ink; we will need to hide and show the photo a lot, and it's much easier to do when it's in a layer of its own. It makes sense to reduce the opacity of the photo and lock its layer so you don't move it accidentally. After that, just start to trace over the outlines and the boundaries between colors in the photo (Figure 24-1).

Calligraphic pen

imported photo in layer *background*

Figure 24-1: Importing the image and setting up tracing using the Calligraphic pen

Which tool to use for tracing an image depends on the nature of the image and the result you want to get. If you're tracing geometric shapes, easily representable by straight lines and Bézier segments, use the Pen tool. If you need more freeform and artistic shapes while still minimizing the number of paths and nodes, the Pencil tool is a better choice. Finally, if you are after an especially expressive, possibly even "untidy" style, use the Calligraphic pen. I wanted my drawing to be laconic but artistic and natural, and I had no reason to save on the number of nodes, so I used the Calligraphic pen:

Figure 24-2: Tracing complete: 106 path objects in ink

I used a pressure-sensitive tablet pen that allowed me to vary the width of the brush stroke depending on how hard I pressed the pen. However, you can achieve a similar result with nothing but a regular mouse. Why? Because controlling the stroke thickness with pen pressure, while easy in theory, rarely comes out exactly as desired on the first try. A much more efficient approach is to draw with a limited range of width in the Calligraphic pen and then apply the Tweak tool's Shrink/Grow mode (**12.6.4**) to thicken or thin your strokes where appropriate:

Shrink/Grow mode,
Shift-S

Tweak tool

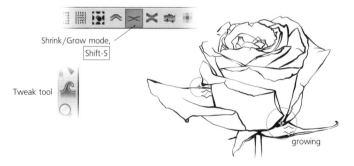

growing

Figure 24-3: Tweaking the drawing with the Tweak tool

The black and white outline is ready—now we need to add color to it. With a crisp ink outline, it makes sense to try a softer method of coloring. First, hide the background layer. Then, create a new layer, watercolor, and put it below your ink layer. After that, with wide calligraphic strokes, make a few wild brush strokes: red under the rose, green under the stalk and leaf, and various shades of blue around those. Finally, blur these strokes by a large enough radius that they begin to blend together:

Figure 24-4: Adding blurred background

This already looks nice—but not nice enough. The smoothly blurred blotches are *too* smooth—and boring. In a quest to make them look more natural, I tried to expand the simple **Gaussian Blur** filter which I had applied to the background by adding more primitives. First, I added a **Turbulence** primitive, composited with the blur, to imitate paper grain. This looked better but still too uniform, too obviously computer-generated. I then added another **Turbulence** component with a much larger period, which I used twice: once, via a **Displacement Map**, for making the overall watercolor more blotchy and splotchy; and then, via a **Composite** operator, for modulating the small-scale paper grain to imitate a more realistic paper where some areas are smoother and others are more rough and grainy:

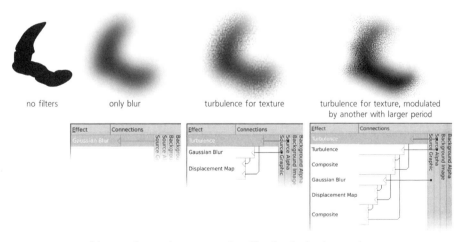

Figure 24-5: Building up the "realistic watercolor" filter for the background

The final composite filter, which I called *Sandy Blur* (see **17.4.2** for more on it), looked a lot more realistic—although much slower to render. At this point I had to switch to working mostly in the Outline (**3.11**) or No Filters modes (**17.4.4**).

As a final step (see the cover for the end result), according to taste, you could duplicate the content of the ink layer and blur it to form a shadow, or (as I did) soften the ink lines slightly by outsetting (thickening) the duplicated ink paths and making them semitransparent.

24.1   Treatment 1: Engraving

After finishing the ink and watercolor layers, I went on to create a number of other treatments of the drawing—variations on the same basic theme. My goal was to demonstrate several characteristic treatments in one image, so I overlaid the rose with five randomly scattered squares and limited each treatment to its own square.

First comes an engraving-like rendition composed of lattices of curved variable-width pen strokes. For this treatment, I chose an area of the rose where the curving and shading of the petals was especially deep and prominent. Engraving is an intricate art; I do not claim that my simulation of it is any good—but I was surprised to find how easy it was to do using Inkscape's tools.

Once you have an outline drawing and want to turn it into an engraving, the first step is planning: Think about the best and most natural way to direct the engraving lines in each part of the drawing. Create a new layer and draw several wide-spaced test strokes with the Calligraphic pen, looking for the best way to capture the changing curvature of each area while maintaining the best directional contrast at the boundaries where areas of different curvature meet:

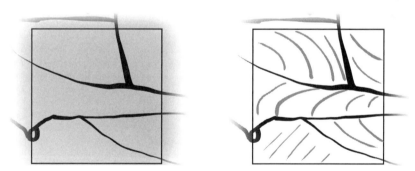

Figure 24-6: *Choosing the engraving square and doing test strokes*

Once you get an idea of how you want the engraving strokes to go, move the test strokes aside (but keep them for reference) and use Calligraphic pen's guide tracking feature (**14.3.7**) to fill each area with evenly spaced uniform-width strokes, as shown in Figure 24-7. Don't worry if the direction or curvature of your strokes drifts off somewhat; you will be able to fix that later. What matters more at this stage is the uniformity of spacing. You can temporarily rotate the entire drawing so it's more natural for stroking. Try to draw beyond the edges of the area you're filling; it will be much easier to trim strokes that are too long than to extend those which fell short.

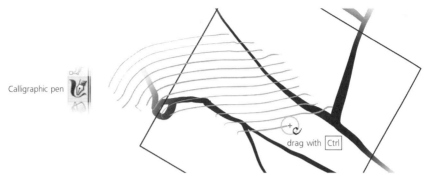

Calligraphic pen

Figure 24-7: Creating an evenly spaced lattice with the Calligraphic pen

The rest of the work is done in the Tweak tool—without which, really, the task of creating a decent looking engraving would be impossible. Use the Shrink mode to trim line ends and thin them, the Grow mode to make them thicker, and the Push mode to move and curve the entire lattice (you must have all strokes of the lattice selected to affect them all at once). Don't worry about the unsightly ends of the trimmed strokes—in the final result they will be covered by the wide boundary strokes of the ink layer:

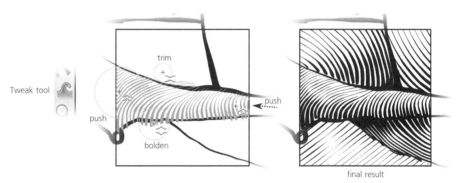

Tweak tool

Figure 24-8: Finalizing the engraving with the Tweak tool

In a real, physical engraving, you typically cut away areas which are to appear white, rather than directly drawing areas which are to be black. This is one of the reasons the example looks less like authentic engraving than it otherwise might.

24.2 Treatment 2: Tessellation

This treatment is easier to do than others because it's mostly automatic. The only tricky part is creating the tessellation itself—that is, a pattern of complex interlocked tiles that cover the entire plane without holes or overlapping.

Draw a shape—any shape!—and create a pattern of tiled clones from it (**Edit ▸ Clone ▸ Create Tiled Clones**, 16.6) with any nontrivial symmetry group;

in this example I used P3. At first, the clones do not form any kind of tessellation; it is your task to reshape the source shape—with its clones already in place—until the clones meet and smoothly interlock. It is much easier than it might seem; the fact that the clones immediately reflect any change in the source shape makes it almost trivial. Just add nodes and move them to grow appendages in your shape. Each of the clones will grow similar appendages. Simply keep adjusting them until the shapes meet all the way around and cover the plane:

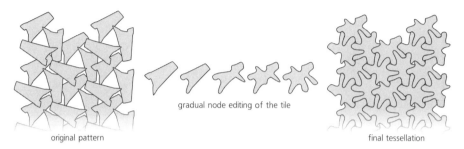

original pattern   gradual node editing of the tile   final tessellation

Figure 24-9: Creating a tessellation

Next, we want the pattern to reflect the colors of the background—so that the rose drawing shows through. Once you set it up, the process is mostly automatic. Make sure the **Use saved size and position of the tile** checkbox is on, delete the existing tiling (**Remove** button), and set the **Width** and **Height** so that the pattern covers all of the area you need covered. Unset the fill color of the original shape (right-click the **Fill:** swatch in the status bar and choose **Unset**). Then, go to the **Trace** tab, enable **Trace the drawing under the tiles**, pick **Color**, and apply the picked value to the clones' **Color** as well:

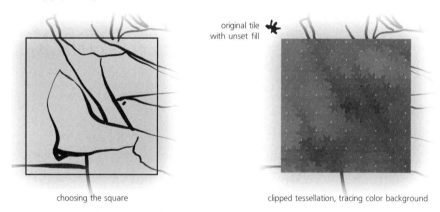

original tile
with unset fill

choosing the square   clipped tessellation, tracing color background

Figure 24-10: Color tracing with the tessellation

The final touch is adding slight glossy highlights to the tiles using filters (Chapter 17). One problem with this is that the gloss filter is not symmetric—it has one special direction from which the light is cast. However, if we apply such a filter to rotated *clones* in the pattern, the filter will be rotated together with the clones and all highlights will appear as if lit from different directions. To work around this, simply group all tiled clones (Ctrl-G) and apply the **Jigsaw Piece** filter from **Filters ▶ Bevels** to the group, as shown in Figure 24-11.

Figure 24-11: Adding highlights

24.3 Treatment 3: A Field of Cubes

This treatment is similar to the color-tracing tessellation in that it is created using the **Create Tiled Clones** dialog. However, in most other respects it is different: It is randomized instead of regular, pseudo-3D instead of flat, and uses three different original objects—and thus three intermingled patterns—instead of a single one.

Let's start by drawing these three original objects by the 3D Box tool. Convert each of them to a group of paths (Shift-Ctrl-C) and duplicate (Ctrl-D). In the bottom copy of a box, enter it as a group, select all six sides and union them (Ctrl-+), then ungroup. This turns a box into a single box-shaped path; unset its fill—in the clones, this one will take the color of the backround. For the second copy of the box, use 50% opacity and white or black color; this will be the shading that will allow each box look like a box despite changing overall color. Finally, group the background shape and the shading into a single group.

Figure 24-12: Original objects for the cube scattering

Now, for each of the prepared cubes, create a P1-symmetry scattering over the area you want to cover, using color-to-color tracing in the **Create Tiled Clones** dialog (16.6.6). Randomize their rotation (slightly, so as to not destroy the perception of all boxes being in a common perspective), their size, and their position. To imitate the effect of a 3D field, set scaling and row spacing to increase from top to bottom (i.e., per row), as shown in Figure 24-13.

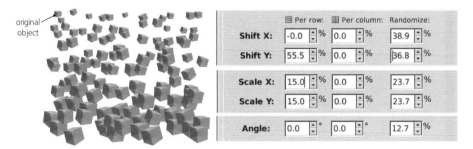

		🗒 Per row:	▥ Per column:	Randomize:
Shift X:		-0.0 ⬍ %	0.0 ⬍ %	38.9 ⬍ %
Shift Y:		55.5 ⬍ %	0.0 ⬍ %	36.8 ⬍ %
Scale X:		15.0 ⬍ %	0.0 ⬍ %	23.7 ⬍ %
Scale Y:		15.0 ⬍ %	0.0 ⬍ %	23.7 ⬍ %
Angle:		0.0 ⬍ °	0.0 ⬍ °	12.7 ⬍ %

original object

Figure 24-13: Scattering the cubes

Now, repeat this procedure for the two other cubes we've prepared, covering the same area. This combined field of cubes doesn't really look like a *field*, yet, because the z-order is wrong: The cubes that are closer to the bottom and larger are supposed to be closer to us and therefore on top of the others, but they are not. To fix this, use the **Restack** extension (from **Extensions ▶ Arrange**) to rearrange the z-order of the boxes so that they stack from top to bottom. Then, perform a single **Unclump** action from the **Align and Distribute** dialog so that there are fewer gaps in the arrangement of cubes.

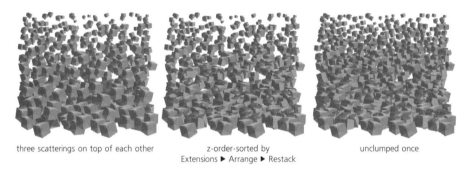

three scatterings on top of each other   z-order-sorted by Extensions ▶ Arrange ▶ Restack   unclumped once

Figure 24-14: Z-order sorting and unclumping the cubes

Remember that our eventual goal is to trace a square area of the rose's background layer. Choose the area you want to trace, group all the cubes, and clip (**18.4**) the group to the chosen square. Now, you may or may not have enabled automatic color-to-color background tracing (as we did in **16.6.6**) for all three patterns; however, even if you did, the colors you got from that are likely quite drab. This is inevitable, as the boxes are relatively large and sample color from large areas, averaging it and therefore making it less saturated than the original background image.

So, it looks like we will need to paint the cubes manually. Just select all the cube clones, choose the Color Paint mode of the Tweak tool (**8.7**), choose a bright red color (or pick it from the background image with Dropper, **8.6**) and paint over the red area of the image. Then, do the same for other colors, including the black ink lines. (If it does not work, it means you forgot to unset fill in the bottom path in each cube, see Figure 24-12.) This smooth, bitmap-like paintjob is a fun way to edit a vector drawing!

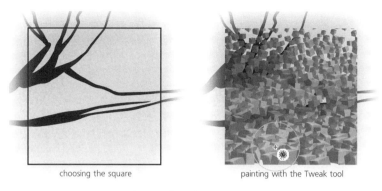

choosing the square   painting with the Tweak tool

Figure 24-15: Painting colors on the cubes

24.4 Treatment 4: A Photorealistic Rendition

This rendition is the most time-consuming of all: We want to recreate the original photograph as closely as possible in this part of our drawing. Absolute photo-realism, of course, is neither possible nor desirable, but we can try to achieve the characteristic "vector photorealism" look which is attractive in its own unique way. The key here is the proper use of shapes, gradient, and blur.

After positioning the square in which we're going to work, reveal the layer where you have the source photo. Then, start by dividing your drawing into areas, each approximated by flat color or a single gradient. Use the Pencil tool (**14.2**) to create these areas and the Gradient tool (**10.1**) to paint and stretch gradients across them. Use the Dropper tool (**8.6**) to pick the exact colors from the photo layer. Overall, try to reduce the contrast between light and dark areas because photos typically overemphasize this contrast compared to human perception.

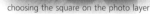

choosing the square on the photo layer   approximating using paths with gradients

Figure 24-16: Approximating areas of the image using paths with gradients

To soften the edges, blur the shapes a bit (no more than 2%) using the **Fill and Stroke** dialog. To apply some naturalistic texture, draw a 40% gray, 10% opaque rectangle over the shapes and apply **Filters ▶ Overlays ▶ Speckle** to it; in the **Filter Editor** dialog, increase the frequency of the random texture (**Base Frequency** in the **Turbulence** primitive). Even using only these simple filters, the drawing starts to acquire a slightly photographic look.

shapes blurred

added a speckle overlay

Figure 24-17: Blurring and texturizing the background

However, our work is far from finished. What we have created is just a layer of rough background paint, upon which the fine details are to be overlaid, reproducing the characteristic wrinkles and texture of the rose petals. Your primary tool will now be the Calligraphic pen (14.3) with relatively small **Width**, zero **Fixation**, and some **Tremor**. Typically you will draw with semitransparent black or white for shading and highlights, correspondingly; you can also try barely saturated versions of complimentary colors (e.g., pale green for red background) which can often yield more "natural" results.

Of course, these layered semitransparent brush strokes need to be blurred as well. However, don't apply blur to each stroke separately; this would be tedious to do (unlike opacity, blur is not retained in the tool's style and therefore not applied to the next created object automatically) and slow to render. Instead, draw a single stroke, group it (Ctrl-G), blur the group, and then enter that group (Ctrl-Enter). Now, each new object you create with Calligraphic pen or any other tool gets added to the blurred group and therefore is blurred along with its siblings. When you're finished drawing within the group, leave it using Ctrl-Backspace.

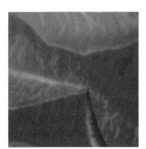
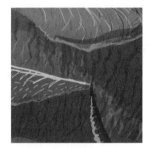

final result with blurred foreground strokes

same, with all blur removed

Figure 24-18: Adding hand-drawn foreground strokes

Pay special attention to the edges of the objects on your "photo"—properly emphasizing these edges with dense highlights and shadows is the key to the attractive painterly look of the drawing. In particular, it's often a good idea to use a slightly more intense highlight on the edge of a highlight and a slightly more intense shadow on the edge of a shadow.

24.5 Treatment 5: A Map

This last treatment is less an example of a practically useful technique than it is a creative reinterpretation of something very straightforward. I was just playing with an eight-color Potrace tracing (**Path ▸ Trace Bitmap**, 18.8.2) of this area of the original photo when I noticed that it acquired an interesting map-like look when I discarded the fill colors and assigned a dashed stroke to the resulting shapes:

 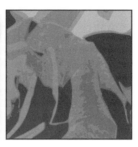 

choosing background square   traced with 8 colors   no fill, dashed strokes

Figure 24-19: Tracing the source photo

All that was left to do is create a yellowish, slightly rough (**Filters ▸ ABCs ▸ Roughen**), semitransparent (so that the background drawing shows through a bit) background rectangle to imitate the surface of an old map, and add some cryptic text labels to complete the picture.

As a final touch, I added dotted frames to all five squares containing various treatments. The final image is on the cover of this book.

AN SVG PRIMER

This appendix is a very high-level glance at the general principles of SVG and its implementation in Inkscape. Some of this material has already been referred to in other chapters. However, this book does not intend to replace the official SVG specification. If you want an absolutely final, complete, and authoritative reference on SVG, you need the SVG specification produced by the W3C. Available versions of this specification can be found at *http://w3.org/Graphics/SVG*; the version that Inkscape currently supports, 1.1, is at *http://w3.org/TR/SVG11*.

Knowledge of SVG and, more generally, XML (SVG is just a specialized variety of XML) is not *strictly* necessary for mastering Inkscape—but it really helps. It will allow you to peek under the hood of Inkscape drawings, and it will often reveal the true reasons behind some of Inkscape's features (or lack thereof). As XML is so widely used these days, this appendix's material may also be useful to you in a lot of other situations not involving Inkscape and SVG at all.

A.1   A Quick Introduction to XML

These days, almost everyone has at least heard of XML, and certainly everyone has used it, though often unknowingly. If you've seen the source code of a web page, you already know what XML looks like, because XHTML, the markup language used on the Web today, is one of the subspecies of XML (more precisely, an *XML vocabulary*). SVG is another such vocabulary.

XML is a standardized way to record structured information in plain text. Its biggest advantage is that it is easy to parse for computers and yet quite understandable for humans. Unlike most other computer-related concepts that are, usually, as complex as you think they are (or more), XML is an unbelievably simple thing. So simple, in fact, that I will now explain it in a few short paragraphs.

The basic building block of an XML document is called an *element*. Here is an example of an element containing some text:

```
<example>Here goes some text.</example>
```

The text inside the element is called its *content*, and that content is delimited by *tags*. Everything between the less-than sign (<) and the greater-than sign (>) is a tag. Here, the opening tag and the closing tag are almost identical, except that the closing one has a forward slash (/) before the element name, which in this case is example.

An element may have no content at all:

```
<example></example>
```

or

```
<example/>
```

These two *empty elements* are absolutely equivalent; the second one, consisting of a single tag, is just a spelling variant of the first. Note the different position of the forward slash (/) in the single-tag empty element.

In addition to text, elements can also contain other elements, but those elements must lie *entirely* within the containing element. For example, this is wrong:

```
<a><b></a></b>
```

because the element b starts inside a but ends outside it. If an element started inside some other element, it must also end within that element. Here is an example of correct XML:

```
<a><b/><c/><d><e/></d></a>
```

One can say that a is the *parent element* of b, c, and d, while d is the parent of e. An element may have many children, but it has only one parent (except for the root element of the document, which has no parent at all). Figure A-1 is a graphic representation of this XML fragment.

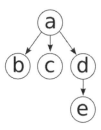

Figure A-1: A tree representing the XML code

NOTE *This explains why groups of objects in Inkscape cannot contain objects from different layers (4.5). A group is a parent element for its children, but so is a layer. A group may be contained inside a single layer, but you can't have it scattered across several layers, because that would result in that group having several parents.*

Apart from children elements, XML elements may have some attributes. Each *attribute* is a name with some associated value. Attributes are specified in the opening tag of an element, for example:

```
<text type="important" font-size="10">Here is some text.</text>
```

Note the use of the equal sign (=) and the double quote marks around attribute values. Both are mandatory.

NOTE *An element cannot have two attributes with the same name. Note that the order of the attributes in the opening tag never affects anything; attributes in XML are unordered.*

Finally, the entire XML document is simply a single element (called *root*) with some text content and children elements, which in turn can have more content and more children, and so on. An XML document can thus be thought of as a tree growing from a single root. For example, here is a complete SVG document whose root element, svg, contains two elements representing a rectangle and a text string:

```
<svg>
  <rect x="100" y="100" width="300" height="50" fill="blue"/>
  <text x="100" y="150">This is a text string.</text>
</svg>
```

A.2 Vocabularies and Namespaces

If this is all there is to XML, what makes it so powerful and so widely used?

XML itself is just a foundation, and on that foundation a lot of buildings have been, are being, and undoubtedly will be erected. You won't believe how many valuable programmer resources were wasted before the advent of XML on inventing new data formats for each application, formulating their rules, writing and testing software to support them, and working around the inevitable bugs, exceptions, and version incompatibilities.

All this misery is now a thing of the past. Now, if you need to record some data, you don't need to go into the low-level details of which characters have special meanings and what are the sizes of various fields. By choosing XML (and you would need serious reasons *not* to choose it) you can concentrate on things that really matter: the structure of your data and how to name elements and attributes that would best express that structure.

Moreover, these days it is quite likely that you won't even need that, because a well-known standardized XML *vocabulary* for your data probably already exists, and you can just make use of it. Each vocabulary defines a set of elements and attributes, detailing what they are supposed to mean, in what contexts they may or may not be used, what is obligatory and what is optional, and so on. SVG is one such vocabulary; XHTML is another. There exist standardized XML vocabularies for a lot of exotic things, from dog genealogies to star catalogs. Many of them reuse parts of other vocabularies.

To be able to mix parts of different vocabularies without confusion, XML uses *namespaces*. A namespace is just a way to indicate where a specific element or attribute comes from. For example, here's an `image` element from SVG vocabulary, representing a linked bitmap image inside an SVG document:

```
<svg:image xlink:href="/dir/file.png" width="200" height="100"/>
```

You can see that the element name and one of the attributes use a colon (`:`). The part of the name before the colon is called the *namespace prefix*. To find out which namespace corresponds with which prefix, we must look for a namespace declaration in the form of a special `xmlns` prefixed attribute (short for *XML NameSpace*), either on the same element or on any of its ancestor elements up the tree. It is customary to place all namespace declaration attributes on the root element. In this case, you will likely find the declarations for `svg` and `xlink` prefixes in the root `svg` element:

```
<svg:svg ...
        xmlns:svg="http://www.w3.org/2000/svg"
        xmlns:xlink="http://www.w3.org/1999/xlink"
        ... >
```

This means that the `svg` prefix is bound to the namespace of `http://www.w3.org/2000/svg` and the `xlink` prefix corresponds to `http://www.w3.org/1999/xlink`. Here, the namespaces are URLs, but they need not be; the only requirement is that they must be globally unique (and URLs are just the easiest way to ensure this uniqueness).

The namespace URL for SVG, `http://www.w3.org/2000/svg`, must look exactly as shown. If the namespace prefix of the elements in your SVG document does not resolve to `http://www.w3.org/2000/svg`, neither Inkscape nor any other software will recognize the document as SVG. The namespace *prefix*, however, may be arbitrary, so long as it's bound to the correct namespace. The prefix may even be empty if you declare it thus:

```
<svg ...
     xmlns="http://www.w3.org/2000/svg"
     ... >
```

Inside the element with that declaration, any element name *without* a prefix will be assumed to be in the SVG namespace. For example, the following will be recognized as a valid image element from SVG, which links an external image file in PNG format:

```
<image xlink:href="/dir/portrait.png" width="200" height="100"/>
```

Namespace errors, such as no namespace declared for a prefix or a wrong namespace URL, are most common when you edit your SVG by hand and then try to load it into Inkscape. Watch out for them!

A.3 Root

Here's a typical root svg element of an Inkscape SVG document with a number of namespace declarations and other attributes:

```
<svg xmlns:dc="http://purl.org/dc/elements/1.1/"
     xmlns:cc="http://web.resource.org/cc/"
     xmlns:rdf="http://www.w3.org/1999/02/22-rdf-syntax-ns#"
     xmlns:svg="http://www.w3.org/2000/svg"
     xmlns="http://www.w3.org/2000/svg"
     xmlns:xlink="http://www.w3.org/1999/xlink"
     xmlns:sodipodi="http://sodipodi.sourceforge.net/DTD/sodipodi-0.dtd"
     xmlns:inkscape="http://www.inkscape.org/namespaces/inkscape"
     sodipodi:docname="file.svg"
     width="1052.3622"
     height="744.09448"
     id="svg2"
     sodipodi:version="0.32"
     inkscape:version="0.46"
     version="1.0">
```

SVG uses the SVG namespace (http://www.w3.org/2000/svg) for its own elements and the XLink namespace (http://www.w3.org/1999/xlink) for the linking attributes (A.9). On top of that, Inkscape adds elements and attributes in the namespaces belonging to Inkscape (http://www.inkscape.org/namespaces/inkscape) and its predecessor Sodipodi (http://sodipodi.sourceforge.net/DTD/sodipodi-0.dtd; see 1.6 for a brief history of Inkscape). Other namespaces declared here are used for metadata elements (general information about the document) and license identifiers (A.4).

The only attributes on the root element that are defined in the SVG standard are width and height (defining the size of the canvas), id, and version. The rest are either namespace declarations or attributes in the custom Inkscape/Sodipodi namespaces.

This root tag specifies the version of Inkscape in which this document was created: inkscape:version="0.46". It also claims that the version of Sodipodi that this document will work with is 0.32 (sodipodi:version="0.32"), because after that version Inkscape forked off Sodipodi. The non-namespaced version attribute refers to the version of the SVG specification this document implements, 1.0.

The only difference between the Inkscape SVG and the Plain SVG formats that Inkscape offers when saving is that Plain SVG strips away all the elements and attributes in Inkscape and Sodipodi namespaces, leaving only the "industry standard" namespaces. Note that no Inkscape-specific elements or attributes are ever allowed to alter how the document *looks*; they can only affect the way it *behaves* when edited in Inkscape (for example, an attribute on a g element may tell Inkscape to edit that element as a 3D box instead of a simple group, see 11.3). Therefore, saving as a Plain SVG is just a way to make a file a little smaller at the cost of losing some of its Inkscape editability. If you find a file that renders differently after being saved as Plain SVG, you've found a bug: Please report it to the developers!

A.4 Defs, View, and Metadata

Now let's descend from the root element of a typical Inkscape SVG document to see what else is in there.

First comes the defs element. As part of the SVG standard, it is a storage bin for things that, by themselves, are not displayed on the canvas, but may be used by other elements that are. This includes gradients, patterns, markers (arrowheads, 9.5), clipping paths, masks, filters, and so on. They are all stored as child elements of the defs element. The SVG specification allows arbitrarily many defs elements placed almost anywhere in the document, but Inkscape always uses a single defs under the root svg. Here's an example defs element containing a gradient:

```
<defs id="defs4">
  <linearGradient inkscape:collect="always" id="linearGradient2798">
    <stop style="stop-color:#000000;stop-opacity:1;" offset="0" id="stop2800" />
    <stop style="stop-color:#000000;stop-opacity:0;" offset="1" id="stop2802" />
  </linearGradient>
</defs>
```

Adding the linearGradient element to defs, by itself, does not change anything on the canvas. Now, however, any object can reference (10.2.1) this gradient for painting its fill or stroke.

Most of the stuff in defs is kept even if no visible element uses it. (The only exceptions are the elements with the inkscape:collect attribute with the value of always; such elements are automatically deleted when no longer used. Inkscape often uses this flag to mark various supplemental elements it creates on its own and can safely dispose of; it will never delete anything that you created without your permission.)

This allows you to reuse things you once defined but then abandoned, but it also may lead to defs growing larger and larger as you work on your document and try out various techniques. To remove the unused definitions from defs, use the **File ▸ Vacuum Defs** command. Unfortunately, even this command may fail to completely delete *all* unused stuff in defs on the first try; you may need to quit, reload the document, and vacuum defs again for it to fully work.

The next element you will see inside an Inkscape SVG document is sodipodi:namedview. This Inkscape-specific element holds, in its attributes, all kinds of options that are specific to this document: the zoom level and scroll position that Inkscape will use upon loading the document, the colors and spacing of the grids, various snapping modes, the current layer, document units, and so on. From within Inkscape, most of these options are settable via the **File ▸ Document Properties** command (3.1.2).

```
<sodipodi:namedview inkscape:window-height="950"
                    inkscape:window-width="1280"
                    inkscape:window-x="0"
                    inkscape:window-y="24"
                    inkscape:pageshadow="2"
                    inkscape:pageopacity="0.0"
                    bordercolor="#666666"
                    pagecolor="#ffffff"
                    inkscape:zoom="0.64306408"
                    inkscape:cx="836.6226"
                    inkscape:cy="619.40089"
                    inkscape:current-layer="layer2"
                    showguides="true" />
```

Finally, just before the actual content of the document starts, there is the metadata element. It stores information about the author of the document, its purpose, date, license, and so on. It corresponds to the **File ▸ Document Metadata** dialog in Inkscape. The elements inside metadata typically represent the information as RDF (see *http://w3.org/RDF*). RDF may employ many additional XML namespaces to describe different sorts of information.

A.5 Layers and Groups

After the metadata element, the actual visible content of the SVG document starts. As you may have guessed, each document object corresponds to an SVG element. Moreover, the order of the elements in the file corresponds to the order in which objects are visually stacked on the canvas (4.3): Elements closer to the end of the file appear atop those nearer the beginning.

When you group several elements together (4.5), they are placed inside a g element. For example, here's a group that contains a rectangle and a text object:

```
<g id="g2893">
  <rect id="rect2310"
        y="350"
        x="100"
        width="300"
        height="150"
        style="opacity:1;fill:#ff0000;stroke:#000000;stroke-width:1px;" />
  <text id="text2889"
        y="400"
        x="200"
        style="font-size:40px;font-style:normal;font-weight:normal;fill:#000000;
               stroke:none;font-family:Bitstream Vera Sans"
        xml:space="preserve">Text in rectangle</text>
</g>
```

Besides groups, another way to organize your objects is by using layers (4.6). SVG does not have a special element type for layers; instead, Inkscape just uses an SVG g element, adding a special attribute so it knows to treat the group as a layer when the file is edited.

```
<g inkscape:groupmode="layer"
   inkscape:label="Layer 1"
   id="layer1">
   ...contents of the layer...
</g>
```

Since layers are thus a special case of groups, it is easy to understand how Inkscape can "enter a group," treating it temporarily as a layer (4.6.1). It also becomes clear why, upon importing Inkscape's SVG file into another vector editor (such as Adobe Illustrator), you usually lose layers but your objects get additional layers of grouping: The other editor simply does not know about Inkscape's convention of using some g elements as layers and treats all the layers as regular groups.

Inside layers and groups, other SVG elements represent the actual objects of your drawing. See *http://w3.org/TR/SVG11/eltindex.html* for a complete list of elements in SVG 1.1, but note that not all of them are supported by Inkscape yet.

A.6 Coordinates and Units

Distances and coordinates in SVG drawings can be expressed in a number of units: centimeters (cm), millimeters (mm), inches (in), points (pt), and a few others. One unit, however, is special: It is the *SVG pixel* (abbreviated px), some-times called the *anonymous unit*, because it can be written without any unit designation at all. For example, in this rect element, x, y, width, and height are expressed in SVG pixels:

```
<rect id="rect2310"
      y="350"
      x="100"
      width="300"
      height="150" />
```

They might just as well be specified in millimeters:

```
<rect id="rect2310"
      y="98.777mm"
      x="28.222mm"
      width="84.667mm"
      height="42.333mm" />
```

and Inkscape would understand this correctly. However, if you change and resave this SVG file, Inkscape will convert all sizes back to SVG pixels.

Despite its name, an SVG pixel is not the same as a *screen pixel*. When you zoom in, a distance of one SVG pixel becomes larger than one pixel on your screen; when you zoom out, it becomes smaller than one screen pixel. However, when your zoom level (displayed at the right end of the status bar of your Inkscape window, see Figure 2-1) is 100 percent, one SVG pixel exactly corresponds to one screen pixel. This makes this unit especially convenient for creating graphics for screen viewing.

In Inkscape, 90 SVG pixels are equal to one inch, so when you export your graphics at the resolution of 90 dpi (pixels per inch), it will show up exactly as displayed in Inkscape at 100 percent zoom. In most places where you can specify sizes or distances in Inkscape UI, there's a way to specify the units, and the px unit (SVG pixel) is the default (although you can choose a different default unit in **Document Properties**).

SVG uses rectangular Cartesian coordinates for specifying objects' positions on canvas. The coordinate origin in SVG is in the top-left corner of the page, and the Y coordinate grows downward. However, in the Inkscape UI the origin is in the bottom-left corner and Y grows upward. Future versions may change this, most likely by making this "coordinate flip" optional to make life easier for those who edit SVG manually as well as in Inkscape.

A.7 Transformations

Every object in SVG has its own natural place on the canvas. For example, for a rectangle, this place is defined by the x and y attributes on the rect element:

```
<rect id="rect2310"
      y="350"
      x="100"
      width="300"
      height="150" />
```

However, one of the most interesting features of SVG is that this position can be affected by the transform attribute. Most often, this attribute contains a sequence of six numbers inside a matrix(...):

```
<rect transform="matrix(0.96333,0.26831,-0.26831,0.96333,203.200,-160.066)"
      id="rect2310"
      y="350"
      x="100"
      width="300"
      height="150" />
```

In this form, the attribute represents an *affine transform matrix*. A complete treatment of matrix algebra is way outside the scope of this book, but you should have an idea of what transformations are called affine:

- Any *moves*, also called *translations* (Figure 6-1)
- Any *scalings*, including both uniform and nonuniform; for example, scaling only width or only height (Figure 6-2)
- Any *rotations* around any center (Figure 6-6)
- Any *skews*, sometimes called *shears* (Figure 6-7)

Not coincidentally, these transformations are exactly those that the Selector tool can perform (Chapter 6). Note that, for example, perspective transformations are not affine: They cannot be expressed by a transform attribute and cannot be performed by the Selector tool.

So, an element with a transform attribute means: "Draw this element at its natural position and size, then move, scale, rotate, or skew it as specified in the transform."

Moreover, the transform value on the element's parent (for example, on a g element that contains this object) affects the object, too. All the transforms on the object and all its ancestors are combined. This is why, for example, when you move or scale a group, all objects belonging to the group are moved and scaled by the same amount, although it is only the parent g element whose transform attribute is modified.

On the **Transforms** tab of the **Inkscape Preferences** dialog (3.1), there's a **Store transformation** option with the values of **Optimized** and **Preserved**. This determines the strategy of Inkscape when transforming objects. If set to **Preserved**, it will always record all transformations of all objects as transform attributes, leaving all other attributes intact. If set to **Optimized** (default), it will try, whenever possible, to record the transformation into the object's other attributes and not transform. For example, when you move a rectangle, in the optimized mode it will change the rectangle's x and y attributes instead of adding or changing its transform. Not all kinds of transformations and not all types of objects allow such optimization, however, so even in the optimized mode transform attributes will still be created. The only object type that can optimize any kinds of transformations and make do without the transform at all times is path.

A.8 Style

Quite naturally, the style properties of an object can be represented as attributes of the corresponding element. Such attributes are called *presentation attributes*. For example, this rectangle has blue fill and black stroke 1 px wide:

```
<rect id="rect2310"
      y="350"
      x="100"
      width="300"
      height="150"
      fill="blue"
      stroke="black"
      stroke-width="1pt" />
```

This, however, is only one possible way to record style properties in XML. Another way is to pack all the properties into a single attribute, called style, using colons (:) to separate the name from the value in each property and semicolons (;) to separate properties:

```
<rect id="rect2310"
      y="350"
      x="100"
      width="300"
      height="150"
      style="fill:blue; stroke:black; stroke-width:1pt" />
```

Inkscape understands both methods but when writing properties to SVG, for historical reasons, only uses the second one, with a single style attribute.

When both are present, the properties in the style attribute take precedence over the same properties in presentation attributes.

Once again, this appendix will not list all the style properties used by SVG (see *http://w3.org/TR/SVG11/propidx.html* for a complete list), but you should at least recognize them when you see them.

SVG prescribes that most (but not all) style properties should be inherited by children from their parents, provided a child does not specify its own value for that property. For example, if a rectangle has no fill property specified but its parent g has fill="blue", the rectangle will be painted blue. In Inkscape, such inheritance rarely plays a role, simply because normally, objects have most of their properties set whether you changed them or not. However, for fill and stroke properties, there's a way to remove, or *unset*, these properties using the UI, making it possible to inherit these properties from the parent element (8.1.1).

A.9 Linking

Often, elements in SVG need to refer, or *link*, to one another. This is most common when visible elements on canvas use some of the definitions in defs. For example, if you have a rectangle filled with linear gradient, the rect element describes only the rectangle itself. Its gradient is described by a different element, called linearGradient, in the document's defs, and the rectangle links to that gradient definition.

In order to be linkable, an element must have an id attribute whose value is unique inside this document. Inkscape provides unique ids for all elements automatically. The URL for linking to an element is simply its id preceded by a hash mark (#)—for example, #linearGradient2128. In order to use this URL from a style property, you need to enclose it in parentheses and prefix it with the string url. For example, here's a linearGradient element and a rectangle linking to it from its fill property:

```
<defs>
  <linearGradient id="linearGradient2128">
    <stop id="stop2286" offset="0" style="stop-color:#0000ff;stop-opacity:0;" />
    <stop id="stop2284" offset="1" style="stop-color:#0000ff;stop-opacity:1;" />
  </linearGradient>
</defs>

...

<rect id="rect2310"
      y="350"
      x="100"
      width="300"
      height="150"
      style="fill:url(#linearGradient2128)" />
```

Linking is not always done by style properties; for example, the SVG standard says that gradients can link to one another in order to share color stops and other attributes. In such cases, the xlink:href attribute is used (in other words, the href attribute in the XLink namespace). (XLink is another

W3C standard, separate from SVG and used in many XML vocabularies for linking; see *http://w3.org/TR/xlink* for the specification.) The xlink:href attribute uses the plain URL without the url() wrapper; for example, xlink:href="#linearGradient2128".

SVG allows you to link not only to other elements in the same document but also to other documents, accessible locally or on the Internet, as well as to elements inside them. As of version 0.47, Inkscape does not yet support such cross-document linking to SVG documents, although it can link to external bitmap files that are used as bitmap objects in a document.

A.10 Object Types

One of the most important features of Inkscape is its ability to create various object types, with each object remembering its type and providing various controls and behaviors specific to that type (Chapter 11). Some of these object types are directly supported by SVG; for example, Inkscape's rectangles are represented by rect elements from SVG. But others are unique to Inkscape; for example, SVG has no special elements for spirals, stars, or 3D boxes. How can Inkscape use these object types while staying compatible with standard SVG?

The solution is the sodipodi:type attribute. Inkscape saves a star as an universal path element that can represent any shape, but adds to it the sodipodi:type indicating it's actually a star, as well as some other extension attributes storing various star-specific parameters. The path's standard d attribute, meanwhile, provides an exact representation of the star's shape:

```
<path sodipodi:type="star"
      style="fill:#ff0000;"
      sodipodi:sides="5"
      sodipodi:cx="342.85715"
      sodipodi:cy="703.79077"
      sodipodi:r1="105.75289"
      sodipodi:r2="40.397606"
      sodipodi:arg1="0.90027477"
      sodipodi:arg2="1.5285933"
      inkscape:flatsided="false"
      inkscape:rounded="0"
      inkscape:randomized="0"
      d="M 408.571,786.647 L 344.561,744.152 L 284.362,791.893
         L 304.997,717.884 L 240.990,675.383 L 317.754,672.139
         L 338.395,598.132 L 365.202,670.135 L 441.965,666.897
         L 381.770,714.642 L 408.571,786.647 z" />
```

When loading a document with such an element, Inkscape recognizes the sodipodi:type and, for editing, treats the object as a star rather than a path. However, when any other SVG software loads the same file, it ignores any Inkscape-specific attributes and interprets this element as a simple path which, however, *looks* exactly the same as the star created in Inkscape. In other words, while only Inkscape can *edit* the star as a star, using the standard path as the base for this object type ensures that it remains compatible with any SVG software.

A.11 Inkscape SVG Extensions

To conclude this necessary but very superficial appendix, let's compile a list of the most important extension elements and attributes that you will see in Inkscape SVG files. Some of them were already discussed in previous sections; others deserve a brief treatment here.

One point bears repeating: None of these additional elements and attributes make Inkscape documents invalid SVG. The X in "XML" stands for "eXtensible" for a reason: The ability to freely mix different vocabularies was one of the goals of XML from the very beginning. In our case, this means that any Inkscape SVG file must—and does—render absolutely the same in all compliant SVG renderers. (There's a single unfortunate exception from this rule, which we discuss in 15.2.2.3.)

- The `inkscape:collect` attribute is added to those elements in `defs` which can be deleted automatically when no longer used (A.4).

- The `sodipodi:namedview` element is the place where Inkscape stores per-document preferences, as described in A.4.

- The `sodipodi:type` attribute is what Inkscape uses to mark objects of non-SVG types (A.10). An element with this attribute usually has a whole bunch of other Inkscape-specific attributes that store various parameters unique to this object type.

- The `inkscape:transform-center-x` and `inkscape:transform-center-y` attributes are set on an object if you dragged its rotation center (6.4). Inkscape remembers the position of this center for each object for which it was changed.

- The `sodipodi:nodetypes` attribute is where Inkscape stores the types of all nodes of a path that you edited with the Node tool. Classifying nodes as smooth, symmetric, and cusp (12.5.5) is something Inkscape allows you to do, but SVG has no provisions for; hence the need for an extension attribute.

- The `inkscape:groupmode` attribute on a g is what differentiates a group from a layer in Inkscape (A.5). For a layer, this attribute stores the value `layer`.

- The `inkscape:label` attribute can be set on any element to provide a human-readable label for the corresponding object (the problem with using the `id` attribute for that purpose is that it cannot contain spaces and punctuation; `inkscape:label` is free from these limitations, 4.1). In this attribute, Inkscape stores the human-readable name of a layer.

- The `inkscape:export-filename` attribute, which can be set on any element, stores the filename (including path) into which this object was last exported as bitmap. This value is automatically placed into the **Filename** field of the **Export Bitmap** dialog (18.9.1), so you can quickly repeat exporting to the same file even after you closed and reopened the file. (This also explains why Inkscape claims that the file has changed and needs resaving after you did a bitmap export from it.)

B

IMPORT AND EXPORT

This appendix is a collection of notes on the capabilities, limitations, and prerequisites of the major import and export formats that Inkscape supports.

NOTE *For importing some formats, Inkscape uses external pieces of software that you will need to download and install if you want to use this format. As a rule, if you don't have this external software installed (or if it is not in* PATH*), Inkscape will simply omit this format from the list of supported formats in the **Open** or **Import** dialogs.*

B.1 Save vs. Export

While this is largely a terminological convention, Inkscape uses "export" only for the **Export Bitmap** dialog (18.9.1) whereas the supported vector formats, including the default Inkscape SVG format, are listed in the **Save as type** list in the **Save**, **Save As**, and **Save a Copy** dialogs. Since all vector formats except Inkscape SVG lose some editability features or even drop some classes of objects, saving in such a format and trying to close the document will display a warning, as shown in Figure B-1.

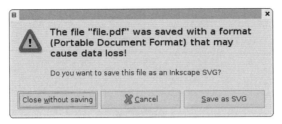

Figure B-1: Data format warning: You are trying to close a non-SVG document.

If you made any changes after saving a non-SVG file, you may have to **Save As** into the original SVG file again. To avoid this annoyance, use the **Save a Copy** command (Shift-Ctrl-Alt-S), which saves a copy of the document in the format and filename you specify. The document is still considered Inkscape SVG and, if it was not changed after last SVG save, no warning is displayed when it is closed.

B.2   SVG Variants

The primary vector format used by Inkscape is called *Inkscape SVG*; as explained in 1.4, it is (almost) standard-compliant SVG with some Inkscape-specific extensions that affect only the editability of various object types in Inkscape, but never change their appearance. It does not make much sense to save as *Plain SVG* except when you are trying to achieve a modest file size gain or encounter some buggy software having problems with Inkscape SVG. Both SVG flavors have *compressed* varieties (using the *.svgz* file name extension), which produce much smaller files but are otherwise the same and should be understood by most SVG software.

SVG files exported from Adobe Illustrator can be opened in Inkscape as usual. However, these files usually contain a lot of AI-specific stuff, which is useless for Inkscape and just blows up the size of the SVG file. It is recommended to save SVG files from AI with the extension *.ai.svg* instead of simply *.svg*. When you open such a *.ai.svg* file in Inkscape, it goes through a special filter which removes the AI-specific binary chunks and converts AI layers into Inkscape layers.

B.3   PDF (Import, Export)

After SVG, PDF is the most powerful, best supported by Inkscape, and most widely recognized vector format (1.5.1.1). While Inkscape cannot yet be recommended for roundtrip PDF editing (i.e., opening a PDF, editing its content, and saving back as PDF) due to the font support limitations (see the following section), PDF is definitely the best option for connecting Inkscape with software which does not support SVG.

Inkscape's *PDF import* is built-in (requires no external software to install) and supports most of static features of latest versions of PDF (shapes, text, images, gradients, opacity, etc.). Interactive PDF features (such as forms) are not supported. Since Inkscape cannot have multiple pages in one document, you will need to specify which single page from a PDF file to import. This choice is the main purpose of the **PDF Import Settings** dialog you see when you try to import or open a PDF file (Figure B-2).

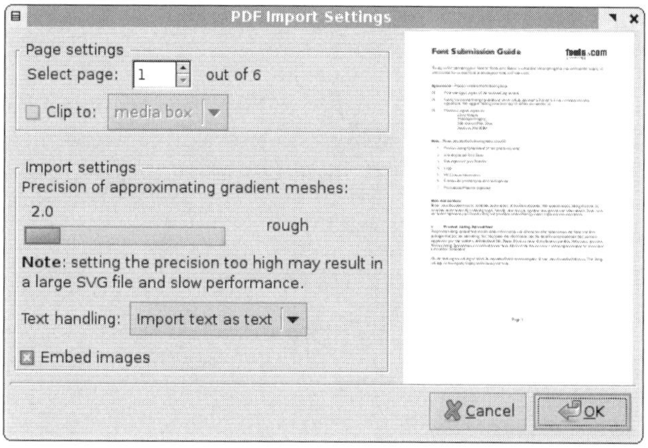

Figure B-2: PDF import options

In the dialog, you can browse the PDF document's pages and choose the one you need, based on the preview image (right pane) that shows the page selected in the counter at top left.

Also, you can optionally clip the imported artwork to the various boxes which may be defined in PDF; for example, clipping to the media box (i.e., page size) hides any objects that the PDF might contain outside the page area (most PDF viewers won't show them anyway, but Inkscape allows you to discover them).

B.3.1 PDF Text

The biggest limitation of the current PDF import support is its treatment of fonts. Most PDF files have their fonts embedded, and Inkscape cannot use these embedded fonts, nor can it convert text to paths on import (the **Text handling** choice in the **PDF Import Settings** dialog has only one option, **Import text as text**). In practice, this means that any text in the imported PDF file will look right if and only if the font it uses is installed on your system; otherwise, a default font will be used which will not only look different but, in most cases, will badly butcher spacing and alignment in text columns.

An additional complication is that most PDFs refer to the font they use by their *PostScript names*, which are slightly different from the names of fonts your operating system shows. For example, PDF may refer to a font called AlbertusMT-Light whereas the same font in your Inkscape list is called Albertus MT Lt. Inkscape tries its best to convert the PostScript names to regular names, but it can only do this for fonts which you have installed, and even then it sometimes fails and chooses a wrong installed font.

NOTE *Whether or not this font name conversion was successful, you can always look up the original PostScript name of the font of any text object in imported PDF by looking at its* style *attribute in XML Editor (4.7). The property you need is* -inkscape-font-specification, *for example:*

-inkscape-font-specification:AlbertusMT-Light

B.3.2 PDF Export

As already mentioned, Inkscape does not have a separate "Export" command for vector formats; instead, you just go to **File ▸ Save** or **File ▸ Save As** and choose the PDF format in the **Save as type** list. After you type the filename and click **OK**, you will be presented with a dialog for setting PDF export options:

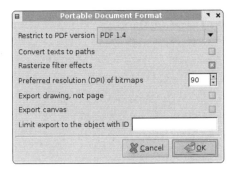

Figure B-3: PDF export options

The version of PDF you can export is limited to 1.4. As for fonts, Inkscape's own export is smarter than its import: Any fonts used in your SVG document will be embedded as subsets (i.e., only the characters actually used in the document) into the PDF it produces. Also, you have the option of converting all text objects to paths on export, in which case even Inkscape itself will be able to import the PDF back, preserving the appearance of text objects.

Filters (Chapter **17**) are a feature of SVG which has no counterpart in PDF. Therefore, you have the option of converting any filtered objects to bitmaps on export (**Rasterize filter effects**). If you uncheck this, filters will be simply ignored (e.g., any blurred object will be crisp). Rasterization has the disadvantage of inflating the file size and losing the vector editability of the objects affected, but it preserves the filtered appearance of the objects. The **resolution** parameter applies to these automatically generated filter bitmaps; set it to 90 dpi for PDFs that are intended for viewing on screen, and to at least 300 dpi for PDFs that are intended for print.

The rest of the options specify which objects and what area of the document to export into PDF. By default, the page size of the PDF is the same as that of your SVG, and any objects outside the page are therefore hidden (but still present in the PDF code). If you enable **Export drawing, not page**, the PDF page will be as big as the bounding box of the entire drawing, regardless of its page size. The **Limit export** option ensures that only the objects whose IDs (**4.1**) you list here will be exported, while all others are ignored. For example, in a file with several logos you can export each logo to its own PDF file using this option; make sure to also enable the **Export drawing, not page**, which in this case interprets "drawing" as "those objects that will be exported."

NOTE *For importing PDF, Inkscape uses the Poppler library* (http://poppler.freedesktop. org). *For exporting PDF, as well as PS and EPS formats, it uses the Cairo library* (http://cairographics.org). *These libraries are being actively developed, and future versions of Inkscape will likely improve the PDF support simply by including newer versions of these libraries.*

B.4 PostScript and EPS (Import, Export)

Once, PostScript was *the* exchange format for vector data. Now, however, it has largely ceded its position to PDF, which supports all practically useful features of PostScript but is at the same time richer (most importantly, it supports transparency) and much easier to support in software. So, whenever you have the choice, use PDF instead of PostScript; however, a lot of old projects and clipart exist as PostScript files, and there's still a lot of obsolete software around which either does not support PDF at all or supports it poorly while trying its best to understand PostScript.

NOTE *EPS is PostScript with some additional limitations which make it better adapted to being imported and inserted into other documents. An EPS file is always a single page, always has all fonts and bitmap images embedded (regular PS files are not obliged to embed stuff, although it is preferable that they do it) and its page size is always exactly clipped to its contents.*

Inkscape supports PS and EPS export natively. The dialog has much the same options as the PDF export dialog:

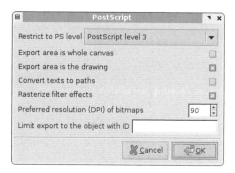

Figure B-4: PS or EPS export options

You can choose the level (i.e., version) of PostScript; most modern software and printers support Level 3. Fonts are always embedded into PS or EPS export (unless you choose to convert them to paths), and filters can be optionally rasterized, just as they are in PDF export. Objects with nonzero opacity are also rasterized automatically (you cannot suppress it) because, unlike PDF, PostScript does not support vector transparency.

For PS and EPS import, you have to install an additional piece of software, the Ghostscript interpreter, which is run automatically to convert the PS or EPS file into PDF format, which is then fed to Inkscape. At *http://pages.cs.wisc.edu/ ~ghost*, you will find its versions for all major operating systems. Make sure the *gs* or (on Windows) *gs.exe* executable file of Ghostscript is in your PATH; if it is not the case, Inkscape will not even list PS and EPS in its file format list in the **Open** or **Import** dialogs.

Since PS/EPS import ends up as PDF import from the Inkscape viewpoint, you will see the same PDF import dialog (Figure B-2). In particular, if a PS file contains more than one page, this dialog will allow you to choose which page to import.

B.5 Printing

Printing can be thought of as a kind of exporting—not only figuratively but also because, to print a document, by default Inkscape exports it to the format that the printer understands—which, depending on the printer driver, is either PostScript or PDF (SVG-capable printers exist but are rare so far). If you select the **Print to file** option from the **Print** dialog, you will get a PS or PDF file that looks exactly the same as if you saved your file with this file type.

Most of the options in your **Print** dialog (such as paper size, margins, print quality, and so on) will depend on your operating system and the printer driver. The only thing that Inkscape adds to this dialog is the **Rendering** tab.

By default, Inkscape prints by exporting the document to a vector format (PostScript or PDF). As explained earlier, Inkscape is smart enough to rasterize those objects using the features these formats don't support: filters (both PS and PDF) and transparency (PS only). However, if for some reason you don't like this selective rasterization, you can render the entire document into bitmap by switching from **Vector** to **Bitmap** on the **Rendering** tab and setting the bitmap resolution. This option is generally safer, as it avoids any kinds of surprises that format conversion may hold, but it may result in very large print files and slow printing.

B.6 AI (Import)

Up to version 8, Adobe Illustrator's native format was based on PostScript (1.5.1.1). It was not fully standard PostScript, however, and importing it into other software has always been a pain. There now exist various scripts on the Web which claim to convert this old AI format into something more tractable, but they are all rather limited and not too reliable. While you can try to use them, officially Inkscape 0.47 does not support import or export of the old AI format.

Starting from version 9, Adobe switched to PDF for the base of its new Illustrator format. The AI files saved by Illustrator still contain many AI-specific extensions; however, they are standard PDF and any PDF-capable software can open and view them as PDF. This is what Inkscape does: It treats any file with the *.ai* extension as a PDF file and presents its standard **PDF Import Settings** dialog to you (B.3). Inkscape will thus lose the AI-specific metadata (such as layers), but at least you will get your vector objects as vectors.

One feature used in complex AI files is *gradient meshes* (1.5.4). Inkscape can import them, but since there's no similar construct in SVG, it has to approximate them with a lattice of small flat-color path "tiles." In the **PDF Import Settings** dialog, you can set the precision of this approximation; raising this parameter will make the imported mesh look smoother, but at the cost of increasing the size of the SVG file and slowing down Inkscape.

NOTE *Imported gradient meshes, with their lattices of small colored paths, are a convenient object for moving, painting, and reshaping in the Tweak tool (6.9, 8.7, 12.6).*

There's no support for AI export in Inkscape, because all recent versions of Adobe Illustrator can import SVG and PDF files without problems.

B.7 CorelDRAW (Import)

For importing the vector files produced by the CorelDRAW vector editor (1.5.2), Inkscape can use the open source Python-based UniConvertor utility. On Linux, simply install the package *python-uniconvertor* from your distribution's repository, and it will fetch all necessary dependencies. On Windows, a copy of UniConvertor is packaged with Inkscape and uses Inkscape's own copy of Python, so you don't need to install anything. Further information and new versions of UniConvertor can be found at *http://sk1project.org*.

Currently, UniConvertor can handle most of the aspects of CorelDRAW files with the exception of text objects. The specific Corel formats it supports are: CDR (CorelDRAW versions 7 to X4), CDT (CorelDRAW template files), CCX (CorelDRAW Compressed Exchange files), and CMX (CorelDRAW Presentation Exchange files).

B.8 EMF (Import/Export), WMF and CGM (Import)

WMF (Windows MetaFile) and EMF (Enhanced MetaFile) are Windows-specific vector formats, used by some Windows-only software (such as Microsoft Office) for data interchange or storing vector clipart. Of these, EMF is more modern and generally preferable (if you have a choice). Inkscape supports EMF import and export natively but only on Windows (because it uses the operating system's support for this format).

Import of WMF as well as another, non-Microsoft vector "metafile" format called CGM is also available on any platform if you have the UniConvertor utility which converts WMF or CGM directly to SVG.

B.9 XAML (Import/Export)

Inkscape can both import and export the XAML (Extensible Application Markup Language) format used by Microsoft in its .NET and Silverlight technologies. No additional software is needed.

B.10 WPG (Import)

WPG (WordPerfect Graphics) is an old vector format that was used by the WordPerfect text processor. There still exist collections of clipart in this format, so it can be very be useful for a vector artist. Inkscape imports WPG natively (no external software is needed).

B.11 DXF and HPGL (Export)

DXF (Drawing Exchange Format) is a common CAD (Computer-Aided Design) format used for plans and technical drawings in software such as AutoCAD. HPGL is a primitive vector format used by some Hewlett-Packard plotters. Inkscape has some native support for exporting to these formats, limited to paths and shapes only; the DXF or HPGL files it exports can then be sent to a plotter or a vinyl cutting device.

B.12 JavaFX (Export)

JavaFX is a new Java-based technology from Sun, designed to build interactive applications for mobile and desktop systems. Inkscape has limited native support (paths and shapes only) for exporting to JavaFX.

B.13 ODG (Export)

OpenDocument Graphics (ODF) is the format used by, among others, the OpenOffice suite and its OpenOffice Draw application. Inkscape's native support for ODG export is limited, but still useful for exchanging data with OpenOffice—as of this writing, OpenOffice still lacks proper support for SVG.

B.14 POV (Export)

POVRay (*http://povray.org*) is a popular open source 3D raytracer, not a vector application. However, Inkscape can export the paths and shapes in its drawing as a 3D scene which POVRay will then render; you can manually edit the text-based *.pov* file to adjust angles, cameras, lighting, etc.

B.15 LATEX (Export)

Users of the old and powerful LATEX document formatting system will be pleased to find out that Inkscape can output its drawings directly into a LATEX document using the PSTricks package (*http://tug.org/PSTricks*) for rendering graphics.

B.16 Bitmap Formats (Import/Export)

As we saw in 18.9, the only bitmap format Inkscape can export is PNG. However, it has built-in import support for a lot more bitmap formats, including all the major ones (PNG, JPG, TIFF, GIF, and others).

B.17 What's Missing?

Among the most often requested, but still unsupported by Inkscape, file formats are Flash (SWF) and Adobe Freehand. For data exchange with Adobe Flash or Adobe Freehand, you can use SVG or PDF formats, but direct support of these important formats would be preferable. Fortunately, it is very easy to plug in a new format into Inkscape; as soon as there's an open source utility which can bridge from one of the known formats (ideally SVG, but PDF would work too) into the unknown, incorporating it into Inkscape is easy.

THE COMMAND LINE

Unlike most vector editors, but like the majority of open source software, Inkscape has a powerful command-line interface. It allows you to perform many tasks (exporting, document modifications, queries, and so on) from scripts or from a console, without using Inkscape's graphical user interface (GUI).

In most cases, ordering Inkscape to perform some task with command-line parameters does not load the GUI at all; after completing the task, Inkscape simply quits. This makes it run faster and consume less memory, since no time and memory are wasted on creating and destroying the GUI.

NOTE *Microsoft Windows treats command-line programs as second-class citizens compared to the "normal" (GUI) applications. You cannot create a single program which can run both as a GUI application and as a command-line application, so the developers of Inkscape on Windows had to make a choice. Naturally, they chose to position Inkscape as a GUI application, which inevitably damaged its command-line functionality.*

More specifically, while Inkscape on Windows takes command-line parameters and acts on them, it cannot output anything to the command prompt window (which makes the query parameters totally unusable). Also, it returns control to the command interpreter immediately, even though the action you have ordered (such as export) may not finish for several more seconds. This makes it nearly impossible to use Inkscape in sequential scripts. One more minor inconvenience is that you must always supply full paths for all files you specify on the command line.

It is possible to recompile Inkscape as a Windows command-line application, which in turn will make it less usable as a GUI application (a separate command prompt window will open every time you run such Inkscape). Consult the Inkscape FAQ on the website if you need to obtain such a command-line version of the program.

C.1 Loading Documents

There's no separate executable for command-line tasks; the regular inkscape (on Linux or Mac OSX) or inkscape.exe (on Windows) will work as a command-line utility if you give it the corresponding parameters. The simplest use of the command line is providing the filename(s) of the document(s) you want to load into the GUI. For example:

```
$ inkscape file.svg some/other/document.svg another/file.pdf
```

will start Inkscape's GUI and load the two SVG documents and one PDF document (automatically imported) into three Inkscape windows. In this case, no task is given to Inkscape, so it simply lets you edit the files. As we will see later, other command-line parameters, usually starting with --, will force it to skip the GUI and do something to the files on its own.

C.2 Export

Most often, the command-line interface is used for exporting SVG documents into other formats. There are command-line parameters for exporting to PNG (18.9), PS, EPS, and PDF (1.5.1.1). For example, exporting to PDF is as simple as:

```
$ inkscape --export-pdf=file.pdf file.svg
```

This will create *file.pdf*; no GUI is loaded, and after completing the export, Inkscape quits. Similarly, you can use --export-ps, --export-eps, and --export-png.

Also, there is --export-plain-svg for converting a document into plain SVG (1.4). It can be used not only for stripping an Inkscape SVG document of Inkscape-specific metadata, but also for converting any of the supported import formats into SVG (Appendix B). For example, this will convert a CorelDRAW file into SVG format:

```
$ inkscape --export-plain-svg=file.svg file.cdr
```

C.2.1 Area

By default, the document's page (2.3) is exported, so objects falling outside the page are invisible in export. You can add --export-area-drawing to make the export cover all visible objects of the document, regardless of its page size. The only exception is EPS, where the default is exporting drawing; for this format, you can limit export to page with --export-area-page (however, due to the limitations of EPS, this area will be contracted inwards to the edge of objects in the page if they do not reach to the edges of the page). For example:

```
$ inkscape --export-png=file.png --export-area-drawing file.svg
```

You can also export single objects out of a document, so that the exported file covers only that object's bounding box. The object you need is specified by its id attribute (A.9):

```
$ inkscape --export-eps=file.eps --export-id=text2054 file.svg
```

If other objects overlap with the exported object's bounding box and are visible, they will also show in the exported PNG file. To suppress them and make a rendering of only the chosen object and nothing else, add --export-id-only. For PDF, PS, and EPS, this is the only possible mode—other objects are always hidden if you specify --export-id.

For PNG export, you can also specify the export area explicitly by specifying the two corner points. For example:

```
$ inkscape --export-png=file.png --export-area=0:0:200:100 file.svg
```

will export the area that spans from the point (0, 0) to the point (200, 100).

Also for PNG export, no matter which method was used for specifying the area, you can "snap" this area to pixel grid, that is, round it to the nearest whole coordinates in px. This is very useful when you export at the default 90 dpi and want your objects drawn to the pixel grid (7.2) to be crisp in the exported bitmap no matter what area you are exporting.

C.2.2 Size and Resolution

For PNG export, you can specify the size of the exported bitmap or its resolution (by default, 90 dpi). For example:

```
$ inkscape --export-png=file.png --export-dpi=600 file.svg
$ inkscape --export-png=file.png --export-width=1000 file.svg
$ inkscape --export-png=file.png --export-height=400 file.svg
```

The first line will export at the resolution of 600 dpi, so that a document page 3 inches wide will export to a bitmap 1800 pixels wide. The other two examples explicitly set the pixel size of the export, and the resolution is calculated to match this requirement.

C.2.3 Background

Areas that have no objects in them come out as transparent in all export formats. However, in PNG export (but not PDF, PS, or EPS), you can specify any background color or opacity for your document during export. For example, if you want a solid opaque black background, use:

```
$ inkscape --export-png=file.png --export-background=#000000 \
    --export-background-opacity=1.0 file.svg
```

NOTE *The \ character in this example shows that the command line was wrapped for display; you should type it as a single line without the \.*

C.2.4 Export Hints

Every time you export a single selected object to PNG via the GUI (18.9), the export filename and resolution are recorded into an export hint added to the document. If, after that, you save the document with these hints, they can later be used for command-line export to PNG as well. For example, if you write:

```
$ inkscape --export-id=text2035 --export-use-hints file.svg
```

only the object with the ID text2035 will be exported to the same file and with the same resolution it was most recently exported from the GUI. Note that the --export-png specifying the filename is not present because the name is derived from the export hint.

C.2.5 Vector Export Options

For PDF, PS, and EPS, there are more export options that correspond to some of the choices in these formats' export dialogs in the GUI. Thus:

```
$ inkscape --export-pdf=file.pdf --export-text-to-path file.svg
```

converts all text objects to paths on export, so that the resulting vector file needs and embeds no fonts, whereas:

```
$ inkscape --export-pdf=file.pdf --export-ignore-filters file.svg
```

will ignore any filters, exporting the filtered objects as if they are not filtered, instead of rasterizing them (which is the default).

C.3 Querying

The textual nature of SVG makes it very easy to generate and edit SVG documents with simple scripts. However, no matter what your script is supposed to do, chances are that you will find it necessary to figure out the bounding boxes of some SVG objects (for example, to check if the text inserted into SVG from a database fits the provided space, or to create a background rectangle or frame for a specific object). Proper calculation of a bounding box, in a general case, is way too complex to do in a script—you would have to reimplement a lot of Inkscape's geometry and rendering code if you want to take into account everything that may affect the bounding box.

Fortunately, instead of all that you can simply ask Inkscape. For example:

```
$ inkscape --query-width --query-id=text1256 file.svg
45.2916
```

Here, we asked Inkscape to tell us the width (in px units) of the object with the id="text1256". It loaded the document, found that object, printed its width back to the console, and then quit.

Similarly, you can --query-height, --query-x, and --query-y to find out the dimensions and coordinates of the object's bounding box. Such Inkscape calls are reasonably fast because they don't load the GUI and don't render the document; however, if you need to query the bounding boxes of many objects, this may add up to quite a delay. In this case, it is better to use the --query-all parameter which returns all bounding box numbers for all objects in a document, as follows:

```
$ inkscape --query-all file.svg
svg2,-55.11053,-29.90404,328.3131,608.6359
layer1,-55.11053,-29.90404,328.3131,608.6359
image2372,-8.917463,349.8089,282.12,212.6382
text2317,-39.85518,454.3014,20.40604,13.32647
tspan2319,-32.58402,454.3014,12.79618,4.989286
tspan2408,-39.85518,462.4921,20.40604,5.135838
path2406,-16.43702,386.617,6.34172,154.7896
text2410,-46.11609,376.8753,34.34841,5.135838
tspan2414,-46.11609,376.8753,34.34841,5.135838
text2418,-55.11053,365.9197,43.02429,5.135838
```

Here, each line is a comma-separated list of: object ID, x, y, width, and height. Parsing such a line in your script should be easy.

C.4 Shell Mode

In order to save the load time (even without a GUI, Inkscape still takes some time to start), you can perform multiple command-line tasks using one instance of the program running in the *shell mode*. For example, this can be used on a server where PNG export requests come from the users and are routed to a shell-mode Inkscape instance for a quick response.

To enter the shell mode, run Inkscape with a single parameter, --shell. You will get a prompt where you can type your commands. There's no special syntax for the shell mode commands; each command is simply a valid command-line invocation of Inkscape, but without the Inkscape program name. For example, if you do:

```
$ inkscape --export-pdf=file.pdf file.svg
```

then in the shell mode, you can type `--export-pdf=file.pdf file.svg` as the shell command. Here is an example shell mode session where one document is exported to PDF and another to PNG:

```
$ inkscape --shell
Inkscape 0.47 interactive shell mode. Type 'quit' to quit.
>file.svg --export-pdf=file.pdf
>otherfile.svg --export-png=bitmap.png
Background RRGGBBAA: ffffff00
Area 0:0:744.094:1052.36 exported to 744 x 1052 pixels (90 dpi)
Bitmap saved as: bitmap.png
>quit
```

C.5 Verbs

Inkscape's command line is not limited to GUI-less export, conversion, and querying tasks. You can script a certain share of regular editing tasks as well. This is done by the `--verb` command-line parameters, which make Inkscape start as usual (with a GUI) and run the specified sequence of verbs on the objects which you select with `--select`. When done, Inkscape does not quit (unless you use the `FileQuit` verb) but simply stops and allows the user to continue editing.

A *verb* typically corresponds to a command that you chose from a menu. It is not a one-to-one mapping, however; some verbs are not available via the menus. On the other hand, many verbs require further interaction from the user, such as adjusting parameters in a dialog; it makes little sense to use them in your script except as a last step, so that the user can "continue from here."

To get a complete list of verbs your version of Inkscape supports (there are more than 750 verbs in version 0.47), run Inkscape with `--verb-list`. Here's just the very top of the list, showing some verbs commonly used in scripting. The verb names are before the ":" and followed by a brief description:

```
$ inkscape --verb-list
FileNew: Create new document from the default template
FileOpen: Open an existing document
FileSave: Save document
FilePrint: Print document
NextWindow: Switch to the next document window
PrevWindow: Switch to the previous document window
FileClose: Close this document window
FileQuit: Quit Inkscape
EditCut: Cut selection to clipboard
EditCopy: Copy selection to clipboard
EditPaste: Paste objects from clipboard to mouse point, or paste text
EditPasteStyle: Apply the style of the copied object to selection
EditPasteSize: Scale selection to match the size of the copied object
```

Apart from the regular Inkscape commands, all preset filters (17.3) and extensions (13.3) have two verbs each: One is the same as running this filter or extension from the menu (which may or may not display a dialog with parameters); the other, with .noprefs appended, always runs without a dialog, using default values. For example:

```
org.inkscape.effect.filter.filter2573v: Glossy clumpy jam spread
org.inkscape.effect.filter.filter2573v.noprefs: Jam spread (No preferences)
org.inkscape.text.uppercase: UPPERCASE
org.inkscape.text.uppercase.noprefs: UPPERCASE (No preferences)
```

For scripting, of course, the .noprefs variants are preferable.

Usually, one or more --verb parameters in a command-line script are preceded by a --select parameter which selects some object by its ID. You can specify multiple --select parameters to select multiple objects. If you want to do something to all objects at once, or to objects one by one, you don't need --select; instead, just use the verbs --verb=EditSelectAll or iterate through the objects with --verb=EditSelectNext.

Here are a few examples. Open the document, select all objects, convert them to paths, save the document, and quit:

```
$ inkscape a.svg --verb=EditSelectAll --verb=ObjectToPath --verb=FileSave \
  --verb=FileQuit
```

Open the document, select a specific group by ID, ungroup it, save, and quit:

```
$ inkscape a.svg --select=g2038 --verb=SelectionUnGroup --verb=FileSave \
  --verb=FileQuit
```

Open a document, select an object by ID, copy it, select another object, paste style, remove any filters it may have had, apply a **Pixel smear** preset filter, save, and quit:

```
$ inkscape file.svg --select=text2328 --verb=EditCopy --verb=EditDeselect \
  --select=text2322 --verb=EditPasteStyle --verb=RemoveFilter \
  --verb=org.inkscape.effect.filter.filter3707-6-6-0.noprefs \
  --verb=FileSave --verb=FileQuit
```

C.6   Getting Help

To get a brief listing of the command-line parameters known to your version of Inkscape, run it with --help. A more detailed reference is available from Inkscape's UI in **Help ▶ Command Line Options** (this opens a web browser and fetches the page from the Internet) or by typing man inkscape on the command line (Linux only).

A very useful parameter (especially if you are going to report a bug or request a feature from Inkscape developers) is --version which prints the exact version and even the SVN revision number of your copy of Inkscape.

KEYBOARD SHORTCUTS

D.1 Tools

F1, s	Selector (5.4)
Space	Selector (temporary)

Space switches to the Selector tool temporarily; another Space switches back. You can make Space-drag pan canvas instead of switching to Selector by turning on the **Left mouse button pans when Space is pressed** option in **Inkscape Preferences**.

F2, n	Node tool (12.5)
Shift-F2, w	Tweak tool (6.9, 8.7, 12.6)
F3, z	Zoom tool (3.9)
F4, r	Rectangle tool (11.2)
Shift-F4, x	3D Box tool (11.3)
F5, e	Ellipse tool (11.4)
F6, p	Pencil tool (14.2)
Shift-F6, b	Pen tool (14.1)
Ctrl-F6, c	Calligraphic pen tool (14.3)
Shift-E	Eraser tool (5.8, 14.3.6)
Shift-F7, u	Paint bucket tool (14.4)
Ctrl-F1, g	Gradient tool (10.1)
F7, d	Dropper tool (8.6)

F8, t	Text tool (Chapter 15)
F9, i	Spiral tool (11.6)
Shift-F9, *	Star tool (11.5)
Ctrl-F2, o	Connector tool (1.2)

Double-clicking on a tool button opens the **Inkscape Preferences** dialog (11.1.2) with the page of the corresponding tool.

D.2 Dialogs

D.2.1 Open

Shift-Ctrl-F	Fill and Stroke (8.1.1)
Shift-Ctrl-W	Swatches (8.3)
Shift-Ctrl-T	Text and Font (15.4.2)
Shift-Ctrl-M	Transform (6.7)
Shift-Ctrl-L	Layers (4.6.4)
Shift-Ctrl-A	Align and Distribute (7.4, 7.5)
Shift-Ctrl-O	Object Properties (4.1)
Shift-Ctrl-H	Undo History
Shift-Ctrl-X	XML Editor (4.7)
Shift-Ctrl-D	Document Properties (3.1.2)
Shift-Ctrl-P	Inkscape Preferences (3.1.1)
Shift-Ctrl-E	Export Bitmap (18.9.1)
Ctrl-F	Find (5.12)
Shift-Alt-B	Trace Bitmap (18.8.2)
Shift-Ctrl-7	Path Effect Editor (13.1.2)

These shortcuts open a new dialog window if it wasn't open yet; otherwise the dialog is activated.

D.2.2 Toggle Visibility

F12	Toggle dialogs

This temporarily hides all open dialogs; another F12 shows them again.

D.2.3 Within a Dialog

Esc	Return focus to the canvas
Ctrl-F4, Ctrl-W	Close the dialog
Tab	Jump to next widget
Shift-Tab	Jump to previous widget
Enter	Set the new value
Ctrl-Enter	In XML Editor, set the attribute value

When editing an attribute value in XML Editor (4.7), Ctrl-Enter writes the new value (same as clicking the **Set attribute** button).

Space, Enter	Activate current button or list
Ctrl-Page Up, Ctrl-Page Down	In a multitab dialog, switch tabs

D.3 The Controls Bar
D.3.1 Access
Alt-X	Jump to the first editable field

D.3.2 Navigate
Tab	Jump to next field
Shift-Tab	Jump to previous field

These navigate between fields in the controls bar (the value in the field you leave, if changed, becomes accepted).

D.4 The Canvas (2.2)
D.4.1 Zoom (3.8)
=, +	Zoom in
-	Zoom out

The keypad +/- keys zoom even when you are editing a text object, unless NumLock is on.

middle click, Ctrl-**right click**	Zoom in
Shift-**middle click,** Shift-**right click**	Zoom out
Ctrl-**wheel**	Zoom in or out

To swap functions of wheel and Ctrl-wheel, turn on the **Mouse wheel zooms by default** option in **Inkscape Preferences**; then Ctrl-wheel will scroll and wheel without Ctrl will zoom.

Shift-**middle drag**	Zoom into the area
Alt-Z	Activate zoom field

The zoom field in the bottom-right corner of the window allows you to specify zoom level precisely.

D.4.2 Preset Zooms (3.9)
1	Zoom 1:1
2	Zoom 1:2
3	Zoom to selection
4	Zoom to drawing
5	Zoom to page
Ctrl-E, 6	Zoom to page width

D.4.3 Zoom History (3.9)
`	Previous zoom
Shift-`	Next zoom

With these keys, you can travel back and forth through the history of zooms in this session.

D.4.4 Scroll (Pan, 3.10)

Ctrl-←, Ctrl-→, Ctrl-↑, Ctrl-↓   Scroll canvas

Scrolling by keys is *accelerated*—it speeds up when you press Ctrl-arrows in quick succession, or press and hold.

middle drag	Pan canvas
Shift-**right drag**, Ctrl-**right drag**	Pan canvas
wheel	Scroll canvas vertically
Shift-**wheel**	Scroll canvas horizontally

When the **Left mouse button pans when Space is pressed** option is on in **Inkscape Preferences**, Space-drag also pans canvas.

D.4.5 Guides, Grids, and Snapping (Chapter 7)

drag   Drag off a ruler to create guide

Drag off the horizontal or vertical ruler into the canvas to create a new guideline. Drag a guideline onto the ruler to delete it.

drag	Drag a guide to move it
Shift-**drag**	Drag a guide (not near anchor) to rotate it
Shift-Ctrl-**drag**	Rotate guide with angle snapping
Ctrl-**click**	Delete guide
|, Shift-\	Toggle guides and snapping to guides

If you want to see the guides but not snap to them, use the global snapping toggle (%). When you create a new guide by dragging off the ruler, guide visibility is turned on.

#, Shift-3   Toggle grids and snapping to grids

If you want to see the grids but not snap to them, use the global snapping toggle (%). Only the 3 on the main keyboard works, not on the keypad.

%   Toggle snapping on and off

This global toggle affects snapping to grids, guides, and objects in all tools.

D.4.6 Display Mode (3.11)

Ctrl-5   Toggle Normal/Outline mode (keypad 5 only)

D.5 The Palette (8.3)

These keys work both in the floating **Swatches** dialog and in the docked palette at the bottom of the window.

click	Set fill color on selection
Shift-**click**	Set stroke color on selection
right click	Open pop-up menu
drag	Drag fill color to objects
Shift-**drag**	Drag stroke color to objects

To change the fill or stroke of an object by dragging color onto it, that object need not be selected. You can also drag colors to the **Fill** (**F**) and **Stroke** (**S**) indicators in the status bar to change the selection.

D.6 Files

Ctrl-N	Create new document (3.2)
Ctrl-O	Open a document (3.5)
Shift-Ctrl-E	Export to PNG (18.9.1)
Ctrl-I	Import bitmap or vector (18.1)
Ctrl-P	Print document (B.5)
Ctrl-S	Save document (2.9)
Shift-Ctrl-S	Save under a new name (B.1)
Shift-Ctrl-Alt-S	Save a copy (B.1)
Ctrl-Q	Exit Inkscape

D.7 The Document Window (3.6)

Ctrl-R	Toggle rulers
Ctrl-B	Toggle scrollbars
F11	Toggle fullscreen
F10	Main menu

Menus can also be activated by Alt with the letter underscored in the menu name.

Shift-F10, **right click**	Drop-down (context) menu
Ctrl-F4, Ctrl-W	Close document window

This shuts down Inkscape if this was the only document window open.

Ctrl-Tab	Next document window
Shift-Ctrl-Tab	Previous document window

These shortcuts cycle through the active document windows forward and backward.

D.8 Layers (4.6)

Shift-Ctrl-N	Create new layer
Shift-Page Up	Move to layer above
Shift-Page Down	Move to layer below

These commands move the selected objects from one layer to another.

Shift-Ctrl-Page Up	Raise layer
Shift-Ctrl-Page Down	Lower layer
Shift-Ctrl-Home	Raise layer to top
Shift-Ctrl-End	Lower layer to bottom

These commands move the current layer among its siblings (normally other layers).

D.9 Objects (Chapter 4)

D.9.1 Undo/Redo

`Shift-Ctrl-Y`, `Ctrl-Z`	Undo
`Shift-Ctrl-Z`, `Ctrl-Y`	Redo

D.9.2 The Clipboard (4.4)

`Ctrl-C`	Copy selection
`Ctrl-X`	Cut selection (copy and then delete)
`Ctrl-V`	Paste clipboard

This places the clipboard objects at the mouse cursor, or at the center of the window if the mouse is outside the canvas. When editing text with the Text tool, this inserts the text from the clipboard into the current text object.

`Ctrl-Alt-V`	Paste in place

This places the clipboard objects into the original location from which they were copied.

`Shift-Ctrl-V`	Paste style

This applies the style of the (first of the) copied object(s) to the current selection. If a gradient handle (in the Gradient tool) or a text span (in the Text tool) are selected, they get the pasted style instead of the entire object.

`Ctrl-7`	Paste path effect

This applies the path effect of the copied path to the paths/shapes in the current selection.

D.9.3 Duplicate (4.4)

`Ctrl-D`	Duplicate selection

New object(s) are placed exactly over the original(s) and selected. Clones may be relinked if you enabled that (16.5).

D.9.4 Clone (Chapter 16)

`Alt-D`	Clone object

The clone is placed exactly over the original object and is selected. You can only clone one object at a time; if you want to clone several objects together, group them and clone the group.

`Shift-Alt-D`	Unlink clone
`Shift-D`	Select original

D.9.5 Bitmaps (Chapter 18)

`Alt-B`	Create a bitmap copy

The imported bitmap is placed over the original selection and is selected.

`Shift-Alt-B`	Open **Trace Bitmap** dialog

D.9.6 Patterns (*10.8*)

Alt-I	Object(s) to pattern

This converts the selection to a rectangle with tiled pattern fill.

Shift-Alt-I	Pattern to object(s)

Each selected object with pattern fill is broken into the same object without fill and a single pattern object.

D.9.7 Group (*4.5*)

Shift-Ctrl-U, Ctrl-G	Group selected objects
Shift-Ctrl-G, Ctrl-U	Ungroup selected group(s)

This removes only one level of grouping; press Ctrl-U repeatedly to ungroup nested groups.

D.9.8 Z-Order (*4.3*)

Home	Raise selection to top
End	Lower selection to bottom
Page Up	Raise selection one step
Page Down	Lower selection one step

D.10 Paths (Chapter *12*)

D.10.1 Object to Path

Shift-Ctrl-C	Convert selected object(s) to path (Chapter *11*)
Ctrl-Alt-C	Convert stroke to path (*12.1.3*)

D.10.2 Boolean Operations (*12.2*)

Ctrl-+	Union
Ctrl-−	Difference
Ctrl-*	Intersection
Ctrl-^	Exclusion (XOR)
Ctrl-/	Division (cut)
Ctrl-Alt-/	Cut Path

The result of **Union**, **Difference**, **Intersection**, and **Exclusion** inherits the id attribute (*A.9*) and therefore the clones, if any, of the bottom object. **Division** and **Cut Path** normally produce several objects; of them, one inherits the id of the bottom source object.

D.10.3 Offsets (*12.4*)

Ctrl-(	Inset path (towards center)
Ctrl-)	Outset path (away from center)

The default offset distance is 2 px units.[1]

Alt-(	Inset path by 1 pixel[2]
Alt-)	Outset path by 1 pixel
Shift-Alt-(	Inset path by 10 pixels
Shift-Alt-)	Outset path by 10 pixels

All the [(,)] commands convert the object to path, if necessary, and produce a regular path.

Ctrl-J	Create dynamic offset
Ctrl-Alt-J	Create linked offset

These commands produce an offset object (13.2), editable by the Node tool, standalone or linked to the original.

Shift-D	Select source

Selecting a linked offset and giving this command will select the source path of the linked offset.

D.10.4 Combine (12.1.1)

Ctrl-K	Combine paths
Shift-Ctrl-K	Break paths apart

D.10.5 Simplify (12.3)

Ctrl-L	Simplify

If you invoke this command several times in quick succession, it will act more and more aggressively. Invoking **Simplify** again after a pause restores the default threshold (settable in the **Inkscape Preferences** dialog).

D.11 The Selector Tool (5.4)

D.11.1 Select (Mouse, 5.4)

click	Select an object

When you left-click on an object, the previous selection is deselected.

Shift-**click**	Toggle selection

This adds an object to the current selection if it was not selected, otherwise removes the object from the current selection.

double click	Edit the object

This switches to the object's most natural editing tool (the Node tool for paths, a corresponding shape tool for shapes, and the Text tool for text). For groups, double-clicking performs the **Enter group** command (the group becomes a temporary layer, 4.6.1). Double-clicking in empty space switches to the parent layer in the hierarchy, if any.

---

[1] A *px unit* refers the absolute unit equal to 1/90 of an inch (A.6).

[2] A *pixel* refers one screen pixel, which is a relative distance that depends on your zoom level (3.8). You can zoom in closer for finer adjustment.

D.11.2   Rubber Band (5.7), Touch Selection (5.8)

drag	Select by rubber band
Shift-**drag**	Add objects to selection

Normally, you need to start from an empty space to initiate a rubber band. However, if you press Shift before dragging, Inkscape will do rubber band selection even if you start from an object.

Alt-**drag**, Shift-Alt-**drag**	Select by touch

Alt-dragging over objects selects those objects that are touched by the path. To start touch selection with Alt, you must have nothing selected; otherwise use Shift-Alt. You can switch rubber band selection to touch selection and back while dragging by pressing/releasing Alt.

D.11.3   Select (Keyboard, 5.11)

Tab	Select next object
Shift-Tab	Select previous object

These keys pick objects in their z-order (Tab cycles from bottom to top, Shift-Tab cycles from top to bottom). This works on objects within the current layer (4.6).

Ctrl-A	Select all (current layer)

This works on objects within the current layer (unless you change that in **Inkscape Preferences**).

Ctrl-Alt-A	Select all (all layers)

This works on objects in all visible and unlocked layers.

!	Invert selection (current layer)

This inverts the selection (deselects what was selected and vice versa) in the current layer.

Alt-!	Invert selection (all layers)

This inverts the selection (deselects what was selected and vice versa) in visible and unlocked layers.

Esc	Deselect
Backspace, Delete	Delete selection

D.11.4   Select Within Group (5.10), Select Under (5.9)

Ctrl-**click**	Select within group

This selects the object at click point disregarding any levels of grouping that this object might belong to.

Shift-Ctrl-**click**	Toggle selection within group
Alt-**click**	Select under

Alt-click selects the object at click point which is beneath (in z-order) the lowest selected object at click point. If the bottom object is reached, Alt-click again selects the top object. So, several Alt-clicks cycle through the z-order stack at click point. On Linux, Alt-click and Alt-drag may be reserved by the window manager. If you reconfigure your window manager to not map Alt-click, then it will be free for Inkscape to use. If your keyboard has a Meta key, you may wish to set your **Modifier key** to use it instead of Alt. (Sometimes you can also use Ctrl-Alt-click (select under, in groups) with the same effect as Alt-click.)

Shift-Alt-**click**	Toggle under
Ctrl-Alt-**click**	Select under, in groups
Shift-Ctrl-Alt-**click**	Toggle under, in groups

| `Ctrl-Enter` | Enter group |
| `Ctrl-Backspace` | Go to parent group/layer |

D.11.5 Move (Mouse, *6.1*)

| **drag** | Select + move |

Dragging an object selects it if it was not selected, then moves the selection.

| `Alt`-**drag** | Move selected |

This moves the current selection (without selecting what is under the cursor), no matter where you start the drag. On Linux, `Alt`-click and `Alt`-drag may be reserved by the window manager. Reconfigure it so you can use them in Inkscape.

| `Ctrl`-**drag** | Restrict movement to horizontal or vertical |
| `Shift`-**drag** | Temporarily disable snapping |

This temporarily disables snapping to grid or guides when you are dragging with grid or guides on.

| **drag**-`Space` | Drop a copy |

When dragging or transforming with the mouse, each `Space` leaves a copy of the selected object. You can press and hold `Space` while dragging for a nice "trail."

D.11.6 Move (Keyboard, *6.1*)

| `←`, `→`, `↑`, `↓` | Move selection by the nudge distance |
| `Shift-←`, `Shift-→`, `Shift-↑`, `Shift-↓` | Move selection by 10 times the nudge distance |

The default nudge distance is 2 px units.

| `Alt-←`, `Alt-→`, `Alt-↑`, `Alt-↓` | Move selection by 1 pixel |
| `Shift-Alt-←`, `Shift-Alt-→`, `Shift-Alt-↑`, `Shift-Alt-↓` | Move selection by 10 pixels |

D.11.7 Transform (Mouse, *6.2, 6.3*)

click, `Shift-S`	Toggle scale/rotation handles
drag	Scale (with scale handles)
drag	Rotate or skew (with rotation or skew handles)

D.11.8 Scale with Handles (*6.2*)

drag	Scale
`Ctrl`-**drag**	Scale preserving aspect ratio
`Shift`-**drag**	Symmetric transformation

Holding `Shift` while transforming makes transformation symmetric around the center of the selection.

| `Alt`-**drag** | Scale by integer |

Hold `Alt` while scaling to limit scale to 2, 3, 4, etc. or 1/2, 1/3, 1/4, etc. of the initial size.

D.11.9 Scale (Keyboard, 6.5.2)

| `.`, `>` | Scale selection up by the scale step |
| `,`, `<` | Scale selection down by the scale step |

The default scale step is 2 px units.

`Ctrl-.`, `Ctrl->`	Scale selection to 200%
`Ctrl-,`, `Ctrl-<`	Scale selection to 50%
`Alt-.`, `Alt->`	Scale selection up by 1 pixel
`Alt-,`, `Alt-<`	Scale selection down by 1 pixel

Scaling is uniform around the center, so the size increment applies to the larger of the two dimensions.

D.11.10 Rotate/Skew with Handles (6.3)

| **drag** | Rotate or skew |
| `Ctrl`-**drag** | Snap skew angle |

Holding `Ctrl` when dragging a skew (noncorner) handle snaps the skew angle to the angle steps. The default angle step is 15 degrees; it can be changed in **Inkscape Preferences**, **Steps**.

| `Ctrl`-**drag** | Snap rotation angle |

Holding `Ctrl` when dragging a rotation (corner) handle snaps the rotation angle to angle steps.

D.11.11 Rotate (Keyboard, 6.5.3)

`[`, `]`	Rotate selection by the angle step[3]
`Ctrl-[`, `Ctrl-]`	Rotate selection by 90 degrees
`Alt-[`, `Alt-]`	Rotate selection by 1 pixel

These commands use the rotation center, draggable in Selector (by default it is in the geometric center).

D.11.12 Flip (6.5.3)

| `h` | Flip selection horizontally |
| `v` | Flip selection vertically |

If the tool is in rotate mode (rotation center visible), that center becomes the axis of flipping; otherwise it flips around the geometric center of the selection.

D.11.13 The Rotation Center (6.4)

| **drag** | Move rotation center |

Dragging the center snaps it to the centerlines and bounding box edges of the selection.

| `Shift`-**drag** | Move without snapping |
| `Shift`-**click** | Reset rotation center |

Resetting the rotation center moves it back to the geometric center of the object's or selection's bounding box.

---

[3] Throughout Inkscape, `]`, `)`, `}` rotate clockwise, `[`, `(`, `{` rotate counterclockwise.

D.11.14 Cancel

Esc	Cancel rubber band, move, transformation

Press Esc while the mouse button is still down to cancel rubber band selection, move, or transformation of any kind.

D.12 The Node Tool (12.5)

D.12.1 Select Objects (Mouse)

click	Select a nonselected object
Alt-**click**	Select under
Shift-**click**	Toggle selection

D.12.2 Select Nodes (Mouse)

click	Select/deselect node(s)

Click on a node to select it; click on the path between two adjacent nodes to select them. Clicking in an empty space deselects all selected nodes (next click will deselect the object).

Shift-**click**	Toggle selection

This adds/removes a node (if clicked on node) or two nodes (if clicked on path) to/from the node selection.

D.12.3 Rubber Band Selection (12.5.2)

drag	Select multiple nodes

Dragging around nodes does a rubber band selection; previous node selection is deselected.

Shift-**drag**	Add nodes to selection

Normally, you need to not be over a path or a node to initiate a rubber band. However, if you press Shift before dragging, Inkscape will do a rubber band selection even if you start over a path.

D.12.4 Select Nodes (Keyboard, 12.5.2)

Tab	Select next node
Shift-Tab	Select previous node

These keys select nodes within the selected path.

Ctrl-A	Select all nodes in subpath(s)

If the path has multiple subpaths and some nodes selected, this selects all only in subpaths with already selected nodes.

Ctrl-Alt-A	Select all nodes in path

This selects all nodes in the entire path.

!	Invert selection in subpath(s)

If the path has multiple subpaths and some nodes selected, this inverts the selection (deselects what was selected and vice versa) only in subpaths with already selected nodes.

Alt-!	Invert selection in path

This inverts selection in the entire path.

Esc   Deselect all nodes

D.12.5 Grow/Shrink Node Selection (12.5.2)

Page Up, Page Down, **wheel**   Grow/shrink selection (spatial)
Ctrl-Page Up, Ctrl-Page Down,   Grow/shrink selection (along path)
Ctrl-**wheel**

Your mouse pointer must be over a node for growing/shrinking. Each key press or wheel click selects the nearest unselected node or deselects the farthest selected node.

D.12.6 Move Nodes (Mouse, 12.5.7)

drag   Move selected nodes
Ctrl-**drag**   Move nodes, restricting to horizontal or vertical
Ctrl-Alt-**drag**   Move along the selected node's handles

This restricts movement to the directions of the node's handles, their continuations, and perpendiculars (total eight snaps). If the node has straight lines on one or both sides, this will snap it to these lines' directions and perpendiculars instead.

Shift-**drag**   Temporarily disable snapping
Shift-**drag**   Drag out handle

If a node has a retracted handle, hold Shift to drag a handle out of the node.

drag-Space   Drop a copy

When dragging nodes with the mouse, each Space leaves a copy of the selected object.

Alt-**drag**   Sculpt selected nodes (12.5.7.2)

To stop sculpting without losing the pressure-sensitive profile, release Alt first and then lift the pen.

D.12.7 Move Nodes (Keyboard, 12.5.7)

←, →, ↑, ↓   Move selected node(s) by the nudge distance
Shift-←, Shift-→, Shift-↑, Shift-↓ Move selected node(s) by 10 times the nudge distance

The default nudge distance is 2 px units.

Alt-←, Alt-→, Alt-↑, Alt-↓   Move selected node(s) by 1 pixel
Shift-Alt-←, Shift-Alt-→,   Move selected node(s) by 10 pixels
Shift-Alt-↑, Shift-Alt-↓

D.12.8 Move Node Handle (Mouse, 12.5.7)

drag   Move a node handle
Ctrl-**drag**   Snap the handle to angle steps

This also snaps to the handle's original angle, its continuation, and perpendiculars.

Shift-**drag**   Rotate both handles
Alt-**drag**   Lock the handle length

Ctrl, Shift, Alt can be combined when dragging handles.

`Ctrl`-**click**   Retract the handle

Retracted handle has zero length; use `Shift`-drag to extract it back out.

D.12.9   Scale Handle (One Node Selected, *12.5.6*)

`<`, `>`   Contract/expand both handles by scale step

The default scale step is 2 px units. This may apply to more than one selected node.

`Left Ctrl-<`, `Left Ctrl->`	Scale left handle by the scale step
`Right Ctrl-<`, `Right Ctrl->`	Scale right handle by the scale step
`Left Alt-<`, `Left Alt->`	Scale left handle by 1 pixel
`Right Alt-<`, `Right Alt->`	Scale right handle by 1 pixel

Instead of the `<` and `>`, you can use the `,` (comma) and `.` (period) keys, respectively.

D.12.10   Rotate Handle (One Node Selected, *12.5.6*)

`[`, `]`   Rotate both handles by the angle step

This may apply to more than one selected node.

`Left Ctrl-[`, `Left Ctrl-]`	Rotate left handle by the angle step
`Right Ctrl-[`, `Right Ctrl-]`	Rotate right handle by the angle step
`Left Alt-[`, `Left Alt-]`	Rotate left handle by 1 pixel
`Right Alt-[`, `Right Alt-]`	Rotate right handle by 1 pixel

D.12.11   Scale Nodes (Two or More Nodes Selected, *12.5.7.3*)

These commands scale the selected nodes as if they were an object. If the mouse is over a node, that node becomes the axis of scaling; otherwise it scales around the geometric center of the selected nodes.

`.`, `>`	Scale nodes up by the scale step
`,`, `<`	Scale nodes down by the scale step

The default scale step is 2 px units.

`Alt-.`, `Alt->`	Scale nodes up by 1 pixel
`Alt-,`, `Alt-<`	Scale nodes down by 1 pixel

Scaling is uniform around the center, so that the size increment applies to the larger of the two dimensions.

D.12.12   Rotate Nodes (Two or More Nodes Selected, *12.5.7.3*)

These commands rotate the selected nodes as if they were an object. If the mouse is over a node, that node becomes the axis of rotation; otherwise it rotates around the geometric center of the selected nodes.

`[`, `]`	Rotate nodes by the angle step
`Alt-[`, `Alt-]`	Rotate nodes by 1 pixel

D.12.13 Flip Nodes (Two or More Nodes Selected, 12.5.7.3)

These commands flip the selected nodes as if they were an object, around the center of that object.

| `h` | Flip nodes horizontally |
| `v` | Flip nodes vertically |

If the mouse is over a node, that node becomes the axis of flipping; otherwise it flips around the geometric center of the selected nodes.

D.12.14 Change Segments (12.5.6)

| `Shift-L` | Make line |
| `Shift-U` | Make curve |

These commands require that two or more adjacent nodes be selected.

D.12.15 Change Node Type (12.5.5)

| `Shift-C` | Make cusp |

This changes the type of node; if you do another `Shift-C` on an already cusp node, it retracts its handles.

| `Shift-S` | Make smooth |

If a cusp node is adjacent to a line segment, `Shift-S` makes it half-smooth with one handle collinear with the segment; another `Shift-S` will expand a second handle.

| `Shift-Y` | Make symmetric |

When making smooth or symmetric, you can lock the position of one of the handles by hovering the mouse over it.

| `Shift-A` | Make auto |
| `Ctrl`-**click** | Toggle smooth/cusp/symmetric/auto |

D.12.16 Join/Break (12.5.4)

| `Shift-J` | Join selected nodes |

This requires that exactly two end nodes within the path be selected. You can lock the position of one of the two joined nodes by hovering the mouse over it.

| `Shift-B` | Break selected node(s) |

After break, only one of each two new nodes is selected. This may apply to more than one selected node.

D.12.17 Delete, Create, and Duplicate (12.5.3)

| `Backspace`, `Delete` | Delete selected node(s) |
| `Ctrl-Backspace`, `Ctrl-Delete` | Delete without preserving shape |

Deleting without `Ctrl` adjusts handles on the remaining nodes to preserve the shape of the curve as much as possible. Deleting with `Ctrl` does not touch the remaining nodes.

| `Ctrl-Alt`-**click** | Create/delete node |

Ctrl-Alt-click on a node deletes it; Ctrl-Alt-click on the path between nodes creates a new node in the click point. Deleting nodes this way always tries to preserve the shape of the curve (same as Delete / Backspace).

double-click   Create node

Double-clicking the path between nodes creates a node at the click point.

Insert   Insert new node(s)

This adds new nodes in the middle of the selected segments, so it requires that two or more adjacent nodes be selected.

Shift-D   Duplicate selected node(s)

New nodes are created on the same path; they are placed exactly over the old ones and are selected.

D.12.18 Reverse (12.1.1)

Shift-R   Reverse path direction

D.12.19 Edit Shapes

The Node tool can also drag the handles of shapes (rectangles, ellipses, stars, spirals). Click on a shape to select it. See the corresponding shape tools for their editing shortcuts, all of which also work in the Node tool.

D.12.20 Edit Fills and Path Effects

The Node tool can also edit the handles of a pattern fill, a gradient fill, and the editable handles of path effects.

D.12.21 Cancel

Esc   Cancel rubber band or move

Press Esc while the mouse button is still down to cancel rubber band selection, node move, or handle move.

D.13 The Tweak Tool (6.9, 8.7, 12.6)

D.13.1 Operation

drag   Act on selected paths in the current mode
Shift-**drag**   Reverse current mode (when applicable)
Ctrl-**drag**   Act temporarily in Shrink mode
Shift-Ctrl-**drag**   Act temporarily in Grow mode

D.13.2 Modes

Shift-M   Move mode
Shift-I   Move in/out mode

Drag moves objects inward to the cursor, drag with Shift moves outward from the cursor.

| `Shift-Z` | Move Jitter mode |
| `Shift-<`, `Shift->` | Scale mode |

Drag scales objects down, drag with `Shift` scales up.

| `Shift-[`, `Shift-]` | Rotate mode |

Drag rotates objects clockwise, drag with `Shift`, counterclockwise.

| `Shift-D` | Duplicate/Delete mode |

Drag randomly duplicates objects, drag with `Shift` randomly deletes.

| `Shift-P` | Push path mode (12.6.3) |
| `Shift-S` | Grow/Shrink path mode (12.6.4) |

Drag insets paths, drag with `Shift` outsets.

| `Shift-A` | Attract/Repel path mode (12.6.5) |

Drag attracts paths to the cursor, drag with `Shift` repels.

`Shift-R`	Roughen mode (12.6.6)
`Shift-C`	Color Paint mode (8.7.1)
`Shift-J`	Color Jitter mode (8.7.2)
`Shift-B`	Blur mode

D.13.3 Parameters (12.6.1)

`←`, `→`	Adjust brush width by 1
`Home`, `End`	Set brush width to 1 or 100
`↑`, `↓`	Adjust tweaking force

Width and force can be adjusted while drawing. With a pressure-sensitive tablet, force also depends on pen pressure.

D.14 The Rectangle Tool (11.2)

D.14.1 Draw

| **drag** | Draw a rectangle |
| `Ctrl`-**drag** | Make a square or integer-ratio rectangle |

This restricts the rectangle so its height/width ratio is a whole number.

| `Shift`-**drag** | Draw around the starting point |

This creates a rectangle symmetric around the starting point of the mouse drag.

D.14.2 Select

click	Select
`Alt`-**click**, `Ctrl-Alt`-**click**	Select under
`Shift`-**click**	Toggle selection

In this tool, selecting by click disregards any grouping (i.e., acts as clicking with `Ctrl` in Selector).

| `Esc` | Deselect |

D.14.3 Resize with Handles (11.2.1)

drag	Drag a square handle to resize

Initially, the two resize (square) handles are in the top-left and bottom-right corners. Resize handles change the width and height of the rectangle in its own coordinate system, before any transforms are applied.

Ctrl-**drag**	Lock width, height, or ratio

D.14.4 Round Corners with Handles (11.2.2)

drag	Drag a circular handle to round corners

Initially, the two rounding handles are in the top-right corner of the rectangle.

Ctrl-**drag**	Lock the corner circular
Ctrl-**click**	Set the corner circular

When rounding corners, dragging one rounding handle keeps the corner circular if the other remains at the corner. You can drag each of the handles independently for an elliptic rounded corner, or drag/click one handle with Ctrl to make it circular again.

Shift-**click**	Remove corner rounding

D.15 The 3D Box Tool (11.3)

D.15.1 Draw (11.3.2)

drag	Draw a 3D box (X/Y plane)
Shift-**drag**	Draw a 3D box (extrude in Z)

D.15.2 Select

click	Select
Alt-**click**, Ctrl-Alt-**click**	Select under
Shift-**click**	Toggle selection
Esc	Deselect

D.15.3 Edit with Handles (11.3.4)

All editing operations occur "in perspective," that is, either along perspective lines or within planes spanned by these.

drag	Resize or move box

The four front handles and the center normally move within the X/Y plane, and the four rear handles along the Z axis; with Shift it is the other way around.

Ctrl-**drag**	Resize or move, snapping handles to axes or diagonals

D.15.4 Edit Perspectives (11.3.3)

drag	Drag square handles to move the vanishing points
[,]	Rotate X perspective lines (if parallel) by the angle step
Alt-[, Alt-]	Rotate X perspective lines (if parallel) by 1 pixel

(,)	Rotate Y perspective lines (if parallel) by the angle step
Alt-(, Alt-)	Rotate Y perspective lines (if parallel) by 1 pixel
{, }	Rotate Z perspective lines (if parallel) by the angle step
Alt-{, Alt-}	Rotate Z perspective lines (if parallel) by 1 pixel

D.16 The Ellipse Tool (11.4)

D.16.1 Draw (11.4.1)

Without Alt, the starting and ending points of the mouse drag mark the corners of the bounding box. With Alt, the ellipse is enlarged so that its circumference passes through these two points (Ctrl-Alt is a special case, see below).

drag	Draw an ellipse
Ctrl-**drag**	Make circle or integer-ratio ellipse

This restricts the ellipse so its height/width ratio is a whole number.

Shift-**drag**	Draw around the starting point

This creates an ellipse symmetric around the starting point of the mouse drag.

Ctrl-Alt-**drag**	

This creates a perfect circle whose diameter is defined by the starting and ending points of the mouse drag.

D.16.2 Select

click	Select
Alt-**click**, Ctrl-Alt-**click**	Select under
Shift-**click**	Toggle selection

In this tool, selecting by click disregards any grouping (i.e., acts as clicking with Ctrl in Selector).

Esc	Deselect

D.16.3 Edit with Handles (11.4.2)

drag	Resize, make arc or segment

Initially, the two resize handles are at the topmost and leftmost points; the two arc/segment handles are at the rightmost point.

Ctrl-**drag**	Lock circle (resize handles)
Ctrl-**drag**	Snap to angle steps (arc/segment handles)

Resize handles change the width and height of the ellipse in its own coordinate system, before any transforms are applied.

Shift-**click**	Make whole (arc/segment handles)

D.17 The Star Tool (11.5)

D.17.1 Draw (11.5.1)

drag	Draw a star
Ctrl-**drag**	Snap star to angle steps

D.17.2 Select

click	Select
Alt-**click,** Ctrl-Alt-**click**	Select under
Shift-**click**	Toggle selection

In this tool, selecting by click disregards any grouping (i.e., acts as clicking with Ctrl in Selector).

Esc	Deselect

D.17.3 Edit with Handles (11.5.2)

drag	Drag a handle to vary the star shape
Ctrl-**drag**	Keep star rays radial (no skew)
Shift-**drag**	Round the star
Shift-**click**	Remove rounding
Alt-**drag**	Randomize the star
Alt-**click,** Ctrl-Alt-**click**	Remove randomization

D.18 The Spiral Tool (11.6)

D.18.1 Draw

drag	Draw a spiral
Ctrl-**drag**	Snap spiral to angle steps

D.18.2 Select

click	Select
Alt-**click,** Ctrl-Alt-**click**	Select under
Shift-**click**	Toggle selection

In this tool, selecting by click disregards any grouping (i.e., acts as clicking with Ctrl in Selector).

Esc	Deselect

D.18.3 Edit with Handles

drag	Roll/unroll from inside (inner handle)

Dragging the inner handle adjusts the **Inner radius** parameter.

Alt-**drag**	Converge/diverge (inner handle)
Alt-**click,** Ctrl-Alt-**click**	Reset divergence (inner handle)

Vertical Alt-drag of the inner handle adjusts the **Divergence** parameter; Alt-click resets it to 1.

Shift-**click**	Zero inner radius (inner handle)

Shift-click on the inner handle makes the spiral start from the center.

drag	Roll/unroll from outside (outer handle)

Dragging the outer handle adjusts the **Turns** parameter. Use Shift-Alt-drag to roll/unroll without changing the radius.

`Shift`-**drag**	Scale/rotate (outer handle)

Use `Shift-Alt` to rotate only (locks the radius of the spiral).

`Ctrl`-**drag**	Snap handles to angle steps

This works for both handles.

D.19 The Zoom Tool (3.9)

click	Zoom in
`Shift`-**click**	Zoom out
drag	Zoom into the area

D.20 The Pencil Tool (14.2)

drag	Draw a freehand line
`Shift`-**drag**	Add to selected path

If a path is selected, `Shift`-dragging anywhere creates a new subpath.

`Shift`-**drag**	Temporarily disable snapping

`Shift` temporarily disables snapping to grid or guides when you are drawing with grid or guides on.

`Alt`-**drag**	Averaging draw (sketch mode)

D.21 The Pen (Bézier) Tool (14.1)

D.21.1 Create Nodes (14.1.1)

click	Create a sharp node

If no path is being created, this starts a new path.

`Shift`-**click**	Add to selected path

If a path is selected, `Shift`-clicking anywhere starts a new subpath.

drag	Create a Bézier node with two handles
`Shift`-**drag**	Move only one handle

This moves only one handle (instead of both) while creating a node, making it cusp.

`Ctrl`-**drag**	Snap the handle to angle steps

D.21.2 Move Last Node (14.1.2)

These commands move the most recently created node (at the start of the red segment) while creating a path.

`←`, `→`, `↑`, `↓`	Move last node by the nudge distance
`Shift-←`, `Shift-→`, `Shift-↑`, `Shift-↓`	Move last node by 10 times the nudge distance

The default nudge distance is 2 px units.

`Alt-←`, `Alt-→`, `Alt-↑`, `Alt-↓`	Move last node by 1 pixel
`Shift-Alt-←`, `Shift-Alt-→`, `Shift-Alt-↑`, `Shift-Alt-↓`	Move last node by 10 pixels

D.21.3 Create/Modify Segments

Ctrl	Snap last segment to angle steps

This snaps the new node's angle, relative to the previous node, to angle steps.

Shift-L	Make last segment line
Shift-U	Make last segment curve

These commands change the last (red) segment of the path to a straight line or curve.

D.21.4 Create Dots (14.1.4)

These shortcuts only work in the Straight lines or Paraxial modes of the tool.

Ctrl-**click**	Create a dot

This creates a small circle whose size (relative to the current stroke width) can be set in **Inkscape Preferences**.

Shift-Ctrl-**click**	Create a double-sized dot
Ctrl-Alt-**click**	Create a random-sized dot

D.21.5 Finish

Enter, **right click, double click**	Finish current line

D.21.6 Cancel

Esc, Ctrl-z	Cancel current line
Backspace, Delete	Erase last segment of current line

D.22 The Calligraphic Pen Tool (14.3)

drag	Draw a calligraphic line
Shift-**drag**	Add to selected path
Alt-**drag**	Subtract from selected path
Ctrl-**drag**	Track a guide path
←, →	Adjust pen width by 1
Home, End	Set pen width to 1 or 100
↑, ↓	Adjust pen angle

Width and angle can be adjusted while drawing.

Esc	Deselect

D.23 The Paint Bucket Tool (14.4)

click	Fill a bounded area
Shift-**click**	Add to selected path

Clicking with Shift unions the newly created fill with the previous selection.

drag	Fill from each point

From each point, the fill spreads to the neighbors with the colors similar to that point. This can be used to fill an area currently filled with a gradient or blur.

Alt-**drag**	Fill from each point same as initial point

From each point, the fill spreads to the neighbors with the colors similar to the initial point of the drag. This can be used to fill several disjoint bounded areas by starting in one and dragging over all of the areas.

Ctrl-**click**	Set fill color
Shift-Ctrl-**click**	Set stroke color

Ctrl-clicking an object sets its fill (or stroke with Shift) to the tool's current style; the object need not be selected.

D.24   The Gradient Tool (10.1)

D.24.1   Select Objects

click	Select
Alt-**click**	Select under
Shift-**click**	Toggle selection

D.24.2   Create Gradients

drag	Create gradient

This creates a gradient on selected objects. The controls bar lets you select linear/radial and fill/stroke for the new gradient.

double click	Create default gradient

This creates default (horizontal edge-to-edge for linear, centered edge-to-edge-to-edge for radial) gradient on clicked object.

D.24.3   Select Handles

click	Select a handle
Shift-**click**	Add handle to selection
Shift-**drag**	Select by rubber band
Tab	Select next handle
Shift-Tab	Select previous handle
Ctrl-A	Select all handles
Esc	Deselect all handles

A single click outside all handles also deselects all handles.

D.24.4   Create/Delete Intermediate Stops (10.5.1)

double click	Create a stop
Ctrl-Alt-**click**	Create/delete a stop

Ctrl-Alt-click on a stop's handle deletes the stop; if it was an end stop, the gradient shortens; if that leaves a single stop, the gradient disappears into flat color.

Insert	Insert new stop(s)

This adds new stops in the middle of the selected segments, so it requires that two or more adjacent handles be selected.

| Delete | Delete selected stops |

D.24.5 Move Handles/Stops (10.5.2)

| **drag** | Move selected handle(s) |
| Ctrl-**drag** | Move stops in 1/10 range increments |

Ctrl-dragging the selected intermediate stops moves them, snapping to 1/10 steps of the available range.

| Alt-**drag** | Sculpt selected stops |

Sculpting moves the selected intermediate stops; the distance traveled by each stop depends on how far it is from the stop being dragged (similar to node sculpting in the Node tool).

| ←, →, ↑, ↓ | Move selected handle by the nudge distance |
| Shift-←, Shift-→, Shift-↑, Shift-↓ | Move selected handle by 10 times the nudge distance |

The default nudge distance is 2 px units.

| Alt-←, Alt-→, Alt-↑, Alt-↓ | Move selected handle by 1 pixel |
| Shift-Alt-←, Shift-Alt-→, Shift-Alt-↑, Shift-Alt-↓ | Move selected handle by 10 pixels |

If at least one end handle is selected, arrow keys move the end handle freely, thereby moving or resizing the entire gradient line. If only mid stops are selected, arrow keys move the selected stops *along* the gradient line.

D.24.6 Reverse (10.2)

| Shift-R | Reverse gradient definition |

This mirrors the stop positions of the current gradient without moving the gradient handles.

D.24.7 Gradient Editor

| **double click** | Open **Gradient Editor** |

Double-clicking a gradient handle opens the **Gradient Editor** with that gradient and the clicked handle chosen in the stops list.

D.25 The Dropper Tool (8.6)

click	Pick fill color
Shift-**click**	Pick stroke color
drag	Average fill color
Shift-**drag**	Average stroke color

Click applies the color under the cursor to the current selection. Dragging a radius calculates the average color of a circular area. If a gradient handle (in the Gradient tool) is selected, that handle gets the color instead of the entire object.

| Alt-**click,** Alt-**drag,** Ctrl-Alt-**click,** Ctrl-Alt-**drag** | Pick inverse color |

If $\boxed{\text{Alt}}$ is pressed, picking the color (with or without $\boxed{\text{Shift}}$, by click or by drag) picks the inverse of the color.

$\boxed{\text{Ctrl-C}}$	Copy color

This copies the color under the cursor to the clipboard, as text in RRGGBBAA format (eight hexadecimal digits).

D.26 The Text Tool (Chapter 15)

D.26.1 Select/Create

click	Create/select a text object

Clicking in an empty space or on a nontext object *creates* a text object; now you can type your text. Clicking a text object *selects* it; the cursor is placed near the click point.

$\boxed{\text{Esc}}$	Deselect the text object

D.26.2 Navigate in Text

$\boxed{\leftarrow}, \boxed{\rightarrow}, \boxed{\uparrow}, \boxed{\downarrow}$	Move cursor by one character
$\boxed{\text{Ctrl-}\leftarrow}, \boxed{\text{Ctrl-}\rightarrow}$	Move cursor by one word
$\boxed{\text{Ctrl-}\uparrow}, \boxed{\text{Ctrl-}\downarrow}$	Move cursor by one paragraph
$\boxed{\text{Home}}, \boxed{\text{End}}$	Go to beginning/end of line
$\boxed{\text{Ctrl-Home}}, \boxed{\text{Ctrl-End}}$	Go to beginning/end of text
$\boxed{\text{Page Up}}, \boxed{\text{Page Down}}$	Move cursor by one screen

All of these commands cancel the current text selection, if any. Use them with $\boxed{\text{Shift}}$ to extend the selection instead.

D.26.3 Flowed Text (Internal Frame, 15.2.2)

drag	Create flowed text

Clicking and dragging in an empty space or on a nontext object creates a flowed text object with an internal rectangular frame.

drag	Adjust frame size

Dragging the handle in the bottom-right corner of the selected flowed text changes the width/height of the frame.

$\boxed{\text{Ctrl}}$**-drag**	Lock width, height, or ratio of frame

Dragging the corner handle with $\boxed{\text{Ctrl}}$ resizes the frame, preserving either width, or height, or ratio.

D.26.4 Flowed Text (External Frame, 15.2.2.2)

$\boxed{\text{Alt-W}}$	Flow text into frame

With a text object and a shape/path selected, this flows text into the shape/path. Both remain separate objects, but are linked; editing the shape/path causes the text to reflow.

$\boxed{\text{Shift-Alt-W}}$	Unflow text from frame

This cuts the flowed text's link to the shape/path, producing a single-line regular text object.

$\boxed{\text{Shift-D}}$	Select external frame

To find out which object is the frame of this flowed text, select it and press Shift-D. The frame will be selected.

D.26.5   Text on a Path (15.2.3)

Shift-D	Select path from text

To find out which path this text is put on, select it and press Shift-D. The path will be selected.

D.26.6   Edit Text

To type + and - characters, use the main keyboard; keypad + and - are reserved for zoom (unless NumLock is on).

Enter	Start a new line or paragraph

Enter in regular text creates new line; in flowed text it creates a new paragraph.

Ctrl-U	Toggle Unicode entry (15.6.1)

To insert an arbitrary Unicode character, type Ctrl-U, then the hexadecimal code point, then Enter. To stay in the Unicode mode after inserting the character, press Space instead of Enter. Press Esc or another Ctrl-U to cancel the Unicode mode without inserting the character.

Ctrl-Space	Insert no-break space

A no-break space is visible even in a text object without xml:space="preserve".

D.26.7   Select Text (15.1.1)

drag	Select text

Left-dragging over a text object selects a text span.

Shift-←, Shift-→, Shift-↑, Shift-↓	Select text by character
Shift-Ctrl-←, Shift-Ctrl-→, Shift-Ctrl-↑, Shift-Ctrl-↓	Select text by word
Shift-Home, Shift-End	Select to beginning/end of line
Shift-Ctrl-Home, Shift-Ctrl-End	Select to beginning/end of text
Shift-Page Up, Shift-Page Down	Select one screen up/down
double click	Select word
triple click	Select line
Ctrl-A	Select all text

This selects the entire text of the current text object.

D.26.8   Style Selection (15.4.2)

Ctrl-B	Make selection bold
Ctrl-I	Make selection italic

D.26.9   Letter Spacing (15.3.4)

Alt->	Expand line/paragraph by 1 pixel
Shift-Alt->	Expand line/paragraph by 10 pixels
Alt-<	Contract line/paragraph by 1 pixel

| Shift-Alt-< | Contract line/paragraph by 10 pixels |

These commands (only when editing text) adjust letter spacing in the current line (regular text) or current paragraph (flowed text).

D.26.10 Line Spacing (15.3.4)

Ctrl-Alt->	Make the text object taller by 1 pixel
Shift-Ctrl-Alt->	Make the text object taller by 10 pixels
Ctrl-Alt-<	Make the text object shorter by 1 pixel
Shift-Ctrl-Alt-<	Make the text object shorter by 10 pixels

These commands (only when editing text) adjust line spacing in the entire text object (regular or flowed).

D.26.11 Kerning and Shifting (15.3.3)

| Alt-←, Alt-→, Alt-↑, Alt-↓ | Shift characters by 1 pixel |
| Shift-Alt-←, Shift-Alt-→, Shift-Alt-↑, Shift-Alt-↓ | Shift characters by 10 pixels |

These commands work when editing a regular text object (not in flowed text). With no selection, they shift (horizontally or vertically) the characters after the cursor until the end of line. With selection, they shift the selection relative to the rest of the text (by inserting opposite kerns at both ends of the selection).

D.26.12 Rotate (15.3.3)

| Ctrl-[, Ctrl-] | Rotate character(s) by 90 degrees |
| Alt-[, Alt-] | Rotate character(s) by 1 pixel |

Rotation only works in regular text (not flowed text). These commands rotate the next character (when there is no text selection) or all characters in the selection (when there is a selection).

INDEX

transforming, 304
using in patterns, 120, 306
Blender suite, 6
blend modes, 63, 289–290
blogs, 330
blur, 4, 9, 286–289, 346
and bounding box, 286
applied to
3D boxes, 176
clones, 274, 282, 287
groups, 287–288
multiple bushstrokes, 366
text objects, 264
bitmap editing with, 308
blending bushstrokes with, 342, 359
for shaders, 160
motion, 288, 291
picking color from, 128
rendering, 14
simulated with inset/outset paths, 229
transforming, 287–288
Blur Content preset filter, 291
Blur primitive, *see* Gaussian Blur
Blurs (Filters submenu), 291
BMP format, 303
bounding boxes, 54
and repeated randomization, 113
and rubber band selection, 72
as selection cue, 54, 68
converting to guides, 103
geometric center of, 86, 88
handles around, 83, 85
of blurred objects, 286, 300
of flowed text, 258
querying via command line, 395
types of, 54, 301
Box tool, *see* 3D Box tool
Break Apart command, 188–190
Brighter extension, 133
brightness, 123, 309
browsers
PNG support in, 31, 315
SVG support in, 8–9, 31
bullets
special character for, 268
using clones for, 271
business cards, 321–328

C

CAD (Computer-Aided Design), 6, 349, 389
Cairo library, 386
Calligraphic pen tool, 25, 135, 238, 244–250, 420
applying stroke style, 126
background tracing with, 245, 248–249, 335

bitmap tracing with, 358
Boolean operations on paths with, 193
controls bar of, 244–248, 250
guide tracking with, 245, 248–250, 360, 420
hatching with, 333–335
parameters of
Angle, 246, 343, 420
Caps, 247–248
Fixation, 246, 248, 343, 366
Mass, 247, 250
Pressure Sensitivity, 245–248, 343
Thinning, 245, 248
Tremor, 247–248, 250, 324, 334, 347–348, 366
Width, 33, 244–245, 248, 324, 334, 343, 366, 420
Wiggle, 247–248
presets of, 248
selection cue in, 68
sketching with, 341
switching to, 399
tool style of, 25
Camouflage pattern, 164
canvas, 19–21, 40, 42
background of, 40, 129
current position on, 374
empty, 70, 72, 78
returning focus to, from a dialog, 400
scrolling
automatic, 256
by keys, 402
by mouse, 23, 401
size of, 373
Canvas vector editor, 39
cartoons, 5, 25
adding depth to, 160
drawing, 238
CCX format, 389
CDR format, 389, 392
CDT format, 389
Celtic knots, 222
CGM format, 389
Chalk and Sponge preset filter, 292
Channel extension, 309
channels, 121–123
correcting, 309
removing from bitmaps, 309
tweaking, 132
characters
kerning, 261–263, 425
rotating, 262
selecting, 256
special, 268, 424
Charcoal extension, 309
Check Spelling dialog, 267–268

Find dialog, 76, 400
Firefox browser, 315
fixation, *see* Calligraphic pen tool
Flash, *see* Adobe Flash
Flatten Béziers extension, 231
fLIP cASE extension, 266
flipping, 89
   around rotation center, 409
   by keys, 89, 409, 413
Flow into Frame command, 258
flowcharts, *see* technical drawings
flowed text, 9, 25, 257–259, 261, 263, 266,
      423–424
fonts
   available to Inkscape, 265
   built-in kerning of, 262
   embedded, 385–386, 394
   families of, 264–265
   installing, 322
   names of, 385
   size of, 264, 266, 322
   variants of, 265
force, *see* Tweak tool
forking, 15
forward slash (/), in XML, 370
Fractalize extension, 232
fractals, 7, 227–228
Freehand, *see* Macromedia Freehand
Fullscreen command, 42
fullscreen mode, 6, 21, 42, 403
Function Plotter extension, 233

G

g element, 58, 60, 64, 374–376, 381
Gauss, Carl Friedrich, 286
Gaussian Blur primitive, 14, 229, 286, 288, 296,
     298, 359
Generate from Path (Extensions submenu),
     229–230
generate-layers.py, 330
Gentium font, 322
Ghostscript interpreter, 12, 327, 387
GIF format, 303
   animated, 329, 333
   importing, 390
Gifsicle utility, 333
Gill vector editor, 15
GIMP (GNU Image Manipulation Program),
     5, 15
   color separation in, 320
   drawing shapes in, 7
   palettes on, 125
   PNG converting with, 327
   running from Inkscape, 304
   selecting in, 2
   soft brush in, 132

Google search engine, 344
GPL (General Public License), 15
Gradient Editor dialog, 422
gradient meshes, 4, 14, 132, 388
gradient stops, 150–159
   clipboard operations on, 404
   color of
      adjusting, 126, 128, 133
      assigning, 128, 422
      interpolating between, 122
      picking, 128
   connection lines between, 150, 158
   creating, 421
   deleting, 158, 421–422
   deselecting, 155, 421
   end, 156–157, 422
   for elliptic gradients, 152
   for linear gradients, 151
   middle, 156, 158–159, 421–422
   moving, 156, 158–159, 422
   opacity of, 154
   painting, 155–156, 158
   sculpting, 422
   selecting, 69, 155, 421
   snapping, 106, 157
Gradient tool, 149, 421–422
   controls bar of, 421
   deselecting in, 78, 421
   gradient definitions in, 153
   selecting in, 68–69, 71, 150, 421
   switching to, 399
gradients, 4, 149–161
   approximating nonlinear profiles, 159–160
   bitmap editing with, 308
   creating, 150–152, 421
   default, 421
   definitions of, 150, 153–154, 374, 379
      removing unused, 154
      shared, 154
   editing handles of, *see* gradient stops
   elliptic, 14, 149–153, 336, 421
   from opaque to transparent color, 149–150,
      160, 325
   in Outline mode, 48
   linear, 14, 149–151, 154, 421
   multistage, 158–159
   on fill, 118, 150
   on objects with an existing gradient, 150
   on stroke, 118, 150
   on text objects, 264
   overlaying, 161
   picking color from, 128
   removing, 151, 421
   repeat mode, 154–155
   reversing, 154, 422
   simplifying, 158, 195
   transforming, 97, 156, 159–160
   tweaking, 161

New command, 322, 330
Next Zoom command, 47
No Filters mode, 301, 360
no-break space, in text, 424
Node tool, 197–208, 410–414
  adding nodes in, 144, 195, 233
  aligning and distributing in, 112
  Bézier handles in, 191, 197
  controls bar of, 197–198, 201–202, 207,
      215–216, 227, 242, 306–307
  deselecting in, 78
  editing
    clones in, 272–273
    gradients in, 150, 198, 414
    path effects in, 217, 414
    paths in, 197–198, 208, 215, 227
    patterns in, 163, 306, 414
    shapes in, 166, 198, 414
    text in, 198
  moving guides in, 100
  rotating in, 411–412
  scaling in, 162, 412, 412
  selecting in, 68, 71, 197–199, 410–411
  switching to, 197, 399, 406
nodes, 188, 197
  adding, 144, 191, 195, 200, 207, 231, 233, 331,
      352, 413–414
  adjacent but not connected by segments, 188
  aligning, 205–206
  auto, 202, 204, 413
  breaking, 413
  cusp, 137, 202, 226, 238–239, 241, 310, 381,
      413, 419
  deleting, 144, 191, 195, 199–200, 413
  deselecting, 199, 410–411
  distances between, 199
  distributing, 144
  duplicating, 200–201
  editing, 208
  end, 188–189, 199, 201, 240, 243
  flipping, 207, 413
  half-smooth, 202, 204, 226, 413
  jittering, 231
  joining, 201, 413
  middle, 188, 199, 202
  moving, 204–208, 411, 419
  no styling for, 198
  reducing, see paths, simplifying
  rotating, 207–208, 412
  scaling, 207–208, 412
  sculpting, 206–207, 209, 335, 411
  selecting, 197–199, 410–411
  smooth, 202, 226, 238–239, 241, 381, 413
  snapping, 106, 169–170, 205
  start, 189
  symmetric, 202, 381, 413
  see also Bézier curves, paths, segments,
    subpaths

sodipodi:nodetypes attribute, 381
Noise Fill preset filter, 291
Noise Transparency preset filter, 291
Noisy Blur preset filter, 291
Non Realistic Shaders (Filters submenu), 293
Normalize extension, 309
Normal view mode, 48, 402
Number Nodes extension, 235

O

Object Properties dialog, 51–52, 400
Object to Path command, 171, 215, 229, 242,
    259, 269
objects, 2, 51–65
  arranging, 99, 114–115
  background, 60, 70
  clipboard operations on, 30, 56–57, 59, 61,
      93, 118, 154, 156, 162, 332
  converting
    to guides, 102–103
    to path, 405–406
  coordinates of, 53–54
  creating, 23–26, 55, 59
  deleting, 73
  duplicating, 33–34, 331, 404
  edges of, 160, 287, 291–292, 307, 365
  editing, 2
  exchanging places of, 89
  hidden, 52, 64, 68, 72–73, 76, 78
  IDs of, 51–52, 76, 79, 316, 381
  infinite, 93
  in Outline mode, 48
  interpolating, 230, 331–332, 335
  invisible, 30, 49, 72–73
  labels of, 52, 381
  locked, 52, 64, 68, 72–73, 76, 78
  metadata of, 52
  next/previous, 27
  order of, see z-order
  overlapping, 112, 114–115
  properties of, 5, 51–52
  reusability of, 3
  rotation center of, 85–86, 381
  searching, 76–78
  size of, 53–54, 93
  snapping, 106, 205
  types of, 5, 77, 165
Objects to Guides command, 102
Objects to Marker command, 146
Objects to Pattern command, 162
ODF format, 390
offsets, 196–197, 228, 405–406
  from stars, 183
  searching, 77
  see also dynamic offsets, linked offsets
Oil Painting preset filter, 292

Swatches dialog, 124, 402–403
  opening by keyboard, 124, 400
SWF format, 333, 390
SWF Tools library, 333
Swirl extension, 310
Switch to Layer Above command, 61
Switch to Layer Below command, 61

T

tables of objects, 114–115
tablet pen
  node sculpting with, 207, 411
  pressure-sensitivity of, 94, 96, 131–132, 207,
    209, 244–248, 289, 343, 358, 411, 415
  with Calligraphic pen tool, 244–248, 343,
    348, 358
  with Tweak tool, 94, 96, 131–132, 208–209,
    289, 415
tags, in XML, 370
technical drawings, 5, 135, 233
  connector lines in, 6, 114, 142, 145
  creating, 349–355
  dots in, 241
  geometric bounding boxes in, 54
  isometric, 350
  paths in, 194, 208
  patterns in, 163
  rectangles with rounded corners in, 97, 170
  tracing, 358
templates, 6, 37–39, 322
  creating, 38
  default, 38
  for animations, 330
  initial layers in, 60
tessellation, 280, 361–365
TEX typesetting system, 6
text, 255, 263–269
  aligning, 110, 261
  and automatic hyphenation, 258
  applying filters to, 264, 288
  baseline origin of, 263
  Boolean operations on, 192
  case of, 266
  clipboard operations on, 256–257, 404
  converting to path, 132, 192, 269, 327,
    335, 394
  creating, 25, 256–259, 423
  deselecting, 423
  direction of, 260
  distributing, 112
  editing, 25, 255–256, 424
  flowed, 9, 25, 257–259, 261, 263, 266, 423–424
  formatting, 255–257
  in Outline mode, 49
  in SVG, 64

kerning, 261–263, 323, 425
letter spacing, 263, 323, 424
line spacing, 263, 425
line wrapping, 256–257, 424
on path, 78, 189, 259–261, 263, 424
rotating characters in, 262, 425
scaling, 266
searching, 76–77, 266
selecting, 256–257, 261, 263, 423–424
special characters in, 268
spellchecking, 267–268
styling, 264–266
Text and Font dialog, 263–266, 322
  opening by keyboard, 263, 400
  Text tab, 256
text editing cursor, 255–257
  moving, 255–256, 261, 423
text editors, 255
text element, 257
Text (Extensions submenu), 266, 266
text nodes, in XML, 64
Text tool, 20, 25, 255–269, 423–425
  controls bar of, 260–261, 264–266, 322
  default style of, 265
  deselecting in, 78
  rotating in, 425
  selecting in, 68–69, 71
  status bar messages in, 257, 268
  switching to, 255, 400, 406
  zooming in, 46
textPath element, 260
textures, 4–5
  adding, 164, 326
  imitating, 292–294, 309
  in bitmaps, 308
Textures (Filters submenu), 294
thinning, see Calligraphic pen tool
thumbnails, 94, 115
TIFF format
  color-separated, 320
  converting from PNG, 314, 327–328
  importing, 303, 390
tiffcc utility, 328
Title Case extension, 266
title element, 52
tool controls bar, see controls bar
toolbox, 22, 24–26
  double-clicking a button in, 167, 241, 244,
    253, 400
  hidden, 42
Torn Edges preset filter, 292
touch selection, 72–73
Trace Bitmap dialog, 251, 311–314, 367
  Mode tab, 311–314
  opening by keyboard, 311, 400, 404
  Options tab, 312

vector formats, 4
    and document page, 40
    supporting in Inkscape, 383–390
    see also individual formats
vector graphics, 1–5, 237
    file sizes of, 3
    memory consumption of, 3
    reusing, 7
    scalability of, 2–3, 45
    studying, 8
video, 8
view area, 44
vignettes, 5
Visio, 6
Visualize Path (Extensions submenu), 235
vocabularies, in XML, 370, 372
VonKoch effect, 227–228

W

W3C (World Wide Web Consortium), 9
watercolor imitation, 296–300, 359
Wave extension, 310
Wavy pattern, 164
Whirl extension, 233
wiggle, *see* Calligraphic pen tool
Wikimedia Commons, 8
Wikipedia, 279
Windows
    .7z archive files for, 18
    command-line applications on, 391
    dictionaries on, 267
    Inkscape version for, 18, 391
    palettes on, 125
    UI palette for, 124
WMF format, 389
word processors, 255
WordPerfect text processor, 389
WPG format, 389

X

XAML (Extensible Application Markup
    Language), 389
Xara, 13
    gradients in, 14
    selecting in, 68, 72, 84
    speed of, 13
    UI of, 13–14
Xara LX, 13
Xara Xtreme, 8, 13, 39
XHTML (Extensible HyperText Markup
    Language), 370, 372
XLink, 373, 379–380

XML Editor dialog, 63–65
    adding animation attributes with, 329
    editing
        attributes in, 400
        coordinates in, 53
        dash patterns in, 139
        font names in, 385
        gradient definition names in, 153
        markers in, 146
        patterns, 162
    hidden or locked objects in, 64, 68
    opening by keyboard, 400
    order of layers in, 64
    status bar of, 64
XML (Extensible Markup Language), 8,
    369–373

Z

Zoner Draw vector editor, 39
zoom, 45–47
    amount of, 46
    and grid lines, 104
    and moving by keyboard, 87
    and transformations, 87–88
    by keys, 23, 45, 47, 401
    by mouse, 23, 46, 401, 419
    by tablet pen, 46
    current level of, 45, 374
    depth of, 3, 22, 45
    different in multiple windows, 42
    displayed in status bar, 53
    history of, 47, 401
    in Outline mode, 48
    in Pen tool, 239
    in Text tool, 46
    into an area, 419
    into selection, 47, 401
    saving with documents, 44
    with rubber band, 46
Zoom tool, 23, 46–47, 419
    selection cue in, 68
    switching to, 399
Zoom (View submenu), 47
z-order
    and combining paths, 189
    and document order, 64
    and selection, 75, 86, 407
    of a stroke, 120, 145
    of groups, 59
    of layers, 56–57
    of objects, 49, 55–57, 72–74, 375
    of sides in 3D boxes, 176
    rearranging, 55–56, 61, 364, 405

The Electronic Frontier Foundation (EFF) is the leading organization defending civil liberties in the digital world. We defend free speech on the Internet, fight illegal surveillance, promote the rights of innovators to develop new digital technologies, and work to ensure that the rights and freedoms we enjoy are enhanced — rather than eroded — as our use of technology grows.

PRIVACY EFF has sued telecom giant AT&T for giving the NSA unfettered access to the private communications of millions of their customers. eff.org/nsa

FREE SPEECH EFF's Coders' Rights Project is defending the rights of programmers and security researchers to publish their findings without fear of legal challenges. eff.org/freespeech

INNOVATION EFF's Patent Busting Project challenges overbroad patents that threaten technological innovation. eff.org/patent

FAIR USE EFF is fighting prohibitive standards that would take away your right to receive and use over-the-air television broadcasts any way you choose. eff.org/IP/fairuse

TRANSPARENCY EFF has developed the Switzerland Network Testing Tool to give individuals the tools to test for covert traffic filtering. eff.org/transparency

INTERNATIONAL EFF is working to ensure that international treaties do not restrict our free speech, privacy or digital consumer rights. eff.org/global

EFF.ORG

ELECTRONIC FRONTIER FOUNDATION

Protecting Rights and Promoting Freedom on the Electronic Frontier

EFF is a member-supported organization. Join Now! www.eff.org/support

THE ESSENTIAL BLENDER
Guide to 3D Creation with the Open Source Suite Blender

edited by ROLAND HESS; *produced by* TON ROOSENDAAL

Blender is a free and open source 3D creation suite that is a real alternative to commercially available 3D design software. A cross-platform software package with millions of downloads annually, Blender is now one of the world's most popular 3D design tools. If you've never tried 3D design before, an introductory chapter will familiarize you with relevant terminology and concepts. If you're already experienced with commercial 3D software, *The Essential Blender* will get you up to speed with Blender quickly. The book is modular in its approach, with each topic addressed independently and accompanied by hands-on tutorial sections.

SEPTEMBER 2007, 376 PP. W/ CD, $44.95 ($53.95 CDN)
ISBN 978-1-59327-166-4

THE BLENDER GAMEKIT, 2ND EDITION
Interactive 3D for Artists

edited by CARSTEN WARTMANN

Blender is the first of the 3D packages to integrate a game engine as well as tools for editing game logic and creating interactive animation. *The Blender GameKit, 2nd Edition* starts with an extensive section for people who are new to 3D—explaining all basic concepts—or new to Blender, with a full introduction to the interface. Then it shows in step-by-step tutorials the fun of creating models, adding motion to them, and how to turn them into simple games. Experienced 3D artists will appreciate the more complex game demos, the character animation tutorials, the introduction to Python, a tutorial with the Frankie character, and the advanced reference section.

MAY 2009, 320 PP. W/ CD, $44.95 ($56.95 CDN)
ISBN 978-1-59327-205-0

THE ARTIST'S GUIDE TO GIMP EFFECTS
Creative Techniques for Photographers, Artists, and Designers

by MICHAEL J. HAMMEL

The Artist's Guide to GIMP Effects shows you how to harness the GIMP's powerful features to produce professional-looking advertisements, impressive photographic effects, as well as logos and text effects. The book's extensively illustrated, step-by-step tutorials are perfect for hands-on learning and experimentation. After a crash course in using the GIMP's interface and core tools (such as brushes, patterns, selections, layers, modes, and masks), you'll learn sophisticated photographic and web design techniques, as well as special type and advertising effects.

AUGUST 2007, 348 PP. FULL COLOR, $44.95 ($53.95 CDN)
ISBN 978-1-59327-153-4

UBUNTU FOR NON-GEEKS, 3RD EDITION
A Pain-Free, Project-Based, Get-Things-Done Guidebook

by RICKFORD GRANT

"A fast, crystal-clear topical tour of the amazing collective accomplishment embodied in Ubuntu."

—Cory Doctorow, Boing Boing

Full of tips, tricks, and helpful pointers, *Ubuntu for Non-Geeks, 3rd Edition* is a hands-on, project-based guide to Ubuntu 8.04 for those interested in— but nervous about—switching to the Linux operating system. Step-by-step projects build upon earlier tutorial concepts, helping you absorb and apply what you've learned.

JUNE 2008, 360 PP. W/CD, $34.95 ($34.95 CDN)
ISBN 978-1-59327-180-0

STEAL THIS COMPUTER BOOK 4.0
What They Won't Tell You About the Internet

by WALLACE WANG

This offbeat, non-technical book examines what hackers do, how they do it, and how readers can protect themselves. Informative, irreverent, and entertaining, the completely revised fourth edition of *Steal This Computer Book* contains new chapters that discuss the hacker mentality, lock picking, exploiting P2P filesharing networks, and how people manipulate search engines and pop-up ads. Includes a CD with hundreds of megabytes of hacking and security-related programs that tie in with each chapter of the book.

MAY 2006, 384 PP. W/CD, $29.95 ($38.95 CDN)
ISBN 978-1-59327-105-3

PHONE:
800.420.7240 OR
415.863.9900
MONDAY THROUGH FRIDAY,
9 A.M. TO 5 P.M. (PST)

FAX:
415.863.9950
24 HOURS A DAY,
7 DAYS A WEEK

EMAIL:
SALES@NOSTARCH.COM

WEB:
WWW.NOSTARCH.COM

MAIL:
NO STARCH PRESS
555 DE HARO ST, SUITE 250
SAN FRANCISCO, CA 94107
USA

UPDATES

Visit *http://www.nostarch.com/inkscape.htm* for updates, errata, and other information.

The Book of Inkscape is set in New Baskerville. The book was printed and bound at Malloy Incorporated in Ann Arbor, Michigan. The paper is Glatfelter Spring Forge 60# Smooth Eggshell, which is certified by the Sustainable Forestry Initiative (SFI). The book uses a RepKover binding, which allows it to lay flat when open.